Communications in Computer and Information Science 1542

More information about this series at https://link.springer.com/bookseries/7899

Gabriella Casalino · Marta Cimitile ·
Pietro Ducange · Natalia Padilla Zea ·
Riccardo Pecori · Pietro Picerno ·
Paolo Raviolo (Eds.)

Higher Education Learning Methodologies and Technologies Online

Third International Workshop, HELMeTO 2021
Pisa, Italy, September 9–10, 2021
Revised Selected Papers

Springer

Editors
Gabriella Casalino
University of Bari Aldo Moro
Bari, Italy

Marta Cimitile
Unitelma Sapienza University
Rome, Italy

Pietro Ducange
University of Pisa
Pisa, Italy

Natalia Padilla Zea
Universidad Internacional de La Rioja
Logroño, Spain

Riccardo Pecori
University of Sannio
Benevento, Italy

Pietro Picerno
eCampus University
Novedrate, Italy

Paolo Raviolo
eCampus University
Novedrate, Italy

ISSN 1865-0929 ISSN 1865-0937 (electronic)
Communications in Computer and Information Science
ISBN 978-3-030-96059-9 ISBN 978-3-030-96060-5 (eBook)
https://doi.org/10.1007/978-3-030-96060-5

This Springer imprint is published by the registered company Springer Nature Switzerland AG
The registered company address is: Gewerbestrasse 11, 6330 Cham, Switzerland

In loving memory of
Prof. Antonella Galanti and
Prof. Luigi Sarti

Preface

This volume of Communications in Computer and Information Science (CCIS) contains the post-proceedings of HELMeTO 2021, the third International Workshop on Higher Education Learning Methodologies and Technologies Online, which took place during September 9–10, 2021. This time, the Department of Information Engineering of the University of Pisa organized the event, which was held online one more year due to the restrictions derived from the COVID-19 pandemic.

The conference included three general tracks and five special tracks, previously proposed by their organizers and peer-reviewed by the Program Committee.

The first general track tackled the topic of Methodologies for Distance Learning in Higher Education. In this session, proposals to improve and to innovate in online learning approaches were presented, fostering a wider spectrum of activities farther than the traditional ones. The second general track was about Technologies for Distance Learning in Higher Education. Proposals in this section presented both new tools and new uses of technology to enhance distance learning activities in several areas, including those which need a manipulative or practical approach. The last (but not least) general track dealt with the cross-cutting issue of the pandemic: Facing the COVID-19 Emergency in Higher Education Teaching and Learning. In this session, authors shared their own experiences in different subjects and different contexts, reflecting on what difficulties arose and what worked best.

In the special sessions authors presented their proposals about digital skills in e-learning and continuous assessment; student's perception of online learning, teaching, and assessment in higher education; faculty development, distance education, and online learning systems in higher education; e-learning and disciplinary teaching: issues and innovations in contemporary higher education; and passing from an emergency Distance Didactic to new forms of blended learning via effective methodologies to design, deliver, and evaluate learning. An international Program/Scientific Committee with members from seven countries (Italy, Spain, Morocco, China, the USA, Germany, and the UK) was in charge of peer-reviewing the 65 papers submitted to the conference. A final set of the best 47 papers were finally accepted for the conference, and 26 papers were extended and selected for publication in this book after a separate peer-review process involving three members of the Program/Scientific Committee.

We thank all the authors for their contributions and presentations, for their efforts, and for their presence online at the event. Similarly, we would like to thank all the committee members, organizers, and contributors, for their involvement and help in the process of preparing and hosting both the conference and this book. Our thanks go also to the University of Pisa and to SIREM (Società Italiana di Ricerca sull'Educazione Mediale). Finally, we thank ION Group for kindly sponsoring HELMeTO 2021.

September 2021

Gabriella Casalino
Marta Cimitile
Pietro Ducange
Natalia Padilla Zea
Riccardo Pecori
Pietro Picerno
Paolo Raviolo

Organization

General Chairs

Francesco Marcelloni	University of Pisa, Italy
Cleo Sgouropoulou	University of West Attica, Greece
Pier Cesare Rivoltella	Catholic University of the Sacred Heart, Italy
Priit Reiska	University of Tallinn, Estonia

Program Committee Chairs

Pietro Ducange	University of Pisa, Italy
Natalia Padilla Zea	Universidad Internacional de La Rioja, Spain
Paolo Raviolo	eCampus University, Italy

Steering Committee

Daniel Burgos	Universidad Internacional de la Rioja, Spain
Gabriella Casalino	University of Bari, Italy
Marta Cimitile	University of Rome Unitelma Sapienza, Italy
Pietro Ducange	University of Pisa, Italy
Riccardo Pecori	University of Sannio, Italy
Pietro Picerno	eCampus University, Italy
Paolo Raviolo	eCampus University, Italy
Piercesare Rivoltella	Catholic University of the Sacred Heart, Italy
Christian M. Stracke	University of Bonn, Germany

Program Committee

Laura Sara Agrati	University of Bergamo, Italy
Pasquale Ardimento	University of Bari, Italy
Massimiliano Barattucci	eCampus University, Italy
Fabrizio Barpi	Politecnico di Torino, Italy
Mario Luca Bernardi	University of Sannio, Italy
Gabriella Casalino	University of Bari, Italy
Marta Cimitile	University of Rome Unitelma Sapienza, Italy
Daniele Di Mitri	Goethe University of Frankfurt am Main, Germany
Yannis Dimitriadis	University of Valladolid, Spain
Anna Dipace	University of Modena and Reggio Emilia, Italy
Xu Du	Central China Normal University, China
Stefano Faralli	University of Rome Unitelma Sapienza, Italy
Michela Fazzolari	IIT-CNR, Italy
Simona Ferrari	Catholic University of the Sacred Heart, Italy

Enzo Iuliano	eCampus University, Italy
Paola Magnano	Kore University of Enna, Italy
Tawfik Masrour	Moulay Ismaïl University, Morocco
Riccardo Pecori	University of Sannio, Italy
Pietro Picerno	eCampus University, Italy
Loredana Perla	University of Bari, Italy
Nadia Sansone	University of Rome Unitelma Sapienza, Italy
Maria Grazia Simone	eCampus University, Italy
Georgina Stebbings	Manchester Metropolitan University, UK
Ilaria Terrenghi	Catholic University of the Sacred Heart, Italy
Gaetano Tieri	University of Rome Unitelma Sapienza, Italy
Chih-Hsiung Tu	Northern Arizona University, USA
Gennaro Vessio	University of Bari, Italy
Elena Verdú	Universidad Internacional de La Rioja, Spain
Viviana Vinci	University of Reggio Calabria, Italy

Additional Reviewers

Silvia Margarita Baldiris Navarro
Enrico Bocciolesi
Ilaria Bortolotti
Giambattista Bufalino
Stefano Cacciamani
Alessio Ceccherelli
Ambrogia Cereda
Donatella Cesareni
Alberto Corbi
Miao Dai
Antonella De Blasio
Luis De La Fuente Valentín
Dario De Notaris
Stefano Di Tore
Maka Eradze
Manuela Fabbri
Svetlana Karkina
Onur Karademir
Michele Lanzetta
Maria Beatrice Ligorio
Francesco Lupi
Paola Mangano
Stefania Massaro
Irene Mauro
Martina Pantarotto
Salvatore Patera
Tiziana Ramaci
Alessandro Renda
Marco Rondonotti
Alessia Scarinci
Andrea Tinterri
Fiorella Vinci
Shuoqiu Yang
Fabian Zehner
Lizhao Zhang

Publication Chairs

Marta Cimitile	University of Rome Unitelma Sapienza, Italy
Riccardo Pecori	University of Sannio, Italy

Learning Methodologies and Technologies Online. HELMeTO 2021 Editorial: Introduction to the Scientific Contributions (Editorial)

Gabriella Casalino[1], Marta Cimitile[2], Pietro Ducange[3], Natalia Padilla-Zea[4], Riccardo Pecori[5], Pietro Picerno[6], and Paolo Raviolo[6]

[1] University of Bari, Bari, Italy
[2] University of Rome Unitelma Sapienza, Rome, Italy
[3] University of Pisa, Pisa, Italy
pietro.ducange@unipi.it
[4] Universidad Internacional de La Rioja, Logroño, La Rioja, Spain
[5] University of Sannio, Benevento, Italy
[6] eCampus University, Novedrate CO, Italy

Keywords: Distance learning · Virtual learning environment · Online learning · eLearning

Methodologies and technologies supporting distance learning played a crucial role in the last year and an half, characterized by the COVID-19 pandemic. Indeed, all educational stockholders, at all levels, had to adapt to a new model of distance or blended learning, necessary to ensure social distancing and reduction of viral contagion [1]. On the one hand, students had to reduce their attendance in classrooms and universities to a minimum, if not totally. On the other hand, they were catapulted into a digital learning environment, to which they were not accustomed. Discussions on the effects and perceptions have been analyzed in the specialized literature [2]. Also teachers had to change the paradigms of knowledge transfer and training. Most teachers and managers of training institutions were not trained for the digital transition and experienced lots of difficulties [3].

Luckily, scientific and technological research in the field of education, whether conducted entirely at a distance or in a blended mode, soon showed itself to be rich in proposals and solutions [4]. Starting with the electronic decade, i.e. the 1990s, distance learning technologies and methodologies became mature in the 2010s. The first Massive Open Online Course (MOOC) [5] appeared in 2008 and, since then, new methodological and pedagogical studies have been proposed to support distance learning [6, 7]. Especially in the framework of higher education, such as universities, online education has called for standardization and quality assessment procedures [8]. These aspects have become critical for any academic organization, especially given the framework of the Bologna process and its progressive deployment leading to the European Higher Education Area initiative.

The experiences of a huge number of Higher Education Institutions in handling the COVID-19 emergency have been reported in the scientific literature [9]. As regards the HELMeTO community, a cross-track on "Facing the COVID-19 Emergency in Higher Education Teaching and Learning" was arranged for the first time last year, during the second edition of the workshop, and authors from different countries discussed tools, practices, and frameworks adopted by their institutions for approaching the emergency and the rapid switching of their courses to the distance learning mode [10]. Also this year, for the third edition of the workshop, the cross-track was organized. Moreover, five special tracks were organized by recognized researchers in the field of distance learning. These special tracks ranged from advances in digital skills in e-Learning to issues and innovations in contemporary higher education, from the transition towards new forms of blended learning to the analysis of the student's perception of online learning.

In the following, we briefly summarize the contributions accepted in the present book of HELMeTO 2021. In the first section, we summarize the contributions of the three general tracks on methodologies, technologies for distance learning in higher education, and facing COVID-19. Then, in the second section, we focus on the works dealing with the five special tracks, organized in five subsections. In the following, each contribution is cited by specifying the surname of the first author.

Contributions of the General Tracks

In this section, we briefly summarize the contributions accepted for the three general tracks of HELMeTO 2021. Of the 30 contributions originally selected, 11 extended papers successfully passed the revision process to be included in the present book.

Methodologies for Distance Learning in Higher Education

In the last year, the interest for online learning methodologies in higher education and continuous education has increased significantly. This was mainly due to the fact that the majority of higher education institutions worldwide had to implement online and blended learning solutions in response to the global pandemic. Even with the gradual return to normality of face-to-face teaching, it seems likely that many online learning solutions will remain part of the educational offer of the universities, both as online courses or as contingency measures. This track proposes a reflection on some different perspectives on online learning.

Cecchinato, in his contribution, focuses on the differences between students involved in social annotation activities and those involved in threaded forums as well as the relative impact on learning performance. The study of Renieri et al. addresses the need for training pre-service teachers (PST) and pre-service support teachers (S-PST) on coding and educational robotics. Questionnaires were administered to examine whether their knowledge, beliefs, and self-confidence towards these topics changed after participation in a remote training program on educational robotics. Results helped in the definition of an effective training program able to enhance PST and S-PST self-confidence towards educational robotics. Lupi and Lanzetta focus their paper on one of the key topics in contemporary higher education, namely developing a structured approach to the scientific literature search among students through the use of an online collaborative approach.

These papers show different ways to put methodology in online contexts in the spotlight, so that the actual relevance of this component of the educational ecosystem is highlighted conveniently.

Technologies for Distance Learning in Higher Education

Several initiatives to enrich teaching-learning and assessment processes have arisen in the last few years, which aimed to improve both learning results and work efficiency, together with teachers and students' satisfaction and motivation. In this track, we have examples of such processes.

De-La-Fuente-Valentín et al. outline the PLeNTaS project, which is intended to help teachers in the exam review process by using an automatic tool. This proposal has the rubrics as a core element of a process based on natural language processing. Ardimento et al. focus their contribution on teamwork assessment. Evaluating single students who performed a task in a group is difficult since the teacher cannot know the actual contribution of each of them. The authors present an environment based on extensions of the Fluorite plug-in to solve the problem. Casalino et al. seek the latent abilities of students who answer a mathematical questionnaire. Authors used non-negative matrix factorization together with information visualization techniques to enhance the understandability of the results. Anastasi and Musmarra highlight the relevance of the Internet of Things for current and future ICT jobs, particularly in technological innovations. Their proposal presents a set of bodies of knowledge to cover the main elements of this technology in several educational levels. Chiofalo explains how physics can be more effectively taught if students see how it works in their everyday life. To develop this idea, the author presents the Street Physics Toolbox, which includes the basic concepts of physics, explained with five-minute-long video-pills about daily life situations.

Facing the COVID-19 Emergency in Higher Education Teaching and Learning

The 2021 edition of HELMeTO again tackled the COVID-19 global pandemic, which was still under development during September 2021 because of novel virus variants. As a consequence, a proper special track was arranged, as in the previous edition, in order to deal with the countermeasures adopted in higher education methodologies.

The contribution of Tinterri et al. deals with the strategies enacted to cope with the ongoing COVID-19 pandemic both from the teachers, and the students, perspective to identify a proper relationship. The paper employs a survey made of several demographic and ERT experience-related items to understand the positive or negative aspects that most affected their perceptions. Cappellini et al. describe the distance learning experience of students from 23 different countries as regards the so-called

Foundation Course, a pre-university program introduced in 2016 at the University of Pisa which is primarily aimed at prospective students in countries where the national schooling system does not meet the minimum requirements of the current Italian legislation for university access. Kalatskaya and Latypova describe the challenges and solutions, with a critical insight, as concerns teacher education in Russia (Kazan Federal University) during the COVID-19 pandemic. In particular, they try to find out what organizational solutions need to be offered in order to transfer students to the remote format of conducting practice, what individual assignments can be offered to students with this format of practice, how effective this format of practice is, and what difficulties teachers and students face in the course of distance practice format. Finally, Langenhagen explores the impact of the COVID-19 pandemic by using a gamified mobile learning app to limit its negative effects in the learning process. The core element of the app is a database with over 550 questions covering all nine chapters of the considered accounting course. The questions are single- and multiple-choice, but they also provide sorting and close-text tasks.

Contributions of the Special Tracks

The 3rd edition of HELMeTO launched a call for special tracks to invite scholars all over the world to propose topics focused on distance learning in higher education. Seven special tracks successfully passed the review process and were opened for submissions. Five out of these seven special tracks collected a total of 33 contributions and 15 contributions successfully passed the revision process and have been included in the present book.

Digital Skills in e-Learning and Continuous Online Training

The special track "Digital skills in e-learning and continuous online training" aimed to reflect on and understand the digital skills of young people and young adults and their manifestation in higher education and continuing online training courses. Specifically, it aimed to propose new criteria to encourage the development of digital skills for the development of effective learning, critical thinking, information autonomy, creativity, cooperation, and active digital citizenship.

Lejarreta et al., in their contribution, discuss the strategies adopted by the rural communities of Homa Bay (Kenya) to train digital skills and adapt their capabilities and resources to the needs of incorporating new technological tools. The contribution of Raviolo et al. aims at mapping the specific activities of e-tutoring at the eCampus University with respect to the reference models present in the literature and taking into account the specificity of higher education. The fundamental objective was to analyze the role of the e-tutor and to highlight how this is a key figure in the e-learning process to implement an effective learning experience.

Student's Perception of Online Learning, Teaching, and Assessment in Higher Education

The special track "Student's perception of online learning, teaching, and assessment in higher education" aimed at studying the relations between students' perception of the academic environment (teaching, workload, and assessment), their learning approaches, and outcomes in online academic learning environments. More specifically, since in higher education distance learning environments are different from traditional ones, the special track focused on research and trends in students' perceptions regarding course design and organization, content presentation, learning climate, digital interaction (with peers, tutors, and teachers), feedback, technical competency and workload, teaching methods, and their possible impact on satisfaction, motivation, and learning outcomes.

Carlomagno and Minghelli investigate the perception of space and relation, probing, through the use of CReAP, the DLaD model centered on body, relationship, and performative actions. Their aim was to study perception in relation to interpersonal distance, and to define the characteristics of a space which can assume the necessary relational connotations for didactic activities. The model of performative didactics was implemented during workshops with students and teachers at the Suor Orsola Benincasa University of Naples and at the Catholic University of the Sacred Heart of Milan. Fedeli et al. study the challenges experienced in fostering student engagement in MOOCs by exploring the learning experience of the participants. The experimental environment was "Innovative Teaching: Engaging Adult Learners with Active Learning", a MOOC platform developed at the University of Padua, and the study aimed to promote active learning, enhance cooperative engagement, and develop communities of inquiry.

Faculty Development, Distance Education, and Online Learning Systems in Higher Education

The special track "Faculty development, distance education, and online learning systems in higher education" aimed at illustrating the current trends in online faculty development and at facilitating the exchange of experiences and knowledge between those involved in the development of the teaching skills of academic teachers practicing in distance learning.

Di Tore et al. showcase several educational web resources for the acquisition of 3D printing skills that the University of Salerno used to train teachers of different grades of the school system in the practice of media education. The contribution of Triacca et al. introduces the strategy that the Catholic University of the Sacred Heart planned in response to the COVID-19 pandemic for offering an integrated teaching method that mixes the traditional teaching approach with digital communication to allow students to follow classes from home without any delay and with full access to all learning opportunities. The study of Perla and Massaro puts the basis for the design of a new paradigm, Virtual Patient Education, for experimenting with tele-medicine opportunities in primary and secondary prevention contexts. In particular, the authors present the results of exploratory research aimed at investigating the perceptions of students of Educational Sciences and Primary Education Sciences at the University of

Bari "Aldo Moro" on the social impact of obesity and on citizen/patient involvement in informed lifestyles with health and quality of life outcomes. Vinci and Scarinci administered an online questionnaire to university teachers to investigate their experience of distance learning during the COVID-19 pandemic with a particular focus on didactic mediation and evaluation. Finally, the work of Agrati et al. focuses on how the teaching material of an Assessment Literacy course held in the primary and secondary school teachers training program of three Italian and Russian universities was adapted during the COVID-19 pandemic.

E-Learning and Disciplinary Teaching: Issues and Innovations in Contemporary Higher Education

The special track "E-learning and disciplinary teaching: issues and innovations in contemporary higher education" aimed to collect and analyze e-learning practices that focus on curricular teaching experiences. It was mainly directed to teachers and researchers interested in the learning of disciplinary teaching, its training processes, and its pedagogical consequences.

De Blasio and Vinci focus on some of the possible transformations that digital environments produce in the relationships between teachers, and between teachers and students, by analyzing a specific teaching methodology: narrative learning. Iannella et al. describe a learning activity called Advent Calendar proposed within a calculus course. The purpose is to explore the possible advantages of mixing digital tools and pedagogical techniques in order to keep students engaged and help them to approach the study of mathematics effectively, improving both their satisfaction level and their results. Boffa et al. discuss how to design a set of categories to guide the digital transaction in engineering and beyond by maintaining the alignment of the Teaching Learning Activities (TLA) and Assessment Tasks (AT) to the Intended Learning Outcomes (ILO).

From an Emergency DaD to New Forms of Blended Learning via Effective Methodologies to Design, Deliver, and Evaluate Learning

The special track "From an emergency DaD to new forms of blended learning via effective methodologies to design, deliver, and evaluate learning" aimed at collecting proposals for rich and hybrid learning environments which integrate technology into educational contexts through transformed knowledge practices.

Chipa et al. analyze the experience of Service Learning, developed by three upper secondary schools, through the use of the LifEComp framework, whose competences are able to highlight the parallelism with the purposes of Service Learning. Bruschi et al. consider different drivers for transformation that have been embodied in some online pilot courses delivered during the last academic year at the University of Turin. The joint application of these drivers, through different instances and their combination, has given a vision of what is changing, while inspiring faculty members in the design and delivery of innovative courses to shape the future offer of higher education.

Acknowledgments

The contribution of Pietro Ducange to this work is supported by the Italian Ministry of Education and Research (MIUR), in the framework of the CrossLab project (Departments of Excellence). The work of Riccardo Pecori has been supported by the PON R&I 2014–2020 "AIM: Attraction and International Mobility" project, funded by the Italian Ministry of Education and Research (MIUR), the European Social Fund, and the European Regional Development Fund.

References

1. El Refae, G.A., Kaba, A., Eletter, S.: Distance learning during Covid-19 pandemic: satisfaction, opportunities and challenges as perceived by faculty members and students. Interactive Technology and Smart Education (2021)
2. Giovannella, C.: Effect Induced by the Covid-19 pandemic on students' perception about technologies and distance learning. In: Mealha, Ó., Rehm, M., Rebedea, T. (eds.) Ludic, Co-design and Tools Supporting Smart Learning Ecosystems and Smart Education. Smart Innovation, Systems and Technologies, vol. 197, pp. 105–116. Springer, Singapore (2021). https://doi.org/10.1007/978-981-15-7383-5_9
3. Marek, M.W., Chew, C.S., Wu, W.C.V.: Teacher experiences in converting classes to distance learning in the Covid-19 pandemic. Int. J. Dist. Edu. Technol. **19**(1), 40–60 (2021)
4. Traxler, J.: Distance learning–predictions and possibilities. Educ. Sci. **8**(1), 35 (2018)
5. Stracke, C.M., Downes, S., Conole, G., Burgos, D., Nascimbeni, F., et al.: Are MOOCs open educational resources?: a literature review on history, definitions and typologies of OER and MOOCs. Open Praxis **11**(4), 331 (2019)
6. Burgos, D., et al. (eds.): Higher Education Learning Methodologies and Technologies Online. Springer, Cham (2019). https://doi.org/10.1007/978-3-030-31284-8
7. Agrati, L.S., et al.: Bridges and mediation in higher distance education: HELMeTO 2020 report. Educ. Sci. **11**(7), 334 (2021)
8. Stracke, C.M.: Quality frameworks and learning design for open education. Int. Rev. Res. Open Dist. Learn. **20**(2) (2019)
9. Daniel, J.: Education and the Covid-19 pandemic. Prospects **49**(1), 91–96 (2020)
10. Agrati, L.S., et al. (eds.): Bridges and Mediation in Higher Distance Education. Springer, Cham (2020). https://doi.org/10.1007/978-3-030-67435-9

Contents

Methodologies for Distance Learning in Higher Education

Threaded Forums and Social Annotation in Higher Education: A Comparison in Supporting Collaborative Knowledge Construction

Graziano Cecchinato(✉)

University of Padova, Padua, Italy
graziano.cecchinato@unipd.it

Abstract. This paper documents a comparison between two collaborative knowledge construction practices carried out in a post-graduate course. A quasi-experimental study was conducted to analyse and compare the interactions among students in Moodle threaded forums and the Perusall social annotation system. It has been investigated if and how the different functionalities and affordances of the two environments influence student participation and knowledge construction processes. After a brief explanation of Perusall's functionalities and the activities accomplished by the students, this paper presents a quantitative and content analysis of students' interactions. Results show that the affordances of the two environments led students to different patterns of participation. In Moodle threaded forums, discussions were more oriented to general topics of the course and were intended to express opinions, whereas in the Perusall social annotation system there has been more focus on fostering comprehension about specific issues of study material. Social annotation systems, therefore, could be a productive environment to support students' study.

Keywords: Social annotation · Perusall · Forum

1 Introduction

Over the past three decades, with the progressive spread of e-learning in higher education (HE), online threaded forums, available in almost all Learning Management Systems, have supported students' interactions in various collaborative knowledge construction practices [1]. In the framework of socio-constructivist theory, online threaded forums have been used to foster collaboration among students, accomplish cooperative tasks, promote meaning negotiation, improve social relationships, and so on. Recently, the outbreak of the Covid-19 pandemic, and the following contraction of in-presence classes, has further increased their use.

Despite their wide use, however, there is a common opinion, particularly among students, that these practices are a useless workload that does not really help them to learn [2]. Growing research confirms that forum discussions can be digressing, shallow

G. Casalino et al. (Eds.): HELMeTO 2021, CCIS 1542, pp. 3–15, 2022.
https://doi.org/10.1007/978-3-030-96060-5_1

and inefficient in promoting focused and interactive dialogues on course content [3–7]. Some of the reasons concern the learning practices' design and how the teachers lead the activities [8]; others regard the affordances provided by these environments to meet students' interactions and learning needs [9–12].

A possible way to overcome these downsides could come from alternative collaborative environments produced by the evolution of the digital ecosystem. This contribution explores the use of social annotation (SA) in HE, which could be productive, particularly in supporting online group study in tackling course material.

2 Social Annotation in Higher Education

Forum systems are separate from study materials.

To open a discussion over a course topic, students are discouraged by two constraints: they have to check if there are other open threads on the same topic, which could be a long and annoying task, and, if there are none, they have to reconstruct the context of their comment. Usually, the more selective the reference is to the materials, which could be even a single word, the more demanding the task is. The post's readers also have drawbacks: they have to open the material, find the passage, and read it. So, there is a divorce between the study material and the forum activities [13].

One practice that could overcome the weaknesses of forums and help support students' commitment to study the material is SA, the digital reinvention of one of the essential activities of scholarly inquiry: annotation [14]. The practice of annotation is a function of sustained intellectual engagement consisting of highlighting or underlining chunks of text and writing related notes in the margins. Although the research is poor and not all the results are consistent [15], there is evidence that paper-based annotation can produce remarkable learning benefits [16], improving students' performance in reading and writing [17], providing a helpful memory medium [18], and promoting deep learning [19].

SA can extend these benefits by exploiting new technologies. It is a web service that makes ubiquitous and shareable the notes inserted in a digital resource [20, 21]. Like other practices that have been digitally reinvented, annotation has been deeply changed by the new social dimension. Instead of being a personal tool for reflection and memory, annotation has become a way of asking and giving help to other readers to understand, clarify, and extend their knowledge of the content, facilitating and valorising the social constructivist learning process.

Following this perspective, a growing number of faculties have begun to use SA systems in HE. The literature review by Zhu and colleagues [22] reported that SA is mainly applied in processing domain-specific knowledge, supporting argumentation and inquiry, improving literacy skills, and supporting instructor or peer assessments.

A corpus of research indicates some benefits associated with the use of SA in various educational settings. For example, researchers found improvement in participation and engagement [19, 23, 24], in collaborative learning [25, 26]; in maintaining the focus of discussion [27] in summarising skills [28]; in argumentation and reading strategies [29] in reading comprehension, meta-cognitive skills and peer-critique skills [16, 17, 30–35] and also in learning outcomes [19, 25, 26, 36–38].

Even if a minority of these studies are based on rigorous empirical designs, as most of them rely on self-reported data, the three main literature reviews carried out on SA in HE [22, 39, 40] confirm that it can foster motivation in tackling coursework and in improving collaborative knowledge construction.

As reported by Clapp and colleagues [2], there is also increasing literature that shares practices and reports promising results when applying SA to different educational subjects, e.g., English as a foreign language [41], political science [42], academic writing [43], pathology [44], history [45], pharmacy [46], translation studies [47], education technologies [48], Computer science [49], Humanities [50], attesting to a good maturation level when applying SA to HE.

SA tools designed explicitly for HE have functionalities that improve students' online dialogues and collaborative learning. SA practices in HE are usually self-directed by the students and specifically addressed to understand study materials better. By sharing their questions, remarks, doubts, suggestions, hypotheses, or assumptions on the documents' issues, students realise that they can get a more reliable comprehension, avoid common misconceptions, reduce workload, and extend their social relationships among classmates and teachers [38]. In addition, SA tools have functionalities that promote students' help and valorise their participation, such as upvoting systems that improve a sense of community and social recognition.

Other remarkable aspects refer to affordances and interaction design. For example, SA tools anchor every dialogue to a specific passage of text, showing both in the same window, making the context of the discussions clear to all.

This reduces the level of required explicitness, the amount of text to write and read, possible misunderstanding, thus fostering involvement [51]. Moreover, the aggregation of specific material's passages and all the related annotations avoids dealing with the same issue in different dialogues, an eventuality common in forums, which produces inefficiencies and compromises participation [52].

3 Overview of Perusall

Since the rise of the Web, SA systems have been developed for different purposes, like social bookmarking, collaborative writing, social reviewing, social fact-checking, and collaborative knowledge construction in educational settings. The list of the tools is very long, including CoNote [53], OATS [54], EDUCOSM [55], Diigo (https://www.diigo.com/) [56], HyLighter (https://www.hylighter.com/) [24], Spreadcrumbs (http://spreadcrumbs.l3s.uni-hannover.de/) [57], Hypothesis (https://web.hypothes.is/) [58], and Perusall (https://perusall.com/) [59].

Only a few of these tools are still active and updated with the current functionalities of the Web. Among them, the tool chosen for the educational practices analysed in this study is Perusall. There are many reasons for this choice, covering several aspects. Technical: it is very user-friendly, it is almost the only SA tool that is compliant with all browsers, it does not require add-in software to install, it allows to annotate text as well as images and videos, and it is LTI compliant, allowing integration with the main LMS. Economical: it is completely free for students and teachers and, thanks to agreements with leading publishers, it allows students to access many textbooks at a reduced price.

Ethical: it has fair terms of service, fair privacy policy and tools for special education needs. Educational: it has been designed inside the academy (Harvard) specifically to facilitate socio-constructivist practices in HE [38]. Remarkable Perusall's functionalities are reports that highlight the most challenging material's areas for students and an automated grading system based on a machine learning algorithm that considers data collected from student participation. Other Perusall features aim to improve students' dialogues, fostering their participation and better focusing the discussions on the most interesting issues:

- annotations are inserted by highlighting a chunk of study material, such as a sentence, a single word, part of a page, a detail of an image, or a frame in a video, and visualised on the side in the same windows. So, the annotation, any possible replies and the related course material are strictly anchored;
- with single click students and teachers can express their appreciation by subscribing to an annotation. The number of subscriptions highlights the relevance of a question or the appreciation for a reply to students and teachers;
- viewing settings allow students to focus only on specific annotations, such as those from a specific student, from the teacher or the unread annotations. Students can choose the option to show only the questions without answers, and that encourages students to focus on helping their peers;
- the social recognition that derives from receiving subscriptions from students and teachers rewards student engagement and fosters "social presence" [60], producing a better "sense of community" [61, 62].

Perusall makes it easy and productive for teachers to carry out SA activities. In order to assign materials to study, teachers can load documents from their computers, open scientific papers from the Internet and textbooks from the Perusall catalogue, which includes electronic versions of more than 70,000 textbooks. Teachers can easily create assignments defining work notes, workgroups, annotations parameters and deadlines. They can contribute to the discussions by making comments and upvoting students' annotations.

4 Study

4.1 Research Questions

This contribution documents a study on the application of Perusall in a post-graduate course to support processing domain-specific knowledge through student discussions about course materials. The study aims to analyse whether or not SA practices using Perusall can improve students' participation and meaning's negotiation compared with Moodle threaded forums.

The research questions were:

- are there differences between students' participation using Perusall SA activities compared to Moodle threaded forums?

And, if so:

- what are the differences, and how do they influence learning?

4.2 Related Work

Excluding some experiences that report anecdotal evidence, few quasi-experimental studies compare threaded forums and SA activities in HE.

Brush and colleagues (2002) [13] have compared EPost, a discussion board system, with WebAnn calculating the number of comments, the number of replies and the number of characters posted on both systems. The findings have shown that discussions in the SA environment were more focused and more thoughtful.

In another study comparing the Blackboard forum system with Openlaw Annotation, van der Pol and colleagues (2006) [63] carried out a content analysis of the communications in both environments. Findings have shown that anchored discussions strengthen the link between discussions and study material and that the SA system seems to offer increased communicative efficiency.

Sun and Gao (2014) [64] have carried out a content analysis of the conversations in Diigo and threaded forums identifying focus and types of knowledge construction processes. Results have shown that the SA tool led to more focused discussions, and maybe it is a good alternative for achieving specific learning goals.

In a more recent study (2017) [27], the same authors comparing Blackboard forums with Diigo analysed students participation by calculating the number and the average word count of comments in the two environments. Moreover, a content analysis similar to the previous one has been executed, confirming the former conclusions.

4.3 Procedure

A quasi-experimental study involved 90 students who attended the "E-learning Technologies" post-graduate course of the "Social, Work and Communication Psychology" second cycle degree at the University of Padova in the 2020/2021 academic year. The course aimed to acquaint students with the potential of new e-learning technologies through hands-on activities; thus, they were not involved in unrelated to course activities.

Students were divided into two groups by last name (A-Lor, n = 47 and Los-Z, n = 43). Both groups received the same assignment, the study of two research papers. The A-Lor group used Perusall, and the Los-Z group used a Moodle forum for the first paper and vice versa for the second paper. Students were familiar with Moodle forums, having used them in many other courses, whereas nobody had used Perusall before. Nevertheless, no support was provided. Each assignment lasted three days. The assignments were not mandatory, but by carrying them out, the students received a grade (automatically in Perusall and manually, by the teacher, in the Moodle forum) worth a maximum of 4% of the final course mark. Students were not aware of the evaluation criteria to promote free and genuine participation, only aimed at understanding the two papers. The teacher did not prompt any dialogues with initial questions or post any comments on Perusall or the Moodle forum.

The students' involvement in collaborative knowledge construction was investigated by conducting both quantitative and content analyses comparing students' participation in both environments. For the first analysis, the number of comments, the number of dialogues, the average comments per dialogue, and the average words per comment were considered indicator parameters for the different modes of interaction.

The content analysis evaluated the interactive level of the comments, considering whether they were intended as self-reflection or as a prompt to open a discussion with classmates. A second analysis investigated the granularity level of the comments, evaluating if they tackled a general theme or a specific issue of study materials.

4.4 Results

The computation was executed using Jamovi version 1.6.23. In Table 1 are reported the descriptive data that compares students participation in the two environments.

Table 1. Descriptive data on Perusall and Moodle Forum activities.

Activity	Environment	Number of comments	Number of dialogues	Average comments per dialogue	SD	Average words per comment	SD
1	Perusall A - LOR	614	164	3.74	2.21	27.83	22.27
1	Moodle forum LOS - Z	139	33	4.21	5.18	89.93	67.21
2	Perusall LOS - Z	224	69	3.25	2.37	44.66	26.68
2	Moodle forum A - LOR	180	30	6.00	6.51	95.01	51.48

Data showed that the same activity was considerably different in the two environments. In Perusall, there were a higher number of comments, a higher number of dialogues, a lower number of comments per dialogue and a lower number of words per comment. Overall, the number of comments was 262.69% higher in Perusall when compared with Moodle, and on average, the Moodle forum comments were 287.66% longer than the Perusall comments.

Regarding the number of comments, the results of the two-way ANOVA test showed a statistically significant difference in the two environments [$F(1, 176) = 46.5$, $p < .001$, $\eta_p^2 = .209$]. For the same variable, the results showed a statistically significant difference also taking into account the two activities [$F(1, 176) = 21.7$, $p < .001$, $\eta p^2 = .110$] and the interaction between environments and activities [$F(1, 176) = 27.7$, $p < .001$, $\eta p^2 = .136$] (Table 2).

Table 2. Two-way ANOVA test on the number of comments.

	Sum of squares	df	Mean square	F	p
Environments	1358	1	1358.4	46.5	<.001
Activities	633	1	633.4	21.7	<.001
Environments * Activities	810	1	809.8	27.7	<.001
Residuals	5139	176	29.2		

The same test on the length of comments showed a statistically significant difference when only considering the two different environments [$F(1, 176) = 99.90$, $p < .001$, $\eta_p^2 = 0.362$] (Table 3).

Table 3. Two-way ANOVA test on the length of comments.

	Sum of squares	df	Mean square	F	p
Environments	331111.4	1	331111.4	99.89976	<.001
Activities	11478.0	1	11478.0	3.46303	.064
Environments * Activities	32.5	1	32.5	.00980	.921
Residuals	583340.9	176	3314.4		

The content analysis was carried out by coding the comments with the Pena-Shaff and Nicholls' schema (2004) [65] according to whether they were "Interactive" or "Monologue". Following that schema, questions, replies, support, consensus, clarification/elaboration, social interactions, and comments with references to others were coded as "Interactive". On the other hand, reflective analysis, subjective analysis, assertion, and off-topic comments were coded as "Monologue". Moreover, all the comments were coded "Specific" or "Overall" according to whether their content targeted a specific issue or a general theme of the study material (Table 4).

The Author and the course's teacher assistant coded the comments independently with an agreement rate of 87.7% and Cohen's Kappa of .724, indicating a substantial level of agreement according to estimation guidelines [66]. The coding results are reported in Table 5.

Most of the comments were coded "Interactive" (69.8% forum Moodle and 70.1% Perusall), whereas 26.7% of the Moodle forum and 80.5% of Perusall comments were coded "Specific".

The binomial logistic regression test examined the different distributions of the variables "Interactive/Monologue" and "Specific/Overall" in the two environments. Results showed a statistically significant difference only for the "Specific/Overall" variable (Chisquare $= 49.8$, $df = 1$, $p < .001$) (Table 6).

Table 4. Examples of annotations' classification (translated from Italian).

Specific	Generic
In the paper, they say: "It is unclear from the literature whether there is a relationship between pre-class reading behaviour and in-class exam performance". I think the point is not about how useful it is to present the content before class, but how better is active, shared learning compared to the traditional teaching method	Surely, a shared collaborative attitude influences the final outcome. A common workspace to share reciprocal knowledge and mutual interests and ideas to stimulate motivation among peers is essential
Interactive	Monologue
I agree with XXX, the activation of new methodologies increases learning, but, on the other hand, I do not think that teachers experience less workload. In fact, they have a chance to improve their teaching method and innovate it, making it "user friendly" for young people	I hope that the system will move towards greater use of technological tools. I believe that teachers are pretty unfamiliar with the use of digital tools. However, during the Covid-19 pandemic they have been forced to use technology more than ever, and certainly now they recognise its potential

Table 5. Results of the content analysis.

Environments	Interactive comments	Monologue comments	Specific comments	Overall comments
Perusall	70.12%	29.88%	80.51%	19.49%
Moodle forum	69.83%	30.17%	26.72%	73.28%

Table 6. Binomial logistic regression test on "Interactive/Monologue" and "Specific/Overall".

Variable	χ^2	df	p
Interactive/Monologue	.00254	1	.960
Specific/Overall	49.8	1	<.001

5 Discussion

The descriptive data on Perusall and Moodle Forum activities shows a higher number of dialogues with fewer and shorter comments per dialogue in Perusall (Table 1). This reasonably seems to indicate that the interactions have been focused on more specific issues, considering the distinctive affordances provided by Perusall that strictly links comments to related chunks of study material. Furthermore, this statement is reinforced by the higher number of longer replies in the Moodle forum thread, suggesting more general discussions.

Shorter comments in Perusall (Table 3) could attest to the benefits of the contextual visualisation of text and the related comments that reduce the level of required explicitness. And the upvoting system may also have contributed to reducing the number of comments per dialogue in Perusall.

Findings seem to suggest that the different design of the two environments has influenced students' participation.

Results show that not only the different designs of the two environments but also the different activities have influenced the number of comments (Table 2). This can be explained by the different lengths of the papers tackled in the two activities (six and eleven pages) since the longer paper generated more comments than the shorter. Therefore, the different length of the papers is an element to be avoided in future research.

The results of the content analysis, that is supported by a substantial level of agreement between the two researchers that codded the comments, do not show a significant difference in the dichotomic variable "Interactive/Monologue" but shows a considerable difference for the "Specific/Overall" one, confirming a higher focus on specific key questions of the study materials in Perusall.

Overall, it is reasonable to suppose that some specific interaction affordances provided by Perusall can lead students to be more focused and stick to the study's content dialogues, therefore fostering a better process of collaborative knowledge construction.

Future research could corroborate these results with students' opinions on whether or not different environments influenced their learning interactions and in what ways. In addition, research comparing SA and threaded forum practices with learning outcomes in different subjects could provide other remarkable clues on the different benefits of these two environments on students' learning.

6 Conclusion

The present research findings are consistent with previous studies that compared forums and SA practices using other environments [13, 27, 63, 64].

SA tools seem to foster dialogues more focused on processing the meaning of the materials and more directed to the point. In contrast, forum boards are more suited for discussing general topics and comparing different opinions. Thus, SA tools can be very useful in processing domain-specific knowledge when students struggle to grasp concepts. Therefore, teachers have to carefully consider the most suitable environments to choose according to their teaching goals.

Despite a growing research consensus, SA remains relatively unknown as a collaborative knowledge construction tool; therefore, it could be very useful. For instance, one helpful application could be in the *flipped classroom* context. As known [67], in this approach students are encouraged to tackle the study material before attending the relative class. Using a SA environment can make the students' efforts more productive and provide the teacher with useful tips to set the subsequent lesson to match the students' learning needs. In this way, instead of being a "teacher-centred" lecture focused on predefined topics, the lesson can target the most problematic learning issues that emerged from the students' interactions. SA environments like Perusall facilitate this process by providing reports with the most commented passages and unanswered questions.

Acknowledgements. The Author is very grateful to the students in the class for participating in the study and to Romina Papa for participating in the content analysis.

References

1. Fehrman, S., Watson, S.L.: A systematic review of asynchronous online discussions in online higher education. Am. J. Dist. Educ. **35**(3), 200–213 (2021)
2. Clapp, J., DeCoursey, M., Lee, S.W.S., Li, K.: "Something fruitful for all of us": social annotation as a signature pedagogy for literature education. Arts Humanit. High. Educ. **20**(3), 295–319 (2021)
3. Gao, F., Zhang, T., Franklin, T.: Designing asynchronous online discussion environments: recent progress and possible future directions. Br. J. Edu. Technol. **44**(3), 469–483 (2013)
4. Knowlton, D.S.: Promoting durable knowledge construction through online discussion. In: Proceedings of the Mid-South Instructional Technology Conference (2001)
5. Hara, N., Bonk, C.J., Angeli, C.: Content analysis of online discussion in an applied educational psychology course. Instr. Sci. **28**(2), 115–152 (2000)
6. Larson, B.E., Keiper, T.A.: Classroom discussion and threaded electronic discussion: learning in two arenas. Contemp. Issues Technol. Teach. Educ. **2**(1), 45–62 (2002)
7. Gunawardena, C.N., Lowe, C.A., Anderson, T.: Analysis of a global online debate and the development of an interaction analysis model for examining social construction of knowledge in computer conferencing. J. Educ. Comput. Res. **17**(4), 397–431 (1997)
8. Rourke, L., Kanuka, H.: Learning in communities of inquiry: a review of the literature. Int. J. E-Learn. Dist. Educ. **23**(1), 19–48 (2009)
9. Herring, S.C.: Interactional coherence in CMC. In: Proceedings of the 32nd Annual Hawaii International Conference on Systems Sciences 1999. HICSS-32. IEEE (1999)
10. Hewitt, J.: Beyond threaded discourse. Int. J. Educ. Telecommun. **7**(3), 207–221 (2001)
11. Thomas, M.J.: Learning within incoherent structures: the space of online discussion forums. J. Comput. Assist. Learn. **18**(3), 351–366 (2002)
12. Lambiase, J.J.: Hanging by a thread: topic development and death in an online discussion of breaking news. Language@ Internet **7**(9) (2010)
13. Brush, A.J., Bargeron, D., Grudin, J., Borning, A., Gupta, A.: Supporting interaction outside of class: anchored discussions vs. discussion boards. In: Proceedings of the Conference on Computer Support for Collaborative Learning: Foundations for a CSCL Community, Boulder, CO, USA, pp. 425–434. International Society of the Learning Sciences (2002)
14. Unsworth, J.: Scholarly primitives: what methods do humanities researchers have in common, and how might our tools reflect this. In: Symposium on Humanities Computing: Formal Methods, Experimental Practice, vol. 13, p. 5-00. King's College, London (2000)
15. Dunlosky, J., Rawson, K., Marsh, E., Nathan, M., Willingham, D.: Improving students learning with effective learning techniques: promising directions from cognitive and educational psychology. Psychol. Sci. Public Interest **14**(1), 4–58 (2013)
16. Li, S.C., Pow, J.W.C., Cheung, W.C.: A delineation of the cognitive processes manifested in a social annotation environment. J. Comput. Assist. Learn. **31**(1), 1–13 (2015)
17. Yang, X., Yu, S., Sun, Z.: The effect of collaborative annotation on Chinese reading level in primary schools in China. Br. J. Edu. Technol. **44**, 95–111 (2013)
18. Marshall, C.C.: Annotation: from paper books to the digital library. In: Proceedings of the Second ACM International Conference on Digital Libraries, pp. 131–140 (1997)
19. Nokelainen, P., Miettinen, M., Kurhila, J., Floréen, P., Tirri, H.: A shared document-based annotation tool to support learner-centred collaborative learning. Br. J. Edu. Technol. **36**, 757–770 (2005)

20. Hoff, C., Wehling, U., Rothkugel, S.: From paper and pen annotations to artefact-based mobile learning. J. Comput. Assist. Learn. **25**, 219–237 (2009)
21. Glover, I., Xu, Z., Hardaker, G.: Online annotation–research and practices. Comput. Educ. **49**(4), 1308–1320 (2007)
22. Zhu, X., Chen, B., Avadhanam, R.M., Shui, H., Zhang, R.Z.: Reading and connecting: using social annotation in online classes. Inf. Learn. Sci. **121**, 261–271 (2020)
23. Johnson, T.E., Archibald, T.N., Tenenbaum, G.: Individual and team annotation effects on students' reading comprehension, critical thinking, and meta-cognitive skills. Comput. Hum. Behav. **26**(6), 1496–1507 (2010)
24. Lebow, D.G., Lick, D.W.: HyLighter: an effective interactive annotation innovation for distance education. In: 20th Annual Conference on Distance Teaching and Learning (2005)
25. Hwang, W., Wang, C., Sharples, M.: A study of multimedia annotation of Web based materials. Comput. Educ. **48**(4), 680–699 (2007)
26. Su, A.Y.S., Yang, S.J.H., Hwang, W., Zhang, J.: A web 2.0-based collaborative annotation system for enhancing knowledge sharing in collaborative learning environments. Comput. Educ. **55**(2), 752–766 (2010)
27. Sun, Y., Gao, F.: Comparing the use of a social annotation tool and a threaded discussion forum to support online discussions. Internet High. Educ. **32**, 72–79 (2017)
28. Passig, D., Maidel-Kravetsky, J.: The impact of collaborative online reading on summarising skills. Educ. Inf. Technol. **21**(3), 531–543 (2016)
29. Wolfe, J.: Annotations and the collaborative digital library: effects of an aligned annotation inter-face on student argumentation and reading strategies. Int. J. Comput.-Support. Collab. Learn. **3**(2), 141–164 (2008)
30. Nokelainen, P., Kurhila, J., Miettinen, M., Floreen, P., Tirri, H.: Evaluating the role of a shared document-based annotation tool in learner-centered collaborative learning. Paper Presented at the Advanced Learning Technologies. The 3rd IEEE International Conference (2003)
31. Chen, C.M., Chen, F.Y.: Enhancing digital reading performance with a collaborative reading annotation system. Comput. Educ. **77**, 67–81 (2014)
32. Archibald, T.N.: The effect of the integration of social annotation technology, first principles of instruction, and team-based learning on students' reading comprehension, critical thinking, and meta-cognitive skills. Ph.D. Dissertation, Florida State University, Tallahassee, FL (2010)
33. Chen, C.M., Wang, J.Y., Chen, Y.C.: Facilitating English-language reading performance by a digital reading annotation system with self-regulated learning mechanisms. Educ. Technol. Soc. **17**(1), 102–114 (2014)
34. Yang, S.J.H., Zhang, J., Su, A.Y.S., Tsai, J.J.P.: A collaborative multimedia annotation tool for enhancing knowledge sharing in CSCL. Interact. Learn. Environ. **19**(1), 45–62 (2011)
35. Chen, C.M., Li, M.C., Chen, T.C.: A web-based collaborative reading annotation system with gamification mechanisms to improve reading performance. Comput. Educ. **144**, 1–17 (2020)
36. Wang, Q.: Using online shared workspaces to support group collaborative learning. Comput. Educ. **55**(3), 1270–1276 (2010)
37. Mendenhall, A., Johnson, T.E.: Fostering the development of critical thinking skills, and reading comprehension of undergraduates using a web 2.0 tool coupled with a learning system. Interact. Learn. Environ. **18**(3), 263–276 (2010)
38. Miller, K., Lukoff, B., King, G., Mazur, E.: Use of a social annotation platform for pre-class reading assignments in a flipped introductory physics class. In: Frontiers in Education, vol. 3, p. 8. Frontiers (2018)
39. Novak, E., Razzouk, R., Johnson, T.E.: The educational use of social annotation tools in higher education: a literature review. Internet High. Educ. **15**(1), 39–49 (2012)
40. Ghadirian, H., Salehi, K., Ayub, A.F.M.: Social annotation tools in higher education: a preliminary systematic review. Int. J. Learn. Technol. **13**(2), 130–162 (2018)

41. Chang, C.K., Hsu, C.K.: A mobile-assisted synchronously collaborative translation–annotation system for English as a foreign language (EFL) reading comprehension. Comput. Assist. Lang. Learn. **24**(2), 155–180 (2011)
42. Lightfoot, S.: "Delicious politics"—the use of social bookmarking in politics teaching. J. Polit. Sci. Educ. **8**(1), 94–101 (2012)
43. Pargman, D., Hedin, B., Hrastinski, S.: Using group supervision and social annotation systems to support students' academic writing. Högre utbildning **3**(2), 129–134 (2013)
44. Sahota, M., Leung, B., Dowdell, S., Velan, G.M.: Learning pathology using collaborative vs. individual annotation of whole slide images: a mixed methods trial. BMC Med. Educ. **16**(1), 1–9 (2016)
45. Wood, J., Scorpo, A.L., Taylor, S., Rahman, M., Bell, E., Matthews-Jones, L.: Making historians digitally: social bookmarking and inquiry-based learning in history in higher education in the UK. In: Inquiry-Based Learning for the Arts, Humanities, and Social Sciences: A Conceptual and Practical Resource for Educators. Emerald Group Publishing Limited (2014)
46. Sera, L.: # SocialBookmarking: an overview and primer for use in pharmacy education. Curr. Pharm. Teach. Learn. **7**(3), 342–347 (2015)
47. Zhao, N., Gao, F., Yang, D.: Examining student learning and perceptions in social annotation-based translation activities. Interact. Learn. Environ. **26**(7), 958–969 (2018)
48. Cecchinato, G., Foschi, L.C.: Perusall: university learning-teaching innovation employing social annotation and machine learning. Qwerty-Open Interdisc. J. Technol. Cult. Educ. **15**(2), 45–67 (2020)
49. Peng, Z., Mei, L., Yuhua, N., Yi, Z.: The application of the Diigo-based collaborative learning model in the course "fundamentals of computers". In: 2010 International Conference on Educational and Information Technology, vol. 2, pp. V2-446. IEEE (2010)
50. Schneider, E., Hartman, S., Eshel, A., Johnsrud, B.: Making reading visible: social annotation with lacuna in the humanities classroom. J. Interact. Technol. Pedag. **9** (2016)
51. Dillenbourg, P.: What do you mean by collaborative learning? In: Dillenbourg, P. (ed.) Collaborative-Learning: Cognitive and Computational Approaches, pp. 1–19. Elsevier, Oxford (1999)
52. Herrmann, T., Kienle, A.: KOLUMBUS: context-oriented communication support in a collaborative learning environment. In: van Weert, T.J., Munro, R.K. (eds.) Informatics and the Digital Society. ITIFIP, vol. 116, pp. 251–260. Springer, Boston, MA (2003). https://doi.org/10.1007/978-0-387-35663-1_26
53. Davis, J., Huttenlocher, D.: Shared annotation for cooperative learning. In: Proceedings of CSCL95: First International Conference on Computer Support for Collaborative Learning, pp. 84–88. Lawrence Erlbaum, Mahwah (1995)
54. Bateman, S., Farzan, R., Brusilovsky, P., McCalla, G.: OATS: the open annotation and tagging system. In: Proceedings of I2LOR (2006)
55. Miettinen, M., Nokelainen, P., Floréen, P., Tirri, H., Kurhila, J.: EDUCOSM-personalized writable web for learning communities. In: Proceedings ITCC 2003. International Conference on Information Technology: Coding and Computing, pp. 37–42. IEEE (2003)
56. Estellés, E., Del Moral, E., González, F.: Social bookmarking tools as facilitators of learning and research collaborative processes: the Diigo case. Interdisc. J. E-Learn. Learn. Objects **6**(1), 175–191 (2010)
57. Kawase, R., Herder, E., Nejdl, W.: Annotations and hypertrails with spreadcrumbs. An easy way to annotate, refind and share. In: Proceedings of the 6th International Conference on Web Information Systems and Technology (2010)
58. Ruland Staines, H.: Digital open annotation with hypothesis: supplying the missing capability of the Web. J. Sch. Publ. **49**(3), 345–365 (2018)
59. King, G.: An Introduction to Perusall. Erişim (2016). https://perusall.com/downloads/gary-king-webinar-slides.Pdf

60. Lowenthal, P.R.: Social presence. In: Social Computing: Concepts, Methodologies, Tools, and Applications, pp. 129–136. IGI Global (2010)
61. Rovai, A.P.: Building sense of community at a distance. Int. Rev. Res. Open Distrib. Learn. **3**(1), 1–16 (2002)
62. Kalir, J.H., Morales, E., Fleerackers, A., Alperin, J.P.: "When i saw my peers annotating": student perceptions of social annotation for learning in multiple courses. Inf. Learn. Sci. (2020)
63. Van der Pol, J., Admiraal, W., Simons, P.R.J.: The affordance of anchored discussion for the collaborative processing of academic texts. Int. J. Comput.-Support. Collab. Learn. **1**(3), 339–357 (2006)
64. Sun, Y., Gao, F.: Web annotation and threaded forum: how did learners use the two environments in an online discussion? J. Inf. Technol. Educ. **13**, 69–88 (2014)
65. Pena-Shaff, J.B., Nicholls, C.: Analysing student interactions and meaning construction in computer bulletin board discussions. Comput. Educ. **42**(3), 243–265 (2004)
66. Landis, J.R., Koch, G.G.: The measurement of observer agreement for categorical data. Biometrics **33**(1), 159–174 (1977)
67. Lage, M.J., Platt, G.J., Treglia, M.: Inverting the classroom: a gateway to creating an inclusive learning environment. J. Econ. Educ. **31**(1), 30–43 (2000)

"Experience" on the Screen. Training Pre-service Teachers on Educational Robotics

Francesca Gratani, Lorella Giannandrea, and Alessandra Renieri(✉)

Department of Education, Cultural Heritage and Tourism, University of Macerata, 62100 Macerata, MC, Italy
{f.gratani,lorella.giannandrea,alessandra.renieri}@unimc.it

Abstract. Training teachers is relevant for Educational Robotics' (ER) effective and motivated introduction in schools. Teachers' self-confidence and beliefs about new technologies are crucial elements for the students' proficiency. A lack of self-confidence could often prevent the successful implementation of new activities in schools. For this reason, Pre-Service Teachers (PSTs) are a key category to invest in. Furthermore, given the potential of ER to achieve inclusive education, there is a solid reason to train Pre-Service Support Teachers (S-PST) as well. Coding and ER training is indeed generally provided through in-person and extra-curricular courses aimed primarily at in-service teachers. The present study addresses the need for training PSTs and S-PSTs on those topics, also through experiential distance curricular courses. Specifically, we examined PSTs' and S-PSTs' knowledge and self-confidence towards ER pre-post training, their beliefs and their satisfaction with the courses. The study also investigates whether a distance experiential pathway can be successful despite the lack of a face-to-face experience. The results are satisfactory not only for improving knowledge but also for the effectiveness in enhancing PSTs' self-confidence towards ER and coding. We also achieved positive results in terms of beliefs and satisfaction with the course.

Keywords: Pre-service teacher · Teacher training · Educational robotics · Support teaching · Distance learning

1 Introduction

Training teachers on Educational Robotics (ER) is relevant for its successful and motivated introduction in schools [1]. Despite the proven potential of ER as a learning tool to promote disciplinary and 21st-century transversal skills, robots are still underused in schools. To promote their use, it is necessary to reflect not so much on the tool itself, but rather on the teachers who will use the tool [2]. ER effectiveness is highly influenced by the way teachers propose it to their pupils [3].

Researchers highlight that teachers' self-confidence and beliefs about new technologies are crucial elements for the students' proficiency. A lack of self-confidence or a fear of new technologies could often prevent the successful implementation of new activities in schools [4–6].

G. Casalino et al. (Eds.): HELMeTO 2021, CCIS 1542, pp. 16–30, 2022.
https://doi.org/10.1007/978-3-030-96060-5_2

For this reason, looking at the future of teaching, Pre-Service Teachers (PSTs) are a key category to invest in [7, 8], especially for the topic of ER. Undergraduate education is the stage where PSTs start to build their professional identity [7]. Starting to learn about ER during that period allows them to adapt to new technology trends, understand the pedagogy behind ER, and experience its usefulness. They will gain self-confidence in learning and teaching ER, and they will be encouraged to include it in their future classroom [9].

The aim of ER training courses is not just to know, build and programme a new robot, but, furthermore, to enable teachers on the educational benefits that Robotics can bring [10]. These courses could be an incentive for new insights, encouraging teachers to deepen what they had learned and giving them the confidence to experiment in their classrooms [11].

Moreover, ER has proved to be one of the most promising tools for achieving an inclusive education [12, 13]. Therefore, there are solid reasons and needs also to train support teachers [14] to exploit all the meaningful benefits of technology.

In response to current demands, we need to update the PSTs curriculum knowledge [15] and make them able to use this knowledge in practice, becoming "reflective practitioners" [16]. However, most teacher training courses focus on providing them with simple knowledge and skills, maintaining an approach in which participants are not active protagonists [17]. ER tools and methodologies, being based on a constructivist and embodied approach, support an experiential learning cycle, well synthesized in the four steps of Kolb's model [18]: concrete experience, reflective observation, abstract conceptualization, active experimentation.

This challenge becomes even more daunting considering the recent shift to distance learning due to the covid-19 emergency.

The effective use of technology in education requires thoughtful planning, design, reflection and testing. The trainer should reflect on the impact that a specific strategy has on the learning experience and orient practices to the student needs. Course design has to promote forms of active learning since the more active a student is in the learning process, the more student-centered the learning process is. Distance learning environment can be successful when it encourages: (i) contact between students, (ii) reciprocity and cooperation between students, (iii) prompt feedback, (iv) time on task, (v) active learning techniques, (vi) communication of high expectations, and (vii) respect diversity and ways of learning from each student. Relevant techniques to promote active learning in online environments are problem-based learning, collaborative and cooperative learning, and role-play simulation [19].

Coding and ER training is generally provided through in-person and extra-curricular courses aimed primarily at in-service teachers.

The present study addresses the need for training PSTs and Pre-Service Support Teachers (S-PSTs) on those topics, also through experiential distance curricular courses. Specifically, this study examines whether PSTs' and S-PSTs' knowledge, beliefs and self-confidence towards ER change after participation in the training program. The study also explores the PSTs' (and S-PSTs') satisfaction with the courses.

The paper has the following structure: Sect. 2 describes courses' participants (Sect. 2.1), activities (Sect. 2.2), and assessment methods (Sect. 2.3); Sect. 3 reports the study results and their discussion; the last section outlines our conclusions and final considerations.

2 Methods

The courses were held entirely online between March and April 2021, using the two platforms adopted by the University to support synchronous and asynchronous interactions. The reference platform for asynchronous interactions was OpenOLAT, where materials, tasks, and feedback were shared. Microsoft Teams was instead used for all the synchronous meetings. The next subsections will provide a detailed description of the participants, the course activities, and the assessment instruments/methods.

2.1 Participants

The PST course was attended by 200 students enrolled in the third year of the master's degree course in Primary Education Sciences at the University of Macerata (MC). Instead, the S-PST course was attended by 49 students enrolled at the specialization course for Kindergarten Support Teaching, provided by the University of Macerata (MC). Before beginning the classes, participants were asked to fill in a form to detect personal and professional information and issues connected with the training course topics (previous training experiences, knowledge, self-confidence). Depending on how many participants filled the forms in, we collected data concerning personal/professional information of a sample of 88 PST and 47 S-PST (see Table 1).

Participants in both courses are almost all female. For the PST course, 84.09% of students are between 20 and 25 years old, while students of S-PST fall predominantly in the 40+ age group (70.21%). As for the educational qualification, 77.27% PSTs and 63.83% S-PSTs have only a diploma, 10.23% PSTs and 29.79% S-PSTs have a master's degree, and a minority of both sets have a bachelor's degree. Different perspectives emerge regarding the current employment situation, probably due to the age disparity of the two samples: 76.14% of PSTs do not work, whereas more of the 90% of S-PSTs work (80.85% in the educational field and 10.64% in other fields).

Finally, most of the students (PST: 85.23%, S-PST: 74.47%) stated that they had no previous experiences in coding and/or ER. Among the remaining participants, most had individual training experiences (PST: 11.36%, S-PST: 12.77%), and a smaller percentage had done training courses. In particular, 2.6% of PST and 8.2% of S-PST had attended courses lasting less than 5 h, while 6.1% of S-PST had attended courses of more than 5 h.

2.2 Courses Description

The courses are aimed at introducing coding and ER tools and methodologies, focusing on Kindergarten. We decided to introduce training on these topics, starting with the lower stage of education and then move on to the higher stages in subsequent years, with a view to continuity and verticality.

Both courses were introduced as modules within the Technology Laboratories. These Laboratories are included in the curricular teaching of the two courses and require compulsory attendance of 70% (PST) and 100% of the hours (S-PST).

The courses were mainly divided into two phases. The first phase was aimed at presenting some coding and ER tools and methodologies. In particular, we introduced

Table 1. Summary of data describing PST and S-PST samples.

Features	Index	PST values (%)	S-PST values (%)
Age	20–25	84.09	2.13
	26–30	5.68	2.13
	31–40	9.09	25.53
	>40	1.14	70.21
Gender	F	98.86	97.87
	M	1.14	2.13
Educational qualification	Diploma	77.27	63.83
	Bachelor degree	12.5	6.38
	Master's degree	10.23	29.79
	PhD	–	–
Master	Master (I level)	2.27	97.87
	Master (II level)	–	2.13
Background	High school	87.5	91.49
	Technical institute	11.36	2.13
	Professional institute	1.14	6.38
Currently working	No	76.14	8.51
	Yes, in the educational field	18.18	80.85
	Yes, in other fields	5.68	10.64
Teaching educational stage	Nursery	18.75	–
	Kindergarten	6.25	71.05
	Primary school	50	21.05
	Lower Secondary school	6.25	–
	Upper Secondary School	–	2.63
	Other	18.75	5.26
Support teachers	Yes	/	44.74
	No		55.26

students to Cody Roby [20], Cody Feet [21], and Cody Color cards [22], to Bee-Bot emulator platform [23] and Blue-Bot app, and finally to the Scratch Jr software [24] (available both in-app and desktop version). We have shown distinctive features, functioning, potentiality, difficulties, and possible learning activities for each tool. Instead, the second phase was dedicated to planning a learning path for kindergarten pupils based on coding and/or ER. Every meeting was recorded, and all the material was shared in the OLAT platform; students could thus refer to it at any time, and as many times they wanted.

Although the two courses presented the same basic design, they differed in terms of time and methods due to the number of hours available and the characteristics of the samples.

PST Course. The course schedule is reported in Table 2. It lasted a total of 15 h, distributed in five meetings. In the first phase (meeting I-II), students mainly worked individually, carrying out some individual exercises live (synchronous feedback) and others at home to be submitted for the following week (asynchronous feedback). The live exercises aimed at a practical understanding of the functioning of the Cody Roby, Cody Feet and Cody Color cards. Participants had to compose or apply short paths on a grid to solve the task starting from some guide-tracks. In the second meeting, we assigned a task to be done individually at home after a collective exercise-guide on the use of the Bee Bot platform and Scratch Jr software. Specifically, using the Bee Bot simulator, they had to: choose the background (of the grid); create a short story; build a code to make Bee Bot go through the various stages of the story; take a screenshot that includes the grid and the code; briefly describe the story created. While using the ScratchJr application (from tablet or PC), they had to: customize the character; choose a background; write their name above the background; choose what to make the character do; create a script consisting of (at least) one command per color that makes the character act; take a screenshot that includes the entire ScratchJr window; describe briefly what the character must do. These tasks were then delivered on OLAT, where we subsequently provided feedback.

On the contrary, in the second phase (meeting III-IV), participants had to work in groups to design the learning path during the meetings and at home. We provided some guidance/criteria on which the evaluation would then be based. Outlining the design requires to: define and make explicit the context, the competence(s), the goals and the fields of experience; explain the path highlighting the work phases, what teacher and children do, and the possible strategies, mediator, materials, and evaluation methods; clearly explain the coding and/or ER tools used, describing their characteristics, why they were chosen and how they are used. The group activity began during meeting III to provide any initial support live and then continued at home. The participants had to work and compare themselves virtually in the OLAT Wiki. Each group had their own Wiki environment where they outlined the design in a customizable way. In this environment, it is possible to monitor the activity of each student and the different versions of the work. Moreover, there is a "Discussions" section where students could compare and where we provided our feedback.

S-PST Course. The course schedule is reported in Table 3. It lasted a total of 23 h, distributed in five meetings. In contrast to the other course, this was mainly based on teamwork from the first phase, without homework assignments. This choice was due to the greater amount of time available and the different characteristics of the sample. The participants, indeed, are primarily student-workers, also engaged in the weekend for the mandatory attendance of the specialization course. We also found a lower level of knowledge and training related to the topics than PSTs, which prompted us to provide synchronous support and promote teamwork. The group activities took place in various rooms organized in the Teams platform, where trainers could freely enter to monitor and interact. Restitution then followed the teamwork in the general room.

The activities related to the first tools (Cody cards, Bee bot, ScratchJr) were almost the same assigned in the PST course. Instead, the design task was focused on inclusion. We requested to specify the type(s) of disabilities involved and the methods of inclusion. In addition, as a preparatory activity, we introduced the creation of a shared database of designs. Each group had to collect examples of instructional designs/activities which

Table 2. The training course schedule (PST).

Meeting	Duration	Activities
I	2.5 h	*Preliminary Test;* Introduction to *Coding* and *ER;* Presentation of *Cody Roby, Cody Feet, Cody Color*; Individual exercises
II	2.5 h	Presentation of *Bee-Bot* and *Blue-Bot*; Individual exercises; Presentation of *Scratch Jr*; Individual exercises; Task Assignment on Bee-Bot and Scratch Jr
III	2.5 h	Presentation of OLAT *Wiki;* Task Assignment; Start of Group Activity – planning of a *learning path*
IV	2.5 h	Group Activity – planning of a *learning path*
V	5 h	Restitution and evaluation (asynchronous on OLAT); *Final Test*

Table 3. The training course schedule (S-PST).

Meeting	Duration	Activities
I	3 h	*Preliminary Test*; Introduction to *Coding* and *ER*; Presentation of *Cody Roby, Cody Feet, Cody Color*
II	5 h	Individual exercises; Presentation of *Bee-Bot* and *Blue-Bot*; Individual exercises and group activities
III	5 h	Presentation of *Scratch Jr*; Group activities
IV	10 h	Group activity – creation of a *shared database* Group activity – planning of a *learning path*
V	5 h	Restitution and evaluation, peer and self-evaluation; *Final Test*

used coding and/or ER tools across the various fields of experience. They filled out a table with the following guide-fields: link to the video or resource; section/age of pupils (if indicated); duration; field(s) of Experience; type of disability; coding and/or ER tools; annotations (why you chose it, strengths/weaknesses, etc.). Tables were then uploaded onto the OLAT platform.

2.3 Assessment Instruments and Methods

We administered an Entry-Level (EL) and a Post-Course (PC) questionnaire on basic knowledge (K) and self-confidence (SC) on ER-coding tools and methodologies, inspired by [25]. The PC questionnaire also investigated participants' satisfaction (SAT) with the course, focusing on its organization and activities. Moreover, we detected their "beliefs" (B) on the relevance of such training during their undergraduate education and the possible introduction of ER-coding in schools.

Test K consisted of six multiple-choice questions with three answers: correct, partially correct, incorrect. Questions n. 1, 2, 5, 6 are related to Coding and questions n. 3, 4 to ER. According to the numbers of correct answers we identify three groups with different levels of knowledge: basic, medium and advanced.

The other constructs (SC, SAT, B) presented questions structured according to a 5-point Likert scale. Some of them also included an open-ended question to explore the reasons behind the given answer.

Test K (Knowledge)
With the term "Computational Thinking", we intend:

1. the logical process that allows you to use information technology with familiarity;
2. the logical process that enables you to solve mathematical problems by applying a procedure;
3. the logical-creative process that enables you to solve problems of various kinds by planning a procedure.

With the term "Coding", we intend:

1. a kind of computer data protection, using security codes;
2. the use of Scratch or other visual programming languages;
3. computer programming, performed through the construction of a code.

With the term "Educational Robotics", we intend:

1. the method designed by Lego to use robots in schools and encourage experiential learning;
2. the robotic kits that can be employed to teach the fundamentals of Robotics;
3. the whole set of tools and methodologies based on constructionism, which states that learning derives from the possibility to build an object;

In a generic Educational Robotics kit, a generic sensor can be used

1. make the robot interact with the emotions perceived in the environment;
2. prevent the robot from colliding with obstacles in the environment;
3. acquire data from the environment and allow the robot to interact with its environment;

Cody Roby is:

1. a method for introducing coding to very young children;
2. an unplugged method to introduce coding: the instructions written/drawn on the tiles are passed from Cody to the Lego robot "Roby" which interprets them;
3. an unplugged method to introduce coding: the instructions written/drawn on the tiles are passed from Cody to Roby which reads and executes them.

Cody Feet is:

1. a method of coding that lets children practice pixel art activities using their own feet;
2. a method to introduce coding for school-age children;
3. a coding method that allows you to build paths with square tiles that represent the instructions needed to follow them.

Questionnaire SC (Self-confidence):

- How much do you know about the methodologies related to Educational Robotics?
- How much do you know about the tools (like software, kit, …) to carry out an activity of Educational Robotics in the classroom?
- How much do you know about the methodologies related to Coding?
- How much do you know the tools (like software, kit, …) to carry out an activity of Coding in the classroom?
- How much do you feel able to plan an Educational Robotics activity?
- How much do you feel able to plan a Coding activity?

Questionnaire SAT (Satisfaction)
[Organization]

- Adequacy of information regarding the module (setting, content, how to access materials, etc.)
- Adequacy of documentation provided (teaching materials)
- Adequacy of module timing and activities/deliverables
- Usefulness of the OLAT platform as a working environment.
- Usefulness of the TEAMS platform as a working environment
- Adequacy of support/feedback provided by teachers
- Difficulties in group work carried out "at a distance".
- Why?
- Difficulty in group work done "at a distance".
- Why?

[Activities]

- Usefulness of individual exercises
- Usefulness of group work
- Sustainability of deliverables
- Clarity of deliverables.

[Overall]

- Overall evaluation of the course.

Questionnaire B (Beliefs)

- How important do you think it is for future teachers to be trained on Coding and/or Educational Robotics while in college?
- Why?
- How important do you think it is to introduce Coding and/or Educational Robotics at school?
- Why?

The questionnaires were administered through Google Forms and were not mandatory.

To assess the design of the learning paths, we created a rubric focused on the following descriptors: age pertinence; time pertinence; originality; correct use of tools; conscious use of tools; inclusiveness; internal consistency. The last two descriptors were used only for the S-PST course. These assessment criteria were shared in advance with the participants. Moreover, taking advantage of the final synchronous restitution in the S-PST course, we also included a self and peer-assessment by the authors and the other students. The ratings provided by peers were collected through a Google form and were expressed using a 5-point Likert scale.

3 Results

The statistical analysis was carried out using RStudio (v 1.4.1103). A comparison of the results of the two samples (PST and S-PST) showed no statistically significant differences. We found slightly higher scores in the sample PST. A more detailed analysis of the S-PSTs' results is available in [26]. We thus performed a preliminary analysis by combining the two samples and considering closed-ended questions only.

Data from K-EL, K-PC, SC-EL and SC-PC were recorded. K-EL and K-PC answers were classified into three classes (see Fig. 1. and Fig. 2.) according to the levels of knowledge, mentioned in Sect. 2.3.

For the four Coding-related questions (n. 1–2–5–6), we considered the following correlation between class and correct answers: basic (0 or 1 correct answer), medium (2 or 3 correct answers), and advanced (4 correct answers), while for the two ER-relating questions (n. 3–4): basic (0 correct answers), medium (1 correct answer), and advanced (2 correct answers).

For SC-EL and SC-PC, since SC is a more complex construct, we discretized and divided data into five classes (levels) (see Fig. 3. and Fig. 4.) according to the Likert scale used: very low level (class I), low level (II), medium level (III), good level (IV), very good level (V). We tested the difference between EL and PC to verify the training effectiveness. We decided to verify the differences by separating Coding and ER questions to analyses the improvements better.

Being the variables non-parametric, we chose the McNemar-Bowker test (H0: no correlation between variables, rejected with p-value < 0.05).

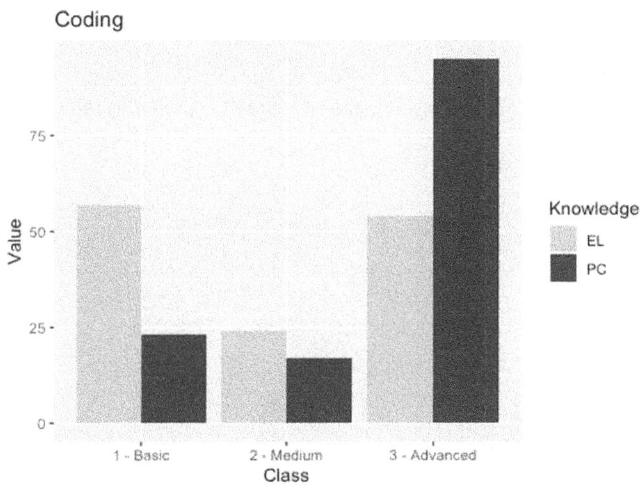

Fig. 1. Histogram reporting data from tests K-EL (light grey) and K-PC (dark grey) related to coding.

Tests show a statistically significant difference between K-EL and K-PC in the Coding related questions. Specifically: from classes I and II (p < 8.15e-01), from classes I and III (p < 1.33e-06) and class II and III (p < 7.35e-02).

Tests show a statistical no-significant difference between K-EL and K-PC tests in the ER related questions: from classes I and II (p < 0.4240), from classes I and III (p < 0.0681) and class II and III (p < 0.3).

Tests show a statistically significant difference between SC-EL and SC-PC questionnaires in the Coding related questions. Specifically, we detected the most significant difference between classes I and IV (p < 5.24e−10) and classes II and IV (2.68e−07).

Between SC-EL and SC-PC questionnaires in the ER related questions, we detected the most significant difference between classes I and IV (p < 1.64e−11) and classes II and IV (p < 2.68e−07).

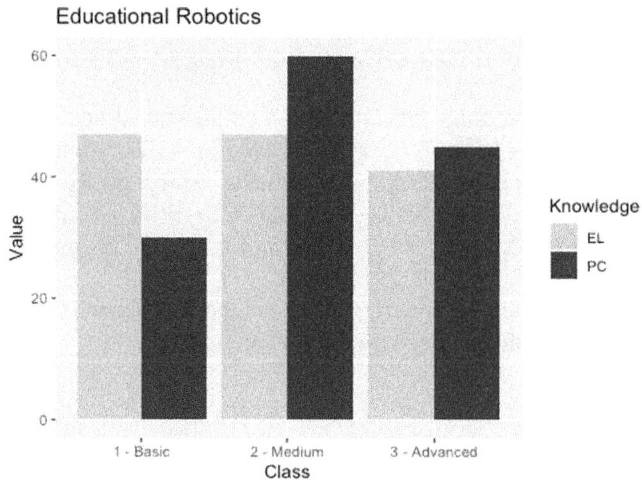

Fig. 2. Histogram reporting data from tests K-EL (light grey) and K-PC (dark grey) related to educational robotics.

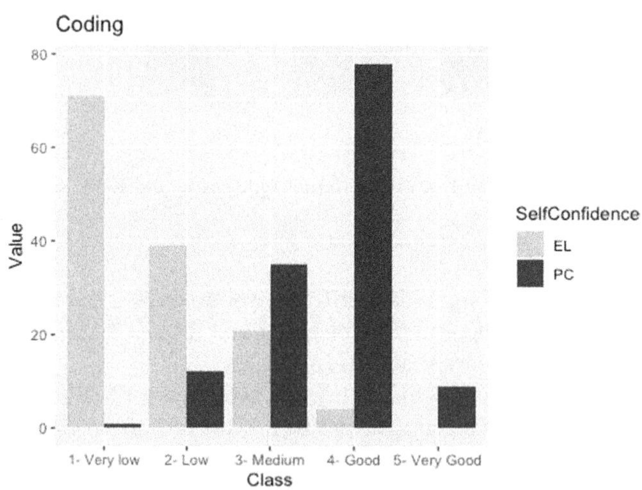

Fig. 3. Histogram reporting data from questionnaires SC-EL (light grey) and SC-PC (dark grey) related to coding.

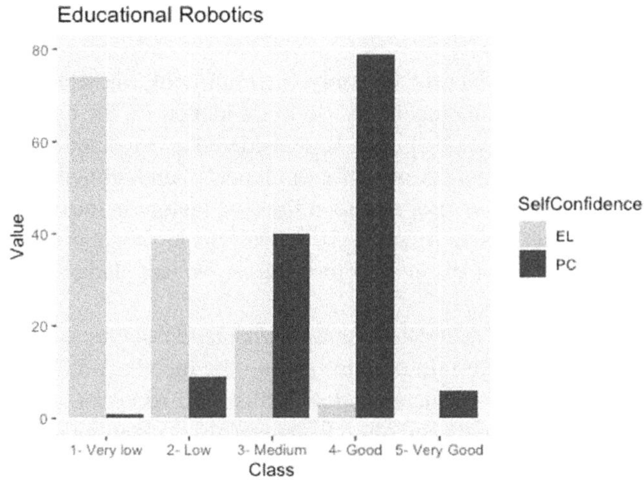

Fig. 4. Histogram reporting data from questionnaires SC-EL (light grey) and SC-PC (dark grey) related to educational robotics.

According to SAT-PC and B-PC, the training achieved mostly positive outcomes (see Table 4 and Table 5):

Table 4. Data from SAT-PC questionnaire.

SAT	Mean
Organization	8,06/10
Activities	8,67/10
Overall	8,59/10

In particular: for SAT-Organization, "Adequacy of support/feedback provided by teachers" reached the higher mean (8,72/10), while for SAT-Activities, "Usefulness of group work" reached the higher mean (9,01/10).

Table 5. Data from B-PC questionnaire.

Beliefs	Mean
Beliefs (1)	7,16/10
Beliefs (2)	7,13/10

4 Conclusions

The course results are satisfactory not only for improving knowledge but especially for the effectiveness in enhancing PSTs' self-confidence in ER and coding. Indeed, while the improvement of knowledge can be considered an expected and usual outcome of a training course, the progress of self-confidence is undoubtedly less predictable. This construct is regarded as one of the main limiting factors in introducing coding-ER activities and methodologies in schools. Moreover, given this and the positive results achieved in beliefs and satisfaction with the course, we can also consider the training pathway as successful.

From the data collected, we believe that this is mainly due to the possibility of: (i) putting theoretical knowledge into practice during the meetings or at home; (ii) experiencing with exercises/tasks of increasing difficulty; (iii) receiving immediate or asynchronous feedback from trainers and often from peers; (iv) planning an activity/pathway in groups using knowledge and methodologies and obtaining a shared repository of paths ready to be implemented; (v) collaborating and sharing. We have also tried to focus on tools and resources that are easily accessible to all, even at a distance (e.g., online emulator platforms, Scratch Jr app, Cody cards and paths that can be printed or reproduced on paper, etc.).

This was an initial effort to introduce these topics into the curricular teaching of PSTs and S-PSTs through an experiential learning approach. The actual effectiveness of this course should be detected more deeply by monitoring the participants during their future work experiences in classrooms.

Moreover, monitoring the activities of the individual and the groups within the LMS could provide further data on the participation of the PSTs involved, valid for a better understanding of the knowledge-building processes.

To improve our Training Proposal for PSTs and S-PSTs, we identified as possible suggestions a more extended schedule and the use of more interactive methods, such as immersive platforms and the support of virtual and augmented reality.

References

1. Alimisis, D. (ed.): Teacher Education on Robotics - Enhanced Constructivist Pedagogical Method. ASPETE, Athens (2009)
2. Negrini, L.: Teachers' attitudes towards educational robotics in compulsory school. Ital. J. Educ. Technol. **28**(1), 77–90 (2020). https://doi.org/10.17471/2499-4324/1136
3. Alimisis, D.: Educational robotics: open questions and new challenges. Themes Sci. Technol. Educ. **6**(1), 63–71 (2013)
4. Mallik, A., Borges Rajguru, S., Kapila, V.: Fundamental: analyzing the effects of a robotics training workshop on the self-efficacy of high school teachers. In: ASEE Annual Conference and Exposition. Salt Lake City (2018). https://doi.org/10.18260/1-2--30548
5. Hew, K.F., Brush, T.: Integrating technology into K-12 teaching and learning: current knowledge gaps and recommendations for future research. Educ. Technol. Res. Dev. **55**(3), 223–252 (2007). https://doi.org/10.1007/s11423-006-9022-5
6. Lawson, T., Comber, C.: Superhighways technology: personnel factors leading to successful integration of information and communications technology in schools and colleges. J. Inf. Technol. Teach. Educ. **8**(1), 41–53 (1999). https://doi.org/10.1080/14759399900200054

7. Giacomassi Luciano, A.P., Altoé Fusinato, P., Carvalhais Gomes, L., Luciano, A., Takai, H.: The educational robotics and Arduino platform: constructionist learning strategies to the teaching of physics. J. Phys: Conf. Ser. **1286**(1), 012044 (2019). https://doi.org/10.1088/1742-6596/1286/1/012044
8. Gabriele, L., Bertacchini, F., Pantano, P., Bilotta, E.: Laboratorio per apprendere le competenze del 21° secolo: percorsi didattici con scratch per i futuri insegnanti della scuola primaria. Ital. J. Educ. Technol. **28**(1), 20–42 (2020). https://doi.org/10.17471/2499-4324/1113
9. Kaya, E., Newley, A., Deniz, H., Yesilyurt, E., Newley, P.: Introducing engineering design to a science teaching methods course through educational robotics and exploring changes in views of preservice elementary teachers. J. Coll. Sci. Teach. **47**(2), 66–75 (2017). https://doi.org/10.2505/4/jcst17_047_02_66
10. Negrini, L.: Teacher training in educational robotics. An experience in Southern Switzerland: the PReSO project. In: Lepuschitz, W., Merdan, M., Koppensteiner, G., Balogh, R., Obdržálek, D. (eds.) RiE 2018. Advances in Intelligent Systems and Computing, vol. 829, pp. 92–97. Springer, Cham (2019). https://doi.org/10.1007/978-3-319-97085-1_10
11. Gratani, F., Giannandrea, L., Renieri, A.: The impact of a teacher training online course on educational robotics. In: Gómez Chova, L., López Martínez, A., Candel Torres, I. (eds.) EDULEARN21 Proceedings, pp. 11527–11533. IATED, Valencia (2021). https://doi.org/10.21125/edulearn.2021.2412
12. Eguchi, A.: Educational robotics for promoting 21st century skills. J. Autom. Mob. Robot. Intell. Syst. **8**(1), 5–11 (2014). https://doi.org/10.14313/JAMRIS_1-2014/1
13. Karna-Lin, E., Pihlainen-Bednarik, K., Sutinen, E., Virnes, M.: Can robots teach? Preliminary results on educational robotics in special education. In: Sixth IEEE International Conference on Advanced Learning Technologies (ICALT 2006), pp. 319–321. Kerkrade, The Netherlands (2006). https://doi.org/10.1109/ICALT.2006.100
14. Agatolio, F., Pivetti, M., Di Battista, S., Menegatti, E., Moro, M.: A training course in educational robotics for learning support teachers. In: Alimisis, D., Moro, M., Menegatti, E. (eds.) Edurobotics 2016 2016. AISC, vol. 560, pp. 43–57. Springer, Cham (2017). https://doi.org/10.1007/978-3-319-55553-9_4
15. Moore, T.J., Glancy, A.W., Kersten, J.A.: NGSS and the landscape of engineering in K–12 state science standards. J. Res. Sci. Teach. **52**, 296–318 (2015). https://doi.org/10.1002/tea.21199
16. Schön, D.: The Reflective Practitioner. Basic Books, New York (1983)
17. Giannandrea, L., Gratani, F., Renieri, A.: Crossing boundaries: documentation of a teacher training course on design, robotics and coding. Res. Educ. Media **12**(1), 85–92 (2020). https://doi.org/10.2478/rem-2020-0010
18. Kolb, D.A.: Experiential Learning: Experience as the Source of Learning and Development. Prentice-Hall, Englewood Cliffs (1984)
19. Sutiah, S., Slamet, S., Shafqat, A., Supriyono, S.: Implementation of distance learning during the COVID-19 in faculty of education and teacher training. Cypriot J. Educ. Sci. **15**(5), 1204–1214 (2020). https://doi.org/10.18844/cjes.v15i5.5151
20. Bogliolo, A.: A scuola con CodyRoby. Il coding come gioco di ruolo. Giunti, Firenze (2020)
21. Bogliolo, A.: Coding in your classroom, now! Giunti, Firenze (2016)
22. Cody Color. http://codemooc.org/codycolor/. Accessed 15 Sept 2021
23. Bee-Bot emulator. https://www.terrapinlogo.com/emu/beebot.html. Accessed 15 Sept 2021
24. Scratch. https://scratch.mit.edu/. Accessed 15 Sept 2021

25. Scaradozzi, D., Screpanti, L., Cesaretti, L., Storti, M., Mazzieri, E.: Implementation and assessment methodologies of teachers' training courses for STEM activities. Technol. Knowl. Learn. **24**(2), 247–268 (2018). https://doi.org/10.1007/s10758-018-9356-1
26. Gratani, F., Renieri, A., Giannandrea, L.: Inclusive designing through educational robotics. A training course for pre-service support teachers. In: Book of Abstracts ATEE Spring Conference 2020–2021. Firenze University Press (2021). https://doi.org/10.36253/978-88-5518-412-0

A Novel Approach for Cooperative Scientific Literature Search and Socialization

Francesco Lupi[1(✉)] and Michele Lanzetta[1,2]

[1] Department of Civil and Industrial Engineering, University of Pisa, Pisa, Italy
francesco.lupi@phd.unipi.it, lanzetta@unipi.it
[2] Interdepartmental Center for Lifelong Learning, Training and Education Research, University of Pisa, Pisa, Italy

Abstract. The scientific literature search is a crucial enabler for the research process and one of the most problematic and inefficient activities that researchers must face. Most University students never experience scientific literature search, although research is the primary mission of the universities and one of the major activities of their professors and a primary parameter for their careers. The aim of this paper is to i) present a new approach for scientific literature search based on virtual team collaboration, ii) explore the team dynamics of the knowledge building process in a virtual environment and, iii) propose a blog tool for open knowledge sharing both for experienced researchers and beginning students. An experiment on a collaborative scientific literature search on five virtual teams for a total of 25 students at the 2nd edition of the 2nd level Master in Valorization of different abilities and education research proposed by the CAFRE Interdepartmental Center for Lifelong Learning, Training and Education Research at Pisa University has been developed. The collaboration result is a Google Sites embedding individual blogs where each virtual team can build and share organized knowledge based on literature search.

Keywords: Methodologies for distance learning · Collaborative literature search · Edublog · Virtual teamwork

1 Introduction

Recent digitalization has expanded the boundaries of self-learning, offering a tremendous amount of easy to access information [1], modernizing tools for students communication [2], and also differentiating forms and methods for teaching [3,4]. At the same time, the increasing size of the Web delivers significant complexities. For example, pertinent information retrieval (IR) via queries (i.e., a structured sequence of keywords used to formalize the search of information on a given database or search engine [5]) has become a big challenge even for experienced users [6]. This fact is mainly due to the big data revolution that made the

G. Casalino et al. (Eds.): HELMeTO 2021, CCIS 1542, pp. 31–45, 2022.
https://doi.org/10.1007/978-3-030-96060-5_3

management of hundreds of gigabytes (i.e., volume) of unstructured (i.e., variety) data uploaded per second (i.e., velocity) on the Web extremely challenging [7]. Bounding our interest in structured information sources (i.e., scientific papers), as depicted by Fig. 1, it is evident that the volume of published articles is growing exponentially. As highlighted in [8], science is a cumulative endeavor as new knowledge is often created in interpreting and combining such existing published works. Therefore, the major challenge is to untangle the explosive growth of scientific papers published in various databases and transmitted over the Internet [9].

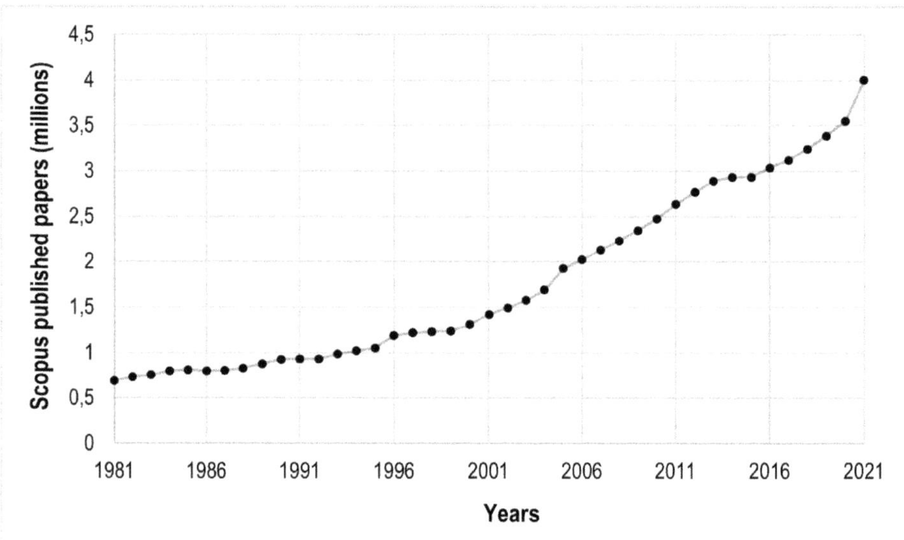

Fig. 1. Global number of scientific published papers in the Scopus database over the last 4 decades. The already massive number of annual papers and its increase seems not yet reaching its asymptote.

Many students in research universities are involved in research projects during or immediately after attending their courses for various reasons: because they choose research for their career as PhD students or hired by research institutions or by the same university by fellowships; during their final projects or in research-oriented teaching projects [10]. This usually happens during graduate degree and master's programs; however, early research involvement may benefit all university students. Not only research, but all the industrial world can benefit from the new knowledge coming from millions of papers published every year. According to these facts, the ability of accessing this latent and enormous potential should be included in the set of skills of every student going through a University level program [11].

At the same time, in a globally and digitally interconnected world, there is a growing need to equip students with crucial competences such as critical thinking, interpersonal communication, collaborative skills, and global awareness [12]. To develop these skills, educational institutions would need to consider innovative teaching methods to provide students with the opportunity for active learning [13,55]. Based on rewarded studies such as [14], cooperative learning has been presented as a useful strategy toward this revolutionary teaching and learning approach. In a nutshell, it can be said that cooperative learning emphasizes cooperation between students in groups helping them in understanding concepts and reaching goals [15]. In view of the above, cooperation learning within and among students' team is highlighted as a critical enabling factor for the proposed method, which aims to improve the students' soft and literature search skills. This method can be especially useful in interdisciplinary study programs, where the hard skills of each student is such that all of them can strongly benefit from a deeper interaction as a learning community [16,17]. In this context, instead of scientific literature searches made by individual users, a group could significantly improve the effectiveness of this activity by enabling a better knowledge space covering and benefit from cooperative learning. Team collaboration provide an actual approach to switch from a single point of view to multiple perspectives [18], increasing the likelihood to retrieve information that autonomous exploration is not [19,20].

In this work we propose a method based on virtual cooperative and active learning [21,22] for cooperative literature search and socialization at a high-level educational framework. Experiments on the proposed methodology via a real case study conducted by five self-controlled virtual teams for a total of 25 students have pointed out the main benefits and criticalities along with a software tool implementation.

2 Background

Significant work has been carried out on literature search optimization, and collaborative search has been identified as a practical solution in the sharing of experts' knowledge that leads to faster and higher quality information seeking. This paper seems one of the first attempts to define a structured approach for virtual collaborative literature search and results in dissemination.

In Sect. 2.1, an overview of cooperative learning theory is provided. Section 2.2. introduce the second ingredient of this article: literature search and share. To conclude, a brief overview of the digital transition is offered in Sect. 2.3.

2.1 Cooperative Learning Theory

Interest in cooperative learning gathered momentum in the early 80s as a structured form of construction of skills and knowledge through the interactions among learners, which results in attaining shared goals at any level of education and domain [13,23,24]. In this framework, the instructor's role concern setting the goals; planning the tasks; assigning students into small group to facilitate social interaction among one another [25]; acting as a coach or facilitator, monitoring the learning process of each group; providing students with ongoing feedback and assess group progress [26]. Two main benefits of cooperative learning can be identified in academic and social competences improvement [13,23]. Concerning the former, scientific methodology are involved in moving the students from a passive to a more active role in the learning process, and exploration of information by reinforcing academic skills [27–29]. It also appears that cooperative learning allows students to analyze problems via multiple perspectives helping them to think in more complex ways [13,30,31]. In addition to academic benefits, emotional (i.e., appreciation, enthusiasm, motivation, values, commitment) and interpersonal social (i.e., communication, leadership, trust, decision making, conflict resolution) skills have been highlighted by several authors as enablers that boost learners to develop better cognitive abilities [23,32–34].

2.2 Literature Search and Share

Systematic literature review refers to the reproducibility of results by following a structured research method based on queries in the IR domain [35–39]. Despite literature search is a crucial milestone for scientific methodology, yet, surprisingly, search is often thought of as a solitary user activity with related limitations on the actual covering of knowledge space given a specific topic [40]. Among promising solutions, the idea of intelligence amplification (i.e., symbiotic interaction between human and machine [41]) has been proposed. Other approaches based on collaborative search (e.g., [40–42]) provide evident benefits. However, significant room for improvements in this field seems to be still present. For example, tools like blogs, in addition to being open access and easy to use platforms, are a valuable way to build an indexed knowledge storage system (e.g., hyperlinks) [43]. Moreover, these tools provide a nourishing environment that encourages collaboration and an interchange of skills among users (e.g., students or other stakeholders) by building a learning community based on shared knowledge [44] and able to improve the amount and pertinence of the retrieved documents. As highlighted in [45] all major search engines (e.g., Google Scholar) are designed for solo use. However, many tasks in both professional and casual settings can benefit from jointly searching the Web with others or through cooperative public sharing (e.g., ResearchGate).

2.3 Digital Transformation

Virtualization is one of the most speculated topics in the transition of the last decades of the "digital era" and which the current pandemic scenario exalted [46]. The digital aspect is an additional opportunity for the proposed method since literature search is suitable for online, blended, and in-person approaches. The current COVID-19 pandemic has imposed virtualization in every context, even in a higher education environment [47]. Virtual teams have been treated and re-discovered in the enhancement of social and professional skills through processes of sharing, exchange, and motivation [48,49]. Contrary to many other activities that have suffered from forced digitization, a collaborative scientific literature search can be boosted by the distance approach and maximize the capabilities of related virtual tools and practices.

3 Methodology

The methodology for a collaborative scientific literature search based on virtual team cooperation to improve the search's performance and teamwork skills is proposed. The main four phases of the methodology presented in this article and boundary conditions are shown in Fig. 2 and summarized below.

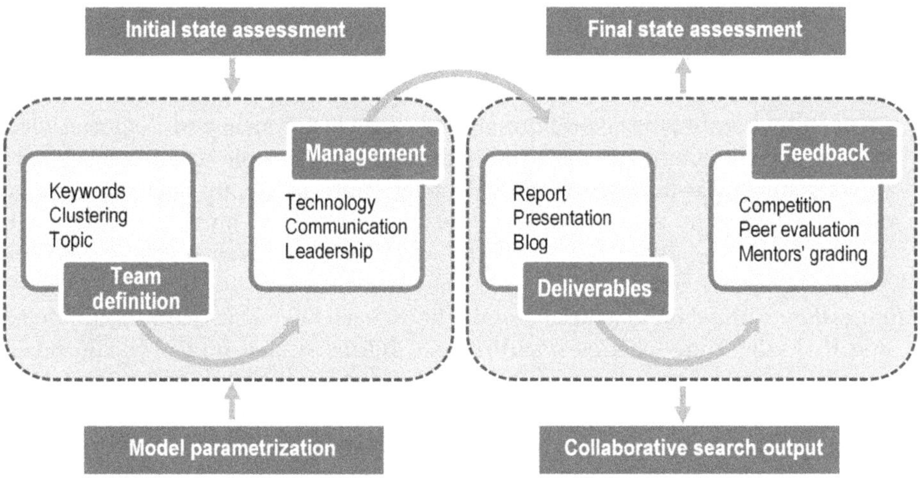

Fig. 2. The methodology of collaborative scientific literature search in a virtual team environment.

Before describing each phase in the linear flow of Fig. 2 (i.e., team definition, management, deliverable, and feedback), a set of boundary conditions must be defined to initiate the model (i.e., initial state assessment, and model parametrization). As detailed in Sect. 2.1 about cooperative learning theory, instructors must be assumed as leaders in all these initial activities and mentors in the operative phases. During the initial state assessment, the number (n) of students involved in the activity must be defined. A lower bound can be at least four students. Moreover, students' skills must be mapped by the instructors (e.g., proficiency in the use of technology, expertise in communication and leadership as well as scientific topics interest). A specific interview mode or questionnaire can be considered in this preliminary activity based on the size of n. According with this assessment, it is possible to set up each phase of the model to maximize the outcome of the process (i.e., the final state assessment and collaborative search output). Peer-review evaluations and mentors' grading are used in the final state assessment to provide feedback on the collaborative search output (e.g., report, presentation, blog). In the following, the main phases of the linear flow are detailed.

Team definition: Firstly, the instructors must define a set of $t \approx n/mean(m)$ topics, where m is the team size. As highlighted in Sect. 2.1, a small group often achieves better cooperation among members, and $3 \leq m \leq 6$ seems to be a good experimental size. If no clear pattern is depicted by the initial assessment of students on scientific interests, it is up to the instructors to choose the topics. Secondly, the students define one keyword (and eventually related synonyms) for at least three of the given topics (if $t > 2$). As additional information, the students are required to specify a degree of interest (e.g., I, II, or III choices) for each topic. Thirdly, the final association of students to a given topic is conducted by the instructors. During this activity, the instructors assign students to teams mainly based on the degree of interest. At the same time, skills in the use of technology, expertise in communication, and leadership assessed in the preliminary stage are also considered. Negotiation in case of not enough or too many students for a given topic could be necessary. To conclude, the instructors provide basic notions about query generation and the literature search process, creating an initial query for each team by arranging the generated keywords and synonyms logically and following proper syntactic rules.

Management: based on instructors' guidelines, each thematic team should define specific tasks, time schedules, and responsibilities to accomplish the literature search starting from the initial query defined in the previous phase. Each group is free to plan the preferred approach for collaborative search. The most crucial aspect is that each student brings hard and soft skills to a contaminated environment with a high level of interaction and specific sub-tasks fulfillment. Formal and informal leaders will emerge in this planning phase. After an internal drafting stage, each group must communicate and discuss the drafted management approach with the instructors. Moreover, at least two iterative rounds of meetings with the instructors to show partial results must be scheduled for ongoing feedback. As for technology and tools for collaboration, Microsoft Teams channels could help formal exchanges or meetings; Google Drive could help in paper collection and analyses; WhatsApp for informal and quick-response discussions. As for the scientific databases, a freely accessible Web search engine such as Google Scholar that indexes the full text or metadata of scholarly literature seems suitable for such initiating activities. Comments, observations, and generated material should be collected and organized for Web communication (e.g., short text and hyperlinks) into the educational blog (aka *edublog*).

Deliverable: each thematic team can develop intermediate (i.e., draft) and final (i.e., rigorous) reports following a given scientific literature review format. For example, the instructors could provide a template embedding the main areas required for the literature search (e.g., problem definition, state of the art solutions, open challenges, and future development). Then, it is up to the instructors to select the preferred report structure. As already highlighted in the management phase concerning digital tools, the material can also be reformatted for *edublog*. A team presentation in front of the class can be considered an additional deliverable to improve the overall collaboration.

Feedback: peer-to-peer feedback must be shared along the whole process. Moreover, a formal vote is assigned by the instructors after the final presentation, and mentors' tips are embedded to improve the final deliverable.

4 Experimental Setting

An actual experiment involving five teams was carried out at the 2nd edition of the 2nd level Master in Valorization of different abilities and education research proposed by the CAFRE Interdepartmental Center for Lifelong Learning, Training, and Education Research at Pisa University. The master provides skills ranging from knowledge and assessment of diversity to tools and technological methodologies, organizational and pedagogical skills transmitted in an interdisciplinary and integrated way for the most profitable enhancement of the person.

In this context, 25 students participated in the experiment. The students' skills levels (i.e., poor, average, good, excellent) on the three main enabling tools of the online cooperative scientific search via a virtual team (i.e., collaborative tools, website editing, search engines) have been summarized in Fig. 3.

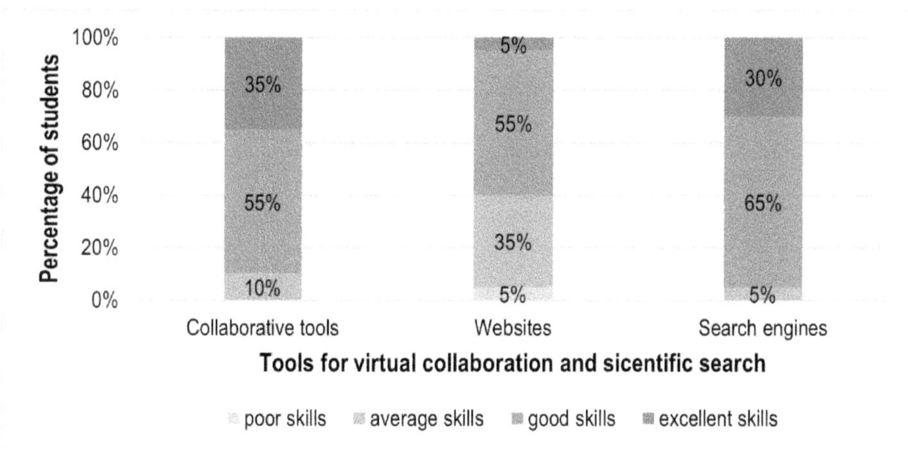

Fig. 3. Collaborative tools: Google Drive, Microsoft teams, Whats App. Websites editing: Blogger, Word Press. Search engines: Google Scholar.

As for additional information, the students ranged from 24 to 59 years old and presented heterogeneous cultural backgrounds and scientific interests (e.g., continuing education and pedagogical sciences, management and control strategy, modern philology, history of art, agricultural sciences, medicine). The defined

Table 1. Thematic teams additional information.

Team name	Members	Website link (in Italian)
T-ILP	6	https://valorizzazione.cafre.unipi.it/didattica-dellitaliano
T-M	5	https://valorizzazione.cafre.unipi.it/motivazione
T-S	4	https://valorizzazione.cafre.unipi.it/attivit%C3%A0-fisica
T-CD	6	https://valorizzazione.cafre.unipi.it/cura-e-disabilit%C3%A0
T-WI	4	https://valorizzazione.cafre.unipi.it/opposta

keywords by each student and scientific interests as well as proficiency in the use of technology, expertise in communication and leadership have been considered in the generation of the five thematic teams (i.e., Italian language pedagogy (T-ILP), motivation (T-M), sport (T-S), caregiving and diversity (T-CD), work and innovation (T-WI)). Additional information can be found in Table 1.

A two-month experiment took place in the middle of a pandemic, which necessitated virtual collaboration. The main results due to the implementation of the phases in Sect. 3 are presented and discussed in Sect. 5.

5 Results

A major deliverable of this work is the *edublog* developed as a platform for a collaborative scientific literature search and results in presentation (Fig. 4).

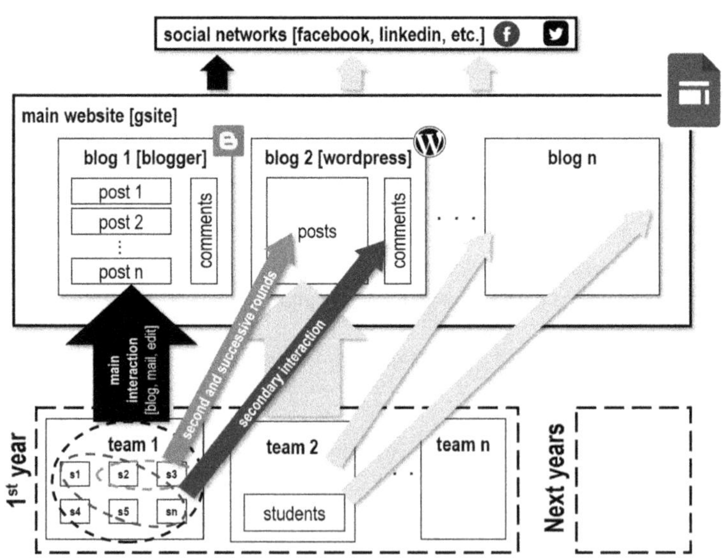

Fig. 4. The proposed *edublog* structure [http://valorizzazione.cafre.unipi.it] (in Italian) showing the intra- and inter-team cooperation.

The *edublog* embeds individual blogs where each virtual team can collaborate in building and sharing organized knowledge. Over 100 original posts that received 2k visits in less than six months have been published. In the following Sects. 5.1 and 5.2, intra- and inter-team socialization and assessment activities of the experiment are reported.

5.1 Socialization During Literature Search and Peer Evaluation

As the main leading social result, the interaction among students via the *edublog* has been pointed out as the most appreciated aspect of the offered master program. Similarly, oral presentations have also benefited from the work done within the teams and cross-comments provided by the external members. In addition, the students set up a survey, filled, analyzed, and reported it. These activities have enormously increased the interaction among students and easier monitoring by the instructors with relatively low load, reliable assessment, objective evaluation tools (i.e., survey), and distributed responsibility among the students. Furthermore, each student has evaluated each other under several parameters, including topic adherence, subtopic organization, search depth, extension, schedule adherence, and presentation quality. This process has significantly impacted their awareness and shows that socialization is a solid enabler for stimulating students' engagement and quality of work.

5.2 Assessment

The two most used parameters that formally assess the performance of the query are precision (i.e., purity of retrieval) and recall (i.e., completeness of retrieval) [50]. Figure 5 offers a representation of three standard sets in IR.

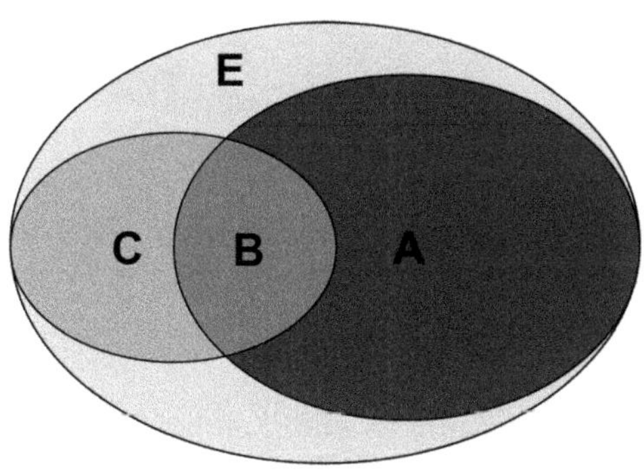

Fig. 5. A = not-retrieved pertinent documents, B = retrieved pertinent documents, C = retrieved not-pertinent documents, E = not-pertinent not-retrieved documents.

Without considering additional sets, precision is quantified as follows:

$$Precision = B/(C + B)$$

This quantity can be computed without approximation since the denominator is directly available as the query's output, and the numerator can be obtained after classifying each retrieved item as pertinent or not-pertinent. The higher the precision, the better the semantic abstraction of the underlying problem. On the other side, the recall is still an open challenge since it can be only "estimated" by the following ratio:

$$Recall = B/(A + B)$$

Unfortunately, even if B can be computed, the denominator is unknown since A can only be estimated. For the above reason, various automatic query expansion (QE) techniques (aka query augmentation) have been implemented to stretch B as close as possible to A [51,52]. In a few words, QE techniques try to add (in a manual, automatic, or user-assisted way) new meaningful terms to the initial query improving its recall [53].

With this aim, the current work can be seen as a practical QE approach based on a collaborative search. As depicted in Fig. 6, clear benefits can emerge on recall calculation by the addition of a new set obtained thought collaborative search (i.e., the additional set D). D reduce the amount of missed good documents (A′ = A − D) and increase the number of the good ones retrieved (B′ = B + D).

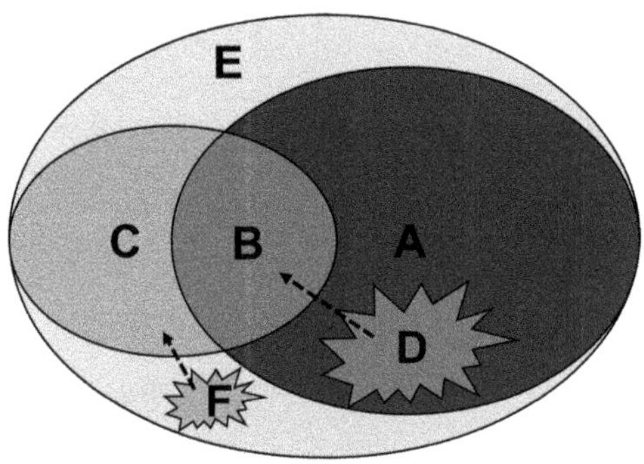

Fig. 6. The additional sets of retrieved documents via collaborative search. D = collaboratively retrieved pertinent documents and F = collaboratively retrieved non-pertinent documents.

In order to compare autonomous and collaborative search from a QE (i.e., recall augmentation) perspective, sets B and D obtained during the experiment have been quantified. Set B has been approximated considering the output of the initial query generated autonomously by the instructors in the preparatory step. Switching to the collaborative mode search, and after the interaction between students and customization of the query, citation-chain search, as well as the two iterative rounds of meetings with the instructors, the set D has been generated. Thus, the initial set B has increased to B′ = B + D. Please note that the "pertinence" or "not pertinence" of a retrieved document has been delegated to the instructors judging if a given article is or not in-scope with respect to the given topic.

Table 2 summarizes the experiment results highlighting the previously defined IR sets and the % variation of the recall (i.e., $\Delta R\%$) switching from autonomous to a collaborative search for each thematic team. Considering $A' = A - D$ and thanks to this relative approach, $\Delta R\%$ can be computed by the following equation although the set A is unknown:

$$\Delta R\% = \frac{B'/(A'+B')}{B/(A+B)} - 1 = \frac{(B+D)/(A+B)}{B/(A+B)} - 1 = \frac{B+D}{B} - 1$$

Table 2. The results of the experiment. IR sets and the % of improved recall switching from an autonomous search (i.e., B) to a cooperative approach (i.e., B′ = B + D) are provided for each thematic team.

Team name	B	D	B′	$\Delta R\%$
T-ILP	30	33	63	+110
T-M	25	60	85	+240
T-S	40	3	43	+8
T-CD	24	15	39	+63
T-WI	52	8	60	+15

Despite these early promising results in the recall augmentation (+87% on average), additional studies and experiments are required to expand the proposed approach further. For example, as previously highlighted, this work aims to improve query recall; however, an analysis about the impact of collaborative search on the overall precision also deserves attention. As shown in Fig. 6, the effect on precision due to collaborative search is highly dependent on the additional set F. In this case, contrary to the recall, direct benefits on precision cannot be claimed a priori since F increases the amount of worst documents retrieved (C′ = C + F), and the relative size of D and F can negatively or positively impact the % variation of precision (i.e., the efficiency). An interesting research topic could be the exploration of the recall and precision relation in a collaborative framework as an extension of the well known inverse correlation in autonomous search (i.e., the trade-off problem [50]). Similarly to the proposed equation for $\Delta R\%$, the following $\Delta P\%$ equation is suggested for those who will explore both the aspects when switching to cooperative search:

$$\Delta P\% = \frac{B'/(C'+B')}{B/(C+B)} - 1 = \frac{(B+D)/(C+F+B+D)}{B/(C+B)} - 1$$

6 Conclusion

In this work, we present an approach for scientific literature search based on virtual team collaboration, explore the team dynamics of the knowledge building process in a virtual environment, and propose a blog tool for open knowledge sharing for experienced researchers and beginning students. Our experience has shown that the method can be adapted to different education environments by developing an initial state assessment and tuning the methodology accordingly.

The developed collaboration platform (i.e., http://valorizzazione.cafre.unipi.it) is a Google Sites (in Italian) embedding individual blogs (i.e., *edublog*) where each virtual team can build and share organized knowledge based on literature search.

Among the key elements of the experience are: team formation and keyword negotiation in a supervised way; platform creation; team oral presentations in two rounds, 5 min per presenter; self-assessment based on a self-created online survey; training on literature search; cooperative editing and blog creation.

The method was tested in an entirely virtual environment due to the pandemic but seemed suitable for blended or in-person as well. This work has several merits, which can be individually explored further: the objective assessment of the deliverable quality coming from a cooperative search in contrast to autonomous search (please refer to the % improved recall in Table 2); the virtual team dynamics generated in an educational environment by enabling the production of new knowledge and soft skills; the infrastructure of the developed *edublog* for sharing knowledge.

Acknowledgment. The following master students (i.e., Maria Pacini, Tecla Arrighini, Noemi Debbi, Tina Ofria, Antonio Bindi) and mentor (i.e., Angela Dini) who contributed to the initial draft and coauthored the extended abstract in [54] are gratefully acknowledged.

References

1. AlRyalat, S.A.S., Malkawi, L.W., Momani, S.M.: Comparing bibliometric analysis using PubMed, Scopus, and web of science databases. JoVE (J. Vis. Exp.) (152), e58494 (2019). https://doi.org/10.3791/58494
2. Santos, H., Batista, J., Marques, R.P.: Digital transformation in higher education: the use of communication technologies by students. Proc. Comput. Sci. **164**, 123–130 (2019)
3. Lupi, F., et al.: Toward a sustainable educational engineer archetype through industry 4.0. Comput. Ind. **134**, 103543 (2022)
4. Frolova, E.V., Rogach, O.V., Ryabova, T.M.: Digitalization of education in modern scientific discourse: new trends and risks analysis. Eur. J. Contemp. Educ. **9**(2), 313–336 (2020)
5. Chiarello, F., Trivelli, L., Bonaccorsi, A., Fantoni, G.: Extracting and mapping industry 4.0 technologies using Wikipedia. Comput. Ind. **100**, 244–257 (2018)
6. Azad, H.K., Deepak, A.: Query expansion techniques for information retrieval: a survey. Inf. Process. Manag. **56**(5), 1698–1735 (2019)

7. Oussous, A., Benjelloun, F.Z., Lahcen, A.A., Belfkih, S.: Big data technologies: a survey. J. King Saud Univ.-Comput. Inf. Sci. **30**(4), 431–448 (2018)
8. Brocke, J.V., et al.: Reconstructing the giant: on the importance of rigour in documenting the literature search process (2009)
9. Mwangi, W., Cheruiyot, W., et al.: A survey of information retrieval techniques. Adv. Netw. **5**(2), 40 (2017)
10. Bhattacharyya, P., Chan, C.W., Waraczynski, M.: How novice researchers see themselves grow. Int. J. Sch. Teach. Learn. **12**(2), 3 (2018)
11. Ruescas-Nicolau, M., Sánchez-Sánchez, M., Espí-López, G.: The use of a cooperative-learning activity about scientific literature search in physiotherapy students: an experience. In: INTED2017 Proceedings, pp. 2196–2203. 11th International Technology, Education and Development Conference, IATED (2017)
12. Johnson, D.W., Johnson, R.T.: An educational psychology success story: social interdependence theory and cooperative learning. Educ. Res. **38**(5), 365–379 (2009)
13. Loh, R.C.Y., Ang, C.S.: Unravelling cooperative learning in higher education: a review of research. Res. Soc. Sci. Technol. **5**(2), 22–39 (2020)
14. Baloche, L., Brody, C.M.: Cooperative learning: exploring challenges, crafting innovations (2017)
15. Silalahi, T.F., Hutauruk, A.F.: The application of cooperative learning model during online learning in the pandemic period. Budapest Int. Res. Critics Inst.-J. (BIRCI-J.) **3**(3), 1683–1691 (2020)
16. Studente, S., Ellis, S.: Enhancing the online student experience through creating learning communities-the benefits of chatbots in higher education. In: McKenzie, S., Garivaldis, F., Dyer, K.R. (eds.) Tertiary Online Teaching and Learning, pp. 25–33. Springer, Singapore (2020). https://doi.org/10.1007/978-981-15-8928-7_3
17. Jan, S.K., Vlachopoulos, P., Parsell, M.: Social network analysis and learning communities in higher education online learning: a systematic literature review. Online Learn. **23**(1) (2019)
18. Kagan, S.: Cooperative Learning. Kagan San Clemente, San Clemente (1994)
19. Tannenbaum, S.I., Traylor, A.M., Thomas, E.J., Salas, E.: Managing teamwork in the face of pandemic: evidence-based tips. BMJ Qual. Saf. **30**(1), 59–63 (2021)
20. Vygotsky, L.S.: Mind in Society: The Development of Higher Psychological Processes. Harvard University Press (1980)
21. Johnson, D.W., Johnson, R.T.: Learning together and alone: the history of our involvement in cooperative learning. In: Pioneering Perspectives in Cooperative Learning, pp. 44–62. Routledge (2021)
22. Venton, B.J., Pompano, R.R.: Strategies for enhancing remote student engagement through active learning (2021)
23. Gillies, R.M.: Cooperative learning: review of research and practice. Aust. J. Teach. Educ. (Online) **41**(3), 39–54 (2016)
24. Johnson, D.W.: Social interdependence: interrelationships among theory, research, and practice. Am. Psychol. **58**(11), 934 (2003)
25. Johnson, D.W., Johnson, R.T.: Cooperative learning: the foundation for active learning. In: Active Learning—Beyond Future (2018)
26. Slavin, R.E.: Classroom applications of cooperative learning. In: APA Educational Psychology Handbook, Vol 3: Application to Learning and Teaching, pp. 359–378 (2012)
27. Biggs, J.: What the student does: teaching for enhanced learning. High. Educ. Res. Dev. **18**(1), 57–75 (1999)
28. Cavanagh, M.: Students' experiences of active engagement through cooperative learning activities in lectures. Act. Learn. High. Educ. **12**(1), 23–33 (2011)

29. Shimazoe, J., Aldrich, H.: Group work can be gratifying: understanding & overcoming resistance to cooperative learning. Coll. Teach. **58**(2), 52–57 (2010)
30. Lim, D.H.: Cross cultural differences in online learning motivation. Educ. Media Int. **41**(2), 163–175 (2004)
31. Van Knippenberg, D., Schippers, M.C.: Work group diversity. Annu. Rev. Psychol. **58**, 515–541 (2007)
32. Du, C.: The effect of cooperative learning on students' attitude in first-year principles of accounting course. Bus. Educ. Innov. J. **7**(2), 107–116 (2015)
33. Thanh, P.T.H., Gillies, R., Renshaw, P.: Cooperative learning (CL) and academic achievement of Asian students: a true story. Int. Educ. Stud. **1**(3), 82–88 (2008)
34. Felder, R.M., Brent, R.: Understanding student differences. J. Eng. Educ. **94**(1), 57–72 (2005)
35. Müller-Bloch, C., Kranz, J.: A framework for rigorously identifying research gaps in qualitative literature reviews (2015)
36. Torres-Carrión, P.V., González-González, C.S., Aciar, S., Rodríguez-Morales, G.: Methodology for systematic literature review applied to engineering and education. In: 2018 IEEE Global Engineering Education Conference (EDUCON), pp. 1364–1373. IEEE (2018)
37. Brendel, A.B., Trang, S., Marrone, M., Lichtenberg, S., Kolbe, L.M.: What to do for a literature review?-a synthesis of literature review practices (2020)
38. Vivekavardhan, J., Chakravarthy, A.S., Ramesh, P.: Search engines and meta search engines great search for knowledge: a frame work on keyword search for information retrieval. In: Satapathy, S.C., Raju, K.S., Shyamala, K., Krishna, D.R., Favorskaya, M.N. (eds.) Advances in Decision Sciences, Image Processing, Security and Computer Vision. LAIS, vol. 3, pp. 435–443. Springer, Cham (2020). https://doi.org/10.1007/978-3-030-24322-7_54
39. Boell, S.K., Cecez-Kecmanovic, D.: On being 'systematic' in literature reviews. In: Formulating Research Methods for Information Systems, pp. 48–78 (2015)
40. Andolina, S., Klouche, K., Ruotsalo, T., Floréen, P., Jacucci, G.: Querytogether: enabling entity-centric exploration in multi-device collaborative search. Inf. Process. Manag. **54**(6), 1182–1202 (2018)
41. Dobrkovic, A., Döppner, D.A., Iacob, M.-E., van Hillegersberg, J.: Collaborative literature search system: an intelligence amplification method for systematic literature search. In: Chatterjee, S., Dutta, K., Sundarraj, R.P. (eds.) DESRIST 2018. LNCS, vol. 10844, pp. 169–183. Springer, Cham (2018). https://doi.org/10.1007/978-3-319-91800-6_12
42. Fu, X., Kelly, D., Shah, C.: Using collaborative queries to improve retrieval for difficult topics. In: Proceedings of the 30th Annual International ACM SIGIR Conference on Research and Development in Information Retrieval, pp. 879–880 (2007)
43. Carley, S., et al.: Social-media-enabled learning in emergency medicine: a case study of the growth, engagement and impact of a free open access medical education blog. Postgrad. Med. J. **94**(1108), 92–96 (2018)
44. Duarte, P.: The use of a group blog to actively support learning activities. Act. Learn. High. Educ. **16**(2), 103–117 (2015)
45. Morris, M.R.: A survey of collaborative web search practices. In: Proceedings of the SIGCHI Conference on Human Factors in Computing Systems, pp. 1657–1660 (2008)
46. Amankwah-Amoah, J., Khan, Z., Wood, G., Knight, G.: COVID-19 and digitalization: the great acceleration. J. Bus. Res. **136**, 602–611 (2021)

47. Crawford, J., et al.: COVID-19: 20 countries' higher education intra-period digital pedagogy responses. J. Appl. Learn. Teach. **3**(1), 1–20 (2020)
48. Gibbs, J.L., Sivunen, A., Boyraz, M.: Investigating the impacts of team type and design on virtual team processes. Hum. Resour. Manag. Rev. **27**(4), 590–603 (2017)
49. Herrera-Pavo, M.Á.: Collaborative learning for virtual higher education. Learn. Cult. Soc. Interact. **28**, 100437 (2021)
50. Buckland, M., Gey, F.: The relationship between recall and precision. J. Am. Soc. Inf. Sci. **45**(1), 12–19 (1994)
51. Sharma, D.K., Pamula, R., Chauhan, D.: A hybrid evolutionary algorithm based automatic query expansion for enhancing document retrieval system. J. Ambient Intell. Hum. Comput. 1–20 (2019). https://doi.org/10.1007/s12652-019-01247-9
52. Choi, J., Park, Y., Yi, M.: A hybrid method for retrieving medical documents with query expansion. In: 2016 International Conference on Big Data and Smart Computing (BigComp), pp. 411–414. IEEE (2016)
53. Bhogal, J., MacFarlane, A., Smith, P.: A review of ontology based query expansion. Inf. Process. Manag. **43**(4), 866–886 (2007)
54. Lupi, F., et al.: Cooperative scientific literature search and socialization through virtual teams. In: 3rd International Workshop on Higher Education Learning Methodologies and Technologies Online, pp. 36–39 (2021). ISBN 978-88-99978-36-5
55. Boffa, E., Lupi, F., Lanzetta, M., Maffei, A.: The Digitalization of Engineering Curricula: Defining the Categories that Preserve Constructive Alignment. In: Higher Education Learning Methodologies and Technologies Online. Springer (2022). https://doi.org/10.1007/978-3-030-96060-5_24

Technologies for Distance Learning in Higher Education

Semiautomatic Grading of Short Texts for Open Answers in Higher Education

Luis de-la-Fuente-Valentín[1](✉), Elena Verdú[1], Natalia Padilla-Zea[1], Claudia Villalonga[2], Xiomara Patricia Blanco Valencia[1], and Silvia Margarita Baldiris Navarro[1]

[1] Universidad Internacional de La Rioja (UNIR), Logroño, Spain
{luis.delafuente,elena.verdu,natalia.padilla, xiomarapatricia.blanco,silvia.baldiris}@unir.net
[2] Universidad de Granada, Granada, Spain
cvillalonga@ugr.es

Abstract. Grading student activities in online courses is a time-expensive task, especially with a high number of students in the course. To avoid a bottleneck in the continuous evaluation process, quizzes with multiple choice questions are frequently used. However, a quiz fails on the provision of formative feedback to the student. This work presents PLeNTaS, a system for the automatic grading of short answers from open domains, that reduces the time required for the grading task and offers formative feedback to the students. It is based on the analysis of the text from the point of view of three different levels: orthography, syntax, and semantics. The validation of the system will consider the correlation of the assigned grade with the human grade, the utility of the automatically generated feedback and the pedagogical impact caused by the system usage in the course.

Keywords: Automated grading · Semantic similarity · Feedback · Readability · Short-answers

1 Introduction

Nowadays, the lifelong learning paradigm is consolidated, allowing to adapt students' knowledge and skills to the evolving labor market. This is being especially relevant during the Covid-19 pandemic, which has meant an abrupt change in the way of working. In this context, online learning is a key alternative for many companies and people looking for self-sustainability.

The success in online learning requires an early and well-justified feedback, which implies a work overload for teachers. Moreover, open-answer questions allow better evaluating the knowledge [1, 2] but evaluating this type of questions is a complex task performed with considerable variability among teachers [3, 4]. This problem of variability can be mitigated by using rubrics, which facilitate a more consistent and transparent evaluation process [5]. On the other hand, techniques based on artificial intelligence may support teachers in the extensive evaluation processes involved in online learning.

G. Casalino et al. (Eds.): HELMeTO 2021, CCIS 1542, pp. 49–62, 2022.
https://doi.org/10.1007/978-3-030-96060-5_4

Specifically, open-answer questions imply writing a text by the student, which can be automatically processed by techniques of Natural Language Processing (NLP), machine learning or semantic based systems, techniques widely used in many different fields [6–8].

The reviewed literature shows that there are several tools that allow the automatic evaluation of short-answer questions. An interesting solution that allows the evaluation of different aspects of a text considering different metrics is ReaderBench [9]. It has integrated the indexes proposed by the systems E-rater [10], iSTART [11] and CohMetrix [12]. This open-source tool allows to evaluate the complexity of a text, summaries and explanations, as well as measuring the social collaboration within a group. It uses text mining techniques, NLP and social network analysis tools. ReaderBench has been used in different experiments. For example, Westera et al. [1] used NLP methods of ReaderBench to generate up to 200 indexes, with the aim of evaluating texts in a game environment in the context of online learning. The result of this evaluation is failing or passing. Panaite et al. [13] used ReaderBench to generate a grade for short answers based on four categories (poor, pass, good, excellent). In the 97% of the cases the grade was close to the grade given by a human expert. Recently, deep learning based solutions have been explored for automatic text complexity evaluation, obtaining limited performance due to the lack of a reliable corpus [14]. The limitations of all the above mentioned systems are the lack of explanations in the evaluations so that the students understand the obtained grades. Giving explainable feedback in artificial intelligence is very important and there is much literature about it in recommender systems and decision support systems, for example [15]. In the educational field, a few examples are found focused on decision makers, as an explainable tool that facilitates decision-making processes incorporating textual and graphical explanations when predicting students' outcomes [16], or a dashboard based approach for explainable student agency analytics [17]. However, there are almost no works related to explainable feedback for automatic evaluation systems in the educational field. From the literature review, we can conclude that the evaluation of learning results via analytics methods is a non-mature field [18].

The PLeNTaS project intends to provide students and teachers with valid explanations as formative feedback. A software platform is being developed to provide a semi-automatic evaluation of activities based on short open-answer questions. For each evaluated characteristic of a given answer, a textual explanation of the grade will be provided starting from the information previously provided by teachers.

The rest of the chapter is organized as follows: Sect. 2 presents a brief overview of the PLeNTaS project, including the different levels of analysis and the validation design. In Sect. 3, the main conclusions are outlined.

2 The PLeNTaS Project

With the focus on the provision of an automatic grade of open questions with a quick and accurate formative feedback, PLeNTaS ("Proyectos I+D+i 2019", PID2019-111430RB-I00) is a three-year project that proposes an evaluation process for short-answer questions for Spanish language. For this purpose, the project requires research from the pedagogical and technological points of view, both described as follows.

2.1 Design Decisions

The automatic evaluation requires the definition of a solid pedagogical approach, which should be the basis of any further development. The first required decision is the type of question to be evaluated. The project is focused on open-answer questions but, within such frame, some relevant decisions have still to be made: Will PLeNTaS support specific domain or open domain questions? Will the questions follow a given template? To answer these questions, during the pedagogical work phase of the project the metrics to be automatically evaluated are being defined. From a catalogue of metrics, teachers will compose the rubrics to evaluate the specific answers, so the technological research goal is the automatic fulfill of those rubrics. Then, to validate the system, automatic and human evaluations based on rubrics will be compared. Some relevant decisions are:

- The grading system will consider different levels of analysis, namely orthography, syntax, and semantics. We consider that none of the three levels is enough by itself to grade an activity. However, through the combination of these three levels, the grade is likely to be more accurate. For example, one of the possible techniques for the semantic level is checking if some key terms are present in the text. Therefore, it would be possible to game the system by only writing a list of key terms without any further explanation. A combination of this analysis with a readability analysis from the syntactic level deactivates the chance to game the system this way and forces a good writing style. Moreover, when the text is manually graded by the teacher, a student that offers a readable answer is more likely to obtain better grades because the teacher better understands its meaning.
- PLeNTaS is oriented towards the evaluation of short answers, with a limit of 200 words. Despite Burrows et al. [19] set the length of short answers in a range from one phrase to one paragraph, it is hard to evaluate the syntax when the text contains only one phrase [20]. In short answers, syntax cannot be used as the only grading criterion. Furthermore, in higher education, syntax is not usually a frequent element of the evaluation model. However, given that a student who writes a more readable text is more likely to obtain a higher grade, it seems reasonable to analyze the readability and clarity of the short answers. Therefore, the PLeNTaS system will promote one or two paragraph answers, so that the readability can be graded by the system as a complement for the semantic analysis.
- The system must provide useful feedback so that the grade can be understood by both teachers and students. This is important for the students who need to learn from the received comments, and for the teacher who should accept or refuse the automatic grade, or even explain it to the students.
- Open Domain questions are candidates to be evaluated. In a domain specific approach, a knowledge model is difficult to build. A system that requires a high effort for the creation of a set of questions is less likely to be widely adopted for instructors and institutions. Furthermore, recent works [21, 22] reveal that deep learning techniques are capable of determining similarity between two texts, and therefore it is possible to determine if the student answer is similar to a known solution.
- The three levels of analysis (orthography, syntax and semantics) will consist in a list of lower-level metrics. For example, the semantic level will be determined by

methods such as checking the occurrence of a set of given keywords and measuring the similarity of the student response with a known valid solution. None of these methods is expected to provide a perfect solution, while their combination might produce a fair evaluation. All the provided metrics will set up the rubric used for the evaluation, and the teacher will be able to configure them, for example by setting their weight on the final grade, the number of allowed spelling mistakes, etc. In other words, the rubric is the instrument that allows the teacher to decide which analysis will be considered for the calculation of the final grade, and what is the weight of each of the analysis. One important fact is that the low-level metrics allow for a more detailed feedback, with at least one sentence for each of the elements being graded.

With all these above-described elements, the PLeNTaS system will be able to answer questions as the following one:

> "In less than 200 words, explain what a cell is. In your response, you have to give answer to the following questions: what parts does a cell have? What types of cells are there? How many cells are required to form a living being?"

This sample question contains two relevant ideas. First, it starts with the limit of words so that the students know that the text should not be long, and that they should put some effort on summarizing their knowledge. Second, it splits the question in several smaller questions. With this, the teacher guides the specific content expected in the answer and allows for a more precise application of the semantic analysis. In other words, text similarity and text analysis with deep learning approaches work better with short sentences. A text of 200 words is hard to analyze, while the division of the question in smaller ones allows for a topic-by-topic analysis.

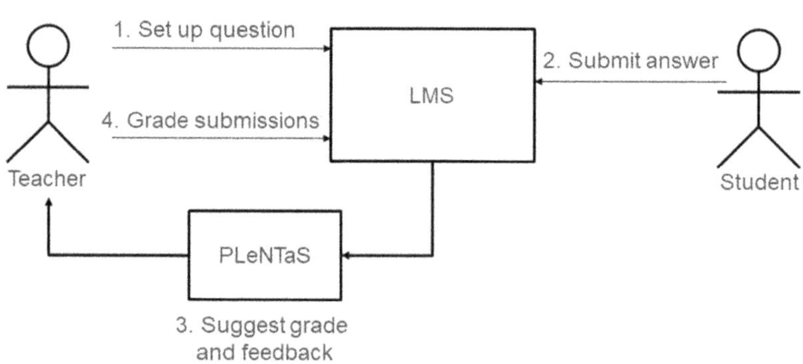

Fig. 1. Pedagogical model for the PLeNTaS support with LMS integration.

Finally, it is important to note that the PLeNTaS system will be used to support teacher's tasks. That is, for each of the answers to grade, the teacher will receive a grade proposal and the feedback sentences. With this, the teacher may accept or refuse the grade, and accept or refuse the feedback comments. This described workflow is depicted in Fig. 1.

2.2 Levels of the Analysis

The automated grade proposed by PLeNTaS is obtained by analyzing the text from three different perspectives, as shown in Fig. 2. The figure summarizes the methodology of the analysis, which is described in this section and can be described in general terms as follows:

- The teacher proposes a question, which divides into sub questions. (S)he writes a set of keywords that should be in the student's response, and provides valid responses for each sub question separately.
- Each student response is analyzed from the orthographical point of view with a spellchecker, which counts the number of mistakes made. This number is one of the values considered in the rubric, which applies the corresponding weight for the final grade calculation.
- The readability of the student response is analyzed with two different instruments (μ index [23] and Fernandez Huerta [24]). The result is averaged and used as an input for the rubric, where the corresponding weight is applied. The calculated ratios are used to build the sentences that serve as feedback.
- The student response is split into sentences, each of which is analyzed separately. First, by comparing a set of keywords with the response; second, with the use of NLP techniques for the calculation of semantic similarity with a given valid response. Each of these analyses are correspondingly weighted, with weights previously defined by the teacher in the configuration options, for the calculation of the final grade.
- The final grade, calculated by applying the rubric specification with the values obtained in each of the levels, and the feedback sentences are then offered to the teacher, who uses this input as a support to assign the grade.

Orthography

Despite orthography is not usually graded by teachers in higher education, a recent study in the Spanish National University of Distance Learning reveals that there is considerable room for improvement in the orthography of university students' asynchronous digital writing, where a total of 71.3% of errors were conditioned by ignorance of the orthographic rules or incorrect use of the language [25].

Kukich [26] divided the types of possible spelling errors depending on their inclusion in a dictionary of correct words. That is:

- non-word errors, where the incorrect word form is not in the dictionary of correct words.
- real-word errors, where the word is spelled incorrectly but its form is in the dictionary of correct words.

While the first type is easy to detect, the second type is more difficult and can be detected with the contextual analysis of the word, that is, with syntactic and semantic information of the surrounding words. Furthermore, correctly spelled words can be syntactically or semantically incorrect in a sentence. This means that a result of zero spelling errors found in the automated analysis does not imply a text with zero errors and thus, as previously stated, the score obtained in the orthographical level cannot represent the grade by itself.

Since many years ago, automatic spellcheckers are very common in word processors and are also integrated in web browsers and almost any software that allows to introduce text as an input. Despite challenges are still present such as improving recommendations that take context into account, or producing spellcheckers for low resource languages [27], automatic spelling correction is a well stablished field.

The output of current spellcheckers is the list of words identified as misspelled. This output allows for very specific feedback, also identifying the words and the evaluation criteria. For example: "you misspelled two words: 'telefone' and 'dadabase'. With these mistakes you have lost 2 points in the final grade".

In summary, spelling errors should not be allowed in higher educational level. Despite automated spellcheckers do not guarantee a perfect detection, the maturity of the field and the simplicity of its integration in the PLeNTaS system are good arguments for its inclusion as a level of analysis. However, orthographic analysis is considered in PLeNTaS a complementary, optional module.

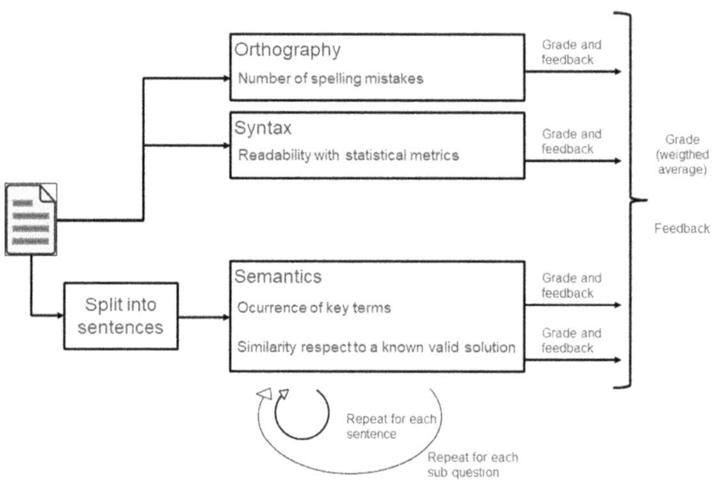

Fig. 2. General workflow of the analysis.

Syntax

George R. Klare [28] defined readability as the ease with which a reader can understand a document due to the style of writing. Of course, understanding a document is a subjective matter that depends on the reader. Therefore, readability should be understood from a statistical viewpoint. Readability is related to the complexity of the sentences and the words used in them. For example, long sentences with several dependent clauses demand more attention and they are therefore harder to understand.

Classical readability formulas such as the Fry Graph [29] or the Raygor estimate graph [30] are based on the sentences length, total number of sentences and number of characters as the most relevant indicators. These statistical methods are language dependent, while they can be easily adapted to other languages by simply adapting the ratios to the proper values.

Other formulas such as Dale Chall [31] rely on the idea that a text is complex to read if the used words are complex to understand. This family of formulas count the average length of the words in the text, the number of longer words and the number of words that appear in a list of unfamiliar words. Depending on the formula, the list of unfamiliar words can be built with different criteria and depends on the educational level of the readers. Given that the list of unfamiliar words is highly language dependent, it is difficult to adapt such formulas to different languages.

Readability formulas has been used for years in many domains such as journalism, insurance, health, laws and, of course, education [32, 33]. According to [34], readability formulas are used with two main goals: first, to predict the readability of a given text; second, to assist in the production of readable writing.

Well known formulas set thresholds for different educational levels, and usually focus on secondary education. Students that enter higher education are supposed to have acquired enough writing skills (which is not necessarily true [35]) and therefore readability is not directly graded at the university. Furthermore, university teachers may have good writing skills, but they are not supposed to have the competence to grade them.

However, readability is still important for students while producing their short-answer texts, because the more readable is a text, the easier the teacher will understand its concepts. In other words, if the teacher does not understand the text, it is unlikely that the student gets a high grade. Furthermore, it is always a good practice to promote the production of readable text, no matter the knowledge field.

In PLeNTaS, readability is measured by applying two classic models for Spanish language, the μ index [23] and Fernandez Huerta [24]. Both models are applied to the whole text provided by the student and will classify it in a scale that ranges from "very easy" to "very difficult". Two indexes will be measured in order to obtain redundancy that ensures the validity of the diagnostic.

When measured from a statistical point of view, readability allows for the composition of formative feedback that explains the application of the grading criteria. It is possible, for example, to identify too long sentences as examples of bad practice, and to mention ratios that are poorly fulfilled. For example: "*the average length of your sentences is 34 words. Good readability requires an average of less than 20 words per sentence. Please consider splitting your long sentences*".

Thus, being readability formulas a widely used method in many domains, PLeNTaS includes such analysis as part of the grading system. Therefore, a valid solution must contain the relevant concepts required in the question and must also have a readable writing style.

Semantics

Given that a correctly written text should be readable and without orthographic errors, the actual grade should come from the semantic analysis. At this level, the following questions can be analyzed: 1) is the answer in the domain of knowledge of the posed question? 2) Is the text answering the question? And 3) is the answer correct? For example, in the question about cells given as example in Sect. 2.1, we could have the following answers:

- "cells and living beings are both in the Earth". This is in the domain of knowledge of the question, but it is not answering the question.
- "living beings require at least twelve cells to be considered as such". This is in the domain of knowledge, provides an answer, but the answer is not correct.

The proposed method for the semantic analysis combines simple techniques such as keyword matching with state-of-the-art techniques for text similarity identification based on Deep Learning NLP.

In PLeNTaS, the teachers create the questions and do the set up (Fig. 1), which means that they provide a set of key terms that are supposed to be included in a valid answer, and a reference response considered correct. There is not a minimum number of key terms required, as this depends on the specific domain and question, although the general recommendation is to include between 4 and 6 keywords. This additional data included by the teachers is latter used to assess the validity of the student answers. Furthermore, as the question should be divided into sub-questions, the reference answer should be also divided into sub-responses, and therefore the analysis is guided by the sub-questions.

In PLeNTaS, we propose a sub-questions based analysis that first analyzes single sentences and then groups of consecutive sentences. For example, in a four-sentence paragraph, the analysis will be executed in the following order: $\{1\}$, $\{2\}$, $\{3\}$, $\{4\}$, $\{1, 2\}$, $\{2, 3\}$, $\{3, 4\}$, $\{1, 2, 3\}$, $\{2, 3, 4\}$, $\{1, 2, 3, 4\}$. This division alleviates the complexity of NLP (which is harder in longer texts) at the time that measures the accuracy of the specific sentences.

One existing approach in automated grading is key term matching. That is, given that the teacher provides a set of key terms that are expected to appear in the student's answer, key term matching can be used. Such type of analysis only provides the answer to the first of the sematic questions: "is the answer in the domain of knowledge of the question?".

As stated in [36], key terms matching has usually been considered a poor method, given that it is difficult to tackle problems such as synonymy or polysemy in the student answers. Despite this known problem, it is a simple approach that provides good enough results. For example, Omran and Ab Aziz [37] use Common Words (COW) as a metric for the distance between the student answer and the reference answer, which counts the number of words that are present in both texts and divide the result by the total of words in the sum of the two answers. Another example of use is the existing module for the Moodle LMS [38], that allows the teacher to configure a set of target phrases that should appear in the answer, and executes the matching with regular expressions.

As stated above, key terms matching has the problem of synonymy in the given terms. The PLeNTaS approach is the augmentation of the catalogue of key terms by checking them in a dictionary and including in the catalogue the direct synonyms. As depicted in Fig. 3, this produces an augmented catalogue that is lemmatized and compared with the lemmatized version of the student answer.

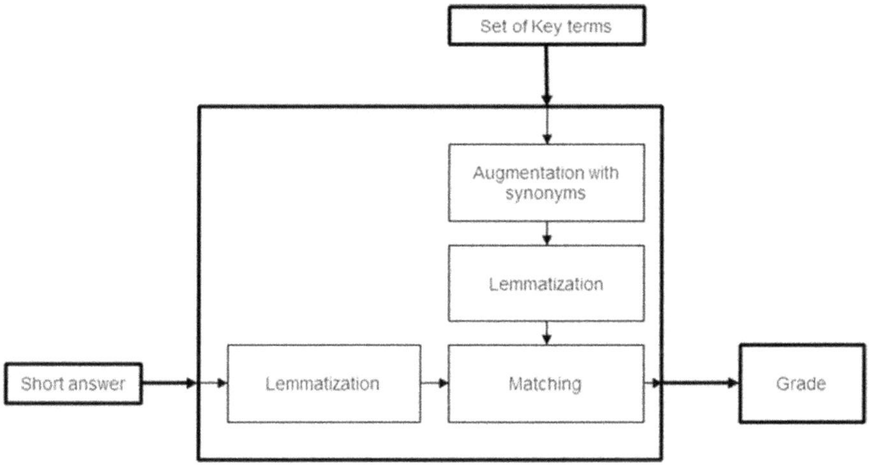

Fig. 3. Key term matching procedure in PLeNTaS.

However, in very specific domains of knowledge, key terms tend to be field specific, and they are unlikely to appear in general dictionaries. The potential result will be an augmented set of key terms equal to the original one. Thus, in the set up of the question the teachers should make their effort on creating a catalogue of key terms as complete as possible, including all the existing correct ways to mention a concept.

Another method to check the semantic correctness of the answer is the calculation of the semantic similarity with respect to the reference solution. There are many techniques reported in the literature for semantic similarity calculation. The existing methods can be divided in Knowledge-based methods, Corpus-based methods and Deep Learning approaches [39]. Knowledge-based methods consider the actual meaning of the words in the text by using knowledge models such as ontologies, thesauri, dictionaries, etc. This approach requires a high effort on building the knowledge model, and the result cannot be adopted in other knowledge domains. The approach of Corpus-based methods is based on the idea that 'similar words occur together, frequently' [40]. With this idea in mind, a large amount of text is processed so that the system finds statistical relations among words, without considering their actual meaning. Those relationships, called word embeddings, can be used to determine if two texts are similar, given that they will be similar if their words have shown to be similar in other texts, which is statistically measured. For example, the log-bilinear regression model GloVe provides word representations that are effective for word analogy, word similarity and named entity recognition tasks [41]. Learning high dimensional word vectors from large datasets, which have a huge number of words in the vocabulary, implies high computational costs. To alleviate these costs, simple model architectures requiring low computational complexity have been proposed, proving to be effective in word similarity tasks [42]. When word embeddings are analyzed with neural network techniques, usually Long Short-Term Memory (LSTM) or Bidirectional LSTM, this is considered a Deep Learning approach. A recent work combines Relational Graph Convolutional Networks (R-GCNs) with Bidirectional Encoder Representations from Transformers (BERT) to learn the contextual similarity between sentences [43]. The latter has shown better performance, but Deep Learning approaches show the problem of their lack of interpretability. That is, given a result, it is difficult to explain how it was calculated.

The semantic similarity approach in PLeNTaS for automated grading offers an approximation for the second and third questions to be solved:

- Is the text answering the question? The approach can tell if the text is similar or not to a given correct answer. Considering that the analysis is performed sentence by sentence and that the whole question is divided into several sub-questions, it can be considered that a sentence with high similarity to the correct sub-answer to a given sub-question is answering the sub-question.
- Is the answer correct? With the current state of the technology in Natural Language Processing, semantic similarity will hardly provide a Yes/No response to this question. However, it can be reworded as "how far is this text from a valid answer?", which is exactly the meaning of semantic similarity.

Feedback provision is a challenging task in the semantic analysis. For example, when applying Deep Learning approaches for Question Answering, the system is able to identify the specific words that are likely the response to a specific question. However, in the case the system finds nothing, it is not able to justify why. This output leads, in most cases, to vague and unspecific feedback. The PLeNTaS project will split the total answer in smaller sentences and analyze them separately. This fact allows identifying the similarity of specific sentences with the real answer. Therefore, the PLeNTaS system will be able to create feedback such as "the question 'What types of cells are there?' has not been answered. Sentence 3 is near to the actual response, but not enough accurate. The expected response is '(...)'.". Although far from the capabilities of a human teacher, this type of feedback allows for the identification of strong and weak aspects in the response.

The PLeNTaS system proposes a hybrid approach that will combine the better results of Deep Learning NLP approaches with the explainability of knowledge-based analysis. As the analysis is repeated for each of the sub-questions and executed at the level of feedback sentence, the grading process is expected to determine the meaningful sentences and therefore provide the useful feedback for the sentences poorly graded. Given that deep learning solutions require large datasets, transfer learning will be adopted. Therefore, a pre-trained model like BERT will be fine-tuned with the set of real answers collected in the project [44].

2.3 Validation

Most of the automated grading systems in the literature are validated from a statistical point of view. That is, they measure the correlation of the grade calculated by the system with the grade assigned by the human teachers. While this is a fair and important measure, it is also important to measure the pedagogical effectiveness of the tool. In other words, the PLeNTaS validation stage will measure the achievement of the project from three different perspectives: 1) the system precision on the automatic evaluation task when compared to human evaluations, 2) the appropriateness of the elaborated feedback, and

3) the overall impact on the teaching-learning process. Although the project is still being developed, the validation plan includes the following stages:

In the first stage, in a laboratory setting, we compiled a corpus of 660 short-answers collected from previous real exams. These exams belong to four different master's degrees in an online university in the first semester of 2021. The students completed their answers in a fully online mode, where a proctoring system supervised the proper conduct of the students during the examination. The collected questions were written according to the template given for the PLeNTaS question type, and the answers where valid for the final grade. The teachers graded such answers without any consideration coming from the researchers. This corpus is the base to do preliminary tests of the different aspects of the PLeNTaS system. The *system precision* seeks for the correlation between machine and human grading. To do this evaluation, every question in the corpus includes the grade assigned by the teacher, which will be compared to the one returned by the system. The results obtained will be contrasted to other tools in the state of the art.

For the continuous evaluation pedagogical approach, where formative grading is important, a fair system precision is not enough for a tool to be adopted. It is also important to measure the *validity of the feedback* offered by the system. The validation of the feedback will combine quantitative and qualitative methods. First, the teachers will receive the feedback and the grade for the automatically graded answers and will be asked if (i) the feedback is in agreement with the calculated grade and (ii) the feedback allows for the identification of the aspects for improvement. A qualitative analysis of those answers will give the opportunity to adjust the system.

In a second stage, further tests of validity of the feedback will be developed, together with the *educational impact*. To widen the validity of the feedback, the same questions will be presented to a set of volunteer students. The evaluation of the *effects on educational quality and student experience,* which is highly relevant for automated grading systems [45], will be performed in a pilot course that incorporates automated grading and feedback as a part of the course. During a 15-weeks course, the students will answer 3–4 PLeNTaS-templated questions and the teacher will grade them with the support of the developed system. During the course, the researchers will annotate any observation from the teacher and, after the course, they will interview the teacher to understand the impact of the system in the course. Additionally, a TAM (Technology Acceptance Model) [46] test will be delivered both to teachers and students in order to evaluate their perceived ease of use and usefulness.

3 Conclusions

PLeNTaS is an on-going project that finalizes in june'2023 and whose main objective is the development and validation of an automated grading system. This project is especially relevant for online, higher education, where frequent sub-missions would create better engagement in the course experience.

Automated grade is calculated with a hybrid approach that considers three levels of analysis: orthography, syntax and semantics. While the first two levels are well established in the state of the art, their use in conjunction to the semantic level will offer more complete feedback to the students.

The analysis of the semantic level is divided in two ways: firstly, the question posed by the teachers is divided into sub-questions, according to the template proposed by the project PLeNTaS. Each of these sub-questions are analyzed separately, which allows for a more accurate analysis and feedback. Secondly, the 200-words answer provided by the student is divided into separate sentences, which are analyzed one by one. This strategy seeks a more accurate detection of the semantics in the text, and therefore more accurate feedback. The semantic analysis proposes a hybrid approach that combines knowledge-based and deep-learning approaches for the seek of semantic similarity.

The project is still in an initial stage, where next steps are the implementation of the three-levels model and the use of the already collected student answers to validate the proposed model.

Acknowledgements. This Work is partially funded by the PLeNTaS project, "Proyectos I+D+i 2019", PID2019-111430RB-I00, by the PL-NETO project, Proyecto PROPIO UNIR, projectId B0036, and by Universidad Internacional de la Rioja (UNIR), through the Research Institute for Innovation & Technology in Education (UNIR iTED, http://ited.unir.net).

References

1. Westera, W., Dascalu, M., Kurvers, H., et al.: Automated essay scoring in applied games: reducing the teacher bandwidth problem in online training. Comput. Educ. **123**, 212–224 (2018). https://doi.org/10.1016/J.COMPEDU.2018.05.010
2. McNamara, D.S., Crossley, S.A., Roscoe, R.D., et al.: A hierarchical classification approach to automated essay scoring. Assess. Writ. **23**, 35–59 (2015). https://doi.org/10.1016/J.ASW.2014.09.002
3. Campbell, J.R.: Cognitive processes elicited by multiple-choice and constructed-response questions on an assessment of reading comprehension. Temple University (UMI No. 9938651) (1999)
4. Rodrigues, F., Oliveira, P.: A system for formative assessment and monitoring of students' progress. Comput. Educ. **76**, 30–41 (2014). https://doi.org/10.1016/J.COMPEDU.2014.03.001
5. Brame C.J.: Rubrics: tools to make grading more fair and efficient. In: Science Teaching Essentials, pp. 175–184. Academic Press (2019)
6. Prasad Mudigonda, K.S., Sharma, P.: multi-sense embeddings using synonym sets and hypernym information from wordnet. Int. J. Interact. Multimed. Artif. Intell. **6**, 68 (2020). https://doi.org/10.9781/ijimai.2020.07.001
7. Zhou, S., Chen, B., Zhang, Y., et al.: A feature extraction method based on feature fusion and its application in the text-driven failure diagnosis field. Int. J. Interact. Multimed. Artif. Intell. **6**, 121 (2020). https://doi.org/10.9781/ijimai.2020.11.006
8. Rao, S.B.P., Agnihotri, M., Babu Jayagopi, D.: Improving asynchronous interview interaction with follow-up question generation. Int. J. Interact. Multimed. Artif. Intell. **6**, 79 (2021). https://doi.org/10.9781/ijimai.2021.02.010
9. Dascalu, M.: readerbench (1) - cohesion-based discourse analysis and dialogism, pp. 137–160 (2014)
10. Ramineni, C.: Automated essay scoring: psychometric guidelines and practices. Assess. Writ. **18**, 25–39 (2013). https://doi.org/10.1016/J.ASW.2012.10.004

11. McNamara, D.S., Levinstein, I.B., Boonthum, C.: iSTART: interactive strategy training for active reading and thinking. Behav. Res. Methods Instr. Comput. **36**, 222–233 (2004). https://doi.org/10.3758/BF03195567
12. Graesser, A.C., McNamara, D.S., Kulikowich, J.M.: Coh-metrix. Educ. Res. **40**, 223–234 (2011). https://doi.org/10.3102/0013189X11413260
13. Panaite, M., Dascalu, M., Johnson, A., et al.: Bring it on! Challenges encountered while building a comprehensive tutoring system using ReaderBench. In: Penstein, R.C., et al. (eds.) AIED 2018. LNCS (LNAI and LNB), vol. 10947, pp. 409–419. Springer, Cham (2018). https://doi.org/10.1007/978-3-319-93843-1_30
14. Cuzzocrea, A., Bosco, G.L., Pilato, G., Schicchi, D.: Multi-class text complexity evaluation via deep neural networks. In: Yin, H., Camacho, D., Tino, P., Tallón-Ballesteros, A.J., Menezes, R., Allmendinger, R. (eds.) IDEAL 2019. LNCS, vol. 11872, pp. 313–322. Springer, Cham (2019). https://doi.org/10.1007/978-3-030-33617-2_32
15. Zhang, Y., Chen, X.: Explainable Recommendation: A Survey and New Perspectives (2018)
16. Alonso, J.M., Casalino, G.: Explainable artificial intelligence for human-centric data analysis in virtual learning environments. In: Burgos, D., et al. (eds.) HELMeTO 2019. CCIS, vol. 1091, pp. 125–138. Springer, Cham (2019). https://doi.org/10.1007/978-3-030-31284-8_10
17. Saarela, M., Heilala, V., Jaaskela, P., et al.: Explainable student agency analytics. IEEE Access **9**, 137444–137459 (2021). https://doi.org/10.1109/ACCESS.2021.3116664
18. Kent, C., Laslo, E., Rafaeli, S.: Interactivity in online discussions and learning outcomes. Comput. Educ. **97**, 116–128 (2016). https://doi.org/10.1016/J.COMPEDU.2016.03.002
19. Burrows, S., Gurevych, I., Stein, B.: The eras and trends of automatic short answer grading. Int. J. Artif. Intell. Educ. **25**, 60–117 (2015)
20. Pérez-Marín, D., Pascual-Nieto, I., Rodríguez, P.: Computer-assisted assessment of free-text answers. Knowl. Eng. Rev. **24**, 353–374 (2009). https://doi.org/10.1017/S026988890999018X
21. Mohler, M., Mihalcea, R.: Text-to-text semantic similarity for automatic short answer grading (2009). (3AD)
22. Gautam, D., Rus, V.: Using neural tensor networks for open ended short answer assessment. In: Bittencourt, I.I., Cukurova, M., Muldner, K., Luckin, R., Millán, E. (eds.) AIED 2020. LNCS (LNAI), vol. 12163, pp. 191–203. Springer, Cham (2020). https://doi.org/10.1007/978-3-030-52237-7_16
23. Muñoz Baquedano, M.: Legibilidad y variabilidad de los textos. Boletín Investig. Educ. **21**, 13–25 (2006)
24. Fernandez Huerta, J.: Medidas sencillas de lecturabilidad. Consiga **214**, 29–32 (1959)
25. Vázquez-Cano, E., González, A.I.H., Sáez-López, J.M.: An analysis of the orthographic errors found in university students' asynchronous digital writing. J. Comput. High. Educ. **31**(1), 1–20 (2018). https://doi.org/10.1007/s12528-018-9189-x
26. Kukich, K.: Techniques for automatically correcting words in text. ACM Comput. Surv. **24**, 377–439 (1992). https://doi.org/10.1145/146370.146380
27. Hládek, D., Staš, J., Pleva, M.: Survey of automatic spelling correction. Electronics **9**, 1–29 (2020)
28. Klare, G.R.: The Measure of Readability. University of Iowa Press, Ames (1963)
29. Fry, E.: A readability formula that saves time. J. Read. 513–516, 575–578 (1968). (8 pages)
30. Raygor, A.L.: The Raygor readability estimate: a quick and easy way to determine difficulty. Read. Theory Res. Pract. **1977**, 259–263 (1977)
31. Dale, E., Chall, J.S.: A formula for predicting readability. Educ. Res. Bull. **27**(1), 11–28 (1948). http://www.jstor.org/stable/1473169
32. Crossley, S.A., Skalicky, S., Dascalu, M.: Moving beyond classic readability formulas: new methods and new models. J. Res. Read. **42**, 541–561 (2019). https://doi.org/10.1111/1467-9817.12283

33. Morato, J., Iglesias, A., Campillo, A., Sanchez-Cuadrado, S.: Automated readability assessment for spanish e-government information. J. Inf. Syst. Eng. Manag. **6**, em0137 (2021). https://doi.org/10.29333/jisem/9620
34. Klare, G.R.: A second look at the validityl of readability formulas. J. Read. Behav. **8**, 129–152 (1976). https://doi.org/10.1080/10862967609547171
35. Taylor, Z.W.: College admissions for L2 students: comparing L1 and L2 readability of admissions materials for U.S. higher education. J. Coll. Access. **5**(1) (2020). https://scholarworks.wmich.edu/jca/vol5/iss1/6. Article 6
36. Selvi, P., Bnerjee, D.A.K.: Automatic short-answer grading system (ASAGS) (2010)
37. Ben, O.A.M., Ab Aziz, M.J.: Automatic essay grading system for short answers in English language. J. Comput. Sci. **9**, 1369–1382 (2013). https://doi.org/10.3844/jcssp.2013.1369.1382
38. Essay (auto-grade) question type - MoodleDocs
39. Chandrasekaran, D., Mago, V.: Evolution of semantic similarity – a survey. ACM Comput. Surv. **54** (2020). https://doi.org/10.1145/3440755
40. Gorman, J., Curran, J.R.: Scaling distributional similarity to large corpora. In: COLING/ACL 2006 - 21st International Conference on Computational Linguistics and 44th Annual Meeting of the Association for Computational Linguistics, Proceedings of the Conference, pp. 361–368. Association for Computational Linguistics (ACL), Morristown (2006)
41. Pennington, J., Socher, R., Manning, C.D.: GloVe: global vectors for word representation. In: EMNLP 2014 – Proceedings of 2014 Conference on Empirical Methods in Natural Language Processing, pp. 1532–1543 (2014). https://doi.org/10.3115/V1/D14-1162
42. Mikolov, T., Chen, K., Corrado, G., Dean, J.: Efficient estimation of word representations in vector space (2013)
43. Xu, S., Shen, X., Fukumoto, F., et al.: Paraphrase identification with lexical, syntactic and sentential encodings. Appl. Sci. **10**, 4144 (2020). https://doi.org/10.3390/APP10124144
44. Qiu, X., Sun, T., Xu, Y., Shao, Y., Dai, N., Huang, X.: Pre-trained models for natural language processing: a survey. Sci. China Technol. Sci. **63**(10), 1872–1897 (2020). https://doi.org/10.1007/s11431-020-1647-3
45. Hahn, M.G., Navarro, S.M.B., De La Fuente, V.L., Burgos, D.: A systematic review of the effects of automatic scoring and automatic feedback in educational settings. IEEE Access **9**, 108190–108198 (2021). https://doi.org/10.1109/ACCESS.2021.3100890
46. Davis, F.D.: Perceived usefulness, perceived ease of use, and user acceptance of information technology. MIS Q. **13**, 319–339 (1989). https://doi.org/10.2307/249008

Using Process Mining to Understand Students' and Teams' Dynamics

Pasquale Ardimento[1(✉)], Mario Luca Bernardi[2], and Marta Cimitile[3]

[1] University of Bari Aldo Moro, Bari, Italy
pasquale.ardimento@uniba.it
[2] University of Sannio, Benevento, Italy
bernardi@unisannio.it
[3] University UnitelmaSapienza, Rome, Italy
marta.cimitile@unitelmasapienza.it

Abstract. In Software Engineering courses several team activities are proposed to improve not only students' technical skills but also their capability to collaborate. However, the evaluation of the activity of each student relative to the whole team is very hard for the teacher. For this reason, several studies aim to investigate how to support teachers in the evaluation of the activities of students involved in software development teams. This study proposes an approach to extract information about software team members' behavior by mining the data gathered by the interactions of students with the coding environment. The paper also describes an exploratory study consisting to use the proposed approach to analyze the activities of the students involved in a team project assigned at the computer programming II course held at the University of Bari Aldo Moro. The results show the effectiveness of the proposed approach to support the comprehension of students' team dynamics and single student contribution along with the teamwork.

1 Introduction

Software development projects are usually performed by locally and globally distributed teams and for this reason, their success requires not only technical skills but also the capability to communicate, organize and collaborate [1]. This allows several teachers to include in their programming courses some team activities and enhance students' collaboration with the adoption of integrated development environments (IDEs) (where students perform their programming assignments) and version control systems (VCS) (where students manage their commits). However, the teamwork activity is sometimes not easy to evaluate and monitor while the teacher is not able to understand the contribution of each student with respect to the team activities. According to this, several approaches are proposed to achieve software teamwork. Some of them are based on qualitative and subjective data captured via surveys and peer evaluation [2,3]. Other approaches [4] use a reputation system to compute individual contributions in a team. Finally, several authors propose a collaborative learning system also

G. Casalino et al. (Eds.): HELMeTO 2021, CCIS 1542, pp. 63–73, 2022.
https://doi.org/10.1007/978-3-030-96060-5_5

supporting the mining of students' activities from a computer supported based on a peer-to-peer network [5,6]. This study proposes a process mining approach to extract information about team members' behavior in a team working. The main assumption at the base of the proposed approach is that the interactions of students with the IDEs and with the VCS can be captured and mined to monitor students' behavior when they are involved in a set of programming tasks [7,8]. However, this study proposes a framework to capture the interactions of students involved in a team project with the Eclipse IDE and with the VCS and record both of them as event logs. The logs are then mined with a declarative process mining technique [9] to discover the coding workflow executed by each student and support the teacher to evaluate and understand the behavior of the single student of the group. The novelty introduced by this work consists in the extraction of the individual and team development workflows from both the IDE and the VCS. However, the analysis of such models should give a great contribution to understanding and evaluating the team working dynamics and drive the teacher in the identification of the team tasks. Moreover, even if process mining is adopted in some recent studies to model coding activities of students and developers that interact with IDEs [8,10,11], it is the first time that it is used on both IDEs and VCS data. This paper also proposes an exploratory study mining event logs captured in the development of a team project assigned at the computer programming II course, a second-year course for programmers learning the Object-Oriented Paradigm and the Java language, held at the University of Bari Aldo Moro. The collected logs pertain to 5 teams of students where each team is composed of 2 or 3 students. The rest of the paper is structured as follows. Section 2 provides some background material on existing approaches to capture the interactions of software developers and related process mining notions. Section 3, instead, provides some background material on studies conducted to measure and evaluate software development processes in software engineering courses. Section 4 shows the proposed miner framework introduced whereas in Sect. 5 a case study showing the use of the miner approach in a real domain is presented and discussed. Section 6 provides the conclusions.

2 Background

In this section, a discussion of the existing approaches to capture the interactions of software developers with the coding environment is proposed (Sect. 2.1). The section (Sect. 2.2) also introduces the required process mining notions useful to understand the proposed mining approach.

2.1 Capturing Students Activities

In the proposed approach the students' activities are monitored by capturing their interactions with the IDEs and with the VCS [7,8]. The monitoring of the interactions of each student with the IDE gives the teacher indications about the student's behavior and how the student writes the code [12]. Differently, the monitoring of the interactions of each student with the VCS helps to understand the overall software development process [13]. For example, authors in [14] analyze data extracted from VCS to study how developers collaborate. The adoption of an integrated development environment (IDE) and a VCS in software development courses is very diffused since teachers usually desire that students use authentic tools [15]. In particular, in the educational contexts, several VCS tools (i.e.Git/Github) offer to the software educational community ad-hoc educational resources to improve students' and teachers' experience [16]. Moreover, an advantage of using VCS tools can be derived from analyzing the data that are generated when the student interacts with this tool. Looking for example at the Github API, it provides information that can be input for learning analytics and educational data mining [17]. Recent studies use information collected by the VCS tool to compute a set of indicators useful to evaluate project quality, student behavior, student individual, team contributions [18].

2.2 Declarative Process Mining

Process Mining (PM) is a set of data mining algorithms able to perform analysis of operational processes based on event logs recorded by an information system to discover, monitor, and improve real processes [19,20]. Looking to the PM approaches, the so-called declarative techniques take as input/output a process represented with a declarative language [21,22]. This representation of the process is more flexible and it is suitable to represent processes in unstable environments such as code development processes where multiple execution paths are involved. In this study, the so-called Declare Miner [9,23] is used to mine from the extracted logs, a process model representing the student's behavior. The process model is represented using the Declare language. It consists of a set of constraints that are concrete instantiations of templates. These templates are abstract entities defining parametrized classes of properties with a formal semantics based on the Linear Temporal Logic (LTL) formulas related to an intuitive graphical representation. The LTL formulas are related to non-deterministic Finite State Automatons (FSA) useful to represent all the traces of a log that satisfy the constraint. Table 1 reports some examples of templates (their meaning and the graphical notation are also included).

3 Related Work

Measuring and evaluating software development processes in software engineering courses is becoming very critical for teachers. According to this, several studies propose metrics mined from software development systems for monitoring and observing students' development processes [18]. Other studies propose PM approaches to study and discover the typical software development processes [24,25]. In particular, PM techniques can be used to mine development processes starting from Software Configuration Management (SCM), VCS, or IDE systems [24]. Authors in [24], introduce a PM framework able to identify software development process models to optimize software development activities. In [26], a

Table 1. Graphical notation and description of the discovered Declare templates.

Template	Description	Notation
Init(A)	A must be the first activity to be executed	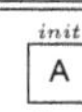
Existence(A)	A must be executed at least one time	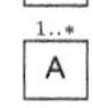
Existence2(A)	A must be executed at least two times	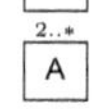
Existence3(A)	A must be executed at least three times	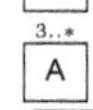
Co-Existence(A,B)	Neither A nor B is executed, or they are both executed	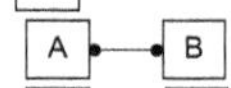
Response(A,B)	If A is executed, then B has to be executed at any time after A	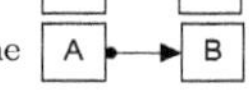
Precedence(A,B)	B can be executed only if A has been at some time previously executed	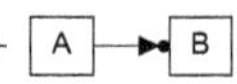
Succession(A,B)	A and B must be executed in succession	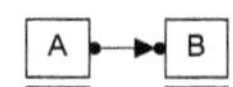
Alternate Response(A,B)	if A occurs then eventually B occurs after A without other occurrences of A in between	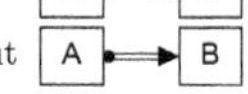
Alternate Precedence(A,B)	if B occurs then eventually B occurs after A without other occurrences of B in between	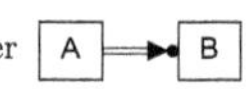

PM approach is used to analyze logs captured by the Issue Tracking System (ITS) and mine student bug fixing process. In this study, the evaluation of each single student contribution is performed using a set of metrics (learning analytics) that provide feedback about the process. The students' development process is also evaluated in [8,10]. Here authors use a declarative approach to mine students' development process starting from the information extracted by the IDE. Starting from this contributes, the approach proposed in this study has two main novelties. The first novelty consists to use both the data extracted from IDE and the VCS. The second novelty regards the goal of this study. However, differently from similar process mining-based approaches, in this study, the single student model and the team model are compared to evaluate the contribution of each student to the team.

4 The Proposed Approach

The proposed approach is depicted in Fig. 1. The figure describes the interaction of two students (A and B) involved in the same team project (for briefly we consider a group composed of two students). Each student interacts with the Eclipse IDE by generating a stream of human-computer interaction (HCI) events and committing events. For each student, all the events are captured in Eclipse: the HCI Processor captures any interaction with IDE (low level and high-level events) while the Commit Monitor captures any interaction with VCS (e.g., commits and push events). All the events captured for each student are then processed by the Log Generator that generates a unique log, containing all the events. The Log Generator is obtained by extending the functionality

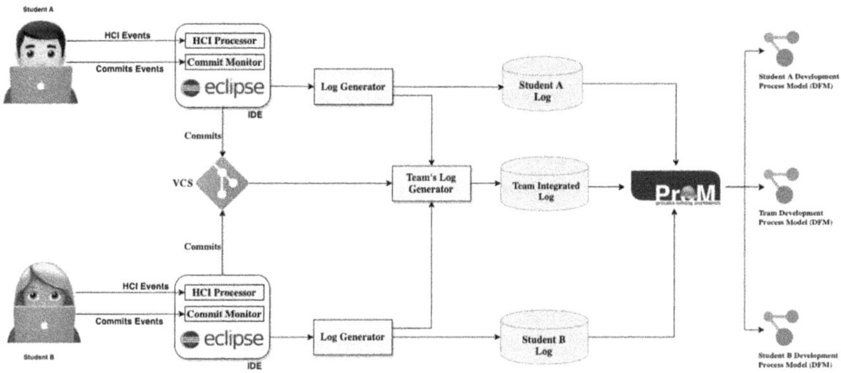

Fig. 1. The environment architecture.

of Fluorite [8], an open-source instrumentation plugin able to capture the low-level interactions of the student with the IDE and VCS (for example, shortcuts, keyboard key presses, and gestures). The proposed extension mainly allows to capture i) additional contextual information to the low-level events and ii) high-level events (for example, open or generate a file). A more detailed description of the proposed Fluorite plugin and the proposed extensions is reported in [8]. The Commits events are also stored in a remote repository, hosted either on the GitHub platform or BitBucket and managed by a VCS for collaborative software development. All the captured interactions (HCI events and Commit events) are then cleaned and filtered out. The cleaning activity consists to remove the students' interactions that are unrelated to the project's activity and correct inconsistencies. The described interactions are then processed by the Log Generator (one for each student) to become event logs.

Finally, the logs are converted into XES[1]. For each student, the XES logs are collected in a Student log repository. The students' logs are also sent to the Team's Log Generator component. This component collects the logs generated by all the students of the same team to generate a unique log of events stored on the Team integrated log repository. Finally, the mining of the student and the team integrated logs is performed using the Declare Miner described in Sect. 2. This allows obtaining the declare process describing the coding process executed by every single student involved in a team project and by all the team. These process models can be used to evaluate each students' contribution relative to the entire team.

5 Case Study

The preliminary evaluation of our proposed approach is performed on 5 teams (Gr.1, Gr.2, Gr.3, Gr.4, Gr.5), each one composed of 2 or 3 students from an

[1] http://www.xes-standard.org.

advanced Java course held at the University of Bari Aldo Moro (Italy). The project work assigned to the teams consists of implementing a simple software system by using the Java programming language. The teams had 3 months to complete their project and each student had a personal copy of the Eclipse environment including the HCI Processor, the Commit Monitor and a personal account to the software development team platform. After the project completion, officially communicated to the teachers, the HCIs and the students' commits are processed by the Log Generator and transformed into logs. Following the cleaning step a total number of 926 logs are collected. Afterward, the students' and team logs are mined using the Declare Miner to discover the process model.

In this step, we set both "Min Constraint Support" and "Min Activity Support" Declare Miner parameters to 50% which means that both constraints and activities satisfied in at least 50% of the traces in the log are discovered. The obtained models allow both to compare teams based on their activities and compare for each team the single-member contribution.

5.1 Single Students' Evaluation

An example of Declare process model of two students belonging to the same team, named Gr.1, is depicted in Figs. 2 and 3. For briefly, in this discussion we indicate respectively these students as "follower" and "leader". The number of occurrences for each activity and the relation between them is reported in the rectangles and the more frequent activities are highlighted in blue (increasing tone corresponds to increasing frequency). Discovered constraints, instead, are reported on the edges linking two activities. For example, in Fig. 2, the co-existence constraint between the activity "InsertString" and "MoveCaret" means that in 78.60% if "InsertString" occurs then "MoveCaret" occurs before or after "InsertString". Moreover, the description of the discovered activities is reported in Table 2.

In general, based on the figures, we can observe that the "FileOpen", "Save", "MoveCaret" activities are the most frequent activities while all the interactions always start and return on the global commands. Starting from global commands, the developers move to other activities related to other functions clusters. The process models also highlight that the activities can be grouped in two clusters corresponding to the principal IDE functions. The first group is composed of the global functions that alter the IDE behavior and allow to switch working contexts. The second group consists of all the editor functions for writing the code, (for example "InsertString", "SelectText", "ColumnNext"). Hence, comparing the models, a different behavior between the two students can be observed.

The leader not only performs more frequently functional activities during a development session (the frequency for the leader is almost double with respect to the follower) but he also makes more frequently commit commands, 35.29% versus 21.43% of traces in the log. Moreover, often (71.4% of the cases) for the follower the activity "file open" is immediately after a "save" command without, therefore, any changes have been made. Finally, there is a significant difference between the absolute values of activities executed by the two students and the number of commits executed. Follower student executed 4104 activities belonging to 42 different types, while leader student executed 11021 activities belonging to 50 different types.

This suggests to the teacher that student leader gives a higher contribution to the project than student follower. Moreover, comparing the leader and follower processes with the team process as described in Fig. 4 we can observe that the leader gives a larger contribution with respect to the follower involved in the project. A general overview of the involved teams highlights that more than one of them is not well-balanced (not all the students contribute similarly) and, in particular, is possible to recognize the leader student and in what consists his/her most valuable contribution.

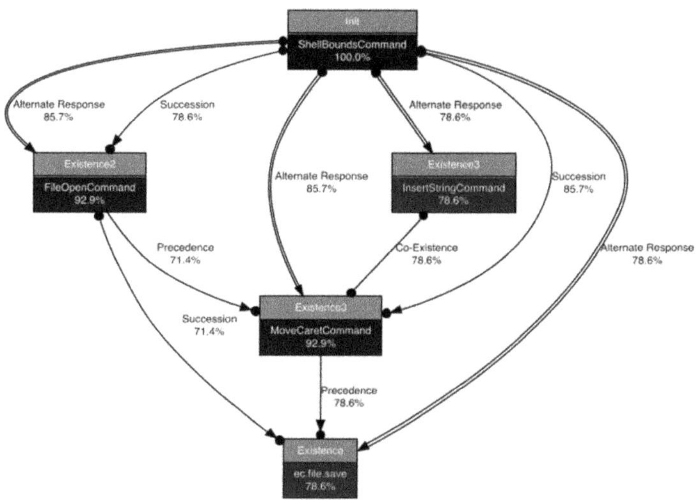

Fig. 2. Declare process model of the follower member of Gr.1. (Min. Constraint/Activity Support set to 50%)

5.2 Teacher Feedbacks

To further evaluate the team dynamics and extract some feedbacks useful to the teacher, Table 2 shows the main activities executed by all the involved groups. For each activity we reported the relative frequency of its occurrence for all development sessions belonging to a group; a development session corresponds to a single trace in the log. The groups executed, respectively from the Gr1 to Gr.5: 36795 activities, 219695 activities, 97025 activities, 24108 activities, 49932 activities.

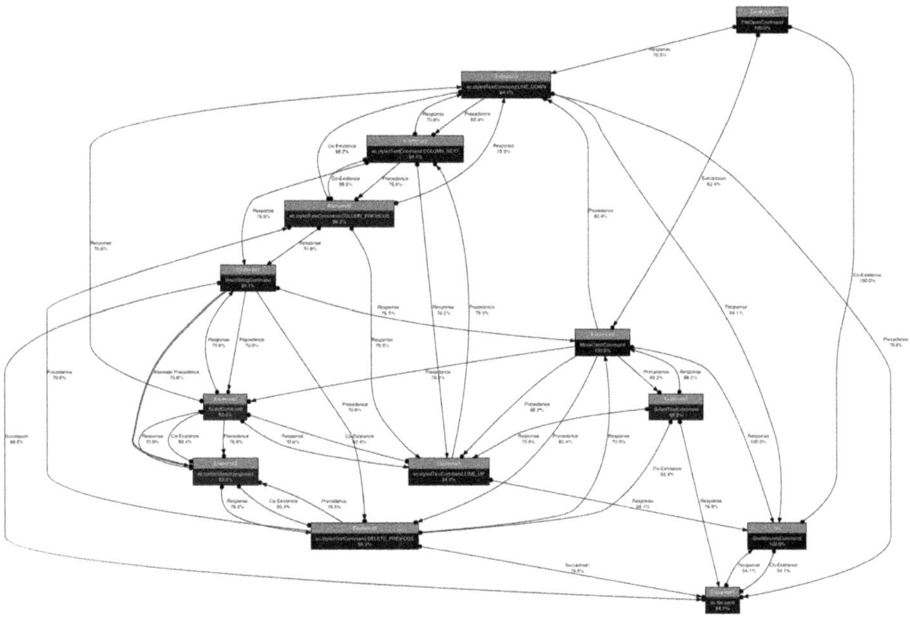

Fig. 3. Declare process model of the leader member of Gr.1 (Min. Constraint/Activity Support set to 50%)

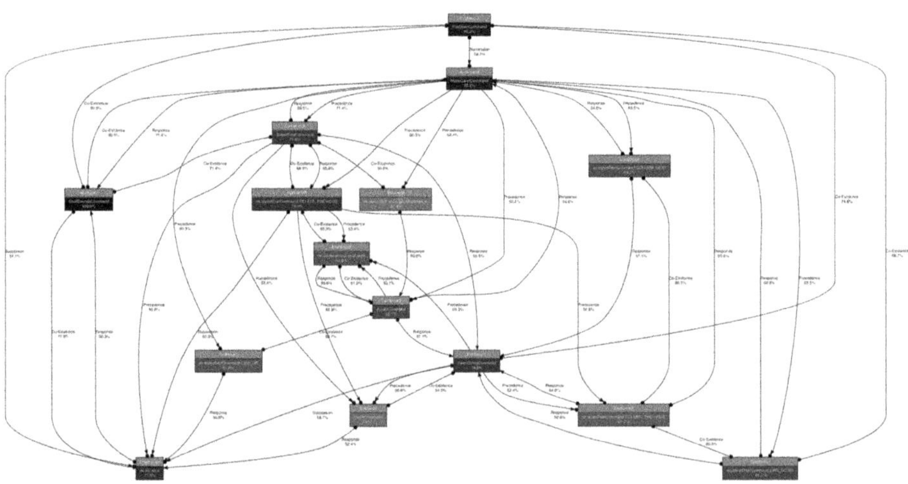

Fig. 4. Declare process model of the Gr.1 (Min. Constraint/Activity Support set to 50%)

Table 2. The distributions of the main activities.

Activity	Description	Gr.1	Gr.2	Gr.3	Gr.4	Gr.5
Getter/Setter	When the user automatically generates setters and getters	0,04%	~0%	0.02%	0%	~0%
File open	Occurs whenever a file is brought into focus. Ex: Opening files, switching tabs, closing other tabs, etc.	4.49%	7.81%	6.56%	7.89%	2.34%
Move caret	When the user moves the editor caret	10.21%	19.44%	18.55%	27.99%	19.92%
Assist command	Assistance when editing files, the AutoComplete in Eclipse	12.35%	9.91%	11.51%	2.92%	5.59%
Save	Saving a specific file	2.90%	4.57%	4.81%	1.36%	1.18%
Select text	When a user selects/highlights text	2.65%	6.46%	5.68%	7.23%	11.83%
Delete previous	When a user using the keyboard deletes the previous character	9.37%	10.18%	8.18%	12.95%	8,23%
Insert string	Inserting data	32.87%	28.17%	27.73%	27.16%	35.66%
Copy	Copying data	0.35%	0.87%	0.58%	2.11%	2.60%
Paste	Pasting data	0.61%	1.55%	1.12%	2.80%	5.07%
Run	Run the program	1,07%	3.19%	4.21%	1.31%	0.96%
Debug	Run the program in debugging mode	0%	0%	0%	0%	0%
Push commit	When the user commits the changes made to the remote repository	0.31%	0.09%	0.16%	0.24%	0.1%
Repo commit	When the user commits the changes made to the local repository	0.05%	0%	0.01%	~0%	0%
Pull	When the user fetch and download content from the remote repository	1,58%	0,07%	0.14%	0.12%	0.01%

Observing the table, a series of considerations useful in understanding the essence of students' team behavior can be made:

- Generally, we notice a poor use of IDE facilities (i.e., getter/setter generation). This can indicate that students have a poor knowledge of IDE functionalities supporting code generation.
- Search activities are absent: no group made search activities on the source code. A possible explanation is that the program to be developed was very small and maybe it was quicker navigating files than using the search functionality.
- We noticed a low frequency of commits and pulls: this can indicate that students have little mastery with collaborative development. As a consequence, they are more prone to perform few commits with bigger changes by introducing more errors.
- There is an absence of debugging activities that suggest (as also highlighted in some related work [27]) to the teacher to highlight the importance of determining the correctness of the program at least in all the main scenarios requested by the customer.

6 Conclusions and Future Work

This paper describes a process mining approach for the analysis of software student team activities. The aim is to analyze and compare single student contributions in the teamwork starting from data extracted by the IDEs and VCS.

The described case study shows that the proposed approach is useful to support teachers to evaluate team dynamics and students' contribution in the team working. It also allows extracting some feedbacks useful to improve the course. In the future, process mining techniques can be applied to perform a quantitative analysis of the team working dynamics. Conformance checking can also be used to identify deviations of students' activities from the team models. Moreover, it could be useful to provide data results by systems able to communicate in a human-understandable way as, for example, the tool developed in [28] used to predict students' outcomes, in both graphical and textual explanations.

References

1. Charette, R.N.: Why software fails [software failure]. IEEE Spectr. **42**(9), 42–49 (2005)
2. Mahmood, A., Choudhary, M.A., Qurashi, A.H.: Redesigning the way teams work smarter using comprehensive assessment of team member effectiveness (CATME). In: 2016 Portland International Conference on Management of Engineering and Technology (PICMET), pp. 1713–1718 (2016)
3. Smarkusky, D., Dempsey, R., Ludka, J., de Quillettes, F.: Enhancing team knowledge: instruction vs. experience. SIGCSE Bull. **37**(1), 460–464 (2005)
4. Kilamo, T., Hammouda, I., Chatti, M.A.: Teaching collaborative software development: a case study. In: 2012 34th International Conference on Software Engineering (ICSE), pp. 1165–1174 (2012)
5. Dietsch, D., Podelski, A., Nam, J., Papadopoulos, P.M., Schäf, M.: Monitoring student activity in collaborative software development. CoRR, abs/1305.0787 (2013)
6. Ji, H., Park, K., Jo, J., Lim, H.S.: Mining students activities from a computer supported collaborative learning system based on peer to peer network. Peer-to-Peer Netw. Appl. **9**(3), 465–476 (2016)
7. Hundhausen, C.D., Olivares, D.M., Carter, A.S.: IDE-based learning analytics for computing education: a process model, critical review, and research agenda. ACM Trans. Comput. Educ. **17**(3), 1–26 (2017)
8. Ardimento, P., Bernardi, M.L., Cimitile, M., Maggi, F.M.: Evaluating coding behavior in software development processes: a process mining approach. In: Sutton Jr., S.M., Armbrust, O., Hebig, R. (eds.) Proceedings of the International Conference on Software and System Processes, ICSSP 2019, Montreal, QC, Canada, 25–26 May 2019, pp. 84–93. IEEE/ACM (2019)
9. Maggi, F.M.: Declarative Process Mining, pp. 625–632. Springer, Cham (2019). https://doi.org/10.1007/978-3-319-77525-8_92
10. Ardimento, P., Bernardi, M.L., Cimitile, M., De Ruvo, G.: Mining developer's behavior from web-based IDE logs. In: Reddy, S. (ed.) 28th IEEE International Conference on Enabling Technologies: Infrastructure for Collaborative Enterprises, WETICE 2019, Naples, Italy, 12–14 June 2019, pp. 277–282. IEEE (2019)
11. Ardimento, P., Bernardi, M.L., Cimitile, M., De Ruvo, G.: Learning analytics to improve coding abilities: a fuzzy-based process mining approach. In: 2019 IEEE International Conference on Fuzzy Systems (FUZZ-IEEE), pp. 1–7 (2019)
12. Gu, Z.: Capturing and exploiting fine-grained ide interactions. In: 2012 34th International Conference on Software Engineering (ICSE), pp. 1630–1631 (2012)
13. de Moura, M.H.D., do Nascimento, H.A.D., Rosa, T.C.: Extracting new metrics from version control system for the comparison of software developers. In: 2014 Brazilian Symposium on Software Engineering, pp. 41–50 (2014)

14. Huang, S.-K., Liu, K.: Mining version histories to verify the learning process of legitimate peripheral participants. SIGSOFT Softw. Eng. Notes **30**(4), 1–5 (2005)
15. Glassey, R.: Adopting Git/Github within teaching: a survey of tool support. In: Proceedings of the ACM Conference on Global Computing Education, CompEd 2019, pp. 143–149. Association for Computing Machinery, New York (2019)
16. Feliciano, J., Storey, M.-A., Zagalsky, A.: Student experiences using Github in software engineering courses: a case study. In: 2016 IEEE/ACM 38th International Conference on Software Engineering Companion (ICSE-C), pp. 422–431 (2016)
17. Kalliamvakou, E., Gousios, G., Blincoe, K., Singer, L., German, D.M., Damian, D.: An in-depth study of the promises and perils of mining GitHub. Empir. Softw. Eng. **21**(5), 2035–2071 (2016)
18. Ju, A., Fox, A.: TEAMSCOPE: measuring software engineering processes with teamwork telemetry. In: Proceedings of the 23rd Annual ACM Conference on Innovation and Technology in Computer Science Education, ITiCSE 2018, pp. 123–128. Association for Computing Machinery, New York (2018)
19. van der Aalst, W.M.P.: Process Mining: Discovery, Conformance and Enhancement of Business Processes, 1st edn. Springer, Heidelberg (2011). https://doi.org/10.1007/978-3-642-19345-3
20. Tamburis, O.: Bridging the gap between process mining and des modeling in the healthcare domain. In: 2019 E-Health and Bioengineering Conference (EHB), pp. 1–4 (2019)
21. Bernardi, M.L., Cimitile, M., Di Lucca, G., Maggi, F.M.: Using declarative workflow languages to develop process-centric web applications. In: 2012 IEEE 16th International Enterprise Distributed Object Computing Conference Workshops, pp. 56–65 (2012)
22. Burattin, A., Cimitile, M., Maggi, F.M.: Lights, camera, action! business process movies for online process discovery. In: Fournier, F., Mendling, J. (eds.) BPM 2014. LNBIP, vol. 202, pp. 408–419. Springer, Cham (2015). https://doi.org/10.1007/978-3-319-15895-2_34
23. Haisjackl, C., et al.: Understanding declare models: strategies, pitfalls, empirical results. Softw. Syst. Model. **15**(2), 325–352 (2016)
24. Rubin, V., Günther, C.W., van der Aalst, W.M.P., Kindler, E., van Dongen, B.F., Schäfer, W.: Process mining framework for software processes. In: Wang, Q., Pfahl, D., Raffo, D.M. (eds.) ICSP 2007. LNCS, vol. 4470, pp. 169–181. Springer, Heidelberg (2007). https://doi.org/10.1007/978-3-540-72426-1_15
25. Bernardi, M.L., Cimitile, M., Martinelli, F., Mercaldo, F.: A fuzzy-based process mining approach for dynamic malware detection. In: 2017 IEEE International Conference on Fuzzy Systems, FUZZ-IEEE 2017, Naples, Italy, 9–12 July 2017, pp. 1–8. IEEE (2017)
26. Mittal, M., Sureka, A.: Process mining software repositories from student projects in an undergraduate software engineering course. In: Companion Proceedings of the 36th International Conference on Software Engineering, ICSE Companion 2014, pp. 344–353. Association for Computing Machinery, New York (2014)
27. Ardimento, P., Bernardi, M.L., Cimitile, M., De Ruvo, G.: Reusing bugged source code to support novice programmers in debugging tasks. ACM Trans. Comput. Educ. **20**(1), 1–24 (2019)
28. Alonso, J.M., Casalino, G.: Explainable artificial intelligence for human-centric data analysis in virtual learning environments. In: Burgos, D., et al. (eds.) HELMeTO 2019. CCIS, vol. 1091, pp. 125–138. Springer, Cham (2019). https://doi.org/10.1007/978-3-030-31284-8_10

Intelligent Knowledge Understanding from Students Questionnaires: A Case Study

Gabriella Casalino[1](✉), Luca Grilli[2], Alfonso Guarino[2], Daniele Schicchi[3](✉), and Davide Taibi[3]

[1] Department of Computer Science, University of Bari, Bari, Italy
gabriella.casalino@uniba.it

[2] Department of Economics, Management and Territory, University of Foggia, Foggia, Italy
{luca.grilli,alfonso.guarino}@unifg.it

[3] Institute for Educational Technology, National Research Council of Italy, Palermo, Italy
{daniele.schicchi,davide.taibi}@itd.cnr.it

Abstract. Learning Analytics techniques are widely used to improve students' performance. Data collected from students' assessments are helpful to predict their success and questionnaires are extensively adopted to assess students' knowledge. Several mathematical models studying the correlation between students' *hidden skills* and their performance to questionnaires' items have been introduced. Among them, Non-negative matrix factorizations (NMFs) have been proven to be effective in automatically extracting hidden skills, a time-consuming activity that is usually tackled manually prone to subjective interpretations. In this paper, we present an intelligent data analysis approach based upon NMF. Data are collected from a competition, namely *MathsChallenge*, performed by the University of Foggia. In 2021 the competition has been held, for the first time, online due to the Covid-19 pandemic.

Keywords: Non-negative matrix factorization · Latent skills · Questionnaires · Learning analytics

1 Introduction

Learning Analytics is an evolving field that is attracting growing attention. Indeed, it consists of the *"measurement, collection, analysis and reporting of data about learners and their contexts, for purposes of understanding and optimizing learning and the environments in which it occurs"* [1]. This model involves four dimensions: the data (*What*), the data analysis methods (*How*), the goal (*Why*), and the stakeholders involved (*Who*) [2].

Several applications – exploring different areas of Artificial Intelligence – have been proposed in the literature. To mention a few, we find proposals to assess the students' engagement and behavior [3], students' behavior during a

G. Casalino et al. (Eds.): HELMeTO 2021, CCIS 1542, pp. 74–86, 2022.
https://doi.org/10.1007/978-3-030-96060-5_6

test/exam [4], or to estimate their performance through virtual learning environments [5,6]. There are also applications based on the Internet of Things (IoT) [7–9], augmented reality [10], or that revolve around information visualization approaches [11]. Other authors provided explainable tools for educational data analysis in virtual environments [12].

Learning Analytics uses different categories of online assessment approaches to monitor students' signs of progress. Among these, questionnaires are a valuable aid to assess students' performance [13]. In this perspective, it is essential to investigate the relationship between questionnaire answers and students' skills.

Different mathematical methods study the relationships between the answers to questionnaires and hidden latent concepts leading to those results.

In the educational domain, the aim of such methods, e.g., Item Response Theory [14], is to provide a mathematical model to predict and evaluate students' *abilities* that are measured through a questionnaire. The main idea behind this theory is that *latent abilities* underlie both the students' performances and the test items. The term "ability" embeds different cognitive students' skills, that are strictly related to the topic under evaluation (e.g., solving a mathematical problem requires different skills compared to text understanding).

Thus, students' performance on a test item can be predicted or explained by a set of latent skills, and a mathematical model can be used to represent the relationships between students' performances on questionnaire items and latent skills underlying items, that is the skills that are required to successfully perform the task related to the item. Of course, the more the student possesses a given skill, the highest is the probability of a correct response to an item that requires such a skill [15].

Understanding students' skills, or the lack of such, can be used as feedback for supporting students in the identification of their learning needs, to measure teaching effectiveness, and discover difficult topics [16]. However, latent skills are difficult to be manually extracted since they are topic-specific, thus requiring a domain expert analysis.

Non-negative matrix factorizations (NMFs) are dimensionality reduction techniques that can describe original data as an additive linear combination of hidden factors [17]. In the educational domain, they have been proven to be effective for extracting hidden skills from questionnaires' items responses, and for profiling students in terms of these skills [18]. NMFs are highly interpretable since hidden skills are described in the same feature space as the original data, thus enabling an intelligent analysis of the results from domain experts. However, differently from other techniques that model the learning behavior of a single student during the time [19], NMF gives a static representation of all the students involved in the evaluation, without taking into account the time factor.

Our Proposal. In this work, students' answers to the *MathsChallenge* competition, which has been carried out in 2021 at the University of Foggia, have been analyzed through NMF. Moreover, results have been explained in terms of *a-priori* knowledge on item's topics, and mathematical assessment measures. Thus, referring to the four dimensions of Learning Analytics, in this work the *What* are questionnaire's answers, the *How* is the NMF, the *Why* is for exploratory data analysis, and finally *Who* are both students and teachers involved in the evaluations, other than different subjects involved in the learning environment, such as tutors, managers, etc. which can also benefit from the outcomes of the analysis. This work aims at showing how NMF can be effectively used to intelligently analyze students' questionnaires by combining the hidden skills emerging from the computation with the *a-priori* information related to the items.

Paper's Organization. This article is structured as follows: the problem and the data will be detailed in Sect. 2. Then the use of NMF algorithms in the educational domain will be briefly described in Sect. 3. Results will be discussed in Sect. 4. Lastly, conclusions and future works will be detailed in Sect. 5.

2 Materials

The *MathsChallenge* is one of the university guidance activities that the Department of Economics, Management, and Territory at the University of Foggia carries out, every year, for supporting high school students in choosing the most suitable University course. Once per year, a relevant number of senior high school students (in the geographic area around Foggia, Southern Italy) compete on mathematical problems. The contest is split into two phases. The first phase takes place at each high school to select the best students allowed to participate in the second phase, named "the final". Next, in the Final phase, the competition winner is selected together with the best student in each high school. The primary aim of such competition is to provide a bridge between high school and University. It represents an important step in the direction of finding and selecting motivated incoming students. The competition consists of several questions in the main areas of mathematics, such as logic, algebra, geometry, calculus, problem-solving. Due to the Covid-19 pandemic, the 2021 edition was moved to an online form. Thus, Google Forms were used to simultaneously deliver the same questionnaire to a total of 434 students (208 males and 226 females) from seventeen different schools. Students competed on mathematical topics, and particularly the questionnaire was composed of twenty multiple-choice questions with one correct answer (allowed time: 45 min). Items belong to different areas of Maths (Linear Algebra, Geometry, Equations, Logic, etc.) reported in Fig. 1a and, to assess the mathematical literacy, each item has been classified according to three main mathematical assessment measures referring to PISA[1], INVALSI[2], and TIMSS[3] whose taxonomies are depicted in Fig. 1b.

[1] PISA 2021 Mathematics Framework Draft available on the web page https://pisa2021-maths.oecd.org/.

[2] INVALSI Istituto nazionale per la valutazione del sistema educativo di istruzione e di formazione (National Institute for the assessment of the educational and training system) more details in the web page (in Italian) https://www.invalsi.it/invalsi/index.php.

[3] TIMSS monitors trends in mathematics and science achievement. For more details, we refer the reader to Mullis, I. V. S., Martin, M. O. (Eds.). (2017). TIMSS 2019 Assessment Frameworks. Retrieved from Boston College, TIMSS & PIRLS International Study Center website: http://timssandpirls.bc.edu/timss2019/frameworks/.

Acronym	Domain
L	Logic
F	Physic
RF	Relations and math functions
E	Calculus – Equations
PR	Probability
N	Numbers
A	Algebra
P	Percentage
Log	Logarithms
D	Calculus
I	Sets
Esp	Exponential
LN	Numerical logic (matrices, series of numbers, etc.)
C	Computation
LP	Propositional logic
G	Geometry
LPS	Problems
GA	Analytic geometry

(a) Math domains/subjects and their acronyms used to classify questions.

Assessment measure	Acronym
INVALSI	
Cognitive domains	
Knowing	DC
Problem Solving	DA
Arguing	DR
PISA 2015	
Process	
Formulating	PF
Interpreting	PU
Employing	PI
TIMSS 2015	
Dimensions	
Knowing	DIC
Applying	DIR
Reasoning	DIA

(b) Taxonomies of mathematical assessment measures with the acronyms adopted for classifying questions.

Fig. 1. Classification schemes used in this paper.

According to the PISA methodology, the mathematical reasoning is evaluated considering three main processes: *(i)* formulating (select a mathematical description or a representation describing a problem; identify the key variables in a model, and so on), *(ii)* interpreting (interpret a mathematical result back into the real-world context; identify the limits of the model used to solve a problem, etc.), and *(iii)* employing (perform a simple calculation; select an appropriate strategy from a list, and so on).

The INVALSI methodology focuses the mathematical reasoning on three main dimensions: *(i)* Knowing (student has the skills required to solve the item); *(ii)* Problem Solving (student can connect the skills to solve a complex problem); *(iii)* Arguing (student produces and supports arguments based on the theoretical knowledge acquired). Similarly, the TIMSS cognitive domains are *Knowing*, *Applying*, and *Reasoning*.

According to the previous assessment methodologies, the classification of items allows us to identify the mathematical reasoning process and the domain associated with each item. We can then better understand the strengths and weaknesses in mathematical literacy arising from the questionnaires, and consider how such a result can be related to the online teaching activity that has characterized the last year due to COVID-19.

Table 1 provides for each question the related subject and the values for each of the three categories mentioned before.

Table 1. Subjects and activities assigned to each question.

Question #	Subject	Cognitive domain	Process	Dimension
D1	N	DC	PU	DIC
D2	Log	DC	PU	DIC
D3	N	DC	PU	DIC
D4	N	DC	PU	DIC
D5	LN	DR	PI	DIR
D6	LP	DC	PU	DIC
D7	GA	DC	PU	DIC
D8	N	DR	PI	DIR
D9	D	DC	PU	DIC
D10	D	DC	PU	DIC
D11	LP	DC	PU	DIC
D12	Esp	DC	PU	DIC
D13	LN	DR	PI	DIR
D14	I	DR	PI	DIR
D15	G	DC	PU	DIC
D16	A	DR	PI	DIR
D17	Log	DR	PI	DIR
D18	LP	DC	PU	DIC
D19	LP	DC	PU	DIC
D20	LP	DC	PU	DIC

3 Method

The NMF machine learning technique has been used to automatically extract the hidden skills that are needed for correctly answering items in the questionnaire. NMF is a dimensionality reduction method that approximates the non-negative data matrix $X \in \mathbb{R}_+^{n \times m}$ with the product of two low-rank non-negative factor matrices $W \in \mathbb{R}_+^{n \times k}$ and $H \in \mathbb{R}_+^{k \times m}$. The factorization rank k defines the number of hidden factors to extract, and it is an input parameter. In the educational domain, a set of m students is described by n-dimensional vectors X_i, such that $X = \{X_1, X_2, \cdots, X_m\}$. Items in the questionnaire are the n items, and each element x_{ij} represents the score obtained by the j-th student at the i-th item. Given the item-student matrix X and the number of hidden skills (k), whose provide semantics for a new vector sub-space, NMF allows a part-based representation of the original data. Each student X_j is described as an additive linear combination of the columns in W, weighted by the coefficients in H_j:

$$X_j \approx W_1 h_{1j} + W_2 h_{2j} + \ldots + W_k h_{kj}. \tag{1}$$

The bases matrix W maps the items with their underlying skills. The columns of the encoding matrix H describe the students through their hidden skills. Therefore, students are represented in a reduced space that simplifies the data while highlighting relationships in them.

Visualization techniques together with the a-priori knowledge given by domain experts (e.g., question subjects/domains and mathematical assessment measures) have been used to intelligently analyze the questionnaire items.

4 Results

The experiments aim to analyze questionnaire data from *MathsChallenge* to identify the hidden factors that students used for answering. Moreover, a priori information regarding the subjects in the questions and the abilities required by each question, according to the three previously described classifications (PISA, INVALSI, and TIMSS), has been used to better describe the knowledge in the hidden factors. Visualization techniques have been used to enhance the understandability of the results. Finally, a proof of concept on the use of NMF for Learning Analytics in the MathsChallenge scenario is discussed.

A sparse variant of the NMF algorithm has been used [20]. Particularly, sparsity constraint has been applied to the bases matrix W to force the hidden factors to contain few non-zero elements, thus enhancing their clarity. Moreover, an SVD based initialization algorithm (Nonnegative Double Singular Value Decomposition – NNDSVD) [21] has been used. This kind of initialization has proven to facilitate the convergence of NMF, thus enhancing the robustness of the results. Finally, the *elbow* method has been used to derive the optimal number of hidden factors. Four has been the suggested value. Thus, students and question items will be described in terms of four hidden skills, which will be automatically extracted from the available data. From now on we will refer to them as $HF1$, $HF2$, $HF3$, $HF4$.

Graphical representations have been used for supporting data analysis by giving immediate insights to discover patterns. Particularly stacked bar plots represent questions and students in terms of proportion of hidden skills in both the bases and encoding matrices W and H. A color schema maps the hidden skills; in particular, we use blue for $HF1$, orange for $HF2$, green for $HF3$, and red for $HF4$.

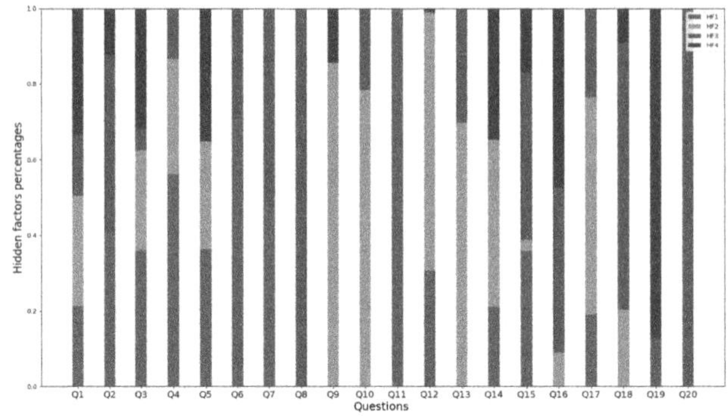

Fig. 2. A representation of the bases matrix W relying on the hidden skills. $HF1$ (blue), $HF2$ (orange), $HF3$ (green), $HF4$ (red). (Color figure online)

Figure 2 illustrates the percentage of required skills for each of the 20 questions. Particularly we can observe that $Q8$ and $Q20$ need only the third hidden factor $HF3$. Similarly, $Q9$, $Q10$, $Q12$, and $Q13$ mostly require $HF2$. Analog analyses can be conducted on the other questions to better understand the skills students used to answer them. These results could be useful to the teachers to assess the effectiveness of the questions. Indeed, they can verify whether the skills that were supposed to be used to answer the questions correctly have been used. Therefore, they could eventually use this feedback to better design the questions.

Since the number of students is too high to visualize all of them, we focused on the first 50 students, ranked by total score (Fig. 3a), and the last 50 (Fig. 3b). As previously discussed, each subject is described in terms of the possessed skills – used to answer the twenty questions in the questionnaire. Some regularities among the best students can be observed, having comparable percentages of the four hidden skills. Different patterns have been identified while moving the analysis through the students' ranks. High differences can be observed from one student to another, and the fourth hidden skill, $HS4$ is mostly represented in those students who obtained low total scores.

Such patterns could be used to identify groups of students with similarities and, building upon such information, to organize support lessons on specific topics that emerged from data analysis.

Furthermore, differently from other dimensionality reduction techniques that cannot explain the extracted hidden factors, as previously discussed, bases vectors in W are in the same feature space as the original data, and thus, they are easily interpretable. The analysis of NMF outcomes leaves room for describing each skill based on the main topics addressed in the challenge. The *a priori* knowledge on the questions given by domain experts has been combined with the NMF part-based representation of the results to obtain further insights.

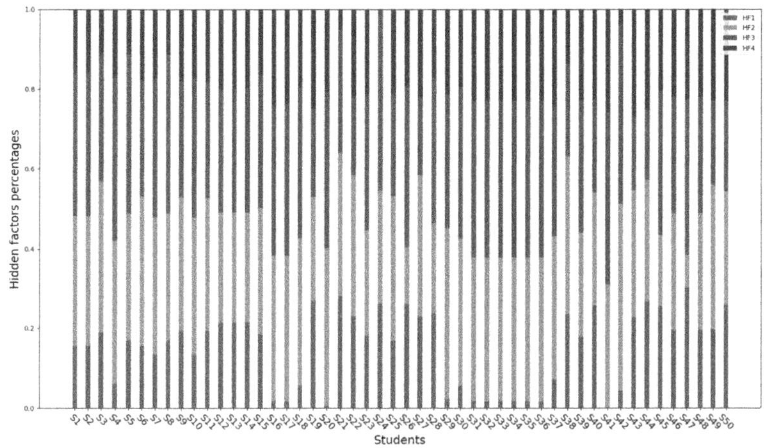

(a)

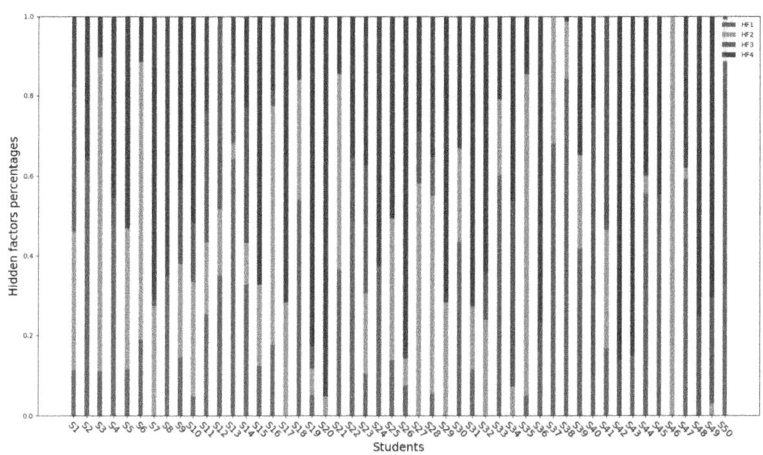

(b)

Fig. 3. An excerpt of encoding matrix H visualized in terms of hidden skills. The first fifty (a) and last fifty (b) students, ranked by total score. $HF1$ (blue), $HF2$ (orange), $HF3$ (green), $HF4$ (red). (Color figure online)

To this aim, we have used the values in the columns W_i to weigh both the subjects and the abilities related to each question (see Table 1). Then the percentages of subjects and abilities required by each hidden skill (columns of W) have been visualized through pie charts to simplify their comprehension. Figures 4 and 5 show, for the four hidden factors, the percentages of subjects and abilities used

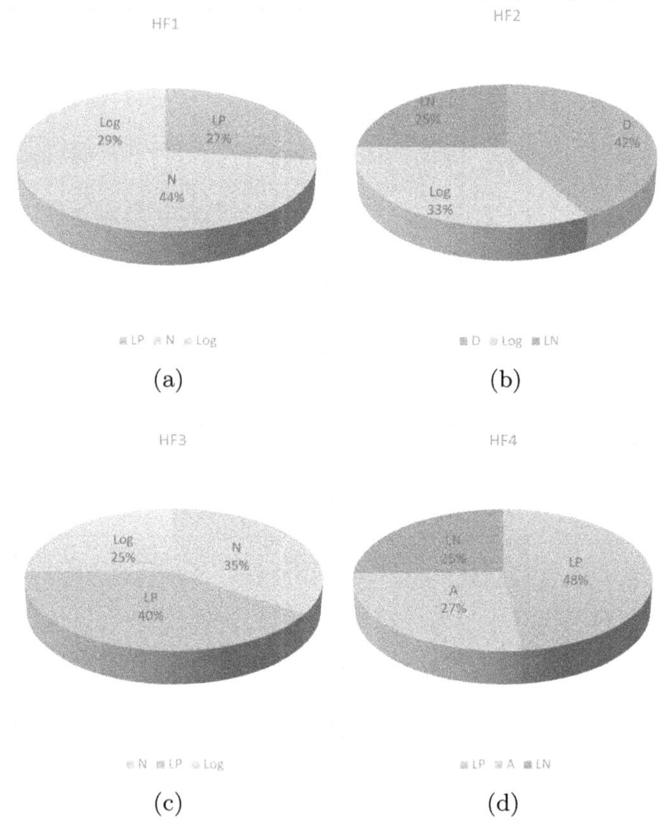

Fig. 4. Three top most important subjects in the description of the hidden factors $HF1$ (a), $HF2$ (b), $HF3$ (c), $HF4$ (d).

to describe them, respectively. In this way, we can *explain* the meaning of each factor in terms of the teacher's knowledge.

In Fig. 4, we can observe that the hidden factors are described by different subjects (hence, different colors). The exception is for the first and third hidden factors, $HF1$ and $HF3$, that are described by the same subject with different percentages. As an example, Fig. 4d describes the fourth hidden factor, $HF4$, by leveraging on a set of most representative topics that need such a skill to be answered correctly. For example, we noted that the fourth hidden skill ($HF4$) concerns *Propositional Logic* (48%), *Calculus* (27%), and *Numerical Logic* (23%), so it seems to be mostly required in these three topics. Indeed, looking at question $Q19$, Fig. 2 shows that it is mostly represented by $HF4$ (red bar). It solves a *Propositional logic* problem, as shown in Fig. 6.

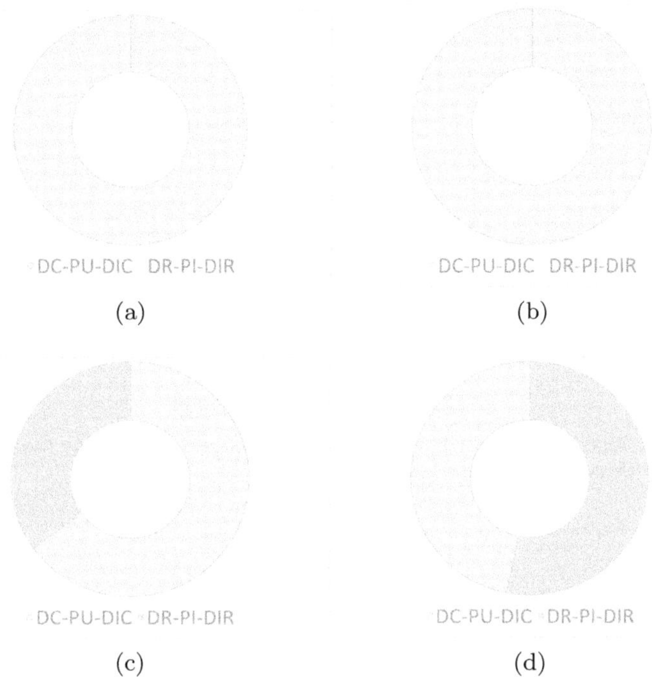

Fig. 5. The image describes how much each factor $HF1$ (a), $HF2$ (b), $HF3$ (c), $HF4$ (d) is involved in the questions concerning both the comprehension topics DC-PU-DIC (yellow), and problem-solving activities DR-PI-DIR (green). (Color figure online)

Similar analyses can be conducted for the other hidden factors.

Moreover, by referring to PISA, INVALSI, and TIMSS classification, we are able to infer the abilities that are required to correctly answer the questions requiring a specific skill. Also, in this case, we can observe that the four hidden skills require different abilities (Fig. 5). Yellow color refers to topic comprehension (identified by the classification values DC-PU-DIC in Table 1b), whilst green color refers to problem-solving activities (DR-PI-DIR). With regards to the example previously discussed, we notice that $Q19$ mostly requires problem-solving abilities, together with topic comprehension. Indeed, the questions matching with $HF4$ mostly require such skills. Furthermore, it is worth noting that although $HF1$ and $HF3$ are described by the same subjects (with different percentages), they differ based on the abilities they require: only topic comprehension for $HF1$, and both topic comprehension and problem-solving for $HF3$.

To conclude, this analysis is useful to investigate the hidden skills required to correctly answer some given questions. These can be used to systematically evaluate students and teaching materials during the time.

E' sicuramente falso che non è vero che è stato dimostrato che è falso che la gara MathsChallenge piace a tutti. 5 punti

Contrassegna solo un ovale.

- La gara MathsChallenge piace a tutti
- Esiste almeno una persona a cui non piace la gara MathsChallenge
- A nessuno piace la gara MathsChallenge
- E' falso che la gara Maths Challenge non piace a tutti
- nessuna delle precedenti risposte è vera.

(a) Original version in Italian.

It is surely false that it is true that it has been proved to be false that everyone likes MathsChallenge 5 points

Check one only oval.

- Everyone likes MathsChallenge
- There exist at least one person that does not like MathsChallenge
- No one likes MathsChallenge
- It is false that not everyone likes MathsChallenge
- None of the above answers

(b) English version.

Fig. 6. Item $Q19$ in the questionnaire.

5 Conclusions

In this work, students' answers to an online questionnaire on mathematical problems have been intelligently analyzed via NMF technique. In particular, our testbed has been the so-called *MathsChallenge* – a yearly contest organized by the University of Foggia to stimulate and select the best students in the choice of the University – that, due to the COVID-19 pandemic, for 2021 edition has been conducted online. The answers to questionnaires of almost 400 students coming from 17 schools have been analyzed. The application of NMF to such questionnaires led us to infer students' latent abilities to answer questions correctly. Visualization techniques have shown to be useful for making NMF results more interpretable and easy to understand. Final results highlight common skills among the best students, and they describe questions based on the main tackled topic. These results are useful feedback for both students and teachers, which can improve their knowledge and their courses, respectively. The approach proposed in this work will be extended in the future. It will be put in place to develop an easy-to-use learning analytic tool that supports teachers in analyzing and predicting the students' performances while providing intuitive visualizations for better grasping phenomena under study [22–24]. Moreover the readability complexity of questions will be taken into account to understand how it affect the students' performances [25,26]. Finally, comparisons with similar methods will be carried out.

Acknowledgment. Gabriella Casalino acknowledges funding from the Italian Ministry of Education, University and Research through the European PON project AIM (Attraction and International Mobility), nr. 1852414, activity 2, line 1. Gabriella Casalino and Daniele Schicchi are members of the INdAM GNCS research group.

References

1. Chatti, M.A., Dyckhoff, A.L., Schroeder, U., Thüs, H.: A reference model for learning analytics. Int. J. Technol. Enhanc. Learn. **4**(5–6), 318–331 (2012)
2. Romero, C., Ventura, S.: Educational data mining and learning analytics: an updated survey. Wiley Interdisc. Rev.: Data Min. Knowl. Discov. **10**(3), e1355 (2020)
3. De Carolis, B., D'Errico, F., Macchiarulo, N., Palestra, G.: Engaged faces: measuring and monitoring student engagement from face and gaze behavior. In: IEEE/WIC/ACM International Conference on Web Intelligence-Companion Volume, pp. 80–85 (2019)
4. Ardimento, P., Bernardi, M.L., Cimitile, M., De Ruvo, G.: Mining developer's behavior from web-based IDE logs. In 2019 IEEE 28th International Conference on Enabling Technologies: Infrastructure for Collaborative Enterprises (WETICE), pp. 277–282. IEEE (2019)
5. Nakayama, M., Sciarrone, F., Uto, M., Temperini, M.: Estimating student's performance based on item response theory in a MOOC environment with peer assessment. In: Kubincová, Z., Lancia, L., Popescu, E., Nakayama, M., Scarano, V., Gil, A.B. (eds.) MIS4TEL 2020. AISC, vol. 1236, pp. 25–35. Springer, Cham (2021). https://doi.org/10.1007/978-3-030-52287-2_3
6. Castellano, G., Fanelli, A.M., Roselli, T.: Mining categories of learners by a competitive neural network. In: Proceedings of the International Joint Conference on Neural Networks, IJCNN 2001, vol. 2, pp. 945–950. IEEE (2001)
7. Picerno, P., Pecori, R., Raviolo, P., Ducange, P.: Smartphones and exergame controllers as BYOD solutions for the e-tivities of an online sport and exercise sciences university program. In: Burgos, D., et al. (eds.) HELMeTO 2019. CCIS, vol. 1091, pp. 217–227. Springer, Cham (2019). https://doi.org/10.1007/978-3-030-31284-8_17
8. Tripathi, G., Ahad, M.A.: IoT in education: an integration of educator community to promote holistic teaching and learning. In: Nayak, J., Abraham, A., Krishna, B.M., Chandra Sekhar, G.T., Das, A.K. (eds.) Soft Computing in Data Analytics. AISC, vol. 758, pp. 675–683. Springer, Singapore (2019). https://doi.org/10.1007/978-981-13-0514-6_64
9. Ahad, M.A., Tripathi, G., Agarwal, P.: Learning analytics for IoE based educational model using deep learning techniques: architecture, challenges and applications. Smart Learn. Environ. **5**(1), 1–16 (2018)

10. Farella, M., Arrigo, M., Chiazzese, G., Tosto, C., Seta, L., Taibi, D.: Integrating xAPI in AR applications for positive behaviour intervention and support. In: 2021 International Conference on Advanced Learning Technologies (ICALT), pp. 406–408. IEEE (2021)
11. Malandrino, D., Guarino, A., Lettieri, N., Zaccagnino, R.: On the visualization of logic: a diagrammatic language based on spatial, graphical and symbolic notations. In: 2019 23rd International Conference Information Visualisation (IV), pp. 7–12. IEEE (2019)
12. Alonso, J.M., Casalino, G.: Explainable artificial intelligence for human-centric data analysis in virtual learning environments. In: Burgos, D., et al. (eds.) HELMeTO 2019. CCIS, vol. 1091, pp. 125–138. Springer, Cham (2019). https://doi.org/10.1007/978-3-030-31284-8_10
13. Gabriella, C., et al.: Framing automatic grading techniques for open-ended questionnaires responses. a short survey. In: Second Workshop on Technology Enhanced Learning Environments for Blended Education-The Italian e-Learning Conference. CEUR-WS (2021)
14. Lord, F.: A theory of test scores. Psychometric monographs (1952)
15. Hambleton, R.K., Shavelson, R.J., Webb, N.M., Swaminathan, H., Rogers, H.J.: Fundamentals of Item Response Theory, vol. 2. Sage (1991)
16. Barnes, T.: The q-matrix method: mining student response data for knowledge. In: American Association for Artificial Intelligence 2005 Educational Data Mining Workshop, pp. 1–8. AAAI Press, Pittsburgh (2005)
17. Gillis, N.: Nonnegative Matrix Factorization. SIAM (2020)
18. Casalino, G., Castiello, C., Del Buono, N., Esposito, F., Mencar, C.: Q-matrix extraction from real response data using nonnegative matrix factorizations. In: Gervasi, O., et al. (eds.) ICCSA 2017. LNCS, vol. 10404, pp. 203–216. Springer, Cham (2017). https://doi.org/10.1007/978-3-319-62392-4_15
19. Gabriella, C., Grilli, L., Limone, P., Domenico, S., Daniele, S.: Deep learning for knowledge tracing in learning analytics: an overview. In: First Workshop on Technology Enhanced Learning Environments for Blended Education-The Italian e-Learning Conference 2021, vol. 2817, pp. 1–10. CEUR-WS (2021)
20. Hoyer, P.O.: Non-negative sparse coding. In: Proceedings of the 12th IEEE Workshop on Neural Networks for Signal Processing, pp. 557–565. IEEE (2002)
21. Boutsidis, C., Gallopoulos, E.: SVD based initialization: a head start for nonnegative matrix factorization. Pattern Recogn. **41**(4), 1350–1362 (2008)
22. Guarino, A., Lettieri, N., Malandrino, D., Zaccagnino, R.: A machine learning-based approach to identify unlawful practices in online terms of service: analysis, implementation and evaluation. Neural Comput. Appl. **33**(24), 17569–17587 (2021). https://doi.org/10.1007/s00521-021-06343-6
23. Lettieri, N., Guarino, A., Malandrino, D., Zaccagnino, R.: The sight of justice. Visual knowledge mining, legal data and computational crime analysis. In: 2021 25th International Conference Information Visualisation (IV), pp. 267–272. IEEE Computer Society (2021)
24. Limongelli, C., Schicchi, D., Taibi, D.: Enriching didactic similarity measures of concept maps by a deep learning based approach. In: 2021 25th International Conference Information Visualisation (IV), pp. 261–266. IEEE Computer Society (2021)
25. Schicchi, D., Pilato, G., Lo Bosco, G.: Attention-based model for evaluating the complexity of sentences in English language. In: 2020 IEEE 20th Mediterranean Electrotechnical Conference (MELECON), pp. 221–225. IEEE (2020)
26. Schicchi, D., Pilato, G., Lo Bosco, G.: Deep neural attention-based model for the evaluation of Italian sentences complexity. In: 2020 IEEE 14th International Conference on Semantic Computing (ICSC), pp. 253–256. IEEE (2020)

Teaching IoT in the Classroom and Remotely

Gaetano Francesco Anastasi[1(✉)] and Paolo Musmarra[2]

[1] ITET G. Garibaldi, Marsala, TP, Italy
gaetanofrancesco.anastasi@posta.istruzione.it
[2] Computer Science Department, University of Salerno, Fisciano, Italy

Abstract. The Internet of Things (IoT) paradigm is widely seen as revolutionary in manufacturing, large-scale industries and many other aspects of our every-day life, e.g. Smart Homes and Smart Cities. In this paper we describe our learning project focused on IoT. We propose principles and contents for specifically addressing IoT in the computer science education since the beginning of technical studies, allowing students to learn computer science and engineering pillars IoT is built upon. We believe that this kind of approach could motivate students to enthusiastically embrace Information Technology and Computer Science.

We implemented our learning project at the high school level, coping with the COVID-19 pandemic period. The technologies used for remote learning in that period are also described, with an emphasis on our virtual lab approach.

Keywords: Internet of Things · Computer science education

1 Introduction

In the greatly changing world of computing, with the near-zero cost of networking and processing, the Internet of Things (IoT) is rising, a global computing architecture of trillions of connected devices that display the world we live in. IoT is bringing a new revolution in manufacturing, large-scale industries and many other aspects of our every-day life, e.g. Smart Homes and Smart Cities [1,2]. The rise and affirmation of IoT will have a strong impact on our society, requiring us to rethink and redesign what is the best way to educate the young generation of engineers and computer scientists.

Emerging jobs require different skills. Green energy, achievements in computing and improvements in transportation will likely play a key role in what Rifkin calls the "Third Industrial Revolution" [3], that will create a demand for new jobs, which will be strongly connected to the IoT. This trend requires an education that can empower a new generation of digital citizens who understand the technology that underpins IoT. All higher-education programs need to make sure that the next generation of data scientists and engineers understands how to build and develop technological systems that reflect and embrace ongoing

G. Casalino et al. (Eds.): HELMeTO 2021, CCIS 1542, pp. 87–99, 2022.
https://doi.org/10.1007/978-3-030-96060-5_7

changes from economic and social point-of-view. In the Information Technology (IT) Curricula 2017 report [4,5], IoT is considered one of the driving forces towards innovation and it is reported as the fastest growing IT skill. However, the same document reports IoT as one of the supplemental IT domains. Instead, we believe that IoT can be considered one the fundamental IT domains yet and thus it deserves to be put on the center of learning curricula.

We envision a curriculum that specifically addresses IoT as the key point for learning computer science and engineering pillars of this paradigm. Our proposal is structured in the form of different Bodies of Knowledge (BoK) that can provide both domain foundations and useful practical understandings, to foster the career of new technicians particularly interested in this field. Upon our conceptual framework we built the **IoT in the classroom** learning project, detailed in this paper and implemented in an Italian High School for technicians, the *Istituto Tecnico "Girolamo Caruso"* of Alcamo (TP), former institution of one of the authors. The project started as an extracurricular activity and then it was brought into the curricular framework, carried on even in the first coronavirus pandemic period of 2020.

The structure of this paper is detailed as follows. Section 2 describes related work focused on teaching IoT. In our work we leveraged a well-known background framework for IoT education. It is briefly described in Sect. 3 for the reader's convenience. Section 4 details the conceptual structure of our proposal in the form of different BoK. Upon our conceptual structure, we actually implemented our learning project: methodologies, contents and pandemic adjustments related to our implementation are described in Sect. 5. Section 6 conducts some analysis and relative corrections on assessment that we made based on gathered results. Section 7 concludes the paper.

2 Related Work

In this section we cite relevant academic work discussing the topic of this paper. It is worth mentioning that the term "IoT in Education" can refer both to the technological tools for improving education [6,7] and to the subject of teaching.

This work belongs to the second category and thus we focus on the literature relevant to that meaning. The work by Voas and Laplante [8] is particularly interesting in providing some appropriate recommendations for an IoT-focused computer science bachelor's degree. Their work identifies five IoT primitives [9] (sensor, aggregator, communication channel, external utility and decision trigger) that serve as indications for choosing fundamental topics. Our work is checked against their conceptual framework, briefly described in Sect. 3. However, with respect to the their work, we make the effort of detailing BoK for an IoT curriculum, establishing priorities among them and providing some experiences related to our implementation.

The work by Burd et al. [10] individuates four major approaches computer science educators are using to integrate IoT concepts and courses into their curricula. It also summarizes choices and challenges related to teaching IoT and describes some tools that allow IoT teachers to get started. Our work does not propose courses but bodies of knowledge that may be mapped in multiple courses, so we believe it is difficult to categorize our proposal by using their model. Nevertheless, in this paper we give some suggestions on tools and technologies for educational purposes: since the work by Burd et al. provides a detailed list, their work can be useful for finding alternatives to the tools and technologies proposed by us.

The work by Koo [11] defines the description and the learning outcomes of a graduate-level course on IoT. It presents the weekly schedule and includes a list of reference materials used in the course. It also presents the feedback and comments received from the students as a form of initial evaluation of on-course performances. Instead, our work, conceptually conceived in the form of BoK, has been implemented at the high school level and focuses on the learning project structure. It is out of the scope of this paper to provide detailed information on courses, such as weekly schedules or reference materials. Additional courses on IoT are cited in the work by De Franco and Kassab [12].

In the work by Tortoriello e Veronesi [13], IoT is considered a new educational resource for developing a transdisciplinary teaching model in which mathematics is the center of an articulated didactic action and acts as a link between the different disciplinary areas, promoting an innovative and fruitful dialogue between scientific and humanistic cultures. In particular, their work describes projects that deal with the issue of pollution and environmental protection by using "smart objects" conceptualized by students. Their work is focused on an interdisciplinary approach, whilst our work is primarily focused on teaching subjects related to computer science. However, we share with the authors the idea that a laboratory methodology in a learning-by-doing approach is nowadays fundamental. By analyzing their work, we believe that their approach and the one proposed in this paper can be considered orthogonal and can mutually benefit one each other when integrated in suitable learning contexts.

One of the aspect of our work about IoT education is that it has been implemented at the high school level. The work of Lensing and Friedhoff [14] also targets high school students along with graduated and undergraduated ones. However, their work focuses on IoT aspects related to the "Makers' world", thus privileges contents to foster creativity and hands-on practice. Instead, our work considers IoT laboratory just as one piece of a broad curriculum to convey IT pillars.

3 Background Framework

For building the content of our learning project we leveraged the work by Voas et al. [8,9,15], that represents a widely-accepted conceptual framework for building curricula specifically intended for the IoT.

In the background framework, the concept of Network of Things (NoT) is introduced. NoT can be defined as the underlying science for IoT and it is built upon five primitives that constitute the fundamental building blocks that govern the operation, trustworthiness, and lifecycle of IoT. In this framework, IoT can be considered as an instantiation of a NoT: more specifically, IoT has its 'things' tethered to the Internet.

The five primitives can be described as follows.

- P1 A *sensor* is any device that uses mechanical, electrical, chemical, optical, or other effects to measure physical properties such as temperature, location, presence, identity, etc.
- P2 An *aggregator* is a software that leverages mathematical functions to transform raw data from any source into an intermediate form for further processing. The software may need a dedicated device with proper computational power for consolidating large volumes of data into lesser amounts.
- P3 A *communication channel* is a medium by which data is securely and reliably transmitted in a NoT. It can be physical (e.g. via Universal Serial Bus), wireless, or wired for moving data between computing, sensing, and actuation.
- P4 An *eUtility* is a software or hardware product or service that hosts various logical IoT components. The concept may include databases, mobile devices, laptops, and clouds. Humans may be viewed as eUtilities.
- P5 A *decision trigger* creates the final results, needed to satisfy purposes, specifications and requirements. Decision triggers abstractly define the end-purpose of a NoT, usually in the shape of a conditional expression that triggers an action. A decision trigger's output can control actuators and transactions or it can feed the NoT, creating a continuous feedback loop.

All the five primitives should be covered when designing a curriculum for the IoT, because they embody the fundamental knowledge for an IoT workforce.

4 Project Structure

Our work aims to individuate some BoK that can be used for building our project. Such BoK emerged from a thorough discussion among the authors, started from the definition of the following learning objectives, presented in difficulty order (from the easiest to the harder):

1. Knowing the basic programming structures;
2. Knowing the internals of a generic smart device;
3. Knowing the fundamentals notions of the networks interconnecting different smart devices;
4. Being able to program and/or assemble simple smart devices;
5. Being able to create mobile apps for monitoring and controlling smart devices;
6. Being able to design and realize a local network composed of several smart devices;
7. Knowing the features of object-oriented programming;
8. Being able to design and develop web services for interactions of *things* among them and/or in the Cloud.

Table 1. Project structure

Body of knowledge	Abbreviation
Computational Thinking	CT
Microcontrollers	MC
Sensing/Actuation Paradigm	SAP
Operating Systems	OS
Computer Networks	CN
The Internet and the Web	IW
IoT Laboratory	ILAB
Object-oriented Programming	OOP
Web Services	WS
Cloud Computing	CC
Security	SEC

Table 2. NoT coverage

	P1 (sensor)	P2 (aggregator)	P3 (communic.)	P4 (eUtility)	P5 (dec. trigger)
CT		x			
MC		x			
SAP	x				x
OS		x		x	
CN			x		
IW			x	x	
ILAB	x	x	x	x	x
OOP				x	x
WS				x	x
CC				x	
SEC			x		

The proposed BoK can provide both domain foundations and useful practical understandings. At a glance, they are listed in Table 1 with the corresponding abbreviation. The first seven BoK (CT, MC, SAP, OS, CN, IW, ILAB) cover learning objectives from number 1 to 6. The remaining ones (OOP, WS, CC, SEC) cover learning objectives number 7 and 8. To verify the compliance of our proposal with the reference background framework described in Sect. 3, we match the proposed BoK with the five NoT primitives (sensor, aggregator, communication channel, external utility, and decision trigger), indicated as P1, P2, and so on. The result is presented in Table 2, where the first column indicates the abbreviation name for each body of knowledge and the "x" indicates that a primitive is covered. Results show that our proposal is adherent with the reference background, since each primitive is covered by at least two BoK.

We propose priorities between each BoK. The precedence graph is depicted in Fig. 1. It can help in choosing contents for courses and eventually identifying mandatory exams.

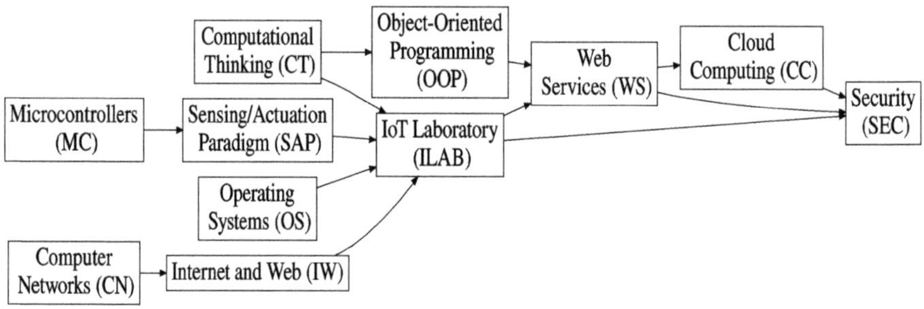

Fig. 1. Precedence graph

The proposed structure allows for maximum flexibility in building courses that can adapt to the students, by considering their background. For instance, we implemented the projects in the 11th grade by using the following BoK: CT, MC, SAP, OS, CN, IW, ILAB. Instead, in the 13th grade we built the course by using ILAB, WS, CC and SEC, since the other BoK were already covered in the students' curricula. Courses were built by considering a time frame of at least 30 h.

5 Methodologies, Contents and Pandemic Adjustments

The project methodologies focused on action research, collaboration and experimentation to create inclusive learning environments. The following teaching strategies and methodologies were used throughout the whole project.

Cooperative learning. Students work in pairs and/or small groups, in order to collaborate for completing tasks towards learning goals, that can be expressed as a project work. Such methodology stimulates collaborative strategies for structuring a positive social interdependence, paying attention to the classroom atmosphere. Students learning cooperatively can benefit one each other of different attitudes and skills, to succeed as a group.

Laboratory teaching. Practical work should occupy an important place in the education of scientists and engineers, since learning by doing reveals to be an effective method for acquiring technical skills. Laboratory teaching is an active way of learning, where students become protagonists by putting their baggage of knowledge into practice. By combining laboratory teaching with cooperative learning, students can develop metacognitive skills, by teaching themselves and each other.

Reinforcement Learning. With the use of immediate feedback and formative evaluation, it is possible to trigger the learner's self-assessment capacity and support self-esteem within the educational path. Through the feedback, the teacher provides to students a comparison of their performance with the educational objectives, helping them in achieving or exceeding their goals. The feedback must be positive, in order to reinforce appropriate behaviors through gratification. Inadequate behaviors must be minimized through the suspension of positive reinforcement because a negative feedback creates unwanted emotional responses such as anxiety and fear, which interfere with the usefulness of the feedback itself. For this reason, formative evaluation should be used during the learning process: negative marks are typical examples of a negative feedback.

Widespread and state-of-the-art technologies were used as regards technical aspects. In particular, low-cost and easy-to-use microcontrollers such as Arduino [16] and Raspberry were used because of the availability and the presence of many Open Educational Resources (OERs) on the Web, that can favor didactic innovation in schools. Following the direction of innovation, we leveraged a visual block environment, MIT App Inventor [17] as the reference programming environment for introducing students to software programming. By using visual block languages w.r.t. traditional programming languages, students can concentrate on problem solving and computational thinking aspects rather than on the side aspects of programming, such as the syntax language or the data size. Moreover, MIT App Inventor uses mobile phones as targets and this aspect can offer a real-world motivation to students [18] because of the pervasiveness of mobile phones. Some positive reports on the effectiveness of teaching fundamentals of programming to non-majors and/or undergraduates by using MIT App Inventor already exist [19,20].

As can be seen by Table 2, the laboratory (ILAB BoK) is very important in our project structure, since it covers all the main aspects for the IoT fundamental knowledge. Obviously, the COVID-19 pandemic period forced us to rethink laboratory activities since the physical presence was not guaranteed anymore. To overcome this problem we acted on two sides.

On one side we made use of online simulator and prototyping platforms, such as Tinkercad[1], that could fulfill our needs for lectures and exercises. In particular, The Tinkercad platform allowed us to set up a virtual lab related to Arduino by effectively simulating the microcontroller itself and a lot of components, as can be seen in Fig. 2. The behavior of the system can be programmed by using visual blocks or the Arduino traditional programming language. Students can share their work with the teacher and receive immediate feedback.

On the other side, we encouraged students to build the simulated IoT projects on their own and provide documentation in the form of technical reports or tutorial videos. Examples of the outcomes realized by students can be found on the web [21].

[1] https://www.tinkercad.com/.

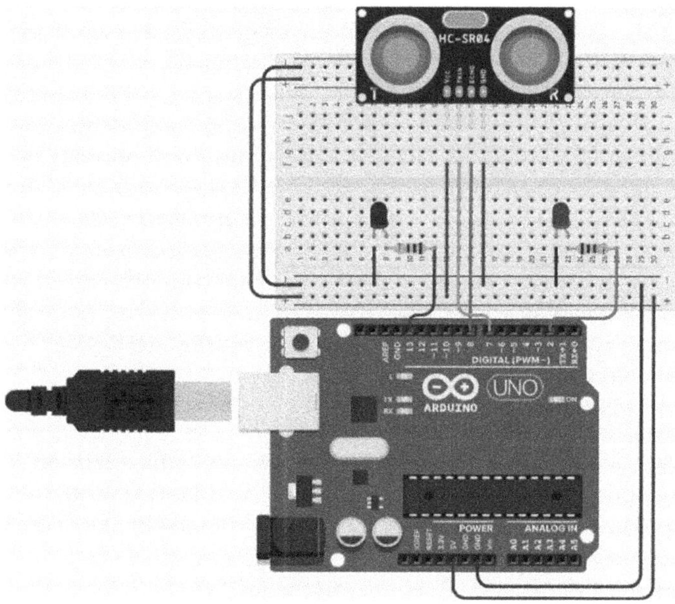

Fig. 2. Arduino virtual project simulated in the Tinkercad platform

Obviously, the emotional state of the students had to be taken into account during the COVID-19 pandemic, since the climate of uncertainty and the period of forced isolation created a certain despair in some moments. For this reason, the students were also supported on the motivational point-of-view and we proceeded to use non-mandatory deadlines.

During the pandemic period, we leveraged common learning platforms, such as Google Classroom[2] and Edmodo [22] for the remote teaching activities, including videoconferences, feedback and assessment. By looking at the related work [23–25], it appears that our approach on lab activities has been shared by other researchers during the pandemic period.

6 Analysis and Assessment

Our experience shows that new technologies excite students, by having a strong motivational impact on their educational path.

At the end of the first year of implementation, a survey has been proposed to 44 students, in order to analyze students' perception about their educational training and, in particular, about IoT has a vehicle to boost their upcoming job career. Their answers have been reported in Table 3 in a Likert scale (1 = strongly disagree, 5 = strongly agree). As can be seen from the answers, the students are

[2] https://classroom.google.com.

Table 3. Opinions of all students

Question	Answer
Do you believe that working with IoT technologies can be useful to improve your programming skills?	3.84
Do you believe knowing how to use IoT technologies can be useful for finding a job?	3.79
Would you like to introduce/deepen IoT technologies in your curriculum?	3.88

Table 4. Opinions of female students

Question	Answer
Do you believe that working with IoT technologies can be useful to improve your programming skills?	3.33
Do you believe knowing how to use IoT technologies can be useful for finding a job?	3.66
Would you like to introduce/deepen IoT technologies in your curriculum?	3

quite enthusiastic about these new technologies, considering them as useful to enrich their formative path, even for a future perspective.

However, we must point out that there is some difference in the data analysis if we also take gender into account. First of all, only the 7.3% of students were female. Table 4 shows the answers given in Likert scale (1 = strongly disagree, 5 = strongly agree) by only female students. We notice that the score is lower for all the answers with respect to the previous table. Furthermore, none of them stated that they were familiar with IoT technologies, so they were not included in the aggregates mentioned in the next table.

In fact, a deeper analysis showed us that the more they knew the subject, the more enthusiastic they were. For instance, the question 'Would you like to deepen IoT technologies in your curriculum?' has collected 3.88, considering all students. However, only the 50% of the students were familiar with IoT before the class and the score increases to 4.43 when the analysis is limited to them. The score further increases to 4.69 when limited to students who had worked with IoT. Table 5 shows the answers given in Likert scale (1 = strongly disagree, 5 = strongly agree) by students who were familiar with IoT. We notice that the score is higher for all the answers with respect to the previous tables.

In general, the opinions provided by the students are very clear regarding their desire to introduce/deepen IoT technologies within their training. However, a further step was necessary in this direction. In fact, the methodologies discussed in Sect. 5, that have been chosen and tested in this article, are typically combined with formative assessment. In order to implement our project in

Table 5. Opinions of students who are familiar with IoT technologies

Question	Answer
Do you believe that working with IoT technologies can be useful to improve your programming skills?	4.34
Do you believe knowing how to use IoT technologies can be useful for finding a job?	4.21
Would you like to introduce/deepen IoT technologies in your curriculum?	4.43

Table 6. Project rubric

	Initial	Basic	Intermediate	Advanced
Choose devices and tools based on their functional characteristics	The student is able to identify tools and devices by leveraging the help giving by teachers or peers	The student is able to identify tools and devices, in an almost completely autonomous way	The student is able to satisfactorily identify tools and devices, in a completely autonomous way	The student is able to satisfactorily and effectively identify tools and devices, in a completely autonomous way
Knowing how to read technical reports and document individual/group activities	The student is able to understand essential information by leveraging the help giving by teachers or peers	The student is able to understand and report essential information, in an almost completely autonomous way	The student is able to understand and report information with a certain degree of detail, in a completely autonomous way	The student is able to understand and report information with a wealth of detail, in a completely autonomous and personal way

curricular teaching, we needed to reconcile such methodologies with summative assessment, since this kind of assessment is required in the Italian high school system.

Some effort has been put in order to provide both formative and summative assessment in a smooth way. In particular, we started thinking about the formative evaluation, which was then translated into summative evaluation at the end of the learning process. For the formative assessment of our learning project implementation, we adopted a simple project rubric, as shown in Table 6, which highlights the fundamental skills being assessed and the levels achieved.

The goal of the project rubric is the evaluation of the result of competent action in terms of application of knowledge and solution strategies. The project rubric can then be accompanied by other rubrics, such as the behavioral rubric, which describes knowing act during the course of the reality task and the metacognitive rubric that describes the ability to reconstruct and illustrate the path carried out in terms of methods, contents, strategies, personal involvement.

Table 7. Marks for competence levels

Level	Mark
Initial	4
Basic	6
Intermediate	8
Advanced	10

In order to use our learning project also in curricular planning, it was necessary to have a summative evaluation with marks in tenth, as a requirement of the Italian school system. In our case, we used an approach that can be considered a little bit unorthodox, since it admits the possibility of translating the formative evaluation into marks in tenths. This approach is corroborated by two observations:

- competences include knowledge and skills and thus by evaluating the former ones we also evaluate the latter ones;
- in our case the project outcome can be a prototype and/or a technical-divulgative documentation to expose contents and techniques: such objects present aspects that lend themselves to the summative assessment.

We point out that the contrary translation from marks to competences should never be done, since the evaluation of knowledge and skills, especially if conducted by traditional tests, satisfies only a partial aspect of competences. Competence levels are then translated into marks only at the end of the learning process and not during the process, because this would lead to the disadvantages mentioned above: frustration, focus on the mark and not on the learning process, and so on.

At the end, to obtain marks from the observation of competence levels, we adopted the translation proposed in Table 7: such translation was done for each competence under observation and the final mark was given by the average of the assessments evaluated for each competence.

7 Conclusion

IoT is a trend topic in ICT and IoT skills are one of the most required by industries for bringing technological innovations. However, the educational system takes time for adapting to evolving industrial and cultural needs. We believe that it is possible and necessary to include IoT early in computer science education, in order to direct students toward the future of computing and society.

For this reason, this paper presented different Bodies of Knowledge for the development of a curriculum on IoT. Upon our conceptual proposal we implemented a learning project to be introduced early in technical education. We discussed some aspects of our implementation, including assessment, methodology, technology, contents and pandemic adjustments for carrying on laboratory activities. We hope that our proposal breaks new grounds and feeds the discussion towards a new framework for computer science and engineering education.

References

1. Ghayvat, H., Liu, J., Babu, A., Alahi, E., Gui, X., Mukhopadhyay, S.: Internet of things for smart homes and buildings: opportunities and challenges. J. Telecommun. Digit. Econ. **3**(4), 33–47 (2015)
2. Zanella, A., Bui, N., Castellani, A., Vangelista, L., Zorzi, M.: Internet of things for smart cities. IEEE Internet Things J. **1**(1), 22–32 (2014)
3. Rifkin, J.: The Third Industrial Revolution: How Lateral Power is Transforming Energy, The Economy, and the World, 2011. Palgrave Macmillan (2012). ISBN 978(0) 230
4. Alrumaih, H., Sabin, M., Impagliazzo, J.: An overview of the new ACM/IEEE information technology curricular framework. In: 2018 IEEE World Engineering Education Conference (EDUNINE), pp. 1–6 (2018). https://doi.org/10.1109/EDUNINE.2018.8450997
5. Task Group on Information Technology Curricula: Information Technology Curricula 2017: Curriculum Guidelines for Baccalaureate Degree Programs in Information Technology. ACM, New York (2017)
6. Ming-Xuan, Y.D.H.C.: The application of the internet of things in digital campus. Mod. Educ. Technol. **6**, 027 (2011)
7. Hui-Xiaoa, B., Shu-Sheng, J.: The internet of things and higher vocational education reforms. J. Shijiazhuang Vocat. Technol. Inst. (2011)
8. Voas, J., Laplante, P.: Curriculum considerations for the internet of things. Computer **50**(1), 72–75 (2017). https://doi.org/10.1109/MC.2017.27
9. Voas, J.: Networks of 'things'. NIST Spec. Publ. **800**(183), 1–30 (2016). 800-183
10. Burd, B., et al.: Courses, content, and tools for internet of things in computer science education. In: Proceedings of the 2017 ITiCSE Conference on Working Group Reports, ITiCSE-WGR 2017, pp. 125–139. ACM, New York (2017). https://doi.org/10.1145/3174781.3174788. http://doi.acm.org/10.1145/3174781.3174788
11. Koo, S.G.M.: An integrated curriculum for internet of things: experience and evaluation. In: 2015 IEEE Frontiers in Education Conference (FIE), pp. 1–4, October 2015. https://doi.org/10.1109/FIE.2015.7344347
12. DeFranco, J., Kassab, M.: Internet of things education. In: Proceedings of the 52nd Hawaii International Conference on System Sciences (2019)
13. Tortoriello, F.S., Veronesi, I.: Internet of things to protect the environment: a technological transdisciplinary project to develop mathematics with ethical effects. Soft Comput. **25**(13), 8159–8168 (2021). https://doi.org/10.1007/s00500-021-05737-x
14. Lensing, K., Friedhoff, J.: Designing a curriculum for the internet-of-things-laboratory to foster creativity and a maker mindset within varying target groups. Proc. Manuf. **23**, 231–236 (2018)
15. DeFranco, J., Kassab, M., Voas, J.: How do you create an internet of things workforce? IT Prof. **20**(4), 8–12 (2018)
16. Banzi, M., Shiloh, M.: Getting started with Arduino: the open source electronics prototyping platform. Maker Media, Inc. (2014)
17. MIT App Inventor. App Inventor Website (2018). http://appinventor.mit.edu/explore. Accessed 22 Aug 2018

18. Wolber, D.: App inventor and real-world motivation. In: Proceedings of the 42nd ACM Technical Symposium on Computer Science Education, pp. 601–606. ACM (2011)
19. Morelli, R., De Lanerolle, T., Lake, P., Limardo, N., Tamotsu, E., Uche, C.: Can Android app inventor bring computational thinking to K-12. In: Proceedings of the 42nd ACM Technical Symposium on Computer Science Education (SIGCSE 2011), pp. 1–6 (2011)
20. Spertus, E., Chang, M.L., Gestwicki, P., Wolber, D.: Novel approaches to CS 0 with app inventor for android. In: Proceedings of the 41st ACM Technical Symposium on Computer Science Education, pp. 325–326. ACM (2010)
21. Arduino Projects. https://www.youtube.com/watch?v=B55yz6y5spI&list=PLohu_r9AZYiv9GNF9jZCVYH6R8uLCqsDx
22. Borg, N., O'Hara, J., Hutter, C.: About Edmodo. https://go.edmodo.com/about/ (2019)
23. Basha, R.F.K., Venusamy, K.: A detailed study of effective online technical teaching aids for augmented learning in Covid'19 pandemic. In: 2020 Sixth International Conference on e-Learning (eConf), pp. 267–270. IEEE (2020)
24. Khant, S., Patel, A.: Covid19 remote engineering education: learning of an embedded system with practical perspective. In: 2021 International Conference on Innovative Practices in Technology and Management (ICIPTM), pp. 15–19. IEEE (2021)
25. Rocca, P.L., Riggi, F., Pinto, C.: Remotely teaching Arduino by means of an online simulator. Phys. Educ. **55**(6), 063003 (2020). https://doi.org/10.1088/1361-6552/abaa21

The Physics of Everyday Life Toolbox for Basic Physics Courses

Marilú Chiofalo(✉)

Department of Physics, University of Pisa and INFN, 56126 Pisa, Italy
marilu.chiofalo@unipi.it
https://people.unipi.it/maria_luisa_chiofalo/

Abstract. The Physics of Everyday Life (PEL) teaching environment is illustrated, developed since 2007 at the University of Pisa in physics courses for life-sciences and for physicists considering a future career in school teaching. Sourcing inspiration from How things work by Lou Bloomfield, PEL aims at explicitly restoring the functional process of scientific thinking, with observation and creation of hypotheses preceding their formalization for subsequent experimental verification, so that intuition is first educated through classroom demonstrations.

The early educational project is illustrated along with its adaptations to different contexts, including high-school situated environments, teachers training, and outreach activities. Then, the evolution of the PEL environment is focused, aimed at enhancing its impact and overturning weak points. This amounts to the Street-Physics Toolbox (SPT), conceived just before the pandemic in the form of 60 video-pills exhausting the full physics program, and resulted to be of significant utility within the perimeter of distance teaching. Implementation examples in real different context are discussed, also in relationship with the general Inquired-Based Learning cycle and of flipped-classroom approaches. Future perspectives include a systematic assessment of the PEL and SPT environment and extending contents for quantum physics and technologies education.

Keywords: General physics teaching · Inquiry-based learning · Flipped classroom

1 Introduction

Einstein and Infeld [1] compare scientific research to a mystery, where Nature is responsible for the "misdeed" and the scientist is the detective who, by means of clues, intuition, and bodies of evidence gets to the mystery solving. Scientific thinking hinges on starting from some form of reality, creating understanding, formalize this creative act in some very dense symbolic system, maths for science, and connecting back again to experiment. In this process, every single tiny

Supported by organization University of Pisa.

G. Casalino et al. (Eds.): HELMeTO 2021, CCIS 1542, pp. 100–114, 2022.
https://doi.org/10.1007/978-3-030-96060-5_8

piece of mind is involved and interconnected, linking abstraction to reality via creativity. Interestingly, this parallels artistic thinking [2] and not by chance science involves visual thinking as one part of mathematical language to boost creativity [3,4]. Developing the abilities required in scientific thinking, as introduced by Galileo, represents for everyone at any age a revolution in our way of looking at reality via one own's multiple intelligences [5,6].

The enormous potential of physics thinking while nurturing minds in educational processes includes the development of abilities as problem solvers; builds up awareness on how errors and error correction work for problem solving; empowers the ability of translating among a number of languages different than the verbal one and often characterized by highest density of information; stands on the idea that things are not right or wrong but the result of a comparison between theory (affected by approximations) and experiments (affected by errors); switches on critical thinking; enhances creativity. These are solid motivations why science is important in our lives, besides fostering technologies and answering the wonderful mysteries of the Universe, and why we should be strongly committed to educate everyone to scientific thinking. However, physics thinking is not essential part of education processes starting from the kindergarten up to middle school. In high school, physics instruction is too often performed by means of a set of equations in a deductive manner [7], in fact placing math beforehand than observation and creative guessing of explanations of phenomena [8,9]. As a result, we remain in the infancy of the knowledge of humankind until adolescence. Students arriving at the first year of college, either still suffer from conceptual mistakes about basic phenomena, or have not developed an intuition about how basic concepts can be combined to explain what it is observed in everyday life.

In non-specialized physics courses, like general physics courses in scientific (non physics) bachelor's degrees, one additional critical issue is about keeping students engaged and motivated students [10,11], while the mathematical tools they can master are still limited. On the opposite side, even in the specialized context of physics courses for physicists, it often happens that the (necessary) attention to the mathematical formalization of the problem leads to defocus the essential physical idea. As a result, students tend to deal with the solution of the problem in a preeminently technical way, risking sometimes longer solution procedures, away from physics. The question then arises, on how to bring the focus back on physics ideas, keeping students engaged in the full process of physics thinking, and empowering their competences in each step of the process played in the functional order: observation, creation of hypothesis, formalization, and back to experimental verification.

An innovative approach to overturn the situation has been conceived and developed by Lou Bloomfield at the University of Virginia with the experience "How things work - The physics of everyday life" [12,13]. This is a complete course in physics, from classical dynamics to fluid dynamics, thermodynamics, electromagnetism, optics, materials science, chemistry-physics, and elements of modern and quantum physics, where the learning units are strictly built from the operation of objects and phenomena of daily life. This contribution illustrates the Physics of Everyday Life (PEL) teaching environment that has been developed since 2007 sourcing inspiration from *How things work* [12,13], and implemented in physics courses for scientific bachelor and master degree courses (mainly inherent life sciences), as well as for physicists at the University of Pisa.

The paper is organized as follows. The early educational project is illustrated in Sect. 2 along with its adaptations to different contexts of formal and non-formal education aimed at different beneficiaries, its successes and criticalities. The present evolution of the PEL environment is illustrated in Sect. 3 aimed at enhancing its impact and overturning its weak points. Here, special attention is devoted to the Street-Physics Toolbox (SPT) conceived just before the pandemic in the form of 60 video-pills exhausting the full physics program and granted by the University of Pisa among the special projects for teaching, and resulted significantly useful within the perimeter of distance teaching. Implementation examples of the toolbox in real different context are discussed in Sect. 4, also in terms of its relationship with Inquired-Based Learning and flipped-classroom approaches. Concluding remarks and future perspectives are finally envisioned in Sect. 5.

2 The Educational Project

Started as an additional and optional physics course at the Faculty of Pharmacy in 2007, today The Physics of Everyday Life (PEL) is a course for the Bachelor degree in Physics of the University of Pisa. It is designed for physics students who want to strengthen their scientific thinking practice and understand complex problems in terms of essential ideas before introducing any technicality, students from scientific Bachelor or Master degree courses with a future of teaching in schools at all levels and degrees, and open to students everywhere animated by curiosity for physics. The same approach - after suited modifications - has been used since 2013 in contexts of both non-formal and formal education for secondary school second degree [14], as well as in popularization events.

The methodology of Everyday Physics draws inspiration from the experience How things work [12,13] by Lou Bloomfield. The basic idea of this teaching and learning process is very simple and builds on the process of scientific thinking. Of the three pillars - observation, creation of hypotheses, and their formalization for subsequent experimental verification - the first two are explicitly and fully used, educating intuition through classroom demonstrations. In the PEL realization, the classroom demonstrations are made with items and gadgets that are required to have household origin (not coming from a physics laboratory), so that students might easily reproduce or build up on them in an hands-on approach [8,9]. Since any idea or concept in physics can be discussed starting from a number of different phenomena, care is needed to select those where the given concept is preeminent, and being aware that not all phenomena are equally effective to the aim. This selection process ends up with essentially a table of content for a full physics course, that is recast in terms of phenomena and objects of everyday life. Once the selection is performed at the teaching level, the specific phenomena to be discussed in classroom for any given concept are chosen at the beginning of the course through a participatory process whenever possible, in order to enhance students curiosity and motivations.

Inspired to Bloomfield idea [12,13], a typical adopted program for a full course in (basic) general physics is presented in double-indexed form: the conventional educational scientific agenda (mostly viewed from professor perspective) and, for each agenda's item, a list of possible everyday-life or popular objects and phenomena (mostly viewed from student perspective) that can be used to discuss the preeminent physics concepts. While referring to the table of contents of [12] to form a definite idea of how this works, we refer to Sect. 3 for a detailed account of the program structure evolved within the PEL environment. The rest of this section is devoted to discuss opportunities and constraints which accompany such an approach.

In this general framework indeed, specific choices are in order, depending on the learning context. Physics is first and foremost a way of thinking and solving problems, therefore the primary aim of general physics as a course for non physicists, for example, is to accompany the student to: (i) acquire basic concepts and ideas of physics, (ii) know how to apply them in practical contexts and (iii) combine them together to answer questions or solve more complex problems by method, and (iv) learn the basic operation of the experimental method. In relation to points (i) and (ii), the choice of basic ideas on which to spend more time depends on the disciplinary context in which the course is used. In relation to point (iii), the introduction of different degrees of complexity and mathematical formalization depends on the more general learning goals of the course of study. For example, PEL is used in two different first year courses of the Pharmacy Department of the University of Pisa, the MD in Chemistry and Pharmaceutical Technologies (CPT) and the BS in Sciences of Herbs and Health Products (SHHP), and in a course to teach teaching physics at the BS in Physics. As to (i) and (ii), it has appeared timely to open a special focus on examples about e.g. fluids statics and dynamics in capillaries or medical diagnostics for the Pharmacy courses, while providing an overall sampling of many different examples in the case of the Physics BS-course. As to (iii), the physics course for CPT contains a higher level of mathematical formalization than for SHHP. In the contexts of teaching to teach at the BS in Physics, the focus is on the methodology itself, so that for example it is explicitly discussed how different phenomena can offer different degrees of effectiveness and efficiency in the classroom work on concepts, with fixed educational and scientific agenda. In any event, the crucial trait is that math is introduced only at a second stage, after the concepts have been digged in during the classroom process of realizing the demos and inducing explanation guesses.

2.1 Adaptations to Formal and Non-formal Educational Context

One of the main PEL traits is hinging on the initial engagement with everyday-life examples and demostrations while gradually adding formalization at a second stage, at a level that depends on the context. Even none, in principle. Thus, the PEL approach has been easily implemented also over many years in outreach contexts like, e.g., the European Researchers Night, and in situated high-school educational contexts. In particular, each year from 2013 to 2018, it has been the methodological framework where 16 meetings have been conducted in as many high schools, within the initiative *Pianeta Galileo* in which the Tuscany Region offers a bridged meeting context to high schools and universities to foster science education and thinking [14]. In 2019, it has been used in a three days-longer format at the "Alessandro Volta" Lyceum in Reggio Calabria (Italy) [15]. Lectures were aimed at students and prepared in collaboration with the school teacher, Carmen Petronio. The PEL approach has revealed to be especially fruitful in these conditions, since thanks to the double-index idea the specific lecture contents and formalization level have been easily tailored on students and teachers needs at the same time, depending on the school specialization (as to the Italian system, this may include classic, pedagogical, scientific, technical, and professional studies) and the class year. The PEL approach has been exploited also in contexts of training for teachers or educators from different school degrees [16–18], as it will be detailed in Sect. 4 for the case of the evolved PEL environment.

2.2 Need to Evolve the PEL Environment

While the original PEL approach has indeed been working to support students in building their motivations towards physics learning, developing their intuition, and improving their performances at the exams, two main drawbacks revealed to be in order. First, the severely reduced amount of calculus performed in the early days started to work as a limitation, as evidenced at the course end by those same students who were especially happy to take a physics course almost without maths. Second, the discussion of a single, preeminent concept, requires to break up more complex phenomena into more simple pieces. Once the single concepts are apprehended, then one can increase the level of complexity. Finally, though engaging in classroom, the level of proactive learning within the PEL approach needed a boost, allowing for example to set up Inquiry-Based Learning (IBL) or flipped classroom environments, especially challenging in large classes with 200–300 students (as in SHHP) [19].

3 PEL and the Street Physics Toolbox

These considerations have led to evolve PEL along the above directions. The pedagogical concept has been inspired to the work of Knight [20], i.e. explicitly setting out conceptual, procedural, and factual knowledge. The idea is that knowledge and expertise are progressively built by digging into the single concepts, the relationship among them being provided by the physics laws, then working onto the understanding of general procedures suited to solve given types of problems, and finally developing the capacity of applying the general procedure to specific problems. In fact, classroom activities of problem solving correspond to the reverse process, which starts from the given more complex question and keeps crumbling the latter into simpler pieces, until getting to the simplest questions which can be answered, and then fold back everything into the final solution.

This general idea is implemented into the PEL environment as illustrated in the schematic concept in Fig. 1. A format is created for macrostories involving more complex everyday-life phenomena, whose understanding can be built up from individual simpler concepts. A detailed account of macrostories and single concepts, and of how they are combined into a typical course syllabus, is provided in Tables 1–2. Then, it has been conceived and realized a toolbox (Street Physics Toolbox, SPT) containing 60 essential concepts of physics from Galileo physics to electromagnetism, in the form of videopills about five minutes long each, based on the PEL approach. To the 60 pills are added the so-called quantum pills and resources developed within the QPlayLearn platform www.qplaylearn.com as evidenced in Table 2, whose concept and composition is described in Ref. [21]. Besides the format of the macrostories, also that of the 60 SPT pills is inspired to Bloomfield idea [12]. As illustrated in the right part of Fig. 1, each pill is devoted to one single concept, that is presented starting from a video depicting a real-life very simple situation, which one wishes to understand the operation of. This is followed by a qualitative verbal description of the main concept involved, then a quantitative description in mathematical form, and eventually the explanation of the phenomenon back on the video. Overall then, verbal, graphical, and mathematical languages are used. The format was designed in a professional way with the collaboration of the writer and journalist-expert in communication Chiara Cini. The realization of the format has benefited of the expertise from Media Events of the University of Pisa for videomaking and production, and for the drawings from Ian Carlos Trujillo Duran, a BS-physics student with specific graphic expertise, who had previously attended the Physics of everyday life course.

In a typical class then, one ideally starts with presenting the everyday-life macrostory via classroom or street-physics demonstrations, and then conducts the class into the induction process of creating possible explanations. During this process, the original complex question is crumbled into smaller pieces, until the simplest concepts are introduced and discussed with the help of the SPT videopills. During the process, the level of formalization can easily be adapted to the class expertise in discussing both the single concepts and the procedures. This is possible without loosing any single piece of qualitative physics understanding. Even at the lowest level of calculus usage, the development of procedural knowledge is preserved, at least in the form of physics thinking and connection among different concepts.

Besides the macrostories, a limited set of larger (hyper-)macrostories has been developed, which allow to cover a full program, as envisioned in column IV of Tables 1–2. The modular nature of the PEL+SPT environment favors as well the development of special macrostories, cross-running along the whole program. These have been built over time, in fact under students and/or teachers suggestions. A few examples are (i) the Physics of Harry Potter for muggles, discussing the physics content of the four spells vingardium leviosa (fluid dynamics and electrodynamics), invisibility cloak (metamaterials), portkey (quantum physics and entanglement), time turner (time travel); (ii) time from Galileo to time travel, discussing mechanical clocks, electronic and digital clocks, irreversibility and the second law of thermodynamics, atomic clocks, spacetime and special+general relativity; and (iii) the science of cooking, discussing cross-border concepts between chemistry and physics.

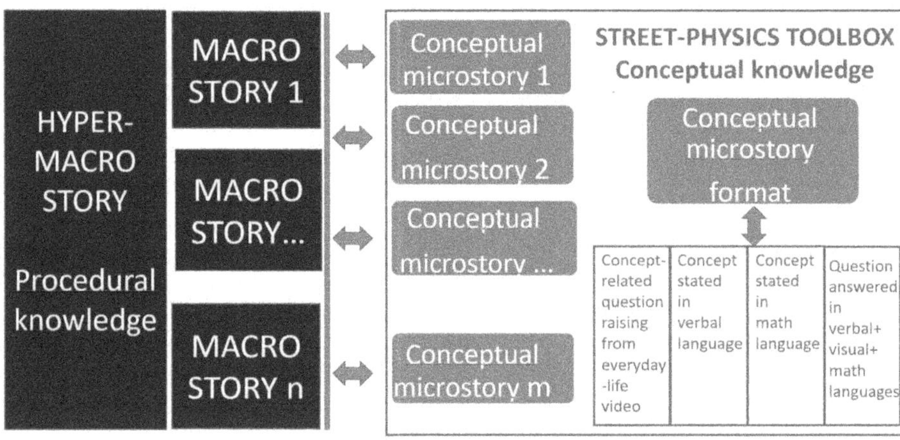

Fig. 1. Schematic concept of PEL+SPT. Conceptual knowledge is built up in the Street-Physics Toolbox (SPT) by discussing each single concept (60 in total) in video-pills according to the format in the legend (see main text). Procedural knowledge is built up in macrostories of everyday-life: macrostories can extend over one (macrostory) or more (hyper-macrostory) lectures, depending on the scientific and pedagogical choices suited to the given physics course. Tables 1–2 provides the detailed structure of the single SPT concepts and the relationship between the macrostories and a conventional general basic physics course. The level of formal tools adopted for both the conceptual and procedural knowledge is tuned, depending on the course context. The macro- and micro-stories formats are both inspired to Lou Bloomfield's How Things Work experience [12], i.e. starting from classroom or street-physics demos to educate intuition.

Table 1. Typical double-indexed conceptual map for a general-physics course in the PEL+SPT environment. From left to right columns runs the professor's perspective, starting from the scientific teaching agenda. From right to left runs the students' perspective, starting from the macrostories. Columns I-IV from left to right: general topic in scientific agenda and specific topic within it (I); single involved concepts entering the SPT, each one treated in a corresponding video-pill according to the format in Fig. 1 (II); macrostories used to discuss the single physics concepts and procedures (III); larger (hyper-) macrostories, requiring on average the number of 2-hours lectures indicated in parenthesis (IV).

Scientific agenda	SPT concepts	Macrostories	Hyper-Macrostories
Dynamics			
Force laws of motion	*Point-like bodies*:	Skateboards	Sports physics (4):
	Vectors		• soccer
	Position		• volleyball
	Velocity		• tennis
	Acceleration		• basket
	Inertial mass		
	Force		
	3 Dynamics laws (3 pills)		
	Initial conditions	Falling balls	
	Constraints	Ramps	
	Gravitational force		
	Elastic force	Spring scales	
	Static friction	Wheels	
	Dynamic friction	& bykes	
	Rigid bodies:	Seesaws	
	Angular position	Carousels	
	Angular velocity		
	Angular acceleration		
	Rotational mass		
	Center of mass		
	Torque		
	3 Dynamics laws		
	Fluids:		
	Pressure	Balloons	
	Archimede's & Bouyant force	Diving	
Momentum & Energy conservation	*Point-like bodies*:	Bouncing balls	
	Momentum		
	Momentum conservation		
	Impulse		
	Impulse theorem		
	Anelastic collisions		
	Elastic collisions		
	Work & Energy	Ramps	
	Kinetic energy		
	Potential energies		
	Thermal energy		
	Energy conservation		
	Power		
	Rigid bodies:	Bumper cars	
	Angular momentum		
	Angular impulse and collisions		
	Rotational kinetic energy		
	Fluids:		
	Matter conservation in flow	Water distribution	
	Energy conservation (Bernoulli)	Water gardening	
	Lift forces	Airplanes & airfoils	
	Viscous and pressure-drag forces	Vacuum cleaners	

Table 2. Follows Table 1. (*) Quantum physics concepts are beyond the 60 SPT pills and are borrowed from the Quest section of the QPlayLearn platform www.qplaylearn.com [21].

Scientific agenda	SPT concepts	Macrostories	Hyper-Macrostories
Resonance & waves			Musical
Natural resonance	Forced damped h.o	Clocks	instruments (2)
Generalities on waves	Freq., wavelength, speed	Sea & surf	
	Stationary waves		
Thermodynamics			
Dictionary	Temperature & Eq. of state	Heaters	Atmospheric weather (2)
	T-forces: thermal expansion		
	Internal energy		
	Thermo work		
	Heat		
Heat transport	Conduction	Thermos	
	Convection	Clothes	
	Radiation	Lamps	
Thermo laws	0, 1, 2 (3 pills)	Air conditioners & engines	
Electromagnetism			
Sources	*Electricity*		Medical imaging (2)
	Charges	Xerocopiers	
	Polarization		
	Induction		
	Magnetism	Household magnets	
	Charges in motion and spins		
Fields & forces	*Electricity*		
	Coulomb & Gauss	Static electricity	
	Magnetism	Household magnets	
	Biot-Savart & Ampère	Magnetic tapes	
	Lorentz force		
Energy	Electrostatic energy	Static electricity	
EM waves	Faraday and Maxwell laws	Microwave oven	
		Radio and TV	
		Cellphones	
		Levitating trains	
		Gen. & dist. electric power	
Light & optics		Sunlight. Paints	
		Analogic & digital cameras	
		Micro-& tele-scopes	
Quantum Physics (*)	Quantum state	Resources	Teleportation (2)
	Quantum measurement	from Quest	
	Superposition	& Discover	
	Entanglement	section at	
	Wavelike behavior	qplaylearn.com	
	Spin		
	Heisenberg principle		
	Tunnelling		

4 Applications

As anticipated, the PEL+SPT environment has been used for high-school teachers training events. In one case for example [18], teachers have been offered the proposal for an educational path mainstreamed on a civic topic especially engaging for young students, that is safe driving. One begins with videos of e.g. a car running tight curves at high speeds, or hard breaking with and without ABS/EBS, or performing a crash test (with a mannequin). Starting from the real situation, all essential concepts in classical dynamics have been discussed, disassembling each complex question into a number of simpler ones within a problem-solving procedure made explicit. The simplest questions were then traced back to three different types of conceptual maps to be discussed back-stage with teachers and useful also with students: solving the problem by: (i) Galileo-Newton's force laws of motion as illustrated in Fig. 2; (ii) energy in Fig. 3; and/or (iii) momentum conservation in Fig. 4. The three conceptual maps were built from 21 out of the 60 video-pills of the SPT, each of them involving only one single concept (like position, velocity, inertial mass, force,...). The single concept was worked out starting from a street-physics experiment, qualitatively conceptualized, elaborated in its formal content, and finally discussed and explained. During the whole process, the SPT is in fact re-organized in conceptual maps, drawn as in Figs. 2, 3 and 4 by connecting the different concepts into procedures: clicking in correspondence to each concept, opens up the corresponding hyper-referred SPT video-pill.

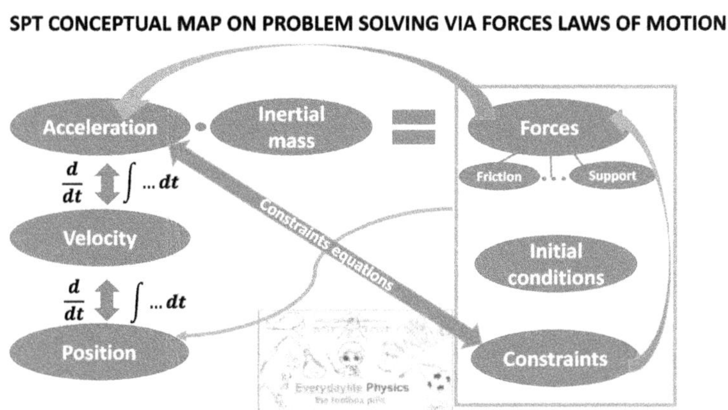

Fig. 2. SPT in teachers-training context. Example of a back-stage conceptual map used to discuss the physics of safe driving [18]. Here, the everyday-life question was how to safely drive a curve at high speed. The problem is discussed by using the procedure involving the forces laws of motion. In the training activity, the initial question is disassembled into simpler questions, until the level of the single concepts is reached (see Fig. 1). Then, the appropriate conceptual map is drawn connecting the different concepts into a procedure: clicking on the presentation in correspondence of each concept, opens up the corresponding hyper-referred SPT video-pill. Credits for the SPT cover: Ian Carlos Trujillo Duran.

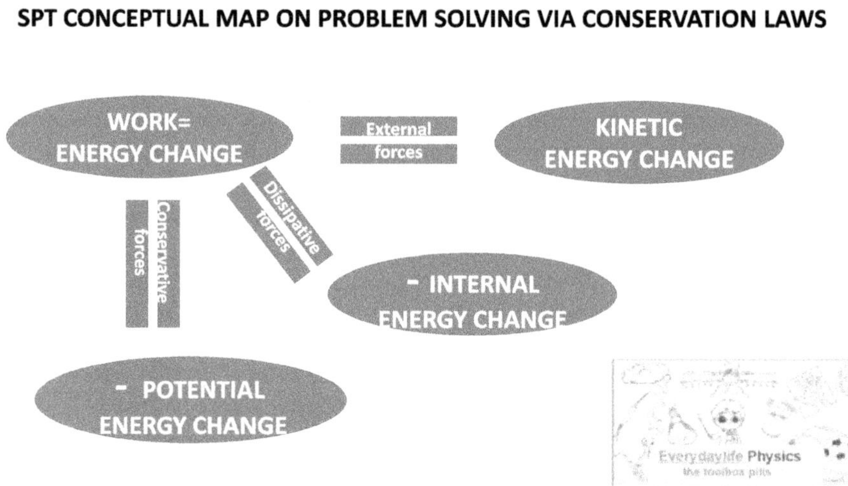

Fig. 3. SPT in teachers-training context. As in Fig. 2 but here, the everyday-life question was how to safely break and the role of ABS and EBS systems, and the problem is discussed by using the procedure involving the energy conservation laws.

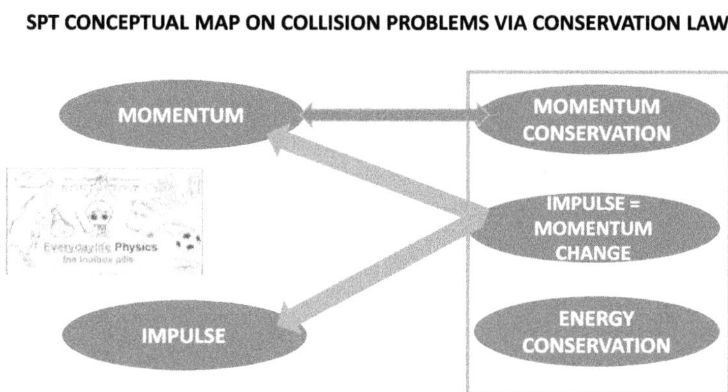

Fig. 4. SPT in teachers training context. As in Fig. 3 but here, the everyday-life question was about how crashes and collisions work (and must be avoided), and the problem is discussed by using the procedure involving the momentum conservation law and impulse theorem, along with energy conservation.

4.1 The Typical Class Problem-Solving Process Using PEL+SPT

As an example of typical class activity, we now schematically illustrate the process of answering one of the questions, i.e. how to safely drive a tight curve by car at constant (possibly high) speed. The question is disassembled into the following questions to be translated and answered with physics language: (a) what does a curvilinear trajectory means? (b) what does constant speed means? (c) what does "safe" means? Answers to questions (a) and (b) imply working on the concept of velocity as a vector providing at each instant of time the direction of motion, and on the concept that a change in the velocity direction leads to a (centripetal-like) acceleration. Thus, the sub-question arises (d) on who is causing that acceleration, leading to the concepts of force, inertial mass, and Newton's law. Question (e) is now about the microscopic nature of the force sustaining that acceleration, and thus to the concept of friction. It is now time to answer question (c), by noticing that safe-curve driving requires that the car is not sliding radially, nor sliding tangentially while wheels are revolving. Elaborating on this question (c) the distinction between static and sliding friction is timely discussed along with their simplest modelling, bringing in also the description of the physics occurring in direction perpendicular to the road plane, and thus introduces the concepts of support and gravity forces and of constraints and constraints equations. The need to determine the amount of static friction in radial direction brings in again the concept of constraints and how constraints equations work. The discussion about rolling friction brings in the essentials of rigid-body kinematics and laws of motion, and leads to answer what ABS and EBS are, and how they work (at least conceptually). Notice how the problem solving procedure leads to the crumbling of the original question into single essential concepts connected by physical laws and/or procedural steps, as depicted in Figs. 2, 3 and 4. In any event, the condition for a safe curve driving is finally derived in terms of speed, curvature, and adhesion force - thus gravity acceleration and static friction coefficient. At this point, additional complications of the original question can be added, by discussing for example what happens if the car is climbing up a bump, or why highways are designed with loose and possibly tilted (with respect to the horizontal) curves, and draining asphalt.

A few remarks are here in order. First, one may notice that the answer to just the first question may imply a number of class lessons, like one would do in an engaging story-telling, where questions leads to questions, until one is finally able to answer the essential ones, and recombine everything back into the big picture. Similar considerations hold for the other questions on the crash test: in fact, for example the analysis of how the airbag works brings in concepts and laws regarding other parts of a traditional physics syllabus, like thermodynamics, electrical circuitry, and material science (how our muscle-skeleton system is able to respond to external stresses). Second, one may notice that these conceptual maps can be exploited at all possible levels of instruction in calculus and mathematical formalization. Zooming in the formalization simply amounts to clicking on the videopill and addressing the "Concept stated in math language", as depicted in the right panel of Fig. 1. The theoretical and practical reference here is definitively the one pushed forward by Randall D. Knight [20], that is centered on the sequential development of conceptual, procedural, and factual knowledge as effective and efficient process for problem solving.

4.2 Application to Basic Bachelor and Master Physics Courses

The SPT within the PEL environment has been used in the two CPT and SHHP courses at Pharmacy and in the Physics of Everyday Life Course at Physics during the pandemic in distant teaching. Though harder to be played under such circumstances, using the described PEL context with the SPT naturally lead to elaborate on physics problems by posing questions as in an IBL cycle, where induction and deduction coexist [22]. In fact, the presently proposed PEL environment - even at the single-concept level - follows all steps of a general IBL process. As evidenced by the synthesis of 72 studies in [23], a general IBL cycle includes Orientation, Conceptualization, Investigation, Conclusion and Discussion, like in the typical process flow described in Sect. 4.1. In addition, in the CPT course, a flipped classroom setup has been briefly experimented during the pandemic, to enhance students' responsible approach and collaborative learning in an increased active environment [24], as well as to free class time for guided exercises and collaborative learning in small group activities [25]. In fact, flipping the classroom required to maintain the ordinary class time [26], due to inadequate students preparation prior to class [24]. In the PEL+SPT environment, class flipping can be performed in different manners. One most natural way, that has been experimented during one semester, amounts to pre-assign the study of specific videopills prior to class time, and then use class time to deeper work on the process of physics thinking while connecting the single concepts. Evaluation of the outcomes of this educational experiment is planned for the next semester, by means of on-purpose conceived questionnaires at the beginning, mid-term, and end of the courses, to be analyzed in a qualitative conceptual classes framework.

5 Conclusions

The PEL environment with associated SPT focuses the learner attention on essential ideas and favors the constant practice of scientific thinking. The technicalities of formalization are naturally sowed in the soil made fertile by curiosity. In this manner, formalization remains a resource - in proportion to the level of instruction - rather than an obstacle to language. A profound cultural change becomes potentially accessible, functional to school and university contexts at all levels. The PEL and SPT process is consistent with a IBL cycle, potentially sharing its known positive effects depending on the type of chosen guidance [23]. The SPT can be a valuable tool to facilitate classroom flipping, though a number of feasibility questions need further research and understanding [24,26].

Future work must necessarily begin with a definite assessment of the present PEL and SPT environment in the different training activities where it has been introduced. A number of future perspectives can also be envisioned both on the content and on the methodological sides. As to the contents, SPT might be interestingly developed for basic materials science and chemistry-physics, where macrostories are already available from Bloomfield [12], and especially in the direction of quantum technologies based on the QPlayLearn resources [21]. On the methodological side, it is worth exploring to which extent PEL+SPT can innovate an IBL-type approach and be effective to implement flipped-classroom settings.

Ackowledgments. This work has benefited over years from many valuable inputs and I'd like to deeply thank Massimiliano Labardi Lou Bloomfield, my colleagues at the Pharmacy Department of the University of Pisa, Chiara Cini, UNIPI MediaEventi, Ian Carlos Trujillo Duran, Dianora Bardi, Zanichelli Editor, Caterina Foti, Sabrina Maniscalco, Carmen Petronio, and Marisa Michelini.

References

1. Einstein, A., Infeld, L.: Evolution of Physics. Cambridge University Press, London (1938)
2. Gardner, H.: A Synthesizing Mind: A Memoir from the Creator of Multiple Intelligences Theory. The MIT Press, Cambridge (2020)
3. Ainsworth, S., Vaughan, P., Russell, T.: Drawing to learn in science. Science **333**(6046), 1096–1097 (1993)
4. Hadzigeorgiou, Y., Fotinos, N.: Imaginative thinking and the learning of science. Sci. Educ. Rev. **6**(1), 15–23 (2007)
5. Gardner, H.: Frames of Mind: The Theory of Multiple Intelligences. Basic Books, New York (1983)
6. Universal Design for Learning. https://www.cast.org/impact/universal-design-for-learning-udl
7. Wieman, C., Perkins, K.: Transforming physics education. Phys. Today **58**, 36–41 (2005)
8. Dorrío, B.V., Blanco-Garcìa, J., Costa, M.F.M.: Hands-on Physics Experiments for Classroom. Selected Papers on Hands-on Science II. https://core.ac.uk/download/pdf/154272769.pdf
9. Flick, L.: The meanings of hands-on science. J. Sci. Teach. Educ. **4**(1), 1–8 (1993)
10. Cooper, P., McIntyre, D.: Effective Teaching and Learning: Teachers' and Students' Perspectives. Open University Press, Buckingham (1996)
11. Pehmer, A.-K., Gröschner, A., Seidel, T.: How teacher professional development regarding classroom dialogue affects students' higher-order learning. Teach. Teach. Educ. **47**, 108–119 (2015)
12. Bloomfield, L.: How things work - The physics of everyday life. Wiley, New York (2001). Table of contents directly. https://www.wiley.com/en-us/How+Things+Work%3A+The+Physics+of+Everyday+Life%2C+6th+Edition-p-9781119013846
13. Bloomfield, L.: How Everything Works - Making Physics out of the Ordinary. Wiley, New York (2007)
14. Pianeta Galileo Homepage (2013–2020). https://www.consiglio.regione.toscana.it/pianeta-galileo/. Pianeta Galileo
15. Chiofalo, M.: Time, from the Pendulum Law to time Travel. Roccella Philosophy School: Lectures at the Lyceum "Volta" (Reggio Cal., Italy) (2019)
16. Chiofalo, M.: Educating to scientific thinking as a route for inclusive learning environments. Lecture at the Master CAFRE: empowering diverse skills and inclusive teaching. University of Pisa (2020 and 2021 editions). https://master.cafre.unipi.it/
17. Chiofalo, M.: Educating to scientific thinking as inclusive teaching. Webinar at the States General for Digital School, Bergamo (2020)
18. Chiofalo, M.: From endangering adolescents behavior to safe driving: scientific thinking for civic education. Webinar for High-School Teachers, Zanichelli (2021)

19. Walker, J.D., Cotner, S.H., Baepler, P.M., Decker, M.D.: A delicate balance: integrating active learning into a large lecture course CBE-life sciences. Education **7**, 361–367 (2017)
20. Knight, R. D.: Five Easy Lessons: Strategies for Successful Physics Teaching. Pearson (2003)
21. Foti, C., Anttila, D., Maniscalco, S., Chiofalo, M.L.: Quantum physics literacy aimed at K12 and the general public. Universe **7**, 86 (2021)
22. Pedaste, M., et al.: Phases of inquiry-based learning: definitions and the inquiry cycle. Educ. Res. Rev. **14**, 47–61 (2015)
23. Lazonder, A.W., Harmsen, R.: Meta-analysis of inquiry-based learning: effects of guidance. Rev. Educ. Res. **86**(3), 681–718 (2016)
24. Akçayir, G., Akçayir, M.: The flipped classroom: a review of its advantages and challenges. Comput. Educ. **126**, 334–345 (2018)
25. DeLozier, S.J., Rhodes, M.G.: Flipped classrooms: a review of key ideas and recommendations for practice. Educ. Psychol. Rev. **29**(1), 141–151 (2016). https://doi.org/10.1007/s10648-015-9356-9
26. van Alten, D.C.D., Phielix, C., Janssen, J., Kester, L.: Effects of flipping the classroom on learning outcomes and satisfaction: a meta-analysis. Educ. Res. Rev. **28**, 100281 (2019)

Facing COVID19 Emergency in Higher Education Teaching

Students' Coping and Study Strategies: Did Emergency Remote Teaching Support the Students During the Pandemic?

Andrea Tinterri[1(✉)], Maka Eradze[2], Pierpaolo Limone[2], and Anna Dipace[1]

[1] Department of Education and Human Sciences, The University of Modena and Reggio Emilia, Viale Antonio Allegri, 9, 42121 Reggio Emilia, Italy

[2] Department of Humanities, Literature, Cultural Heritage and Education Sciences, The University of Foggia, Via Arpi 176, 71100 Foggia, Italy

Abstract. Starting from winter 2020, the COVID-19 pandemic has introduced many challenges in all areas of human life in many countries. It also disrupted the usual functioning of educational institutions, generating an educational emergency where necessary changes needed to be introduced to continue the learning process. While distance learning as a field existed long before the advent of modern technologies, it has never been adopted on such a huge scale. On the one hand, it ensured access to education; on the other, it may have posed further challenges on students' lives and affected their sense of isolation. The current paper is an attempt to understand university students' Emergency Remote Teaching (ERT) experiences: their perceptions of such a large-scale change in their lives, the change in their study modes and methods, and the factors associated with students' appreciation of ERT. The results indicate that the students valued quite highly the ERT experience. Furthermore, it also partly allowed them to cope with the pandemic stress. ERT was especially effective when characterized by good organization of online lessons and interaction with teachers, while the synchronous or asynchronous modality of teaching didn't appear to play a significant role in students' appreciation.

1 Introduction, Rationale, and Literature Review

The Covid-19 pandemic changed the landscape of education with the use of educational technology and its tools. The unprecedented use of educational technology in the learner population has, on one hand, ensured access to education; on the other, created additional challenges. The pandemic not only increased the stress levels due to many different factors such as lockdowns, sudden changes in lifestyle and learning habits, it also changed the learning mode: students, as well as teachers, had to switch to online learning overnight. Before the pandemic, most distance learning programs, or courses, were planned for and implemented in an asynchronous mode. Undoubtedly, the distance learning implemented during the pandemic was different from the preplanned distance learning courses or/and programs that existed before. Moreover, while before

G. Casalino et al. (Eds.): HELMeTO 2021, CCIS 1542, pp. 117–128, 2022.
https://doi.org/10.1007/978-3-030-96060-5_9

the pandemic distance learning was implemented mainly in an asynchronous mode, during the pandemic many switched to synchronous online learning, often without proper reorganization of teaching and learning processes.

Distance learning (DL) is not a new field; it has existed well before the current cutting-edge technologies. In the past, it did not necessarily mean the use of the internet as a medium of communication; as of now, however, it is almost always internet based. DL is "*The family of instructional methods in which the teaching behaviors are executed apart from the learning behaviors... so that communication between the learner and the teacher must be facilitated by print, electronic, mechanical or other device*" [1].

Distance learning can be synchronous or asynchronous. It is worth noting, however, that before the pandemic the widespread form was mainly asynchronous and the most widely used framework to design or study distance learning experiences has been the Community of Inquiry Framework. This mainly addresses the challenges of asynchronous communication during distance learning [2], creating different types of interactions to narrow the transactional distance and increase the learner autonomy [1]. At the same time, such experiences are design specific, and influenced by both learning and interaction designs of learning environments [3].

DL as a discipline has historically problematized and focused on the main topics of research and practice: interaction [4], sense of isolation (overcoming a transactional distance) [5] and supporting learner autonomy and self-regulation [6] of learning by reinforcing metacognitive strategies [7]. Main research directions in the field are directed at alleviating these concerns; moreover, one of the main, original theories in distance education focuses on the interactions between student-teacher, student environment and student-student relationships and developments in the metacognitive processes [8]. However, the pandemic increased the sense of isolation and anxiety in the general population and decreased the social interaction levels. The sudden fall of social interaction levels could have also contributed to the sense of isolation in the learning contexts, or vice-versa.

In the context of the current pandemic, the difference between traditional distance learning and the current situation were denoted by the term "emergency remote teaching" (ERT) [9]. The term stresses the unplanned, unorganized, temporary nature of the current situation, bolstered by the need to guarantee mere access to education. To some, this experience has nothing to do with real DL; however, this unprecedented situation still calls for analysis of the current educational emergency to understand what it can mean for the field and what opportunities it may bring [10].

One of the characteristics of the ERT is the synchronicity of the online teaching experiences. We can hypothesize that this phenomenon happened first to respond to the emergency reorganization need and secondly to offer more social interaction opportunities to the learners; this lead, among other factors, to so-called Zoom fatigue, a complex and understudied phenomenon [11]. However, from existing research, we can theorize its causes and origins from an increased cognitive load [12], non-verbal overload, eye gaze at close distance etc. [11].

We posit that studying pandemic-imposed ERT is highly relevant [13] to the field of DL; first of all, to understand how these changes influence students' learning, study strategies and experiences in general. Second, to reflect on the lessons learned by the educational emergency. To understand how university students fared in the pandemic remote teaching scenario, the current paper focuses on several aspects of ERT: the interplay between synchronous/asynchronous modalities, interactivity of teaching, and student's coping and study strategies. In this study, we investigated the students' DL experiences: their perceptions of such a large-scale change in their lives, the change in their study modes and methods, and the factors associated with students' perceptions of the distance learning experience.

This paper is a case study based on one Italian university case, where we have administered a survey containing several items on remote teaching experiences and demographic information in the first phase of the pandemic (May 2020).

2 Methodology and Data Analysis

This research uses a survey methodology to collect data on the experiences. The survey consisted of several demographic and ERT experience-related items, to understand student appreciation of ERT, as well as the positive or negative aspects that factored most in this perception. A standard stress management questionnaire (COPE), a standard happiness test (UCLA LS3), a 12-item general health questionnaire (GHQ-12) was also included but were not included in the current study. The main research question of this paper is: Is there a relationship between the coping and study strategies and the mode of teaching and learning during the pandemic?

We limited our sample to students that reported participation in at least one online course in 2020 (n = 619). We asked them to rate:

- (i) Their overall appreciation of ERT
- (ii) Their digital competencies,
- (iii) The quality of their Internet connection
- (iv) The rate of synchronous vs asynchronous teaching
- (v) How interactive/non-interactive online courses were
- (vi) How good the organization of courses on their university portal was
- (vii) How much they had to change their study method
- (viii) How much they missed courses in presence
- (ix) How much they missed collaboration with other students
- (x) The quality of their interaction with the teachers
- (xi) The quality of interaction with their colleagues, and
- (xii) How much DL helped them cope with the pandemic.

The first five items were rated on a 1–5 Likert scale, whereas items from five to twelve used a 1–7 Likert scale. Survey results were analyzed using SPSS software[1] The statistical test is indicated for every measure. Mean values are presented ± standard deviation. Due to the non-normal distribution of answers, we used nonparametric tests (Spearman's Rho) to test the association between variables (Table 5).

3 Results

3.1 Demographics

Of the 619 survey participants that reported undergoing at least one online course during the current academic year, 436 were females (70.4%) and 161 males (26%), with 3 participants indicating the option "other" (0.5%) and 19 participants not indicating their gender (3.1%). Most participants (506, 81.7%) are not married whereas 74 of them are (12.0%), 4 are divorced (0.6%) and 35 did not indicate their civil state (5.7%). Most respondents did not have any children (562, 90.8%), with only 21 (3.4%) having one or more and 36 (5.8%) did not answer the question (Table 1).

Table 1. Survey respondents' distribution according to gender, civil state, and family situation

Gender	N	%
Female	436	70.4
Male	161	26.0
Other/Unspecified	3	0.5
Missing	19	3.1
Total	**619**	**100**
Civil State	N	%
Married	74	12.0
Not Married	506	81.7
Divorced	4	0.6
Missing	35	5.7
Total	**619**	**100**
Children(s)	N	%
Yes	21	3.4
No	562	90.8
Missing	36	5.8
Total	**793**	**100**

[1] https://www.ibm.com/analytics/spss-statistics-software.

Table 2. Average number of online classes for students per disciplinary area

Disciplinary area	N	%	Online classes (Mean)	Online classes (Std. Dev)	Online classes (Range)
Area 06 – Medical Sciences	170	27.9	4.44	2.271	1–9
Area 07 – Veterinary and agronomy	52	8.4	3.60	1.537	1–8
Area 10 – Antiquity studies	29	4.7	2.66	1.289	1–6
Area 11 – Historical and philosophical sciences, pedagogy, psychology	73	12.1	2.51	1.324	1–6
Area 12 – Juridical Sciences	70	11.3	2.64	1.384	1–7
Area 13 – Economy and statistics	138	22.8	2.48	1.204	1–6
Other Areas	35	5.6	3.77	1.911	1–9
Total	**566**	**100**	**3.28**	**1.896**	**1–9**

Respondents were students in different disciplinary areas (Table 2), with Area 06 (Medical sciences) or Area 13 (Economy and Statistics) being the most represented. The overall mean of online classes taken during 2020 was 3.28 ± 1.896; however, the average number of online classes taken varied significantly from a disciplinary area to another (Kruskal-Wallis H test = 104.295, $p < 0.001$), with medical sciences students taking, on average, the highest number of online classes (4.44 ± 2.271) and economy and statistics the lowest (2.48 ± 1.204). We found a statistically significant positive association between the number of online classes taken and the rate of asynchronous teaching (iv) (Spearman's Rho (ρ) test, $\rho = 0.139$, $p = 0.001$). We did not find any other statistically significant association between the number of online classes taken and the items numbered (i)–(xii), therefore indicating that the number of online classes taken did not have a great impact on the overall experience of ERT.

3.2 Students' Experience with Distance Learning Before and After the Pandemic

Most participants reported no previous experience with distance learning (Table 3; N = 509, 82.2%) before the pandemic; only a minority (14.4%) reported undergoing 1 or more courses (Table 3). Participants reported a significant difference when asked to evaluate their use of digital devices before and during the pandemic (paired-sample t-test = 27.373, $p < 0.001$). Before the pandemic, they used their devices (smartphones, computers, tablets) for 5.46 ± 3.60 h per day, whereas during the pandemic the number of hours increased to 9.12 ± 4.18 h per day. We found a modest, but statistically significant association ($\rho = 0.085$, $p = 0.04$) between the number of online classes taken and the use of devices during the pandemic.

Table 3. The table shows student's previous experience with distance learning, summarized as the number of online courses undertook before the pandemic. N = number of respondents; % shows the relative percentage of the total of respondents.

Previous experience with distance learning	N	%
No	509	82.2
1–2 Courses	67	10.8
3–5 Courses	16	2.6
>5 Courses	6	1.0
Missing	21	3.4
Total	**619**	**100**

Students were asked to rate (i) their overall appreciation of ERT (Table 4). On average, students had a good opinion of ERT (3.68 ± 1.219). Indeed, the most frequent answers were "4 = good" (28,4%) or "5 = very good" (36,2%) experience with online teaching. We asked students to rate their digital competencies. On average, students rated rather high their digital competencies (3.86 ± 0.942). This was the only category where we found a significant (Mann-Whitney's U test, $p < 0.001$) difference between genres, with males rating, on average, their digital competencies higher (3.79 ± 0.897) than females (3.57 ± 0.941). The mean reported quality of Internet connection was rather high (3.65 ± 1.046).

3.3 Distance Learning Modes and Methods

When we asked students to report the rate of synchronous vs asynchronous teaching they experienced in online classes, most students reported exclusively synchronous teaching ("1" N = 210, 33.9%), but many reported a mix of the two methods ("3", N = 150, 24.2%) or fully asynchronous teaching ("5" N = 80, 12.9%). Similarly, when we asked to rate whether, on average, their courses were interactive or not interactive, most students reported a high level of interactivity ("5" N = 159, 25.7%) but many also reported "average" ("3" N = 137, 22.1%) or "very little" ("1" N = 105, 18.5%) interaction. Students were asked to rate the perceived quality of didactic organization on the University's online portal. The average rating was high (5.52 ± 01.593 out of 7) with most students reporting "excellent" experience (N = 238, 38.5%). On average, students reported that they did not change their study method during ERT (3.53 ± 1.989 out of 7). The most common answer was that they "did not change at all" ("1" N = 143, 23.1%) their study method. However, many students reported that they changed it in part ("4" N = 118, 19.1% and "5" N = 89, 14.4%). A high number of students reported that they missed "a lot = 7" teaching in the presence (N = 187, 30.2%). Many students also reported that they miss "a lot = 7" collaboration with fellow students (N = 197, 31.8%); however, the second most frequent result was not missing collaboration with other students "at all = 1" (N = 106, 17.1%). Most students report that the interaction with teachers was "great = 7" (N = 123, 19.9%). Conversely, the most frequent answer is that students found that interaction with other students was "very poor = 1" (N = 113, 18.3%) although answers were very heterogeneous. Finally, many students report that distance learning helped them "a lot = 7" in coping with the pandemic situation (N = 268, 43.3%).

3.4 Factors for Coping with the Pandemic and ERT Appreciation

We were interested in understanding which factor might be associated with the students' appreciation of ERT, both in general and to cope with the pandemic situation. Given that the distribution of most answers was not normally distributed (Table 4) we used nonparametric correlation analysis using Spearman's Rho (ρ) test (Table 5) to examine the association between variables.

Students' overall appreciation of Online teaching (item i) has a moderate positive association with (ii) student's digital competencies (ρ = 0.128, $p < 0.005$) and (iii) quality of their internet connection (ρ = 0.138, $p < 0.005$). The strongest positive association is found with (vi) organization of courses in the University's web portal (ρ = 0.503, $p < 0.005$), (x) strong interaction with the teacher (ρ = 0.496, $p < 0.005$), and (xi) quality interaction with fellow students (ρ = 0.362, $p < 0.005$). More interactive versus less interactive teaching (v) also showed a weaker but significant positive correlation (ρ = 0.174, $p < 0.005$) with student's experience of online teaching. Conversely, the need to rethink the study method (vii) correlated negatively with student's overall judgement of ERT (ρ = −0.107, $p < 0.005$). The student's judgement did not appear to be associated with (iv) the rate of synchronous vs asynchronous teaching (ρ = −0.26, $p > 0.05$). We also found a strong positive association between students' overall judgement of distance learning and how much they agreed that ERT allowed them to cope with the COVID-19 situation (ρ = 0.511, $p < 0.005$). Similar associations were indeed found for the latter item (xii), except for item vii (the need to rethink the study method) which was not significantly associated (ρ = −0.050, $p > 0.05$). The results are summarized in Table 5.

Table 4. The table shows the mean values for students' answers to the 12 ERT-related questions that are investigated in this study. N = overall number of answers for each item; Min = minimum rating; Max = maximum rating; Std.D = standard deviation; K-S = Kolmogorov-Smirnoff test of normality; S-W = Shapiro-Wilk test of normality. Only the p-value for the test is shown in the table.

Questions	N	Min	Max	Median	Mean	Std. Dev	K-S test p-value	S-W test p-value
(i) Overall appreciation of ERT	616	1	5	4	3.68	1.219	<0.001	<0.001
(ii) Digital Competencies	601	1	5	4	3.68	0.942	<0.001	<0.001
(iii) Quality of Internet connection	601	1	5	4	3.65	1.046	<0.001	<0.001
(iv) Synchronous vs asynchronous teaching	609	1	5	2	2.50	1.390	<0.001	<0.001
(v) Interactive vs non-interactive teaching	569	1	5	3	3.22	1.451	<0.001	<0.001
(vi) Quality of online content organization	618	1	7	6	5.52	1.593	<0.001	<0.001
(vii) Change study method	618	1	7	4	3.53	1.989	<0.001	<0.001
(viii) Miss courses in the presence	618	1	7	5	4.58	2.175	<0.001	<0.001
(ix) Miss collaboration with students	617	1	7	5	4.48	2.309	<0.001	<0.001
(x) Quality of interaction with the teacher	618	1	7	5	4.54	1.818	<0.001	<0.001
(xi) Quality of interaction with students	617	1	7	4	3.64	1.963	<0.001	<0.001
(xii) ERT help cope with the pandemic	617	1	7	6	5.44	1.845	<0.001	<0.001

Table 5. The table shows the Spearman' rank correlation coefficient (ρ) for each pair of answers to the 12 ERT-related questions examined (i-xii). Asterisks indicate the p-value of the test for each case: * $p < 0.05$; **$p < 0.005$.

	(i)	(ii)	(iii)	(iv)	(v)	(vi)	(vii)	(viii)	(ix)	(x)	(xi)	(xii)
(i)		**0.128****	**0.138****	-0.26	**0.174****	**0.503****	**-0.107****	**-0.406****	**-0.299****	**0.496****	**0.362****	**0.511****
(ii)	**0.128****		**0.182****	0.04	**0.094***	**0.135****	0.054	-0.015	-0.07	**0.101***	**0.103***	**0.156****
(iii)	**0.138****	**0.182****		**0.093***	**0.156****	**0.218****	-0.044	-0.022	-0.034	**0.191****	0.050	**0.124****
(iv)	-0.026	-0.004	**-0.093***		**-0.291****	-0.008	0.023	-0.032	0.017	**-0.085***	0.009	0.027
(v)	**0.174****	**0.094***	**0.156****	**-0.291****		**0.164****	0.040	0.030	0.011	**0.284****	**0.202****	**0.205****
(vi)	**0.503****	**0.135****	**0.218****	-0.008	**0.164****		**-0.126****	**-0.184****	-0.142	**0.512****	**0.349****	**0.525****
(vii)	**-0.107****	0.054	-0.044	0.023	0.040	**-0.126****		**0.245****	**0.168****	-0.033	-0.034	-0.050
(viii)	**-0.406****	-0.015	-0.022	-0.032	0.030	**-0.184****	**0.245****		**0.669****	**-0.209****	**-0.152****	**-0.264****
(ix)	**-0.299****	-0.007	-0.034	0.017	0.011	**-0.142****	**0.168****	**0.669****		**-0.135****	**-0.086***	**-0.222****
(x)	**0.496****	**0.101***	**0.191****	**-0.085***	**0.284****	**0.512****	-0.033	**-0.209****	**-0.135****		**0.561****	**0.378****
(xi)	**0.362****	**0.103***	0.050	0.009	**0.202****	**0.349****	-0.034	**-0.152****	**-0.086***	**0.561****		**0.280****
(xii)	**0.511****	**0.156****	**0.124****	0.027	**0.205****	**0.525****	-0.050	**-0.264****	**-0.222****	**0.378****	**0.280****	

4 Conclusions and Discussion

Our analysis aimed at investigating the characteristics of ERT that factored in university students' evaluation of both their experience with remote teaching and its potential helpfulness in dealing with the stress and isolation induced by the pandemic situation.

Overall, students who underwent more online courses tended to use their devices more and had a higher ratio of asynchronous teaching (possibly due to having to watch recorded video lessons). Still, the number of online courses underwent during ERT did not seem to have significantly influenced students' judgement. Survey respondents had, in general, very limited exposure to digital learning in higher education before the COVID-19 outbreak (Table 2). Despite that, students' judgement on their experience with Distance Learning during the pandemic was generally very positive (item i), and students strongly agreed that undertaking online courses helped them endure the difficulties and the stress of the unprecedented pandemic situation (item xii). In this study, we investigated which factors were associated with students' appreciation of their experience with DL.

4.1 Interaction with Teachers and Other Students Positively Influenced Students' Opinion of ERT and Its Helpfulness in Dealing with the Pandemic

The strongest positive associations with students' appreciation of ERT and of its role in coping with the pandemic concerned the quality of the organization of the online contents (item vi) and the quality of interaction with teachers (item x). The perceived level of interactivity of online classes (item v) was associated positively with quality of interaction with teachers (item x), quality of interaction with other students (item xi), and had a significant positive association with both the overall appreciation of ERT (item i) and the role of ERT in coping with COVID-19 (item xii).

Interestingly, however, the rate of synchronous vs. asynchronous teaching was not significantly associated with the overall appreciation of the experience. It was instead negatively associated with the amount of interaction in online classes ($\rho = -0.291$, $p < 0.005$), possibly indicating that the synchronous teaching that is typical of ERT was considered more interactive by students than the asynchronous fruition that is more representative of ordinary distance learning (see introduction). Therefore, our results suggest that students' appreciation of ERT was not due to the ratio of synchronous vs asynchronous teaching but was related to the possibility of interacting with teachers and students. The organization of online courses was also positively associated with interaction (Table 5).

Additionally, technological aspects like students' digital competencies (ii) and quality of their Internet connection (iii) were factors positively associated with the overall appreciation (i) and perceived helpfulness (xii) of DL.

4.2 The Need to Reorganize Study Strategies Negatively Influenced Students' Opinion of ERT

We investigated students' need to change their study method in the passage to ERT (item vii) and how it is associated with the other factors of ERT included in the analysis. The need to change the study method was negatively associated with the rate of appreciation of ERT (i) but did not significantly impact the perceived usefulness of the latter in helping to deal with COVID-19 (xii). Interestingly, however, this item had a significant positive association with missing learning in the presence (item viii) and missing collaboration with students (item ix). These findings could indicate that the need to change the study strategy was perceived as a negative factor by students, possibly because they suddenly could not rely on the ordinary support dynamics that characterize ordinary presence learning. However, this item was also negatively associated with the organization of content on online courses (item vi) therefore suggesting that quality and ease of access of content in university online platforms could reduce the students' need to reorganize their study habits.

Overall, these results indicate that University students interviewed valued quite highly distance learning, at least in part as it allowed them to cope with the stressful situation of the pandemic. Whereas the need to change study habits negatively influenced their appreciation of ERT, it did not affect its coping effect. ERT was especially effective when characterized by good organization of online lessons and interaction with teachers, whereas the synchronous or asynchronous modality of teaching didn't appear to play a significant role in students 'appreciation. In turn, interaction within ERT could possibly act to compensate at least in part the negative feelings linked to the lack of physical interaction with teachers and other students.

4.3 Limitations of the Current Study and Future Directions

The cohort of survey respondents is composed of students from different Universities and different disciplinary areas and is therefore very heterogeneous in nature. It would have been very interesting to compare more thoroughly the different organization of ERT in different disciplinary areas. However, due to the multi-university nature of this study, it is very difficult to obtain and organize information concerning the organization of teaching and learning in each disciplinary area; at the same time, this would be required for a meaningful data analysis.

Another aspect that limited our analysis is due to the very heterogeneous distribution in the judgement of several items in our survey (Table 4). Naturally, every individual reacted differently to the challenges and stress of the sudden change that was imposed on them by the pandemic. However, a more in-depth characterization of survey respondents 'characteristics is outside the scope of the current study. Further research may help define a more definite framework for the social and cultural context in which ERT took place and give better tools to investigate the issue.

Acknowledgments. The research has been partially supported by Erasmus+ grant 2019-1-ES01-KA203-065558. The authors would like to thank Michele Masini and Tommaso Francesco Piccinno for their valuable contribution to the survey construction.

References

1. Moore, M.G.: Learner autonomy: the second dimension of independent learning. Convergence **5**, 76 (1972)
2. Garrison, D.R.: E-learning in the 21st century: a community of inquiry framework for research and practice, 3rd edn. (2016). https://doi.org/10.4324/9781315667263
3. Eradze, M., Laanpere, M.: Interrelation between pedagogical design and learning interaction patterns in different virtual learning environments. In: Zaphiris, P., Ioannou, A. (eds.) LCT 2014. LNCS, vol. 8524, pp. 23–32. Springer, Cham (2014). https://doi.org/10.1007/978-3-319-07485-6_3
4. Anderson, T.: Modes of interaction in distance education : recent developments and research questions. In: Handbook of Distance Education (2003)
5. Moore, M.G.: Theory of transactional distance. In: Theoretical Principles of Distance Education, pp. 22–38 (1997). https://doi.org/10.2307/3121685

6. Bol, L., Garner, J.K.: Challenges in supporting self-regulation in distance education environments. J. Comput. High. Educ. **23**, 104–123 (2011)
7. Cho, M.-H., Shen, D.: Self-regulation in online learning. Distance Educ. **34**, 290–301 (2013)
8. Garrison, D.R., Akyol, Z.: Toward the development of a metacognition construct for communities of inquiry. Internet High. Educ. **24**, 66–71 (2015)
9. Hodges, C., Moore, S., Lockee, B., Trust, T., Bond, A.: The difference between emergency remote teaching and online learning. Educ. Rev. **27** (2020)
10. Rapanta, C., Botturi, L., Goodyear, P., Guàrdia, L., Koole, M.: Balancing technology, pedagogy and the new normal: post-pandemic challenges for higher education. Postdigit. Sci. Educ. **3**(3), 715–742 (2021). https://doi.org/10.1007/s42438-021-00249-1
11. Bailenson, J.N.: Nonverbal overload: a theoretical argument for the causes of Zoom fatigue. Technol. Mind Behav. **2** (2021)
12. Sweller, J.: Cognitive load theory. In: Psychology of Learning and Motivation, pp. 37–76. Elsevier (2011)
13. Eradze, M., Bardone, E., Dipace, A.: Theorising on Covid-19 educational emergency: magnifying glasses for the field of educational technology. Learn. Media Technol. (2021). https://doi.org/10.1080/17439884.2021.1961802

Managing Students from 23 Different Countries in Distance Learning: The Foundation Course Experience of the University of Pisa

Arianna Biancani, Silvia Bruti, Paola Cappellini(✉), Francesco Marcelloni, Arturo Marzano, Marco Polini, Chiara Roda, and Adio Terranova

University of Pisa, Lungarno Pacinotti 43, Pisa, Italy
cooperations@unipi.it

Abstract. The Foundation Course (FC) is a pre-university program primarily aimed at prospective students coming from countries where the national schooling system does not meet the minimum requirements requested for higher education access in Italy and\or with a not appropriate pre-academic education for the enrollment in an Italian or European University Degree Program. The FC of the University of Pisa, in its fifth edition, up to March 2020 had been always delivered in presence, but in the last year due the COVID-19 emergency it has been moved to online learning mode.

In this paper, we describe the experience of transforming the FC, traditionally an on-campus program, to a distance learning modality, with the management and teaching problems arisen to cope with different time zones, the engagement of very young students, the gap in their basic knowledge, especially in scientific subject and technical problems.

Despite all these issues, the online experience has been positive for several reasons that will be discussed in this paper.

Thus, although online teaching was adopted as an emergency measure, we will certainly take advantage of this mode, along with an on-campus option, even when the pandemic is over, since it will make our FC more flexible and affordable for students.

Keywords: Online teaching · Distance learning · Foundation course · Preparatory course · International curricula

1 Introduction

The University of Pisa, as a centuries-old higher education institution, is a traditional university providing research and teaching activities, both at national and international level, with taught class academic standards approach. In the last year the University

---

This work was partially supported by the Erasmus+ project, in the framework of the "EN-hanced Learning and teaching in International Virtual ENvironments" project (2020-1-IT02-KA226-HE-095637).

G. Casalino et al. (Eds.): HELMeTO 2021, CCIS 1542, pp. 129–140, 2022.
https://doi.org/10.1007/978-3-030-96060-5_10

of Pisa, as most others worldwide Universities, has been forced to manage the effects caused by the COVID-19 emergency and suddenly move to online learning format [1, 2]. The current pandemic has had important repercussions on the higher education sector, pushing the so-called "traditional" universities to face new challenges and grab new opportunities: distance learning has become a crucial part in the educational delivery, in particular in those universities for which internationalization is a strong driving force and it is no longer exclusive to a particular segment in the higher educational systems [3].

In this context, for the University of Pisa the conversion of the Foundation Course, traditionally an on-campus program, to a distance learning modality has been one of the experiences that has mainly put to the test the organizational and teaching skills of the university teachers and staff, by requiring a new management way to run the program. At the same time it has been extremely satisfying in terms of both academic and social training experience.

The Foundation Course is a pre-university program introduced in 2016 at the University of Pisa. It was the first Foundation Course launched in Italy and it is primarily aimed at prospective students coming from countries where the national schooling system does not meet the minimum requirements requested by the current Italian legislation for university access [4]. For the university enrollment, in fact, a secondary school leaving certificate obtained after 12 years of school is normally required. That is why the program is primarily designed for students with a secondary school qualification obtained after 10 or 11 years of school or an American high school diploma without 3 Aps or 1 year of college. The program is also intended to fill the educational gap of students coming from countries whose pre-academic education is not considered appropriate for the enrollment in an Italian or European University Degree Program. The Foundation Course is in its fifth edition and up to March 2020 had been always delivered in presence. We consider this course a success story since the number and quality of enrolled students have grown steadily over the years.

In this paper, we describe the experience of transforming the Foundation Course, traditionally an on-campus program, to a distance learning modality, with the management and teaching problems arisen to cope with different time zones, the engagement of very young students, different educational backgrounds and technical problems, mainly due to unstable and unreliable internet connections.

2 The Context

The Foundation Course of the University of Pisa includes two main study tracks, namely Humanities and Science, and consists of 288 h of lessons taught in English and 320 h of Italian language classes over the whole year of study. It also offers 80 more hours of conversation with Italian native speaking students, in order to help to reach at least a B1 level of Italian knowledge.

Beside these two main study tracks the University of Pisa offers three further study options: 1) for Native Italian Speakers, aimed at Italian native speakers and those who have an excellent Italian language knowledge, but not 12 years of schooling; 2) for candidates with a qualification obtained after 10 years of schooling (96 or 120 Credits

Program); 3) Free Choice Modules, available to students who already have the necessary academic requirements to enroll in an Italian university but want to fill the gap in specific subject.

Generally, most of the students choose the Foundation Course in Science as they are interested in a scientific programme useful to prepare for IMAT (International Medical Admissions Test) or other tests for scientific degree such as Engineering, Computer Science, Math, Physics and so on. Table 1 shows the preferences of the students enrolled in the Foundation Course edition 2020:

Table 1. Study options - Foundation Course edition 2020

Study options	No. students	% of students
FC in Humanities	20	31%
FC in Science	32	50%
FC for Native Italians	4	6%
FC 96 Credits	1	2%
Single Modules	7	11%

The geographical Foundation Course target, in terms of potential candidates, is very wide and goes from countries in South America and the United States, to those in Central Asia (Russia and CIS countries) and Far East, with deep differences in culture, skills and knowledge. In particular, the Foundation Course edition 2020 counts 64 students from 23 different countries with sharp differences in time zone (Fig. 1).

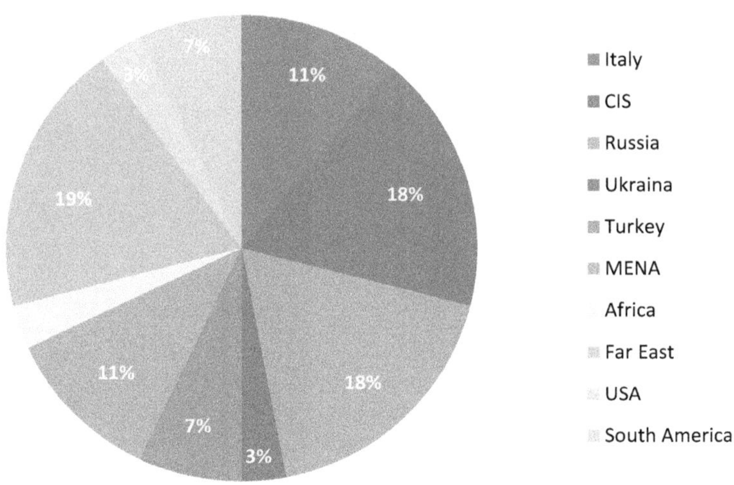

Fig. 1. Foundation Course 2020–2021 students' nationality

In order to overcome the difficulty of coming from very different social and cultural backgrounds, beside traditional classroom lectures, the program also relies on many practical activities, from laboratory exercises to cultural and leisure experiences, such as guided visits to monuments and museums, trips to some of the main Italian cities, organization of social events (e.g. an Italian breakfast morning, one evening in a pizzeria, at the theater and so on) expressly organized in order to encourage the academic and social integration of our very young students (the average age is 18).

The student who successfully completes the Foundation Course will be able to apply for an undergraduate program taught either in Italian or in English.

3 The Transition to Distance Learning: Issues and Solutions

In moving from learning in presence to distance learning we faced several issues. In what follows we list the main issues and the corresponding solutions adopted.

Issue 1: Identify the best time slot for lessons to cope with different time zones without causing too much inconvenience to both students and teachers.

Solution: Considering that it would have been impossible to find a satisfactory time for all the students due to the too many time zones involved, it was chosen a lesson time slot accessible for most students and it was decided to record the lessons to allow the students to watch them whenever they were. At the same time, all students were made aware of the importance of attending live lessons, even if the timetable was uncomfortable, underlining how these courses represented the only means to become familiar with the Italian language, with their classmates and with the teacher.

The final survey done among students highlighted that more than 70% of them had no particular difficulties with the time slots chosen, as shown in Fig. 2. In the survey we used a four-level scale: I strongly disagree, I disagree, I agree and I strongly agree.

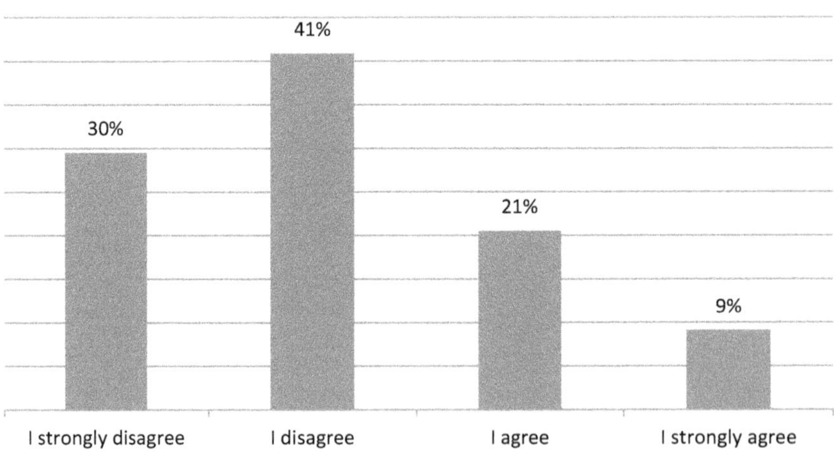

Fig. 2. Final Survey about the Foundation Course 2020: opinions from students about the time slots negative effect on learning

Issue 2: Difficulties in learning Italian, especially online.

Solution: On the basis of the experience gained in previous years, the difficulty in learning the Italian language was clear, especially for students whose language is not neo-Latin and more in general from those who come from not EU countries. This difficulty is also greater when it is not possible to teach in presence and to practice in daily life in Italy. For this reason, before the beginning of the official program, an online very basic Italian course organized through the ICoN platform [5] was delivered in July and August. In particular, absolute beginner students were warmly recommended to attend this preparatory course since it enables them to get acquainted with Italian language and to successfully attend the subsequent A1 class.

The students' comments in the final questionnaire confirmed the difficulty experienced in learning a foreign language outside the social context of the country where the language is spoken and many of them wished to be able to resume studying in a face-to-face mode. About half of the students found Italian classes difficult (Fig. 3), but more than 80% found them useful (Fig. 4).

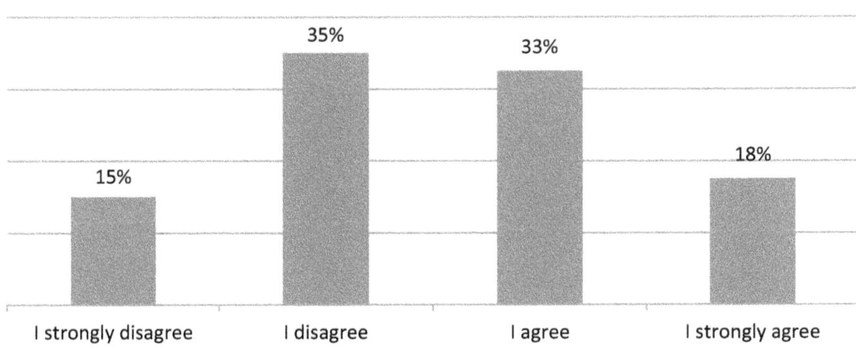

Fig. 3. Final Survey about the Foundation Course 2020: feedback from students about the difficulties of Italian classes

Issue 3: Online lessons are usually more difficult to follow than those in presence due to the lack of face-to-face communication between student and lecturer [6] and to contingent situations such as the poor quality of both internet connection and audio. Furthermore, online lessons can inhibit feedback and interaction, as they often do not encourage the creation of a bond of mutual trust and confidence between lecturer and learner.

Solution: We decided to increase the reception time lecturers dedicate to their students so as to allow them to recover contents they had not learned because of technical and/or personal issues. This was also instrumental to reduce the distance between students and lecturers, by stimulating mutual esteem and trust.

The final opinion of the students was very gratifying as 73% of them declared to be satisfied with the level of interaction and communication achieved with teachers (Fig. 5).

Issue 4: A good percentage of Foundation Course students turned out to be very shy and introverted, with a kind of passive attitude certainly not oriented to a question-asking

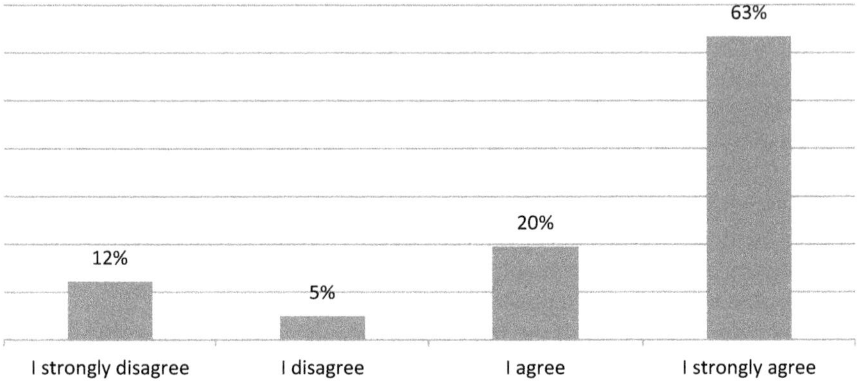

Fig. 4. Final Survey about the Foundation Course 2020: feedback from students about the usefulness of Italian classes

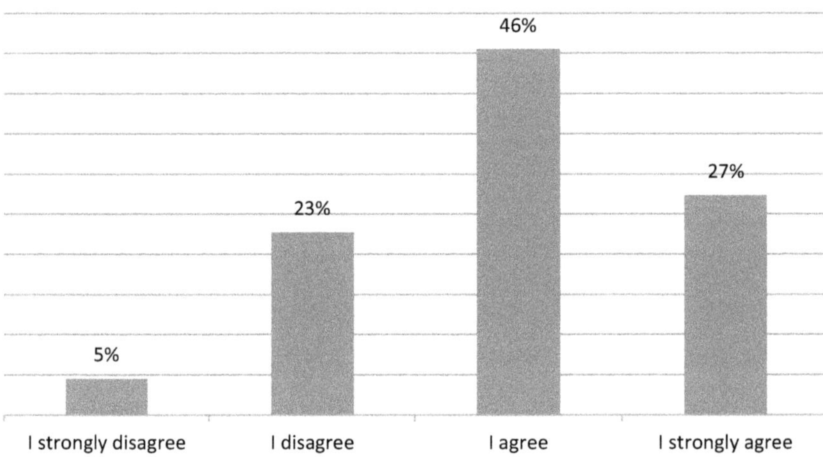

Fig. 5. Final Survey about the Foundation Course 2020: opinions from students about the fruitfulness and effectiveness of interaction and communication with teachers during distance learning

behavior. Besides the online teaching mode, this is presumably due not only to their very young age but also to their educational background, which in many cases prevents them from creating a friendly relation with lecturers and suggests instead treating them with deference. The relationship between teacher and students is to be considered a key element that affects students' progress, engagement and motivation [7].

Solution: As already mentioned above, reception time has been increased to help students to open up with their lecturers, thus developing a more confidential relationship with them. Lecturers were also encouraged to create opportunities for informal discussion in contexts outside the official lesson, such as WhatsApp groups or chat rooms, in order to stimulate the creation of a climate of mutual confidence.

As we already stated in the previous point 3, the students' opinion final survey results about the interaction and the communication with teachers during distance learning was quite good as more than 70% of them found it fruitful and effective (Fig. 5).

Issue 5: A recurring problem with students from different educational backgrounds is the gap in their basic knowledge, especially in scientific subjects. In our experience Mathematics has always been the subject causing most difficulties among students. Indeed, our students' preparation in mathematics was often inadequate and prevented them from attending lectures and completing learning activities without difficulties. In the past years it has often happened that students who had passed all the other courses, found themselves at the end of the year with a serious failure in Mathematics, despite the various attempts we made during the years with the organization of make-up exams and assessment tests.

Solution: Especially in an online context, it is crucial for a teacher to be able to teach to a homogeneous group. To the purpose, we tested the students' initial preparation and designed a Math 0 course for those with most serious gaps to fill, which was taught at the beginning of the program, from September to November, before the annual Math class started.

The results were encouraging as more than 80% of the students found Math 0 course useful (Fig. 6) and declared that it helped them to fill the gaps s they felt to have. Several students left a "thank you" comment for the lecturers for the way they were helped to deal with this subject, still able to scare many of them.

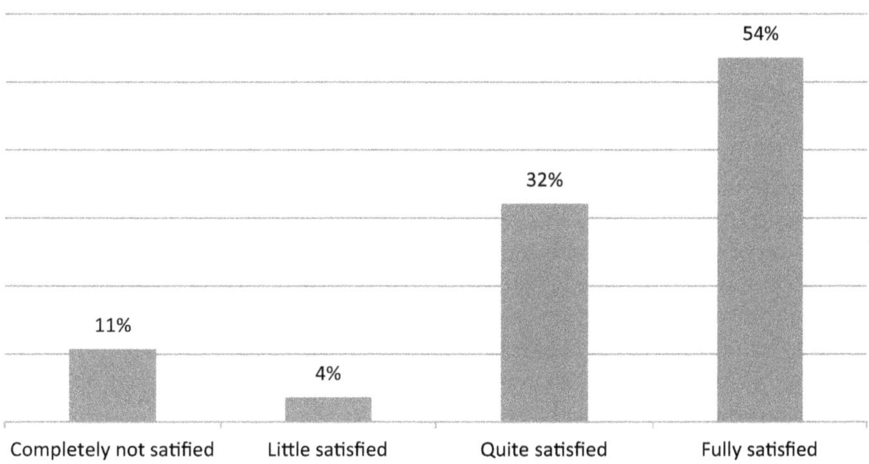

Fig. 6. Final Survey about the Foundation Course 2020: degree of satisfaction from students about Math 0 course

Issue 6: Technical problems, mainly due to unstable and unreliable internet connections, particularly for students from some specific countries, but also problems with microphones and/or video cameras, badly affecting the interaction with lecturers and classmates.

Solution: It is hard to intervene on technical problems. As shown in Fig. 7, a high percentage of students declared that their learning was negatively affected by technical issues. In some cases, it was necessary to deal with situation completely out of control (deriving from the political situation of the student's country such as war) which heavily interfered with the possibility of communication. We tried to partially keep them under control by constantly updating online teaching material and, thanks to our lecturers' willingness to support and help our students, by using other means of communication (i.e., WhatsApp groups and calls).

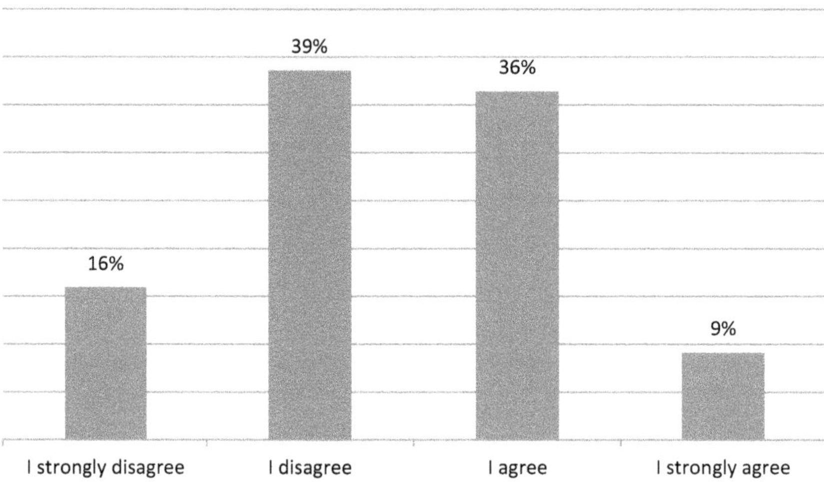

Fig. 7. Final Survey about the Foundation Course 2020: opinions from students about the technical issues negative effect on learning

Issue 7: Individual difficulty in adapting to this new online mode.

Solution: Apart from the more strictly technical aspects and the way in which distance learning was organized and delivered, the individual difficulty in adapting to this new online mode should not be underestimated. Lecturers and administrative and technical staff had to get used to new tools and technologies, and some of them still struggle to become accustomed to them. Students, being digital natives, did not make a great effort to adapt, although they missed an important opportunity for socialization in an academic context that is hard to re-create in online lessons.

The final opinion of the students turned out to be quite positive towards the effectiveness of the interaction and communication developed both with lecturers (Fig. 5) and the administrative staff (Fig. 8).

Issue 8: Online teaching has sacrificed one of the aspects that has always been considered relevant within the Foundation Course program, namely all the cultural and leisure activities provided during on-campus lessons in order to break down cultural boundaries and promote inclusion and socialization among the students, e.g., cultural trips, Italian breakfast and happy hour meetings, eating Pizza together, attending a show at Pisa Theatre.

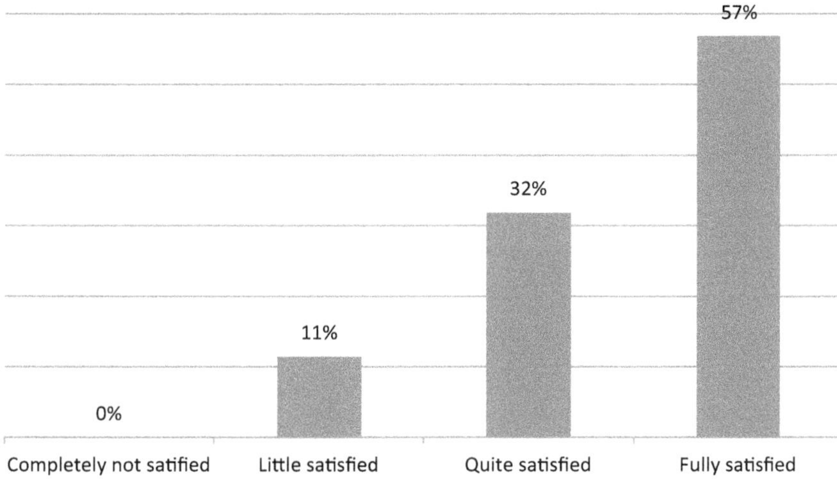

Fig. 8. Final Survey about the Foundation Course 2020: degree of satisfaction from students about the Foundation Course Staff

Solution: In an attempt to compensate this lack, surveys were carried out among the students by asking them to compile ad-hoc questionnaires and to participate in online meetings to identify some of their main interests (cultural, social, political, etc.). A series of themed-seminars and group meetings were organized on the Teams platform to get students to introduce to each other and help them socialize [8]. Students were invited to give small presentations about their home countries using pictures, traditional music, showing films, telling stories that illustrate their customs and habits in order to overcome the cultural gap and to reduce the distance among classmates, and consequently to get them to interact with peers and lecturers. Orientation webinars on the courses offered by the University of Pisa and online meetings with university students' clubs and associations were organized in order to engage students and let them develop a bond with the University and the city.

Final survey about the students' satisfaction showed their appreciation for the efforts made to try to compensate this important aspect through the orientation meetings (nearly 80% in Fig. 9) and through the interaction and communication with teachers (nearly 73% in Fig. 5).

4 Final Remarks

Despite all the issues mentioned above and the difficulties due to the rapidity of the switch and therefore to the lack of a adequate plan necessary to intervene and face this exceptional and unprecedented circumstance, the online experience has been positive.

At the end of the second semester, with one more make-up exam session scheduled in September, the vast majority of the students successfully completed the Foundation Course (respectively 80% in Humanities, 73% in Science and 75% Native Italian, as shown in Table 2). The percentage of student drop-outs was very small, mainly due to

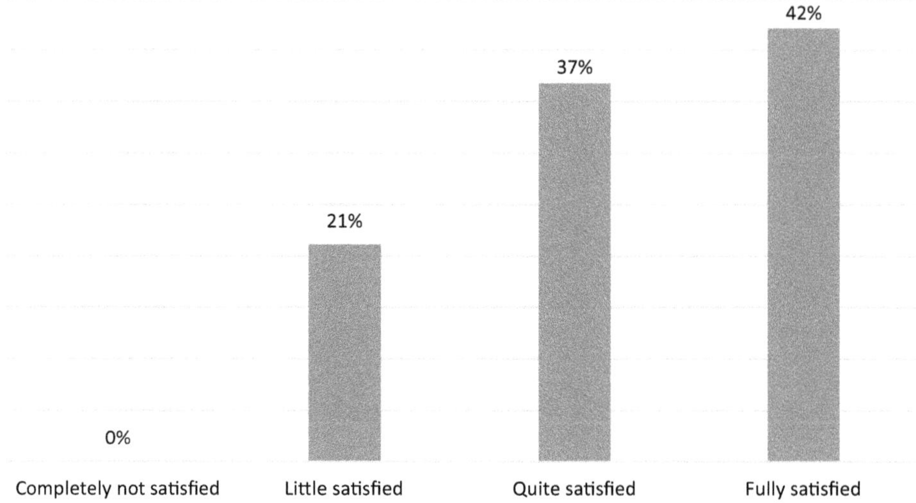

Fig. 9. Final Survey about the Foundation Course 2020: degree of satisfaction from students about the Orientation meetings

the lack of personal motivation and in a couple of cases to personal reasons (family issues and illness).

Table 2. Foundation Course edition 2020 – Final results (updated to July 2021)

Study options	Graduated July 2021	Dropped out
FC in Humanities	80%	5%
FC in Science	73%	6%
FC for Native Italians	75%	–
FC 96 Credits	In progress	–
Single Modules	100%	–

Concerning the Italian language level achieved, at the end of July, 64% of the students reached the minimum level necessary to enroll in an Italian bachelor Degree[1] (Table 3). This quota does not represent the final outcome since students who did not reach the required minimum level will have the possibility to reach it through a make-up exam up to December 2021.

The final survey carried out with questionnaires to evaluate the students' satisfaction level highlighted that 80% of them (Fig. 10) were satisfied with the online classes experience, feeling engaged during the learning process.

[1] According to the MUR Procedures for the entry, stay and enrolment of students applying for visas, no EU students need at least a B1 level of Italian knowledge for enrolling at an Italian bachelor degree.

Table 3. Foundation Course edition 2020 – Italian Language (updated at the end of July 2021)

Italian Language level achieved	July 2021
B2 level	16%
B1 level	48%
A2 level	22%
A1 level	14%

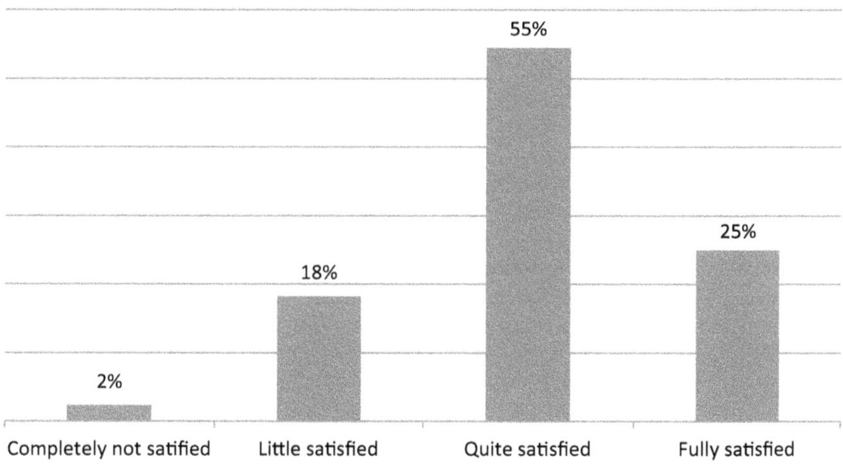

Fig. 10. Final Survey about the Foundation Course 2020: degree of satisfaction from students about the online classes experience

In several comments students praised the way in which the COVID-19 emergency was faced, in particular the ability to switch so swiftly to online and the quality of the contents of the lessons (eg. "not only were the lessons interesting, teachers were able to explain concepts in a way that was easy to understand"). In some cases, students also declared to appreciate having lessons online, because they were working full-time and this gave them the opportunity to be able to keep pace with the lesson.

5 Conclusions

In this paper, we have presented our experience in switching our Foundation course with students coming from 23 different countries from in face-to-face to online teaching.

We highlighted the issues we faced and the solutions we adopted. The survey submitted to the students to assess their satisfaction with the Foundation Course showed that these solutions were adequate and that the students were satisfied.

Online learning also opened up new opportunities. The average number of students of the past editions was 20–25 students per year. In the online 2020 edition the number increased to 64. In fact, the online mode is convenient for international students for several reasons: first of all, there are no problems related to travel restrictions and to Visa procedures. In fact, asking for a Visa very often results in rejections, so students are prevented from participating in the program. This issue is even more crucial for underage students, since they need to find a legal guardian, a requirement that has often been a significant obstacle for them. Instead, by attending a whole year online, they have time to become legally of age and to later come to Italy.

Furthermore, home learning reduces costs for students and their families, which makes it possible for low-income students to choose the program and to continue to study in Italy afterwards.

In conclusion, although online teaching was adopted as an emergency measure, we will certainly take advantage of this mode, along with an on-campus option, even when the pandemic is over, since it will make our Foundation Course more flexible and affordable for students.

References

1. García-Morales, V.J., Garrido-Moreno, A., Martín-Rojas, R.: The transformation of higher education after the COVID disruption: emerging challenges in an online learning scenario. Front. Psychol. **12**(2), 616059 (2021)
2. Chakraborty, P., Mittal, P., Sheel Gupta, M., Yadav, S., Arora, A.: Opinion of students on online education during the COVID-19 pandemic. Hum. Behav. Emerg. Technol. **3**(3), 357–365 (2021)
3. Bergan, S., Gallagher, T., Harkavy, I., Munck, R., Van't Land, H.: Higher education's response to the Covid-19 pandemic: building a more sustainable and democratic future. In: Council of Europe, Higher Education Series No. 25 (2021)
4. MUR: Procedures for the entry, stay and enrolment of students applying for visas (2020). https://www.studiare-in-italia.it/studentistranieri/
5. ICoN: Italian culture on the net (ICoN) (2021). http://www.italicon.education/
6. Hill, K., Fitzgerald, R.: Student perspectives of the impact of covid-19 on learning. All Ireland J. High. Educ. **12**(2), 1–9 (2020)
7. Khan, A., Egbue, O., Palkie, B., Madden, J.: Active learning: engaging students to maximize learning in an online course. Electron. J. E-Learn. **15**(2), 107–115 (2017)
8. Poll, K., Widen, J., Weller, S.: Six instructional best practices for online engagement and retention. J. Online Doct. Educ. **1**(1), 56–72 (2014)

Challenges and Solutions in Teaching Practicum During COVID-19 Pandemic

Natalya N. Kalatskaya(✉) and Liliia A. Latypova

Kazan Federal University, 18 Kremlevskaya, 420008 Kazan, Russia
kalazkay@mail.ru

Abstract. In 2020, due to objective reasons related to the COVID-19 pandemic, universities faced the problem of adjusting the entire educational process. Apart from the introduction of distance learning, there appeared the challenge of organizing the teaching practicum online.

This paper aims to provide a critical insight into teacher education in Russia during coronavirus pandemic; to identify and highlight challenges and solutions to organizing the practicum of student teachers during the pandemic lockdown (the case of Kazan Federal University). The following research questions were posed: (1) What organizational solutions need to be offered to transfer students to the remote format of conducting their practicum? (2) What individual assignments can be offered to students in on-line format of practicum? (3) How effective is this format of practicum? (4) What difficulties do teachers and students face during on-line practicum?

The main data sources are two questionnaires for teachers and students. 82 student teachers and 23 professors of the Institute of Psychology and Education (Kazan Federal University) completed the questionnaires. These professors organized the teaching practicum online during the lockdown. The qualitative analysis that followed helped to reveal the challenges as well as the positive points they learned from the on-line practicum format and allowed to evaluate the effectiveness of distance format.

Keywords: Distance learning · Practice · Students · Pandemic · Russia

1 Introduction

1.1 Relevance of the Problem

The COVID-19 pandemic became a serious challenge for the entire world community in 2020. In the context of the threat of coronavirus infection spread, there was a resolution of the Ministry of Science and Higher Education of the Russian Federation to transfer the educational process of most universities and colleges to distance learning format from March 16, 2020. Distance learning allowed students to stay at home and continue their studies [1]. The Ministry explained this measure was aimed at protecting the health of students and employees of educational and scientific organizations [2]. Such a sudden transition to distance learning was a forced and emergency measure. Not all universities

G. Casalino et al. (Eds.): HELMeTO 2021, CCIS 1542, pp. 141–155, 2022.
https://doi.org/10.1007/978-3-030-96060-5_11

were ready for this cardinal restructuring of the educational process due to different levels of information infrastructure development, the lack of electronic educational resources and reluctance of teachers to use digital platforms and services in the educational process.

The analysis of the relevant literature showed that for the period of the pandemic there were no articles and guidelines for the organization of the learning process and practicum of students in the remote format. The first publications on the problem appeared only in the summer of 2020 [3–9]. The range of scholarly interests was extremely wide. Some scientists enthusiastically discussed the problems of the remote education format in the university and its influence on the quality of higher education as a whole. Other articles were devoted to the study of the positive and negative effects of distance education on students' health [10].

The introduction of various educational technologies, educational services in the educational process and the exchange of experience are presented in the variety of papers [11–15]. There is a number of papers devoted to teacher education in times of COVID-19 in different countries [11, 16–19]. Comparative studies of distance learning organization experience during the lockdown are presented in some works [20–23]. Such scientists raise the problems of social inequality, as well as the effects of distance education on the various areas of human life, including the economy [24–26]. Meanwhile only a few articles highlight the issues of organizing student practicum during the pandemic [27–29].

1.2 Practicum of Future Educational Psychologists in the Russian Federation Before Pandemic

In order to understand changes in the organization of practicum in Russia during the pandemic, it is crucial to disclose its conceptual provisions. The Federal Law of December 29, 2012 No. 273-Federal Law "On Education in the Russian Federation" [30] determines the practicum as "a type of educational activity aimed at formation, consolidation, development of practical skills and competences in the process of performing certain types of work related to future professional engagement". Practicum is carried out by educational institutions through contracts with relevant organizations whose activities meet the educational program implemented. It can also be completed at the university.

The Ministry of Science and Higher Education approved the provision on the practicum of students [31] studying the main professional educational programs of higher education at all levels, of all types, forms and ways. The provision determines the procedure of organizing and conducting students' practicum (as of 11/27/2015 No. 1383). There are three main types of practicum that correspond to a certain stage of mastering the main professional educational program in ascending order: practical training, which is carried out in order to obtain primary professional skills; work experience internship, organized in order to obtain professional skills and professional experience; and pre-service practicum, which is an integral part of the practical training and is carried out if the Federal State Educational Standard provides for the presentation of the graduation thesis. As for the type of practicum, there are research, teaching, technological and other types. Each Federal State Educational Standard provides for its own types of practicum. Currently, the network of educational institutions that train psychologists is extremely diverse, for example, an educational psychologist, a clinical psychologist, a psychology teacher, a counselor psychologist, etc. The content of the practicum of future psychologists in the field of education, as a rule, is developed in accordance with the main areas of work of educational psychologists: psychological counseling, psychocorrection, psychoprophylaxis, psychotherapy, organizational and methodological work, teaching and scientific research.

The specificity of psychologists' work is that they always have to deal with a living being: they change and transform a person. Therefore, the training of a student, as a future specialist, must be carried out only in close contact with the pupil. The practicum of future educational psychologists is carried out in various educational institutions (schools, rehabilitation centers, orphanages, etc.) where this position is offered.

According to Farrakhova [32], Ledovskaya [33], Kalatskaya [34], the content of the practicum of psychology students involves implementation of the following tasks: (1) acquaintance with the psychologist's office, its assessment (assessment of the school psychologist's office, approximate material support for the psychologist's workplace), (2) analysis of a psychologist's work areas and their duration (the approximate duration of various types of work of a psychologist), (3) attending psychology, psychological development, human studies or other classes to get acquainted with the forms and methods of work of a psychologist; taking notes of all attended classes, (4) conducting a psychological analysis of 2–3 classes attended (according to the proposed scheme), (5) observation of general psychological patterns, age characteristics of cognitive processes and pupils' abilities, (6) psychological analysis of pupils' age characteristics in the organization of the lesson and educational activities in general, (7) conducting psychological and pedagogical diagnostics: a) assessment of cognitive processes development level according to the methods proposed by the school psychologist or the supervising teacher, b) a study of the personal characteristics of schoolchildren (psychological analysis of the results obtained; observation of pupils and analysis of psychological observation results with conclusions and recommendations; psychological analysis of the pupils using the results of sociometric survey, referentometry; assistance to the school psychologist and teacher in carrying out psycho-prophylactic work; preparation and conducting extracurricular activities of a psychological profile; conducting credit lessons in psychology), (8) preparation of visual aids, psycho-diagnostic techniques and other tools for the work of a psychologist (on request), (9) observation and analysis of individual consultations, (10) observation and analysis of individual corrective work with a client, (11) observation and analysis of group correctional work, (12) development of a correctional or developmental program (for a specific case of treatment), (13) participation in trainings, (14) observation and analysis of the work and classes of the teacher-psychologist, (15) observation and analysis of the counseling conversation between the teacher-psychologist and the parents, (16) work on a psychological and pedagogical problem to prepare for the graduation thesis.

Supervising teachers from the university are constantly looking for new forms, methods of organizing students' practicum [35].

This paper aims to provide a critical insight into teacher education in Russia during COVID-19 pandemic; to identify and highlight challenges and solutions of organizing the practicum of student teachers during the pandemic lockdown (the case of Kazan Federal University). The following research questions were posed. (RQ1) What organizational solutions need to be offered to transfer students to the remote format of conducting their practicum? (RQ2) What individual assignments can be offered to students with this format of practicum? (RQ3) How effective is this format of practicum? (RQ4) What difficulties do teachers and students face during on-line practicum?

2 Materials and Methods

Research methods include analysis and synthesis of the regulatory, legislative, instructional and teaching papers and materials on management and procedure studies on teacher education during and after lockdown in Russia as well as study and generalization of remote teaching experience. As an illustrative example, we discuss the Kazan Federal University case of teacher education during pandemic and post-pandemic period.

To study the opinion of the students completing their practicum on-line and professors, the organizers of the practicum, we conducted a questionnaire. The survey was created by means of Google forms. The survey was conducted on June 2020. Two questionnaires were drawn up, both for students and teachers.

The questionnaire for students contained 9 questions (Table 1).

Table 1. The questionnaire for students.

Questions	Question type	Research questions
1. I believe that the practicum on-line…	Semi-closed	RQ3
2. Evaluate how the individual tasks you performed during your practicum meet the requirements of training specialists according to your major?	Semi-closed	RQ2
3. How much of the individual assignments were you able to complete?	Semi-closed	RQ2
4. What, do you think, should be changed (improved) in organizing students' practicum on-line?	Open-ended	RQ1
5. What difficulties did you encounter during the practicum on-line?	Open-ended	RQ4
6. What are the positive aspects of conducting the practicum on-line?	Semi-closed	RQ3
7. Evaluate the level of assistance during the practicum by the supervising teacher	Closed type	RQ1
8. Assess the degree of your workload during the practicum	Semi-closed	RQ4
9. Conduct a self-assessment of the competencies you acquired during the practicum on-line	Open-ended	RQ1

The questionnaire for teachers contained 6 questions (Table 2).

Table 2. The questionnaire for teachers

Questions	Question type	Research questions
1. I believe that the on-line format of conducting the practicum…	Semi-closed	RQ3
2. What are the positive aspects of conducting the practicum on-line?	Semi-closed	RQ3
3. What difficulties did you face during the period of organizing the practicum in the remote format?	Semi-closed	RQ4
4. Assess the degree of your workload during the organization of the practicum…	Semi-closed	RQ4
5. I think that the on-line format of the practicum…	Semi-closed	RQ3
6. What interesting methodological solutions in organizing students' practicum in a distance format have you proposed and implemented?	Open	RQ2

The analysis of the survey results involved calculating the distribution of respondents' answers to closed-type questions (forming distribution series, calculating percentages), as well as grouping answers according to the most important features for open-ended and semi-closed questions (calculating percentages). The visualization of the responses involved the construction of histograms. The summary, processing and analysis of data were carried out using a computer program Excel.

The survey sample included students and professors of Kazan Federal University (Russia): 82 student teachers (45 s-year, 21 third-year and 16 fourth-year students, all having experience of completing practicum in the traditional off-line format) and 23 professors representing 5 departments of the Institute of Psychology and Education and those carrying out the organization of the practicum of students - future educational psychologists.

3 Results

3.1 Findings of the First Research Question. Organizational Solutions Need to be Offered to Transfer Students to the Remote Format of Conducting Their Practicum

The first and foremost priority to be solved by Kazan Federal University (KFU) in March 2020 was the adjustment of the entire educational process. After a week's break, the university leadership decided not to stop the educational process at the university and immediately transferred it to a remote format using distance learning technologies and e-learning. For online classes, discussions, group and individual counseling, teachers used various tools like Skype or the Microsoft 365 team space - Microsoft Teams.

Subsequently, the preference was given to the latter, since the office suite of Microsoft 365 applications was purchased by the university, was free for students and teachers and was also supported by the technical services of the university.

The biggest issue on the agenda was the organization of practical training and work experience internship of future teachers and psychologists in the field of education. On the one hand, it was required to ensure the high level of professional training, but on the other hand, it was complicated to organize practicum as there was no access for students to educational institutions due to lockdown and it was impossible to come into direct contact and communicate with children, since pupils studied on the ZOOM platform, whereas KFU students used Microsoft Teams or other platforms. The third problem was the paperwork. There was no experience in organizing the practicum in a remote format; therefore, it was unfeasible to draw up an agreement for the implementation of practical training between the university and an educational institution in a distant format and to sign it during the lockdown period.

3.2 Findings of the Second Research Question. Individual Assignments Offered to Students with this Format of Practice

As of March 16, 2020, at the department of pedagogy of the Institute of Psychology and Education, students of the two groups had already been completing practical training for two months on the practicum sites, according to the signed agreements on practical training. Students received assignments developed according to the program of the practicum. The rest of the students were just getting ready for their practicum. Therefore, the supervising teachers of the students' practicum had to urgently adjust the content and form of the practicum within a week. If the practicum had to be completed in specialized organizations, then the department of pedagogy of the Institute of Psychology and Education was approved as the practicum site.

In addition, the individual assignments for students had to be changed or some corrections had to be made in their wording. The change in the format of assignments was associated with a number of difficulties in resolving such contradictions as "the impossibility of conducting and analyzing the 'real' lessons of teachers", "the impossibility of conducting extracurricular activities, trainings, consultations in the traditional off-line format" and "the impossibility of attending educational institutions, since everyone was quarantined".

Regarding the content of assignments, teachers had to: (1) supplement assignments with electronic resources: classes, master classes presented on the Internet, interactive excursions, links to organizations' websites, (2) revise the very content of the assignments. For example, in the tasks for organizing the activities of children, we were forced to limit ourselves to developing a roadmap for this activity; in the task of studying the duties of the educational psychologist, students were offered to make an analysis of the text of the professional standard and job descriptions, etc., (3) change the wording of the tasks. For example, "on the basis of a conversation with the head of an organization or a school psychologist" had to be replaced with "on the basis of the analysis of the site". This entailed additional detailing, algorithmic presentation of the task, as well as the change in the report forms for these tasks.

Such a restructuring of the content of the assignments made it possible to achieve a partial implementation of the competencies, which is confirmed by the results of a survey of teachers and students.

3.3 Findings of the Third Research Question. Effectiveness and Difficulties Teachers and Students Faced in the Course of Distance Practice Format

Student Survey Results. The survey was conducted after the end of the practicum. According to the results of a students' survey, only 17.9% of respondents answering the first question stated that the on-line format of practicum was a good alternative to the practicum of students in the current situation; 46.4% of students believed it could partially replace the full-time format of practicum. The rest answered more dogmatically explaining that the on-line format practicum cannot replace the traditional, face-to-face format.

Answering the second question, 32.1% of students responded that the new individual assignments the students received for their practicum fully met the requirements for training a specialist in their major. 60.7% of respondents answered that assignments met the requirements only partially. This can be explained by the fact that many tasks that need direct contact with children were replaced. Therefore, the discontent of the students is understandable. 7.1% of the students were categorical and stated that the new assignments did not meet the requirements for training a specialist (See Fig. 1).

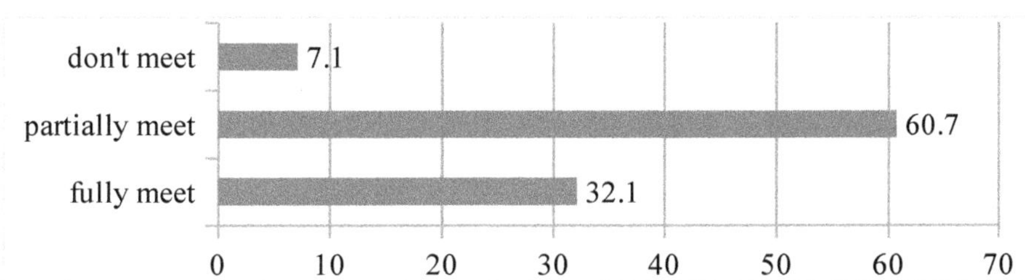

Fig. 1. Students' answers to the question "Evaluate how the individual tasks you performed during your practicum meet the requirements of training specialists according to your major?" (N = 82)

It was significant to find out how feasible the new assignments were. 73.2% of students considered the proposed tasks to be feasible, 23.2% answered that they were partially feasible. Only 3.6% of respondents were categorical in their answer.

It is important to note that 58.9% of students assessed the level of assistance during internship by the supervising teacher as sufficient, 33.9% - as rather sufficient.

The results of the students' answers to the question "What difficulties did you encounter during your practicum on-line?" showed that 33.9% of students did not have any difficulties, 13.9% had technical problems like the poor quality of the Internet, or its disconnection; problems with the headset (microphone, headphones, etc.); no time to pay for mobile communications. Since students were forced to spend a lot of time at the computer, 3.6% of respondents expressed general discontent. In this regard, students' dissatisfaction with the increase in the study load, including the increase in the volume and number of tasks offered, is understandable (for example, some students needed to solve study cases additionally).

10.7% of respondents expressed their dissatisfaction with the organization of the practicum (some did not understand how to complete the assignments; students believed that the teachers did not explain enough, presented incorrect requirements; were unhappy that assignments were changed). This dissatisfaction can be explained by the fact that teachers did not have enough time to develop detailed methodological recommendations for students.

17.9% of students complained about the lack of "live" communication with children, group mates and professors during the practicum on-line. 3.6% believe that the practicum should not take place in a remote format. It was hard to combine the practicum on-line with their work, due to the overlaps in practicum and work schedules. But these difficulties are personal in nature and in no way depend on the organization of the educational process at the university.

Of special interest were students' answers to the question about the positive aspects of participating in the remote format of the practicum (See Fig. 2).

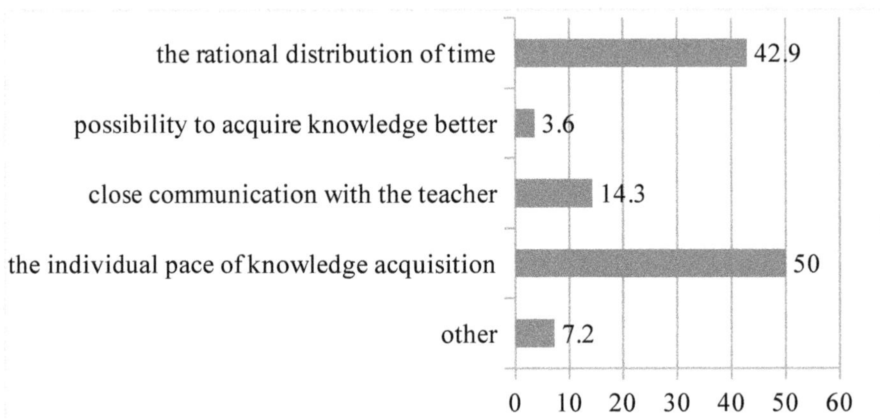

Fig. 2. Students' answers to the question "What are the positive aspects of conducting the practicum on-line?" (N = 82)

Among the open answers, we singled out the following statements (7.2%) - "there are no positive aspects"; "there was an opportunity to be outside the city"; "there was an opportunity to be in a favorable environment (at home, with the family)".

Answering the question "What, in your opinion, needs to be changed (improved) in the organization of practicum on-line?" some students made constructive suggestions. We can say that some of the proposals concerned the organization of practicum in a new format and its methodological support: "It seems to me that in case of the practicum on-line, it is necessary to thoroughly describe the criteria for completing assignments for students", "To formulate assignments more clearly", "Online meetings with specialists of the practicum sites are needed", "Take into account the personal wishes of students, link assignments with the topic of student research", "It was necessary to organize online work with children, school teachers and school psychologists".

There were also such answers like: "Everything possible was done to organize the practicum under the current conditions", "Everything suits me", "Everything that could be done was done", "In general, the practicum was organized well, despite the changed situation, but the problem was only in the lack of live communication, which is difficult to replace with the help of a remote format". It is crucial to note the students' answers to the question "Assess the degree of your workload during the practicum". As students' answers show, slightly more than half of the students (51.8%) began to spend more time on assignments. According to the students, this affected their psychosomatic state and resulted in deterioration of health. At the consultations, students complained of headaches, blurred vision. We believe that the deterioration of students' well-being during the lockdown, the forced transition from the traditional to distance learning, is a separate topic for research [16]. Conducting practicum in a distance format increased the general overload and the amount of time students had to spend at the computer. The rest of the students either did not feel or did not experience overload during the practicum on-line.

The last question in the questionnaire suggested that students conduct a self-assessment of those competencies that had to be mastered during their practicum on a five-point scale, where 5 - competence was completely mastered by me, 1 - competence was mastered at a very low level. The analysis of the received answers of the students showed that those competencies that suggested real contact received low marks (1, 2, 3 points). We will list some of these competencies: Universal Competence (UC) - 3 "the ability to organize and manage the work of a team, developing a team strategy to achieve the goal set", Professional Competence (PC) - 32 "the ability to conduct consultations, professional interviews, trainings to enhance the professional self-determination of students", PC-3 "the ability to organize group and individual activities of children with different types of impaired development in accordance with their age, sensory and intellectual characteristics", etc.

Teachers Survey Results. It was important to learn the experience of supervising teachers who organized the practicum of students in a distance format. 39.1% of teachers stated that the on-line practicum turned out to be a good alternative in the given circumstances, 34.8% noted that this format can partially replace the full-time format of practicum, 21.7% of respondents believed that the distance format cannot replace the full-time format of completing the practicum. Among the open answers, the following can be noted: "Changing the format of practicum is generally possible, but much depends on the major, the direction of training, the program of practicum, the competencies mastered, etc." "It depends on what practicum it is: the research practicum can be carried out, other types of practicum cannot be completed on-line". Most of the teachers (60.9%) noted the positive aspect of the distance format – the possibility to take into account the individual pace of knowledge acquisition in particular. 39.1% of the teachers considered the rational distribution of students' time as the benefit of on-line format. Among the answers to the open-ended question, the following answers can be distinguished: "I consider the remote format to be the only alternative for students' practicum in the given situation";

"I don't find positive aspects in the remote format of the practicum"; "There was no need to waste time on the way to the university"; "It saved time and money".

Here are the results of teachers' answers to the question "What difficulties did you encounter during the period of organizing the practicum on-line?" The problem of ensuring the formation of all competencies in students during the period of training in a distance format caused great difficulty among teachers (56.5%). 17.4% of teachers found it hard to assess the results of the practicum, 8.7% faced difficulties in getting feedback from students. Among the open-ended responses, the following can be distinguished: "Difficulty in controlling the completion of the reports"; "No difficulty"; "There is no live communication with students; it was difficult to talk with an avatar", "It was psychologically difficult to talk to students through the screen".

Assessment of the degree of teachers' workload during the period of organizing the practicum showed not the best-case scenario. 52.2% of teachers began to spend more time checking individual assignments and reporting documents than before; 39.1% did not feel much of a difference - they spent about the same amount of time as before.

Teachers' forecasts about the impact of on-line practicum on the quality of education are contradictory (See Fig. 3).

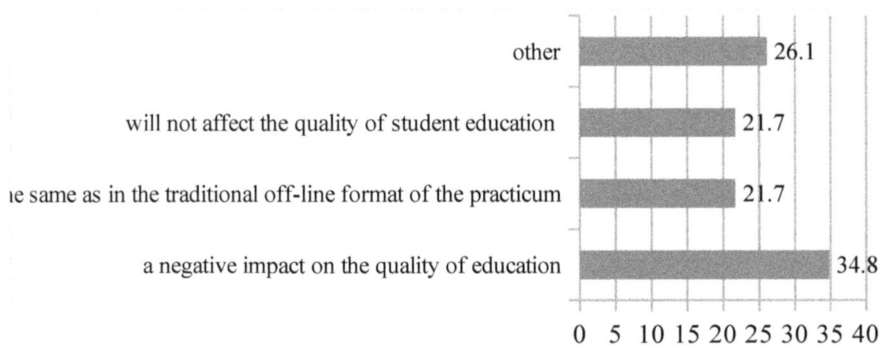

Fig. 3. Teachers' answers to the question «I believe that the on-line format of conducting the practicum ...» (N = 23)

The answers to the open-ended question are of special interest. 26.1% of teachers expressed the following opinions: "Practicum is associated with the development of competencies, and it is very hard to develop them virtually"; "There will be changes, both positive and negative"; "Professional competencies can be formed, but not sufficiently, so it will be necessary to revise the tasks of the practicum programs and the means of assessing the results"; "I will refrain from making forecasts".

The most important and valuable is what was received as a result of the survey of teachers - in our opinion, these are those interesting methodological solutions that teachers were able to find and implement during the period of organizing students' practicum on-line. Below are the examples of tasks selected by the teachers for the period of on-line practicum of students: (1) make a selection of video materials (for example, from 'You tube' resources) with the types of work of educational psychologists: diagnostics of children, conducting correctional, developmental and correctional classes, consultations, trainings, etc., (2) make a selection of videos showing the design of a psychologist's office in educational institutions, the availability of equipment, (3) conduct and record on video the conducted lesson of psychological orientation (training, correctional and developmental lesson, etc.), (4) study regulatory, methodological and other documents; monitor the sites, (5) develop visual materials, assignments for schoolchildren using a variety of programs (Quizlet, etc.) posted on the Microsoft Teams platform, (6) conduct individual and group lessons with groupmates who would play the role of "a student", "a client" in "a virtual group", "video conference" mode on the Microsoft Teams or another platform, (7) prepare an online course "Students' Practicum" in the Moodle system, where teachers posted assignments (case studies, video clips for peer-review, educational films, etc.), (8) conduct an analysis of video lessons, videos with trainings, counseling of practising educational psychologists, (9) develop flow charts and synopses of classes, synopses of trainings, correctional and developmental programs, (10) prepare distance learning materials for the future work of a psychologist with schoolchildren, (11) solve educational cases aimed at processing the results of diagnostics of schoolchildren; carry out statistical processing of the results obtained, (12) carry out diagnostics of schoolchildren using Google forms.

In addition, the teachers noted that the remote format prompted them to use new learning technologies, for example, technologies of level differentiation and problem (heuristic) learning, to apply the methods of Mind mapping (the use of mental maps) and Case-study.

4 Discussion and Conclusions

This article is a tentative attempt to provide a critical analysis of the organization of student teachers' practicum in Russia during the COVID-19 pandemic and highlight the main problems and decisions taken (the case of Kazan Federal University). Similar studies were carried out; however, scholars raised either the issues of organizing only one type of practicum [28, 30, 38], or offered methodological solutions they implemented in organizing the practicum during the lockdown period [28, 36, 38]. It should be noted that while the organization of the educational process in the distance format was, in essence, regulated, then the problem of organizing the practicum of students sustained tense, which is confirmed by other researchers as well [27, 36]. This was especially true of those universities that trained student teachers and psychology students. Finding a solution turned out to be rather challenging, since on the one hand, it was required to ensure the necessary quality of professional training, and on the other, to organize practicum without students' access to the educational institutions and without direct communication with pupils due to lockdown. Besides, it was hard to organize the coordination of the educational process between schools and universities in conditions of uncertainty, when training was carried out on various platforms. To solve the first problem the supervising teachers had to adjust the content and form of the practicum. If the practicum was planned on the basis of specialized organizations, then the Department of Pedagogy of the Institute of Psychology and Education was approved as the official practicum site.

The most serious problem was the adaptation of individual tasks, the fulfillment of which would make it possible to form the necessary competencies. In addition, individual assignments for students had to be changed or some corrections had to be made in their wording. Such a restructuring of the content of the tasks made it possible to achieve a partial implementation of the competencies being formed. The professors of the Institute of Psychology and Education proposed new individual tasks adapted for the distance learning format: compile a selection of videos (for example, from Youtube resources) with the examples of work of educational psychologists: diagnosing children, conducting correctional and developmental classes, consultations, trainings, etc.; conduct and record on video a psychological lesson (training, correctional and developmental lesson, etc.); develop visual materials, assignments for schoolchildren using a variety of programs (Quizlet, etc.) hosted on the Microsoft Teams platform, etc.

A survey of 23 teachers and 82 undergraduate students of 2nd, 3rd and 4th courses revealed the challenges as well as the positive points they learned from the on-line practicum format and allowed to evaluate the effectiveness of distance format. The remote format of the practicum caused an increase in the workload of both students and teachers. Analysis of the answers showed that 51.8% of students began to spend more time completing individual assignments than before. 52.2% of teachers began to spend more time checking individual assignments and reporting documents than they did before. However, it is necessary to consider how to organize work with subjects of education through social networks, unified information platforms and to think over new individual assignments that will be compatible with the remote format of student practicum. This work has already been undertaken by a number of scientists and practitioners [36–38].

The current study confirms the conclusions of Pozdnyakova and Kuleshova [37] that the on-line format of practicum has really a great promising potential. However, the question of a complete transition to distance education is premature. The potential of the traditional format of education will remain in demand due to the unique opportunities that distance education cannot provide. The on-line format of practicum makes it difficult for students to adapt to the real conditions of work in the educational organization due to the lack of "live" contact with students, difficulties in conducting individual and group forms of work with clients. Still there are some researches that indicating the possibilities of using smartphones and exergame controllers for carrying out the interactive learning activities of an online sport and exercise sciences university program [39]. The implementation of blended approach will significantly increase the efficiency of the educational process in the education system in general, and especially in the higher education system during a pandemic and other force majeure circumstances.

Acknowledgements. This paper has been supported by the Kazan Federal University Strategic Academic Leadership Program.

References

1. Ministry of Science and Higher Education of the Russian Federation recommended that universities switch to distance learning [Electronic resource]. RBK: daily internet edition, 15 March 2020. https://www.rbc.ru/society/15/03/2020/5e6e5e109a794717a5e86d27. Accessed 22 July 2021
2. Ministry of Science and Higher Education of the Russian Federation. Decree No. 484 (2020, March 25). On measures for implementing the Order of the President of the Russian Federation of March 25, 2020 No. 206 'On Declaring Non-work Days in the Russian Federation' (2020). https://www.minobrnauki.gov.ru/ru/documents/card/?id_4=1120
3. Yakobyuk, L.I.: Study of the impact of distance learning during a pandemic on learning outcomes. World Sci. Cult. Educ. **5**(84), 179–181 (2020)
4. Aucejo, E.M., French, J., Araya, M.P.U., Zafar, B.: The impact of COVID-19 on student experiences and expectations: evidence from a survey. J. Public Econ. **191**, 104271 (2020). https://doi.org/10.3386/w27392
5. Kerres, M.: Against all odds: education in Germany coping with COVID-19. J. Postdigit. Sci. Educ. **2**, 690–694 (2020)
6. Akimenko, G.V., Seledtsov, A.M., Kirina, Yu.Yu., Nacheva, L.V. Higher education in the era of COVID-19. In: Science, Society, Culture: Problems and Prospects of Interaction in the Modern World: Monograph, pp. 19–31. International Center for Scientific Partnership "New Science", Petrozavodsk (2021)
7. Gafurov, I.R., Ibragimov, G.I., Kalimullin, A.M., Alishev, T.B.: Transformation of education in higher education during a pandemic: pain points. J. High. Educ. Russia **10**, 101–112 (2020)
8. Carrillo, C., Flores, M.A.: COVID-19 and teacher education: a literature review of online teaching and learning practices. Eur. J. Teach. Educ. **43**(4), 466–487 (2020)
9. Flores, M.A., Swennen, A.: The COVID-19 pandemic and its effects on teacher education. Eur. J. Teach. Educ. **43**(4), 453–456 (2020)
10. Zinchenko, Y.P., et al.: The spread of COVID-19 in Russia: immediate impact on mental health of university students. Psychol. Stud. **66**(3), 291–302 (2021). https://doi.org/10.1007/s12646-021-00610-1
11. Zhang, W., Wang, Y., Yang, L., Wang, C.: Suspending classes without stopping learning: China's education emergency management policy in the COVID-19 outbreak. J. Risk Financ. Manag. **13**(3), 55 (2020). https://doi.org/10.3390/jrfm13030055
12. Burns, R.: A COVID-19 panacea in digital technologies? Challenges for democracy and higher education. J. Dialogues Hum. Geogr. **10**(2), 246–249 (2020)
13. Pham, H.-H.: Ho Tien-Thi-Hanh Toward a «new normal» with e-learning in Vietnamese Higher education during the post COVID-19 pandemic. J. High. Educ. Res. Dev. **39**(7), 1327–1331 (2020)
14. Kozyreva, O.N., Olkhova, L.A.: Features of the use of distance learning in a pandemic. In: Society, Pedagogy, Psychology: A Collection of Materials, pp. 37–41. Publishing House "Sreda", Cheboksary (2020)
15. Kathpalia, S.S., Kiat, S.E., Tom, K.M.: A blended scientific communication course for undergraduate students: addressing the challenges posed by the COVID-19 Pandemic. J. ESP Today **8**(2), 182–205 (2020)
16. Flores, M.A., Gago, M.: Teacher education in times of COVID-19 pandemic in Portugal: national, institutional and pedagogical responses. J. Educ. Teach. **46**(1), 1–10 (2020)
17. Kidd, W., Murray, J.: The Covid-19 pandemic and its effects on teacher education in England: how teacher educators moved practicum learning online. Eur. J. Teach. Educ. **43**(4), 542–558 (2020)

18. Nasri, N.M., Husnin, H., Mahmud, S.N.D., Halim, L.: Mitigating the COVID-19 pandemic: a snapshot from Malaysia into the coping strategies for pre-service teachers' education. J. Educ. Teach. **46**, 546–553 (2020)
19. Quezada, R.L., Talbot, C., Quezada-Parker, K.B.: From bricks and mortar to remote teaching: a teacher education programme's response to COVID-19. J. Educ. Teach. **46**(4), 472–483 (2020)
20. Galazhinsky, E.: World higher education: pandemic paradoxes. http://www.tsu.ru/university/rector_page/mirovoe-vysshee-obrazovanie-paradoksy-pandemii/. Accessed 1 Apr 2021
21. Melnik, D.: Higher education in the world: problems highlighted by the pandemic. https://tass.ru/opinions/8306213. Accessed 1 July 2021
22. Marinoni, G.: A severe risk of growing inequality between universities. https://www.universityworldnews.com/post.php?story=20200608154051140. Accessed 05 July 2021
23. Kozhevina, O.V.: New higher education: harmonizing online and offline formats in the face of global challenges. Soc. Secur. Insights **3**(4), 133–140 (2020). https://doi.org/10.14258/ssi(2020)4-10
24. Tishchenko, A.S.: The impact of the pandemic on the economy of education. Econ. Dev. Russia **27**(5), 90–97 (2020)
25. Omelchenko, E.: Education of children from families of international migrants in a pandemic. Ethnodialogues **3**(61), 54–64 (2020)
26. Shtykhno, D.A., Konstantinova, L.V., Gagiev, N.N.: Transition of universities to remote mode during a pandemic: problems and possible risks. Open Educ. **24**(5), 72–81 (2020). http://dx.doi.org/10.21686/1818-4243-2020-5-72-81
27. Silina-Yasinskaya, T.V.: Practice of students in the context of the COVID-19 pandemic: problems and solutions. In: Samusevich, V.M., et al. (eds.) Journalism - 2020: Status, Problems and Prospects: Proceedings of the International Conference, Minsk, 12–13 November 2020, pp. 186–189. Belarusian State University, BSU, Minsk (2020). https://elib.bsu.by/handle/123456789/252428. Accessed 22 Feb 2021
28. Nichagina, A.V.: Electronic educational resource as a means of organizing the pedagogical practicum of bachelors during the quarantine regime. Bull. Pushkin Leningrad State Univ. **2**, 207–223 (2020)
29. Azizova, I.: After School provision on-line as a new form of teaching practicum of students in the transition of schools to remote work (the case of the Herzen state pedagogical university). Sci. Notes Transbaikal State Univ. **16**(2), 82–91 (2021)
30. Federal Law of 29.12.2012 № 273-Federal Law "On Education in the Russian Federation" [Electronic resource] Laws, codes and regulations of the Russian Federation. https://legalacts.ru/doc/273_FZ-ob-obrazovanii/. Accessed 28 July 2021
31. Order of the Ministry of Education and Science of the Russian Federation of November 27, 2015 № 1383 "On approval of the Regulations on the practicum of students mastering the basic professional educational programs of higher education" [Electronic resource] GARANT.RU: daily online edition (2015). https://www.garant.ru/products/ipo/prime/doc/71188178/. Accessed 30 July 2021
32. Farrahova, A.R.: Specifics of psychology students' practicum organization. Bull. Eastern Acad. Econ. Law **1**(39), 102–109 (2009)
33. Ledovskaya, T.V.: Actual problems of educational psychologists' practicum organization. Bull. Donetsk Pedag Inst. **3**, 135–139 (2018)
34. Kalatskaya, N.N., Guryanova, O.A.: Organization of psychological and pedagogical practicum of students in the conditions of modernization of pedagogical education. Educ. Self-Dev. **2**(44), 75–86 (2015)
35. Shirshova, I.A.: Forms of organization and support of student teachers' practicum: generalization of domestic experience. Sci. Notes V.I. Vernadsky Crimean Federal Univ. Sociol. Pedag. Psychol. **1**(67), 64–75 (2015)

36. Solovieva, N.M.: Distance learning technologies in the organization of student teachers' practicum. Teach. XXI Cent. **2–1**, 44–49 (2011)
37. Pozdnyakova, O.K., Kuleshova, E.V.: Experience of organizing student teachers' practicum in the remote format. Samara Sci. Bull. **9**(3), 287–293 (2020). https://doi.org/10.17816/snv202093308
38. Makarova, O.V., Neverovich, G.A., Tsyvareva, M.A.: Tools and methods of organizing primary school teachers' on-line teaching practicum. Pedag. Theory Pract. **6**(2), 318–324 (2021)
39. Picerno, P., Pecori, R., Raviolo, P., Ducange, P.: Smartphones and exergame controllers as BYOD solutions for the e-tivities of an online sport and exercise sciences university program. In: Burgos, D., et al. (eds.) HELMeTO 2019. CCIS, vol. 1091, pp. 217–227. Springer, Cham (2019). https://doi.org/10.1007/978-3-030-31284-8_17

The Use of a Gamified Learning App in Accounting Education: Exploring the Impact of COVID-19

Julian Langenhagen(✉)

Goethe University, Frankfurt, Germany
langenhagen@econ.uni-frankfurt.de

Abstract. In many educational areas, COVID-19 has necessitated a fundamental change in teaching conditions. Students had to immediately adapt themselves and their learning strategy to the new circumstances. This research project offers unique opportunities to investigate the question of what precisely these adaptations looked like. Two semesters before the pandemic started, a gamified learning app was launched in an undergraduate accounting course at a large German university. During the pandemic, the associated course had to be converted from a synchronous face-to-face to an asynchronous online lecture. On the one hand, this work investigates whether the app launch itself had an influence on the learning strategies of the students. On the other hand, it also sheds light on whether the change in teaching had an additional impact on learning strategies, especially on the use of the app. To answer these questions, comprehensive usage data of the app and data from an accompanying survey are examined. The results indicate that both the launch of the app and the changed teaching conditions due to COVID-19 have a distinct impact on students' learning strategies.

Keywords: Learning analytics · Learning strategies · Gamification · COVID-19

1 Introduction

The outbreak of COVID-19 in spring 2020 forced many educators worldwide to instantly adjust their teaching format to the changed circumstances [1]. In many cases, face-to-face courses had to be converted to online-only lectures. Particularly at universities with many students, individual interaction with lecturers was reduced to a minimum. To address this challenge, novel learning tools have been developed and introduced in several settings [2]. However, due to the urgency of implementation, thoughtful concepts were lacking in many cases. Therefore, it is now even more critical to examine the newly developed tools so that they can be adapted if necessary and still be used efficiently after the pandemic [3]. In many cases, the production of the tools required considerable effort and costs. Therefore, those solutions that proved successful during the pandemic should be permanently integrated into post-pandemic teaching [3, 4].

This research project is about a course at a large German public university. Before the pandemic, the undergraduate accounting course was regularly taught face-to-face,

G. Casalino et al. (Eds.): HELMeTO 2021, CCIS 1542, pp. 156–169, 2022.
https://doi.org/10.1007/978-3-030-96060-5_12

with a weekly lecture, a bi-weekly exercise, and bi-weekly tutorials in small groups. In the pandemic, the course was taught with asynchronous online lectures. Prior research suggests that a change in teaching method can have an influence in the student's performance [5, 6]. However, this adaptation was not the only change to the teaching methods in this research project. Two semesters before the switch to online lectures, a gamified learning app was launched for the course.

Education is one of the main application fields of gamification [7, 8], which is commonly defined as "the use of game design elements in non-game contexts" [9]. While there are several studies on the impact of gamification on learning outcomes [10–12], comprehensive studies on the effects of gamified education on learning strategies are scarce [13]. The data basis for the present study contains not only the usage data of the app but also extensive survey data that have been collected since two semesters before the launch of the app. Thus, the present data set covers a total of six semesters. Both the impact of the pandemic and the launch of the app have the potential to result in significant changes to students' behavior and learning strategies. Usually, students are accustomed to a daily learning routine with face-to-face events and corresponding social interaction [14]. Therefore, a switch to online lectures might result in adjusted learning strategies. Online learning has its own strengths and weaknesses compared to traditional face-to-face lectures [15, 16] and prior research suggests that learning strategies can differ substantially in both environments [17–19]. The unique setting will therefore be used to answer the following two research questions:

Research Question 1. Does the introduction of a gamified learning app change the students' learning strategy?

Research Question 2. Does the switch from face-to-face to online lectures due to COVID-19 change the students' learning strategy (and the use of the gamified learning app)?

The chapter continues as follows: Sect. 2 provides a more detailed description of the research setting. In Sect. 3, the results are presented, while Sect. 4 concludes the chapter.

2 Research Setting

2.1 The Lecture: Accounting 1 (BACC)

The study context of this research project is the undergraduate accounting lecture "Accounting 1" (BACC) at a large public university in Germany. The lecture is compulsory and ought to be taken in the third semester of the bachelor's program in business administration and economics. The content of this course includes the basics of cost accounting as well as an overview of their significance and classification in the management accounting context. The course is taken by approximately 600 students per semester and consists of a weekly lecture, a biweekly exercise, and biweekly tutorials (5 meetings in small groups). Lecturing is traditionally done in a face-to-face format with little interaction between students and instructors. Students are encouraged to ask questions during the lecture and to make other verbal contributions. However, due to the size of the group, participation is usually limited. The interaction during the exercises and tutorials is higher, but here, too, the lecturer essentially presents the solutions to the tasks to be discussed. There is no exam-relevant incentive for the students to present solutions themselves. The final exam at the end of the semester is the only assessment. Attending the lecture and the exercise is voluntary.

All before mentioned conditions remained constant in the corona pandemic, with one exception. Lectures, exercises, and tutorials were delivered with asynchronous videos instead of synchronous face-to-face sessions during the two semesters in the pandemic. At this time, students had one week to access each of the lecture videos. All remaining videos (exercise and tutorial) were gradually made available over the course of the semester and were then accessible for the entire semester. In addition, students could reach instructors via chat during specific office hours and via email for the entire semester. However, there were no synchronous live events during the pandemic. The primary learning material consists of a slide deck, a collection of exercises (with solutions), and a trial exam. Moreover, a text book and the associated practice book are recommended by the instructor for a more in-depth study of the lecture content. In the evaluations of past semesters, students often complained that there were no contemporary possibilities to learn the subject matter.

2.2 The App: BaccUp

In response to the previously mentioned student feedback, the responsible chair decided to develop a smartphone app as an additional learning tool. BaccUp, the name of the tool, consists of the abbreviation of the course ("BACC" for basic accounting) and the word "up". "Up" symbolizes the intended development of the learning performance of the students, which should be improved by using the tool (see Fig. 1 for some impressions of the app's design).

The use of BaccUp is voluntary, and no extra credits can be earned by collecting points in the app. The tool is available both via a web version and as an app in the Google Play Store and the Apple App Store. The core element of the app is a database with over 550 questions that cover all nine chapters of the course. The questions are tailored to the subsequent exam by following the exact nine chapters from the lecture so that the students were able to sort the questions well into the other learning materials. In addition to the question types single and multiple-choice, there are also sorting and cloze text tasks.

The app can be used in three different modes: Chapter, Random, and Weekly Challenge. The Chapter Mode can be used to answer specific questions about a single chapter. As soon as a student has mastered the content of one chapter, the next chapter is unlocked. In Random Mode, questions are randomly selected from the chapters that have already been unlocked in chapter mode. In the third mode, the so-called Weekly Challenge, users can compare themselves with other students. Once a week, they have the opportunity to answer 25 questions randomly selected from the chapters already covered in the lecture. The results are subsequently displayed in a weekly and a semester ranking.

For good performances in the Weekly Challenge and other learning achievements (e.g., using the app for several consecutive days), students can earn so-called badges, which are then displayed in their account under their self-chosen username (see Table 1 for an overview of the available badges).

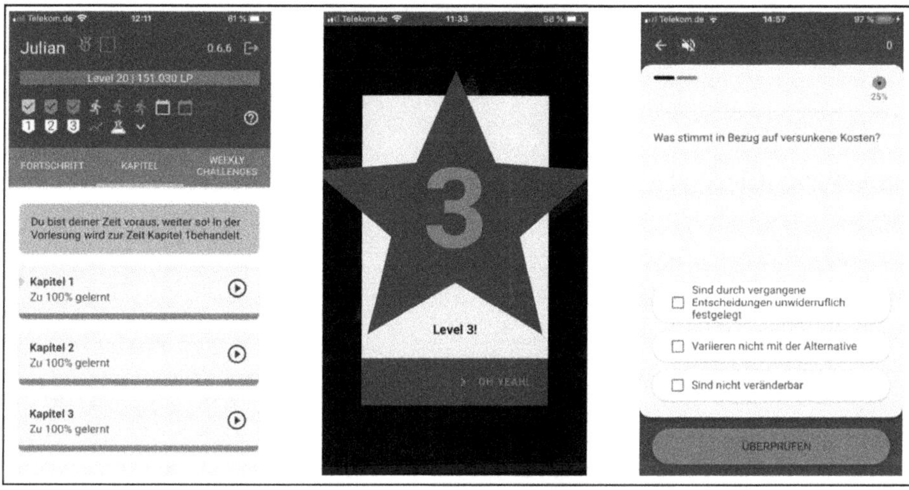

Fig. 1. Screenshots from BaccUp

Table 1. Overview of all available badges in BaccUp

No.	Achievement	Steps	Badge
1	Entered the matriculation number		
2	100% of questions answered in a chapter	1-9	
3	Answered each question correctly once		
4	X consecutive usage days	3, 5, 15	
5	X total answered questions	50, 500, 1000	
6	X perfect weekly challenges	1, 5, 10	

By answering questions (regardless of the mode), students earn learning points and thus increase their learning level. In addition, the progress display of the individual chapters shows students how well they currently master a particular topic. The corresponding progress is measured by the so-called Skill Level Indicator (SLI). If a question is answered correctly, the SLI rises to 100%. This means that the corresponding question will not be displayed again for the time being. However, the SLI decreases over time to indicate that the content of the question might be forgotten. As a result, the question is displayed again over time to check whether its content is still recalled and understood. The app has been specifically designed to complement the existing course and is not intended to replace other learning materials such as the slides or the collection of exercises. The app provides an individual explanation for each question that is displayed if a wrong answer is given. This allows students to work through the catalog of questions regardless of time and place because they do not have to rely on the instructor's availability. The app was launched at the beginning of the summer semester 2019, i.e., two semesters before the teaching style was changed due to the corona pandemic (summer semester 2020).

2.3 Data Sources

The collected data for this research project consists of three different sources: (1) exam scores, (2) usage data of the app users, and (3) survey data (see Table 2).

Table 2. Number of students across semesters

	SS18	WS18	SS19	WS19	SS20	WS20
Exam	590	671	575	648	616	644
App	NA	NA	559	595	447	546
Survey	153	250	127	156	114	167
Teaching	Face-to-face		Face-to-face		Online	

The app data includes details about the usage behavior of each student (e.g., time of use, performance (history) regarding every question, and earned badges). In all four semesters in which the app was available, it could be used in identical form by all students. Therefore, the research setting does not provide a random division in experimental and control groups. In a quasi-experimental setting like this, it is crucial to keep as many parameters as possible constant over time [20, 21]. In the present setting, the lecturer and the learning materials remained constant over all six semesters. Furthermore, the style of the exam was kept constant over all semesters. Since the summer semester 2018, a survey accompanying the lecture has been conducted to capture and compare specific characteristics of the two student cohorts that did not yet have access to the app. Table 3 shows that all six cohorts are very similar regarding basic demographics. The share of female and male students does not differ significantly and the average age, as well as the semester the students are in, are comparable. The survey was divided into four sections: "Time and type of use" (e.g., to which extent the different learning materials were used or where the students typically learn), "Goals" (e.g., which goals were important regarding the course apart from passing the exam), "Satisfaction" (e.g., how satisfied the students were with different parts of the course) and "Other information" (e.g., sex, age, and prior knowledge). In the summer semester 2019, the survey was supplemented with questions on the app (e.g., which elements were exceptionally motivating). The average response rate of the survey is 26%, which is comparable with similar prior studies [22–24].

As of now, the dataset already includes four semesters of app usage and is growing as the research project is still ongoing. According to my knowledge, this is the first study to examine the impact of a gamified mobile learning app on students' learning strategies in a large university course over the duration of several semesters. This research is especially promising as the outbreak of COVID-19 led to an exogenous shock in teaching conditions. The following section first examines app usage data to evaluate whether app usage has changed as a result of the modification of teaching conditions

Table 3. Demographics from the survey samples

	SS18	WS18	SS19	WS19	SS20	WS20
Male	47.17%	47.78%	59.05%	53.70%	47.30%	49.18%
Female	52.83%	52.22%	40.95%	46.30%	52.70%	50.82%
Avg. age	21.84	21.26	21.82	21.10	21.81	21.24
Avg. semester	3.65	3.29	3.73	3.27	3.61	3.41

due to COVID-19. Afterwards, the survey data is analyzed to answer whether the app launch itself has led to changes in students' learning strategies.

3 Results

3.1 App Usage Analysis

Extent of App Usage. The extent of app use can be measured with different key figures, e.g., the total questions answered by a student in a given time. Table 4 shows the total answers per semester as well as the average answers per user. At first glance, there is a clear difference between the summer and winter semesters regarding total answers, indicating that the app was used more in winter terms. However, when looking at the answers per user, the circumstances resulting from COVID-19 also seem to influence the app usage. When the years 2019 and 2020 are pooled together, it becomes clear that the answers per user were significantly higher in the phase with online lectures (484.63 in 2020 vs. 423.38 in 2019, $t = 2.23$, $p = 0.02$).

Table 4. Selected usage data from the app

	SS19	WS19	SS20	WS20
Total answers	196,079	292,503	193,481	287,752
Answers per user	350.77	491.60	432.84	527.02

Temporal Distribution of App Usage. The following analysis examines the temporal distribution of app usage within a given week. During times of face-to-face classes, the lecture took place every Monday from 8 to 10 am and the exercise every two weeks on Tuesdays from 8 to 10 am. Since a smartphone app is likely to be used more while commuting or attending classes, it is reasonable to assume that a focus of usage would be at the beginning of the week, especially around lecture times. Table 5 shows the relative share of answers per weekday in four specific time frames: night (12:00 am to 5:59 am), morning (6:00 am to 11:59 am), afternoon (12:00 pm to 5:59 pm), and evening (6:00 pm to 11:59 pm) for the two semesters in 2019.

Table 5. Share of total answers per weekday and time slot in 2019 (in %)

	Mon.	Tue.	Wed.	Thu.	Fri.	Sat.	Sun.	Total
Night	0.55	0.44	0.36	0.53	0.37	0.18	0.25	2.68
Morning	7.26	6.07	5.45	3.81	4.00	2.85	3.46	32.90
Afternoon	7.63	6.91	6.35	4.72	4.56	4.54	6.23	40.94
Evening	4.64	4.07	3.35	2.71	2.19	2.51	4.02	23.49
Total	20.08	17.49	15.51	11.77	11.12	10.08	13.95	100.00

Table 5 shows that a large proportion of answers were indeed submitted in the corresponding time windows (Monday and Tuesday mornings). Nevertheless, a comparably large proportion can also be observed in the afternoon of these two days and even on Wednesday. The most reasonable explanation for this observation are the two meetings at the beginning of the week. The increase on Sunday could be explained by the fact that students were preparing for the upcoming events in the next two days. However, in the two semesters with online lectures, there were no synchronous sessions with students. The corresponding videos were released at the beginning of the week but could be accessed at any time until the end of the week (lecture) or even until the end of the semester (exercise and tutorials). In this phase, therefore, a focus on use at the beginning of the week is not necessarily to be expected. Table 6 shows the relative proportion of answers per weekday in the four specific time windows for the two semesters in 2020.

Table 6. Share of total answers per weekday and time slot in 2020 (in %)

	Mon.	Tue.	Wed.	Thu.	Fri.	Sat.	Sun.	Total
Night	0.63	0.81	0.80	0.49	0.44	0.46	0.29	3.92
Morning	5.10	4.90	5.60	4.06	3.50	2.97	3.13	29.26
Afternoon	7.02	6.82	6.16	5.18	4.28	4.15	5.98	39.59
Evening	4.24	5.56	4.48	3.15	2.79	2.78	4.22	27.22
Total	17.00	18.09	17.04	12.88	11.01	10.36	13.62	100.00

Table 6 shows, however, that the usage pattern in the semesters with online lectures does not differ substantially from that in the previous semesters. In all four semesters, the focus of the usage is at the beginning of the week, tends to decrease until Saturday, and increases again slightly on Sunday. The pooled data in Table 7 further demonstrates that a general distribution of usage over the week (peak at the beginning, then decreasing until Saturday and increasing again on Sunday) can be identified for all four semesters.

As a result of the app usage analysis, it can be concluded that students use the app more in phases with online lectures. Still, no major differences can be observed in the temporal distribution of usage. The next section examines the survey responses to

Table 7. Share of total answers per weekday (in %)

	Mon.	Tue.	Wed.	Thu.	Fri.	Sat.	Sun.	Total
SS19	19.07	16.17	17.77	12.31	10.88	9.78	14.01	100.00
WS19	20.76	18.37	14.00	11.41	11.28	10.28	13.91	100.00
SS20	17.92	18.74	16.71	12.61	10.19	11.05	12.77	100.00
WS20	16.37	17.65	17.26	13.06	11.57	9.90	14.19	100.00
Total	18.55	17.79	16.27	12.32	11.07	10.22	13.79	100.00

determine if the app launch, as well as the shift to online lectures, had an impact on other student learning activities and corresponding learning strategies.

3.2 Survey Data Analysis

Students' Perception of the App. Table 3 has already shown that the different student cohorts do not have meaningfully different characteristics in terms of demographic data. This result suggests that different personal characteristics of the different groups are rather unlikely as a reason for possible altered learning strategies. Another explanation for alternative learning strategies would be different perceptions of the app. Although no changes were made over the four semesters except for bug fixes, a different perception of the app could be possible, e.g., due to different teaching conditions. Therefore, the following section compares the students' ratings of some essential features of the app across the semesters. Table 13 shows the average scores of the following eleven selected statements from the survey, which could be rated on a 5-point Likert scale from "(1) strongly disagree" to "(5) strongly agree":

1. By using BaccUp, I can better assess my current learning level in BACC than in my other courses.
2. By using BaccUp, I have invested more study time for BACC than for comparable subjects this semester.
3. The app gives me the impression that I have to learn more than in comparable courses without a learning app.
4. For me, the Weekly Challenge was motivating, although no prize was offered.
5. The direct feedback for incorrect answers has helped me in my learning process.
6. The level progress bar has helped me to keep track of my current level of learning.
7. The chapter progress bar helped me to determine my current learning status.
8. I was motivated to complete the collection of badges.
9. By using BaccUp during the semester, I expect to have to invest less time in the learning phase right before the exam.
10. BaccUp is a useful addition to the existing course.
11. I would like a learning app like BaccUp to be used in other courses as well.

Table 8. Average scores of selected statements from the survey

	SS19	WS19	SS20	WS20
1	4.16	4.01	3.97	4.02
2	3.07	3.09	3.07	2.95
3	2.31	2.47	2.24	2.42
4	2.72	2.72	2.61	2.84
5	4.39	4.51	4.43	4.48
6	3.42	3.47	3.57	3.59
7	3.79	3.72	3.82	4.02
8	2.58	2.44	2.63	2.84
9	3.25	3.18	3.13	3.09
10	4.52	4.43	4.25	4.38
11	4.66	4.64	4.57	4.66

The results in Table 8 show that perceptions of the app did not change substantially over the different semesters. All assessments remain at a similar level over time. Statement 1 shows that students are more able to assess their current learning status with the help of the app. The results of statements 2 and 3 indicate that students do not learn more for BACC because they can learn with the app than they do for other subjects in the same semester. Statements 4 to 8 deal with the game elements used in the app. The Weekly Challenge does not seem to be a strong incentive for the students (partly because there is nothing to win). This result also applies to the collection of badges. However, the direct feedback after wrong answers is perceived as very helpful. The level progress bar as well as the chapter progress bar also seem to be beneficial components of the app. Statement 9 suggests that students are unsure if they actually have to study less at the end of the semester by using the app beforehand. Statements 10 and 11, however, clearly show that the app is perceived very positively and that students would like to use similar tools in other courses. In addition, the survey contained one question each on the degree of difficulty and the number of questions. Here, too, the students could rate on a 5-point Likert scale whether the degree of difficulty or the number of questions was "(1) much too low", "(3) exactly right", or "(5) much too high". The result in Table 9 shows that, again, perceptions did not change substantially over time. According to the students, the number of questions was exactly right, but they could well have been a bit more difficult. Since no substantial differences can be identified between the different semester cohorts regarding their perceptions of the app, any possible change in learning strategies over time can most likely be attributed to other factors (such as changes in teaching conditions).

Use of Learning Media. In one of the questions in the survey, the students were asked whether they own certain learning media (PC, laptop, tablet, and smartphone) and use it for learning. They had the choice between "I do not own", "I own" and "I own and use for

Table 9. Students' evaluation of the app's questions

	SS19	WS19	SS20	WS20
Number of questions	3.11	3.14	3.28	3.14
Difficulty of questions	2.77	2.57	2.76	2.68

learning". Table 10 shows the relative shares of the answer "I own and use for learning". The use of the smartphone for learning purposes has risen sharply due to the launch of the app on the one hand but has also declined to a certain degree due to COVID-19 on the other hand. This presumably stems from the fact that the students primarily studied at home in 2020. The slightly increasing rates of other learning media in the last two semesters fit this reasoning.

Table 10. Use of learning media (share of "I own and use for learning" in %)

	SS18	WS18	SS19	WS19	SS20	WS20
PC	16.99	9.60	16.54	12.18	19.30	20.36
Laptop	78.43	80.00	75.59	67.95	78.07	83.23
Tablet	43.14	38.80	41.73	47.44	50.88	51.50
Smartphone	26.80	27.20	64.57	59.62	41.23	47.90

Time Invested in Learning Materials. However, there are further questions in the survey that provide indications of changed learning strategies due to COVID-19 and the introduction of the app. The following question was about the time invested in the specific learning materials. Again, the app is only an addition to the existing learning material and does not offer any new content thematically. Therefore, the question arises whether the introduction of the app resulted in a changed distribution of learning time. In the survey, the students were asked how much time (in minutes per week) they invested in the slide deck, the exercise collection, the text book and the practice book. Table 11 shows that the introduction of the app made students invest less time in the other learning materials, especially in the text book. The results also show a specific effect of the switch to online lectures. In the corresponding semesters, time invested in the slide deck and the exercise collection considerably increased and was even higher than before the introduction of the app.

Share of Learning Time. In the app usage data analysis, we have already seen that the switch to online lectures led to an increase in absolute app usage (and thus learning time). In addition, the app launch also had an impact on absolute learning time with the other learning materials. The question now is whether the app launch or the switch to online lectures has caused a shift in the distribution of learning time between courses. On average, students took about four courses in the given semester the survey was conducted

Table 11. Time invested in learning materials (minutes per week)

	SS18	WS18	SS19	WS19	SS20	WS20
Slide deck	51.18	44.22	39.92	39.13	80.79	75.72
Exercise collection	69.12	55.20	48.54	50.48	75.66	80.12
Text book	22.25	15.66	7.09	9.52	7.11	11.59
Practice book	14.80	10.08	8.39	6.92	7.37	13.47

(see Table 12). This means that if learning time was equally distributed, one quarter of learning time would be spent per course. Whether this was the case for the learning time of BACC was addressed in another question in the survey. In Table 12, we see the results and can see that neither the app launch nor the change in teaching method had a significant impact on the proportionate learning time for BACC. This aligns with the students' evaluation of statements 2 and 3 in Table 8.

Table 12. Number of courses and BACC's share of total learning time

	SS18	WS18	SS19	WS19	SS20	WS20
Number of courses in the given semester	4.50	4.32	4.33	4.39	4.42	4.31
Share of learning time (in %) for BACC	26.27	24.44	24.80	24.23	26.67	25.39

Learning Locations. Another question in the survey asked about the distribution of learning locations (see Table 13). The original idea of the question was to find out if the app launch was making students learn more on the go. The closing of the lecture halls due to COVID-19 added its own dynamic to this question. In the semesters prior to the app launch, students reported learning at home for the most part. Learning on the go accounted for only about two percent. The app launch increased this share slightly to 5.21% (SS19) and 4.17% (WS19). In the semesters during the pandemic, students unsurprisingly reported learning almost exclusively at home. The percentage of learning on the go dropped to 1.02% (SS20) and 1.76% (WS20) during the two semesters, despite the availability of the app.

Performance in Exercise Questions. At the end of the survey, all students could test their current knowledge by answering ten true-or-false questions. For the analysis in Table 14, a correct answer was assigned one point, an incorrect one zero points. The question was intended to test whether the groups that had access to the app were able to score higher than the groups without access to the app at the time of the survey. In the last three semesters, the average score was indeed slightly higher than before. However, the average score of about 8 indicates that the ten test questions were not very challenging for the students.

Table 13. Shares of learning locations (in %)

	SS18	WS18	SS19	WS19	SS20	WS20
Lecture hall	15.87	20.92	22.96	19.93	0.00	0.00
Library	30.46	28.07	26.69	25.98	5.28	7.68
At home	50.19	48.22	44.44	49.74	93.05	90.05
On the go	2.07	1.85	5.21	4.17	1.02	1.76
Other	1.42	0.94	0.69	0.17	0.65	0.50

Table 14. Students' average score in the ten exercise questions

	SS18	WS18	SS19	WS19	SS20	WS20
Average score	8.06	7.97	8.18	8.65	8.78	8.53

4 Conclusion

The analyses in this chapter indicate that both the introduction of a gamified learning app and the switch from face-to-face to online lectures due to COVID-19 can have distinct impacts on the students' learning strategy. By comparing the different cohorts, it was possible to ensure that measured effects could indeed be attributed to the app launch or the change in teaching conditions. It could be shown that the learning app is used considerably more in semesters with online lectures than in semesters with face-to-face lectures. In addition, a temporal focus of use at the beginning of a week could be detected. Lecture and exercise schedules as a presumed explanation for this could not be validated, as similar usage patterns were also shown in semesters without synchronous events. Unsurprisingly, the launch of the app caused a significant increase in smartphone use for learning purposes, which, however, declined slightly again with the switch to online lectures. The introduction of the app was also accompanied by a decrease in the use of the other learning materials. However, in the two semesters during the pandemic, absolute learning time using the other learning materials increased to a new peak level. Nevertheless, the percentage of total learning time spent on BACC was not significantly affected by the app nor by COVID-19. The expectation that students would learn much more on the go due to the availability of the app could not be confirmed. During the pandemic, students unsurprisingly reported learning primarily at home. Overall, the app was perceived as very positive by students. This result can serve as motivation for educators worldwide to develop similar tools. However, it remains an outstanding issue whether students using the app have a greater increase in knowledge at the end of the semester than students who have used the app less or not at all. Evaluations of ten test questions from the survey were used to investigate whether the introduction of the app has led to a measurable increase in understanding the subject matter. No clear result could be found here. Future work on the current research project will therefore investigate in more detail whether the use of the app actually leads to improved performance in the exam.

References

1. Crawford, J., et al.: COVID-19: 20 countries' higher education intra-period digital pedagogy responses. J. Appl. Learn. Teach. **3**, 1–20 (2020)
2. Sangster, A., Stoner, G., Flood, B.: Insights into accounting education in a COVID-19 world. Acc. Educ. **29**, 431–562 (2020)
3. Fogarty, T.J.: Accounting education in the post-COVID world: looking into the mirror of Erised. Acc. Educ. **29**, 563–571 (2020)
4. Calabor, M.S., Mora, A., Moya, S.: The future of "serious games" in accounting education: a Delphi study. J. Account. Educ. **46**, 43–52 (2019)
5. Means, B., Toyama, Y., Murphy, R., Baki, M.: The effectiveness of online and blended learning: a meta-analysis of the empirical literature. Teach. Coll. Rec. **115**, 1–47 (2013)
6. Hurlbut, A.R.: Online vs. traditional learning in teacher education: a comparison of student progress. Am. J. Dist. Educ. **32**, 248–266 (2018)
7. Hamari, J., Koivisto, J., Sarsa, H.: Does gamification work?-a literature review of empirical studies on gamification. In: HICSS, pp. 3025–3034 (2014)
8. Seaborn, K., Fels, D.I.: Gamification in theory and action: a survey. Int. J. Hum. Comput. Stud. **74**, 14–31 (2015)
9. Deterding, S., Dixon, D., Khaled, R., Nacke, L.: From game design elements to gamefulness: defining gamification. In: Proceedings of the 15th International Academic MindTrek Conference: Envisioning Future Media Environments, pp. 9–15. ACM (2011)
10. Sailer, M., Homner, L.: The gamification of learning: a meta-analysis. Educ. Psychol. Rev. **32**(1), 77–112 (2020). https://doi.org/10.1007/s10648-019-09498-w
11. Bai, S., Hew, K.F., Huang, B.: Does gamification improve student learning outcome? Evidence from a meta-analysis and synthesis of qualitative data in educational contexts. Educ. Res. Rev. **30**, 100322 (2020)
12. Huang, R., et al.: The impact of gamification in educational settings on student learning outcomes: a meta-analysis. Educ. Tech. Research Dev. **68**(4), 1875–1901 (2020). https://doi.org/10.1007/s11423-020-09807-z
13. Dichev, C., Dicheva, D.: Gamifying education: what is known, what is believed and what remains uncertain: a critical review. Int. J. Educ. Technol. High. Educ. **14**, 9 (2017)
14. Kővári, E., Bak, G., et al.: University students' online social presence and digital competencies in the COVID-19 virus situation. In: Agrati, L.S., et al. (eds.) HELMeTO 2020. CCIS, vol. 1344, pp. 158–169. Springer, Cham (2021). https://doi.org/10.1007/978-3-030-67435-9_13
15. Adnan, M., Anwar, K.: Online learning amid the COVID-19 pandemic: students' perspectives. J. Pedag. Sociol. Psychol. **2**, 45–51 (2020)
16. Dhawan, S.: Online learning: a panacea in the time of COVID-19 crisis. J. Educ. Technol. Syst. **49**, 5–22 (2020)
17. Clayton, K., Blumberg, F., Auld, D.P.: The relationship between motivation, learning strategies and choice of environment whether traditional or including an online component. Br. J. Edu. Technol. **41**, 349–364 (2010)
18. Broadbent, J.: Comparing online and blended learner's self-regulated learning strategies and academic performance. Internet High. Educ. **33**, 24–32 (2017)
19. Quesada-Pallarès, C., Sánchez-Martí, A., Ciraso-Calí, A., Pineda-Herrero, P.: Online vs. classroom learning: examining motivational and self-regulated learning strategies among vocational education and training students. Front. Psychol. **10**, 2795 (2019)

20. Einig, S.: Supporting students' learning: the use of formative online assessments. Acc. Educ. **22**, 425–444 (2013)
21. Brink, A.G.: The impact of pre-and post-lecture quizzes on performance in intermediate accounting II. Issues Account. Educ. **28**, 461–485 (2013)
22. Sax, L.J., Gilmartin, S.K., Bryant, A.N.: Assessing response rates and nonresponse bias in web and paper surveys. Res. High. Educ. **44**, 409–432 (2003)
23. Kaplowitz, M.D., Hadlock, T.D., Levine, R.: A comparison of web and mail survey response rates. Public Opin. Q. **68**, 94–101 (2004)
24. Shih, T.-H., Fan, X.: Comparing response rates in e-mail and paper surveys: a meta-analysis. Educ. Res. Rev. **4**, 26–40 (2009)

Digital Skills in e-Learning and Continuous Online Training

Online Digital Workshop: An Opportunity for Digital Learning in Kenya

Iratxe Lejarreta[1](✉), Natalia Padilla-Zea[2], and Alberto Corbi[2]

[1] Department of Computer Science, Maristak Durango, Durango, Bizkaia, Spain
ilejarreta@maristak.com
[2] Universidad Internacional de La Rioja (UNIR), Logroño, Spain
{natalia.padilla,alberto.corbi}@unir.net

Abstract. Institutions wishing to introduce e-learning into their educational system need to consider the necessary resources and evaluate the levels of technological literacy of their teaching staff. The teachers' preparation in the field of digital skills is essential to help students to profit their learning period. This requires previous training to allow teachers to achieve an appropriate level in terms of digital competence. This need is especially emphasized in a developing country like Kenya, where digital training for qualified teachers is still emerging. In this paper, we present the work done in a rural area of Homa Bay County (Kenya) and how that face-to-face work has needed to turn into e-learning due to the COVID-19 pandemic. Moreover, we describe the transition from temporary informal remote work to a formal approach, which will use a platform as a training, improvement, and reference plan to ensure the level of digital competence needed by the Kenyan teachers. The proposed solution is based on the Common Digital Competence Framework for Teachers, a Spanish adaptation an of the European frameworks DigComp and DigCompEdu, which allow establishing the criteria to identify digital competence needs and how to prepare digital activities for teachers.

Keywords: Kenya · ICT · DigComp · Digital competence · Teacher training · Digital skills · e-learning · Rural education

1 Introduction

The recent efforts carried out by a developing country like Kenya to provide quality education are remarkable. A proof of this has been the incorporation of basic competences in the Kenyan educational curriculum (Basic Education Curriculum Framework - BECF [1]). This shift to competency-based curriculum was recommended by Kenya Vision 2030 [2] and Sessional Paper No. 2 of 2015 [3], with the goal of providing students with the opportunity to develop and apply their skills and knowledge. BECF considers that basic education students must achieve seven basic competences, one of them being *digital skills*. For the development of digital competence in education, it is necessary to properly integrate technology in the classroom, as well as training teachers and choosing the right technical equipment. According to the vision of the new educational curriculum, the government stated that highly knowledgeable, reflective, professional teachers

G. Casalino et al. (Eds.): HELMeTO 2021, CCIS 1542, pp. 173–186, 2022.
https://doi.org/10.1007/978-3-030-96060-5_13

that have additional enhanced skills and confidence in a range of modern pedagogical tools should be supported and promoted. Teachers, as agents of change, must adapt their capacities and resources to face a methodological change to incorporate digital resources and promote students' active awareness in their learning processes [4]. This means that teachers must assume new demands, which without the necessary resources and training, can cause rejection, stress, anxiety, etc. [5].

We have focused this work on a rural community in Homa Bay County (Kenya). Since 2018, teachers from Maristak Durango school [6] and volunteers from the NGO SED [7] have carried out face-to-face workshops (during summer/vacation period) to improve digital skills among teachers. To provide a complete preparation, it was decided to extend digital training throughout the year by using an online approach. The workshop started informally due to the lack of resources and has since moved towards a more formal strategy, thanks to the construction of a new Community Resource Centre (project financed by the Government of Navarra, Spain) to support the schools in the province of Gwassi (Homa Bay). In this way, electrical and technological equipment will be provided to develop continuous training. However, due to the global coronavirus pandemic [8], the plans were modified, focusing the work on the design of a long-term strategy to support the digital literacy needs for different teacher profiles, since volunteers cannot travel to Kenya. As a solution, an online platform has been proposed to develop digital workshops remotely, through proposed assignments and video call assistance. Even so, the fact of not being present in person makes the initiation tasks very difficult. On the one hand, the devices are new, and they do not have qualified personnel on site to provide help; and on the other hand, some workshop attendees require prior training to the basic use of computers, which is being carried out through some more advanced users who have participated in previous face-to-face workshops.

The rest of the paper is organized as follows: the second section details how the work was done. In the Sect. 2.1 we make an approximation of the situation of online training in Kenya and rural areas, focusing on the place of action. The key aspects of ICT training for Kenyan teachers to launch this workshop are described in Sect. 2.2. The strategy used to arrive at this proposal is included in Sect. 2.3, the workshop design is developed in Sect. 2.4, and the results are presented in Sect. 3. Finally, some conclusions are drawn in Sect. 4.

2 Material and Methods

This section sets the context for this paper and explains why it is important and essential to support the development of digital teaching skills in rural areas of developing countries like Kenya. In this scenario, the design and strategy of the work developed is specified, describing the intervention and the proposed solution.

2.1 E-Learning in Rural Kenya

Online training is an opportunity for developing countries like Kenya to expand access to training and offer quality education. According to [9], e-learning is a way to empower workforce with the skills and knowledge needed to turn change to an advantage, and

[10] explains the effectiveness of various methods that can be implemented in learning processes through e-learning. Although the advantages derived from the adoption of e-learning are clear, its implementation is not easy. Some of the identified challenges are [11]: lack of adequate e-learning policies, inadequate Information and Communication Technology (ICT) infrastructure, the ever evolving technologies, lack of technical and pedagogical competences and training for e-tutors and e-learners, lack of an e-learning theory to underpin the e-learning practice, budgetary constraints and sustainability issues, negative perceptions towards e-learning, quality issues, domination of educational aims by technology and marker forces, and lack of collaboration among the e-learning participants. The results of research [12] on the use of e-learning in Kenya, confirm that there are around eight quality problems that influence e-learning in Kenya and other developing countries: course design, content support, social support, administrative support, course assessment, learner characteristics, instructor characteristics, and institutional factors. However, in line with the above, these challenges must be addressed to minimize their impact and achieve a successful adoption and use of e-learning systems.

In rural areas, where the Digital Divide ("a gap between those able to benefit from digital technology and those who cannot" [13]) is evident, access to the network and technology for residents is practically non-existent. Addressing this problem has become an important development policy for many governments around the world. However, to remove digital barriers and to have current learning opportunities, academic institutions require training processes and educational resources. ICT strengthens teaching processes and provides opportunities to make a connection between school tasks and world reality [14]. Moreover, improving internet access in a country stimulates education [15] and there is a strong correlation between internet access and educational level, employment opportunities, and individual and community economic viability [16]. Thus, access is just one out of the barriers that needs to be addressed alongside with the basic computer training for rural youngsters and adults. Rural areas need support, students in these areas live an educational reality that is very different from that of their peers in the city. They do not have the same educational opportunities and possibilities, and disconnection and poor connectivity are frequent. However, there are some proposed solutions such as that of Hussain et al. [17], who present a model to provide e-learning services to remote/rural areas to promote and facilitate modern education. These authors explain how a dedicated resource centre, hosting the learning management system, facilitates e-learning centres through Internet. The general objective of this model is to have a profitable learning environment equipped with the latest technologies to give students the opportunity to learn about new information and communication technologies and the e-learning environment.

2.2 Kenyan Teacher Training

Results from studies such as [18] indicated a low level of ICT integration in teaching in all teacher-training schools in Kenya. Most teachers would like to learn more about computers, however, there are some who are reluctant to engage and actively participate in ICT initiatives, probably due to insufficient technological resources, lack of time and lack of the needed basic training to integrate ICT in the classroom. Wambiri, G. N. and Ndani, M. N. [19] analysed teacher preparation, arguing that the provision of computers and other infrastructure in schools may not automatically lead to the integration of ICT in schools, unless teachers' beliefs and attitudes are addressed, referring computer competence and its self-efficacy. And they recommend the revision of the primary teacher education preparation curriculum and the training practice of teachers in training in ICT pedagogy to improve their readiness to integrate ICT in their teaching in primary school. The Kenyan government recognizes the need to make ICT available to schools and to support and train teachers, through the ICT Authority corporation, but ICT teacher training has been inadequate [20]. Moving from technology implementation to meaningful integration depends on the technological availability of teachers, support for its use, and curricular connection. Thus, it is necessary to give teachers the opportunity to connect technology with the curriculum they are teaching and to see technology as a vehicle to engage students in understanding these curricular ideas in a deeper way [21].

Defining the requirements of education professionals through teacher competence frameworks can provide reference standards for initial teacher training and for the quality of education professionals throughout their careers. Due to the lack of a specific Kenyan digital skills framework [22], SED and Maristak proposed the use of well-known references to train digital skills, such as the Common Digital Competence Framework for Teachers (INTEF) [23] developed from the results obtained from the DigComp [24] project by the Spanish Government. This choice is motivated because it was designed to be aligned with institutional and contextual requirements in different countries, while remaining open to adaptation and updating. Furthermore, according to [25], it is one of the best valued to be used as a reference, together with the European Digital Competence Framework for Teachers (DigCompEdu) [26]. At the same time, the framework is generic enough to work across different educational settings and to allow adaptation as technological possibilities and limitations evolve [27].

2.3 Digital Workshop Strategy Design

The NGO SED and Maristak Durango school have developed face-to-face workshops in Homa Bay County (Kenya) during the summer periods in 2018 and 2019. However, when the coronavirus pandemic arose, a sudden change to online support was performed to help teachers there to continue learning about ICT. After the summer of 2019 and during 2020, an informal online training began for approximately 12 months. However, this online training was difficult due to the lack of basic infrastructure, so it was not successful (only 2 people were able to connect and not in a stable way), until the Resource Centre was built, and the training could be formalized.

Taking as an example the solutions of other countries [17] and adapting them to the reality of Kenya, the construction of a Resource Centre began in 2020 and currently, Maristak together with SED are working on the e-learning solution for Kenyan qualified teachers. The Resource Centre is considered a place of socialization for the community. It comprises a study and training room, a library, a counselling room, and a conference room. This project promotes the Right to Education and quality learning opportunities and sustainable human development for boys, girls, and young people from 20 rural communities of Homa Bay, through the construction of educational infrastructure and capacity building. This centre guarantees the generation of a space that will reinforce and encourage the participation and training of people in the community and will promote shared initiatives that benefit other rural communities.

As stated above, due to travel restrictions, a more formal online solution has been implemented for the year 2021. Therefore, to start a workshop in online format, users must have a computer with internet access. Thanks to the construction of the Resource Centre, we could count with the minimum resources (devices and internet connection) to launch the training. One router was bought, and a data bundle plan was acquired to have a stable connection. In the centre there are 10 Raspberry Pi [28] devices, an inexpensive solution for the educational environment, which have been used as substitutes for ordinary computers in primary schools in developing countries [29]. It is proven that the Raspberry Pi computer is a very good choice to build computer labs with a low cost and efficient approach [30]. These computers include their own operating system called Raspberry Pi OS [31], with a free and open-source software license. Moreover, to avoid an economic dependency in terms of licenses, all the software installed in these devices is free as well.

The implemented solution [32], has revealed a positive relationship between technology acceptance and e-learning in developing countries. Other studies, such as [33], show that the implementation of e-learning can be effective as a distance learning strategy during the pandemic period. These online digital workshops provide learning and professional development opportunities for teachers in rural communities in the Lake Victoria area, specifically teachers from 20 schools, benefiting around 2,000 students from 20 rural communities in Homa Bay County. The local organizations that work in the development of their community and that are responsible for the centre, have overseen bringing together a group for initial training. For the start-up, a calendar and schedule that best suits the users has been established and during their vacation period, they met in the Resource Centre to carry out the tasks and help each other.

2.4 Formal Online Training

Once the infrastructure and the user's group are ready, an online training plan is established in the Resource Centre. We start from the premise that practically none of the students was able to have an adequate previous online digital training, so the starting point of the proposed training was also basic, allowing everyone to progress on their own at their own pace. The first step was to establish the objective to be achieved in the workshop: teachers have the necessary training to be able to transfer the learning to the students. Once the recommended training is completed, the teachers will feel ready to put the knowledge acquired into practice with students in the classroom. This will allow them to carry out activities for the development of the students' digital competence, as reflected in the educational curriculum of the country.

To strengthen teaching capacities in a guided, practical, and simple way, a virtual Learning Platform was developed. The content structure was designed based on the areas of the reference framework [23]. The selected tool for the platform was Google Classroom [34], which is part of the suite of online productivity applications of Google Apps for Education (GAFE) [35] for teachers and students in learning online. To overcome the obstacles of distance education, educational applications such as Google Classroom should be used [36], as it is easy to use and accessible from all devices. In this case, given that users were not used to using digital resources, it was necessary to choose a simple tool that with a minimal approach that was taught in the face-to-face workshops, would provide the opportunity to enter this environment in the best way possible. As shown in Fig. 1, Google Classroom has a clean and user-friendly interface, and it allows integration with many other digital tools (Gmail, Calendar, Drive and Meet).

The platform contains activities to develop knowledge, skills and attitudes organized around five main areas: 1. Information and data literacy, 2. Communication and collaboration, 3. Digital content creation, 4. Safety, 5. Problem solving. Each area, in turn, is broken down into 21 competences and each of them into six progressive proficiency levels: A1 - Newcomer, A2 - Explorer, B1 - Integrator, B2 - Expert, C1 - Leader, and C2 - Pioneer. These levels are established based on the reference framework [23], which includes the rubric for each level. This proposal updates these levels in 3: foundation (A1, A2), intermediate (B1, B2) and advanced (C1, C2), allowing an easier design of practical activities for each competence and level.

The students solve the tasks individually or in groups and the teacher assists them when they need it through a video call with Google Meet [37], or other means of communication offered by the platform, such as comments, chat or email. A work schedule is established from 9 a.m. to 12 p.m. (GMT + 2) (Kenya Time Zone: GMT + 3), and users attend the Meet room (online) early in the morning to answer questions from the previous tasks and get the explanation of the next task. After that, they work on their own.

To develop the tasks, they need other types of resources such as Google Docs [38]. The files produced with that tool are saved in their Google Drive [39] folder and attached to the assignment before it is delivered. Each day, the teacher reviews the tasks that have been delivered and corrects them remotely, offering comments on whether the task is completed or whether it needs to be corrected or improved. Each interaction on the platform will mean a notification that students will receive through their Gmail inbox [40].

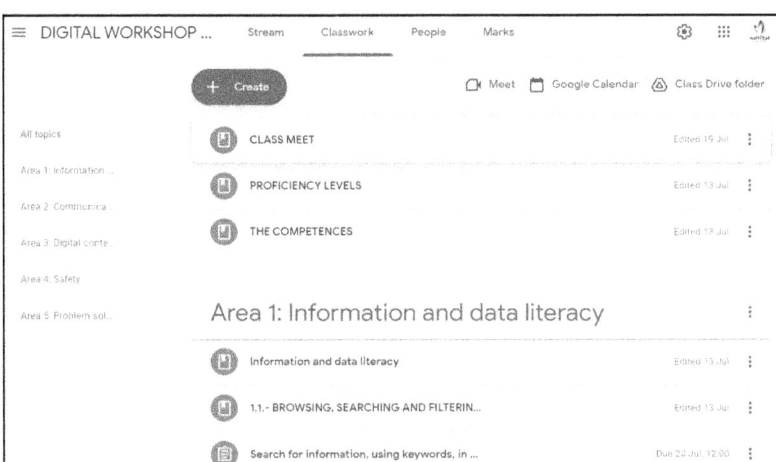

Fig. 1. Screenshot to show the general appearance of the platform.

Planning: A Google Calendar [41] (Fig. 2) with scheduled tasks delivery and teacher support classes was shared. All students have access to the calendar and each task is assigned an estimated due date. Since the pilot test took place during the vacation period (July 2021), teachers could attend the support classes. This schedule was proposed by themselves, but the platform is open so that users can continue with overdue tasks as they wish, each at their own pace. Due to the targeted period, the activities were initially designed to take place one per day. However, we were aware that different difficulties could arise, interrupting the continuous training: absences, connection problems, devices malfunction or ignorance, etc. To avoid dropouts and demotivation, the tasks were planned for an ideal learning rhythm, knowing that several users would advance own their own pace, slower. Thus, activities will be active undefinedly to allow users to solve them reflexively and then, deliver them to the teacher (via de assignment in Goggle Classroom).

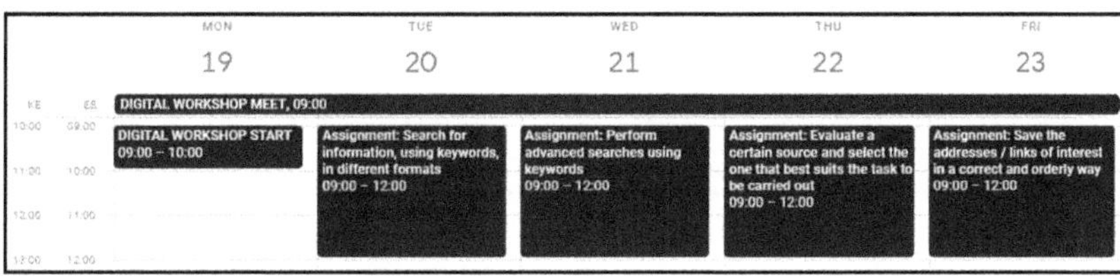

Fig. 2. Calendar with planned assignments.

Participants: The group that participated in the pilot test is made up of 10 users/students, who were assigned a Google account to be able to access the platform safely. The users are mainly teachers, but there are also some members of the local organization and young people who have finished basic education and do not have access to specialized training, nor do they have an occupation and take advantage of this opportunity because they have concerns to continue learning. As in any other aspect of Kenyans' lives, the male sex prevails, but there are also women in the group.

Evaluation: At the end of the tasks of each of the 5 areas defined for the platform, users must complete an evaluation form (Fig. 3) to measure their level of competence and thus be able to design new tasks to develop the progress of each one. The evaluation tests have been prepared through the Google Forms [42] tool, which include multiple choice questions, where users choose the option that most closely matches their knowledge for each question (between 13 and 31 items each area). The forms are based on the evaluation rubric of the reference framework [23], which will allow us to establish an approximatc level for each user, when evaluation forms for all the areas are overtaken.

Users were informed about it is important that they answer the forms sincerely to know the real level that each one has and to be able to progress properly. In addition, knowing the level of competence acquired can help us to organize new future workshops in similar-knowledge groups (if necessary) to work more efficiently.

Finally, as shown in Fig. 4, the results of the tasks and evaluations will be displayed on the platform, only for the teacher (students will only be able to see their own marks).

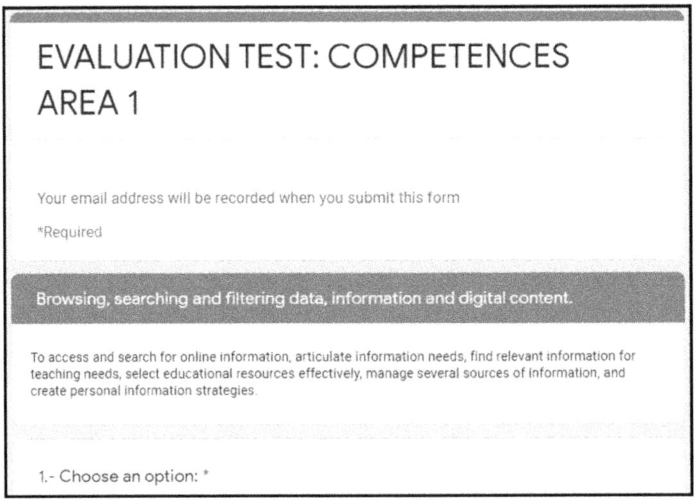

Fig. 3. Form developed with Google Forms to evaluate area 1 assignments.

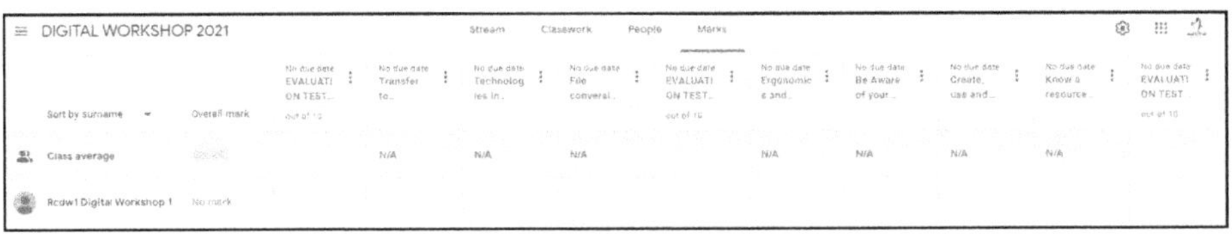

Fig. 4. Section to view all the marks of the tasks carried out by the students.

3 Results and Discussion

The total number of tasks incorporated in the workshop is 29, including the final evaluation of each area: area 1, 6 tasks; area 2, 6 tasks; area 3, 8 tasks; area 4, 5 tasks; and area 5, 4 tasks. The pilot test has been 100% remote and 10 users have participated with frequent attendance, practically daily, except Saturdays.

The first week, the group managed to work on 2 tasks related to the first competence of the first area. Table 1 shows the results of the tasks related to area 1 (planned for the first week), where 90% of the users have delivered a solution, and 10% of the users have completed 33% of the planned tasks. Although the platform indicates the status of the task as "Done", it may not have been completed yet. Students can submit the assignment, even if it is incomplete, but re-submissions can be made on the same assignment, until it is considered as complete. On the other hand, there have been cases in which the user has performed the task, but has not pressed the button to deliver, so in these cases the platform shows the task as "Missing", even if it is complete. Some tasks have not been able to be carried out completely or have had to be adapted to the circumstances of the moment and the place, not due to lack of user skills, but due to resource limitations, so they have been modified or postponed.

Table 1. The result of the tasks in area 1 assigned to users for the first week. The status "Done" means that the task has been submitted by the user and "Missing" that it has not been submitted.

Users/Tasks	Task 1	Task 2	Task 3	Task 4	Task 5	Evaluation Test
User 1	Done	Done	Missing	Missing	Missing	Missing
User 2	Done	Missing	Missing	Missing	Missing	Missing
User 3	Done	Done	Missing	Done	Missing	Done
User 4	Missing	Missing	Missing	Missing	Missing	Missing
User 5	Done	Done	Missing	Missing	Missing	Done
User 6	Done	Done	Missing	Missing	Missing	Missing
User 7	Done	Done	Missing	Missing	Missing	Missing
User 8	Done	Done	Missing	Done	Missing	Done
User 9	Done	Done	Missing	Done	Missing	Done
User 10	Done	Done	Missing	Missing	Missing	Missing

It should be noted that 1 user has managed to complete most of the tasks, almost completing area 3 (digital content creation), successfully reaching the programming competence and thus ranking as the most advanced student. This user has been able to assist the rest of the users who have had to continue at their own pace developing the previous tasks, since the tasks sent had failures and had to be repeated or amended. There have also been cases in which they have worked in a group, so the delivery of the tasks has been collective. By default, the tasks have 3 states: *unreviewed, undelivered and returned*. All the grading notes are always accompanied by comments made by the teacher on the platform itself. Tasks are not assigned a score, but a correction on whether it is complete or not.

The graph represented in Fig. 5 shows the status of the tasks for users after a month of work. We can see area 1 was worked by almost every user. Area 3 (programming) is the most advanced area, reached by only 3 users. User 3 is the one that has delivered more tasks and user 4 has not turned in any of the tasks. It should be noted that user 3 took the initiative to lead the workshop there, and having a higher level, he has been able to help the rest.

The following weeks continued with a positive trend, and although the performance of some users has varied, the results have been positive and high progress has been shown.

Regarding the development of the tasks, the initial planning has not been fulfilled: it has not been possible to move as fast as intended and perform one task per day as originally planned. Remote assistance has made the initial start-up tasks difficult, since there was no one in the Resource Centre with technical knowledge to be able to assist users, give them support and help them with the initial tasks. Later, user 3 took the initiative to help the rest, so we were able to move forward, although more slowly than expected. On the other hand, the attendance has been frequent, but not all users have been able to attend regularly, some of them because of work obligations and

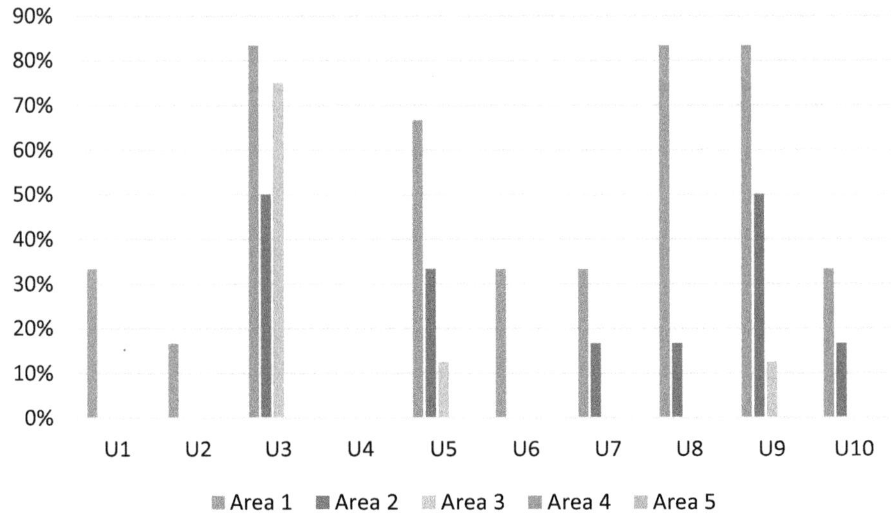

Fig. 5. Number of tasks performed by users per area. Area 1: information and data literacy, Area 2: communication and collaboration, Area 3: digital content creation, Area 4: safety, and Area 5: problem solving.

others because some personal reasons. As mentioned above, the online sessions began with a round of questions about last day task and continued with an explanation of the activity to be carried out during that session. That first part was complex because they lacked the necessary resources to interact properly in the video call through the Meet room: webcam, microphone, and speaker. They had to rely on the smartphone of one of the users. Another trouble we found was that users had difficulties using the Google environment (Classroom, Meet, etc.) because they did not know about it, and this also had an impact on the delay in planning. It was difficult to start, but it was also something that was foreseen, since resources and tools were innovative for our target group that is not familiar with digital resources, except for the use of smartphone, as they currently use commercial applications for purchasing and payment management [43]. As a summary of the main problems encountered during the first online digital workshop, we can highlight:

- Evident difference in the level of digital competence between users.
- Slow connection (sometimes ineffective). Data depletion.
- Lack of infrastructure: headphones, webcam, and microphones.
- Lack of knowledge in the use of the operating system and installed software.
- Lack of knowledge in the use of computers in general.
- Technical ignorance: take a screenshot, attach a file, insert an image into the document, etc.

The final evaluation on the users' digital competence level acquired after the workshop cannot be reported yet, since the tasks in all areas were not completed at the time of writing this section. However, activities performed until now show clear positive progress, considering the low level of pre-basic digital skills of users.

The main findings of this workshop are that the participants in the online digital workshop had a clear interest in the solution proposed. Beyond reaching a specific level of digital competence, the implicit objective of making teachers feel comfortable with the level acquired has been achieved: they expressed it while solving tasks getting easier.

The main contribution of this experience to online training in rural environments is the establishment of the starting point regarding the difficulties found: 1) previous preparation is required in the basic use of computers and applications, and 2) more time is needed to establish a starting level, which can be considered basic in terms of digital competence. Moreover, infrastructure was judged as a good election, since the Raspberry Pi Foundation in conjunction with Google provides low-cost kits, specifically for education [44].

Teachers learn from interaction with other classmates, and collaboration between them becomes an essential tool to promote reflective practice, and an essential resource to achieve maximum teaching effectiveness [45]. To continue promoting the change to digital learning in this area, other alternative ideas are provided to be developed in the future, which may contribute to the improvement of digital competence: developing a resource search engine, designing new learning materials, or collaborating with other professional colleagues.

4 Conclusions

In this paper we have presented a real experience, with the main objective of supporting sustainable educational solutions and improve access to relevant information, education, and training, to boost the economic and social prosperity of Homa Bay County (Kenya), which can be transferred to any other place. Technology linked to the educational environment has evolved, but it is necessary to focus on rural environments to face the digital divide, as is the case in developing countries such as Kenya. Regarding the skills of the competency-based curriculum in force in the country, digital competence is the most complex to face for teachers since it requires specific training and resources. However, this training must be addressed in order that teachers are able to support students at different level in their learning process. Teachers must act as a guide and must be at the level demanded by their students to avoid slowing down their learning.

To contribute to the development of digital skills of teachers in resource-poor schools in rural Kenya, we propose the solution of an online digital workshop to help them through assisted self-training. This solution will allow ICT-backed education and training professionals to develop their digital competence to enhance their knowledge, experience, and skills. This initiative promotes the use of digital technologies, including computers and the Internet, in capacity building and training at all levels and sectors of education and learning in a developing community.

To access online training, it has been essential to have the Resource Centre, which has educational spaces that allow teachers to strengthen their capacities, which will have a favourable impact on optimizing the learning of children from 20 schools in the area. The training has been based on the Common Framework for Teaching Digital Competence, which has served as a reference for the design of practical activities related to each area and competence that build the digital skills at different levels.

The results show positive progress in the acquisition of digital skills of teachers. On the one hand, teachers are given the opportunity to delve into the area that each one considers most necessary and on the other hand, they are provided with help to reach an acceptable level for an effective performance of their teaching activity. The digital workshop is a resource aimed at all teachers who require it, which will serve both to learn, as well as to be able to self-evaluate or discover other skills that they were not aware of. The most important aspect of this training is not finishing the workshop with a certain level, but the progress of each user. This training as a guide for efficient development has been useful to detect basic needs in terms of digital competence. In addition, working to develop the digital competence made possible to bring technology closer to a community with limited resources. Evidence of this is their positive attitude towards technology: they value the positive aspects of technology, they are motivated, they are proactive, and they show curiosity and interest.

But there is still much to do. This initiative is only the starting point for future projects. This work leaves the door open to continue making new contributions to improve the digital educational competence in that region and others with similar features.

Acknowledgments. This research is partially funded by Universidad Internacional de la Rioja (UNIR), through the Research Institute for Innovation & Technology in Education (UNIR iTED, http://ited.unir.net). The authors wish to thank SED and Maristak Durango for their commitment to Kenyan education.

References

1. Kenya Institute of Curriculum Development. Basic Education Curriculum Framework (2017)
2. Kenya Vision 2030. http://vision2030.go.ke/
3. MoEST: Sessional Paper No 2 of 2015: Reforming the Education and Training Sector in Kenya Government Press: Nairobi (2012)
4. Gámiz-Sánchez, V.M.: ICT-based active methodologies. Proc.-Soc. Behav. Sci. **237**, 606–612 (2017)
5. Orejudo, S., Royo, F., Soler, J., Aparicio, L.: Inteligencia emocional y bienestar. Reflexiones, experiencias profesionales e investigaciones. Universidad de Zaragoza, Zaragoza (2014)
6. Maristak Durango. https://maristak.com/
7. NGO SED. https://www.sed-ongd.org/
8. WHO Coronavirus. https://www.who.int/health-topics/coronavirus
9. Oye, N.D., Salleh, M., Iahad, N.A.: E-learning methodologies and tools. Int. J. Adv. Comput. Sci. Appl. (IJACSA), **3**(2), 48–52 (2012)
10. Arunachalam, A.R.: Bringing out the effective learning process by analyzing of E-learning methodologies. Indian J. Sci. Technol. **7**, 41 (2014)
11. Kibuku, R.N., Ochieng, D.O., Wausi, A.N.: e-Learning challenges faced by universities in Kenya: a literature review. Electron. J. e-Learn. **18**(2), 150–161 (2020)
12. Hadullo, K., Oboko, R., Omwenga, E.: Status of e-learning quality in Kenya: case of Jomo Kenyatta university of agriculture and technology postgraduate students. Int. Rev. Res. Open Distrib. Learn. **19**(1), 130–160 (2018)

13. Smyth, G.: Wireless technologies and e-learning: bridging the digital divide. Intel Corporation, December 2006
14. Yusuf, M.O.: Information and communication technology and education: analysing the Nigerian national policy for information technology. Int. Electron. J. **6**(3), 316–321 (2005)
15. Tay, C.: The impact of the internet on trade in education. Technol. Econ. Dev. Econ. **21**(6), 833–854 (2015)
16. Rothberg, A., Bailey, J., Ballard, K.: E-learning in rural environments. In: Southwest Decision Sciences Institute Conference, pp. 1211–1219, February 2012
17. Hussain, S., Wang, Z., Rahim, S.: E-learning services for rural communities. arXiv preprint arXiv:1308.4820 (2013)
18. Chemwei, B.: Relationship between teacher educators' attitude towards computers and their level of ICT integration in instruction in primary teacher training colleges in Kenya. Editon Consortium J. Curric. Educ. Stud. **1**(1), 14–22 (2019)
19. Wambiri, G.N., Ndani, M.N.: Kenya primary school teachers' preparation in ICT teaching: teacher beliefs, attitudes, self-efficacy, computer competence, and age. Afr. J. Teach. Educ. **5**(1), 1–15 (2016)
20. Kenya News Agency. https://www.kenyanews.go.ke/teacher-training-for-ict-integration/
21. Masingila, J.O., Khatete, D.W., Maundu, J.N., Foley, A.R., Ndethiu, S.M., Twoli, N.W.: From implementation to efficacy: factors affecting Kenyan secondary teachers' technology integration. Afr. Educ. Rev. **16**(1), 58–87 (2019)
22. Mwadulo, M.W., Odoyo, C.O.: ICT adoption in the educational management of primary schools in Kenya (2020)
23. National Institute of Educational Technologies and Teacher Training: Common Digital Competence Framework for Teachers (2017)
24. Carretero, S., Vuorikari, R., Punie, Y.: DigComp 2.1: The digital competence framework for citizens with eight proficiency levels and examples of use (No. JRC106281). Joint Research Centre (Seville site) (2017)
25. Cabero-Almenara, J., Romero-Tena, R., Palacios-Rodríguez, A.: Evaluation of Teacher digital competence frameworks through expert judgement: the use of the expert competence coefficient. J. New Approach. Educ. Res. (NAER J.) **9**(2), 275–293 (2020)
26. Redecker, C.: European framework for the digital competence of educators: DigCompEdu (No. JRC107466). Joint Research Centre (Seville site) (2017)
27. Caena, F., Redecker, C.: Aligning teacher competence frameworks to 21st century challenges: the case for the European digital competence framework for educators (Digcompedu). Eur. J. Educ. **54**(3), 356–369 (2019)
28. Raspberry Pi. https://www.raspberrypi.org/
29. Raspberry Pi Developing World. https://www.raspberrypi.org/blog/tag/developing-world/
30. Nuñez-Unda, A., Vera, A., Haz, L., Pinos, V., Zurita, R., Medina, S.: The raspberry Pi as a computer substitute at elementary schools in developing countries: a pilot experiment in Ecuador. In: MATEC Web of Conferences, vol. 210, p. 04023. EDP Sciences (2018)
31. Raspberry Pi OS. https://www.raspberrypi.org/software/operating-systems/
32. Alhumaid, K., Ali, S., Waheed, A., Zahid, E., Habes, M.: COVID-19 & elearning: perceptions & attitudes of teachers towards e-learning acceptance in the developing countries. Multicult. Educ. **6**(2), 100–115 (2020)
33. Prestiadi, D.: Effectiveness of e-learning implementation as a distance learning strategy during coronavirus disease (covid-19) pandemic. In: Proceeding Umsurabaya (2020)
34. Google Classroom. https://classroom.google.com/
35. Google Apps for Education. https://edu.google.com/
36. Sudarsana, I.K., Putra, I.B.M.A., Astawa, I.N.T., Yogantara, I.W.L.: The use of Google classroom in the learning process. In: Journal of Physics: Conference Series, vol. 1175, no. 1, p. 012165. IOP Publishing, March 2019

37. Google Meet. https://meet.google.com/
38. Google Docs. https://docs.google.com/
39. Google Drive. https://drive.google.com/
40. Gmail. https://mail.google.com/
41. Google Calendar. https://calendar.google.com/
42. Google Forms. https://forms.google.com/
43. Ojino, R., Mich, L.: Mobile applications in university education: the case of Kenya. J. e-Learn. Knowl. Soc. **14**(1), 111–125 (2018)
44. Yamanoor, N.S., Yamanoor, S.: High quality, low cost education with the Raspberry Pi. In: 2017 IEEE Global Humanitarian Technology Conference (GHTC), pp. 1–5. IEEE, October 2017
45. Duran, D., Oller, M., Huguet, T.: Docència compartida: aprenentatge docent entre iguals per a l'atenció a la diversitat. GRAI (UAB)-ARMIF, Bellaterra (2018)

E-tutor Profiles in Online Higher Education: Skills and Organizational Models

Paolo Raviolo(✉), Salvatore Messina, Irene Mauro, and Marco Rondonotti

eCampus University, Novedrate, CO, Italia
paolo.raviolo@uniecampus.it

Abstract. This study is focused on the role of e-tutor in Higher Education. The first objective was a systematic literature review, while the second was an analysis of regulations, contracts and other internal University documentation used to define the e-tutor job description. This analysis was developed highlighting the skills required to online tutors and disciplinary tutors. The third step of the research was based on a questionnaire focused on the analysis of the different roles that e-tutors can play in academic contexts. The research sample has been the two e-tutor groups of the eCampus University in the academic year 2020/2021: 220 On Line Tutors (TOL) and 62 Disciplinary Tutors (TD), obtaining 133 complete questionnaires from the TOL group (60.4%) and 42 (67.8%) of the related group of TDs. The e-tutoring model implemented at the university for TOLs clearly focuses on the transversal dimension linked to the use of technological infrastructures and the organizational and administrative processes of the University. On the other hand, the strictly pedagogical dimension remains in the background. The modeling space, intended as a pedagogical practice, could be a space of overlap with the disciplinary tutors but it could become, if well structured, also the space for comparison of the reciprocal practices also articulated on different levels.

Keywords: e-tutoring · Higher education · On-line learning

1 Research Framework

The role of the e-tutor has changed over the years, in light of the changes that digital and social media have introduced in training processes and especially in the e-Learning chain [1, 2].

It is the communicative dimension [3], in particular, which has always been central to the e-tutor's activity, that highlights the need for an update. The skills of online moderation, preparation of group management and animation of online communities, traditionally understandable with reference to the teaching-learning model of Salmon [4], need to be taken up and relocated in a new scenario marked on one side by the spread of Web 2.0 [5], on the other hand by the increasing importance of tutoring

The work is developed together by all the authors; Paolo Raviolo paid more attention to the conclusions, Salvatore Messina the results, Irene Mauro the framework, Marco Rondonotti the objectives and research tools.

G. Casalino et al. (Eds.): HELMeTO 2021, CCIS 1542, pp. 187–196, 2022.
https://doi.org/10.1007/978-3-030-96060-5_14

roles in higher education in which it becomes essential to identify the fundamental competences with respect to online learning contexts [6], in order to to guarantee an effective teaching-learning process.

The tutorial function plays an essential role in training based on online distance learning (ODL) and in training understood in the broadest sense that also includes adult education. Knowledge in online learning paths is built in a context that has significant similarities with lifelong learning [7] in which the learner-tutor-teacher relationship becomes fundamental. The e-tutor, understood as one who "interacts directly with learners to support their learning process when they are separated from the tutor in time and place for some or all these direct interactions" [8], must therefore possess specific skills to manage a personalized approach to each student and collaboratively build a specific path suited to their needs. Above all, he is an essential figure to support group work [9] and to intervene on the sense of isolation and loneliness that students of universities that only deliver online courses report [10].

In Italian telematic universities [11], the training process is based on a didactic setting that presents some specificities compared to that of the present universities; in particular, precise classifications of educational content are introduced [12], the times and paths are extremely personalized and the average age of students is higher. Teaching is organized on two levels: the first based on transmissive teaching, the second on interactive teaching.

The transmissive teaching (DE) or the complex of contents similar to frontal teaching in the classroom, is focused on the presentation/illustration of the contents by the teacher: audio-video recordings, Web conferences, prestigious courses or similar variants.

Interactive teaching (DI), on the other hand, refers to a spectrum of activities including:

- teaching interventions based generally in the form of demonstrations or additional explanations found in FAQs, mailing lists or Web forums (demonstrations or operational tips on how to solve a problem, exercises and the like);
- short interventions made by the participants (for example through discussion or collaboration environments: web forums, blogs, wikis);
- structured e-tivities (individual or collaborative) in reports, exercises, case studies, problem solving, web research, projects, production of artefacts (or similar variants), created by students, with relative feedback;
- forms of assessment such as questionnaires or tests.

The teaching provided in online mode and the organization of face-to-face activities (workshops and internships) require the student to be suitably supported by specialist figures able to support him continuously, guide him in the course of study and in the use of the IT platform, support him in the content, methodological-didactic aspects and from the point of view of motivation.

Support for these activities is guaranteed by two types of e-tutors: the online tutor (TOL) and the disciplinary tutor (TD). This is a debate - whether the tutor should have disciplinary or system skills - that has interested the literature on e-Learning for years. In the context examined, the organizational solution of creating two separate professional figures was adopted.

The TOLs have the task of supporting the student's motivation along the entire didactic path, adequately modulate the study path to the characteristics of each student and promote his active role, favoring the understanding of the context in which his educational path develops. In particular, their role develops around:

- design an individual and personalized didactic plan together with the student, providing support in the temporal organization of the activity;
- provide information on the examination methods and on the articulation of the individual courses: teaching, interactive teaching and eventual laboratory/practical activities in the presence;
- discuss with the student the methodology and planning of the study, encouraging participation in forms of interactive teaching;
- provide information and guidance on the calendars and contents of the virtual classrooms and any laboratory/practical activities in the presence associated with the various courses;
- periodically monitor the progress of the student's learning path;
- support the student in secretarial activities;
- ensure the necessary motivational support.

The TD, on the other hand, is a qualified expert in the discipline who supports the teacher in charge of the teaching, carrying out supplementary didactic activities coordinated by the teacher. It is a figure close to that of the teacher assistant (TAs), an expert who reduces the distance between teachers and students [13], creating a bridge between the specific accompaniment practices of the TOL, students and teachers.

The number and activity of tutors is naturally also related to the number of students, which is currently substantially increasing. The eCampus University in April 2021 had a total of 47,756 students enrolled in degree courses, with an increase of 51% compared to the prepandemic academic year, 2018/19.

These data speak of a different vision of online education, probably also due to the pandemic period that forced students and teachers to use and implement the services of an online university.

2 Methodology

This study is part of a large research project launched on the figure of the e-tutor precisely because of its centrality. In this context, we intend to return the first phase of this work, which consists of:

(1) analysis of the e-tutor's duties in the current landscape;
(2) identification of the two eCampus e-tutor profiles (TOL and TD), developing a mapping of TOL tasks and duties to be compared with the e-tutor models present in the literature [4, 8, 14].
(3) detect the real practices carried out by the TOL and TD tutors, analyzing them in terms of perception of importance and competence;
(4) identify training needs for the design of interventions useful for enhancing the skills possessed by TOLs.

The first objective was pursued through the analysis of the literature, while the second through the documentary analysis of regulations, contracts and other internal University documentation used to build a tutor's job description. This analysis was developed by highlighting the skills required for online tutors and disciplinary tutors.

To achieve the research objectives "3" and "4", the research group identified, thanks to the literary review in the questionnaire by De Metz and Bezuidenhout [13], the tool that best responded to the University e-tutor model precisely because of the theoretical framework underlying the development of this tool. In fact, to define the different roles that e-tutors can play in academic contexts, a three-level classification is used:

- cognitive, declining the tutoring action as a support and development of the learning process through course materials and learning objects;
- affective, indicating attention to creating a peaceful environment and communicative actions that support the student and his self-esteem;
- systemic, referring to all the administrative procedures necessary to guarantee the management and collection of information.
- It is a questionnaire that investigates the e-tutor's perceptions of competence in higher education contexts. Specifically, it investigates:
- how e-tutors perceive their job roles in terms of time, importance and workload;
- what specific skills are needed to carry out their role within the university and to what extent they perceive they have such skills.

The tool is divided into five areas of investigation:

1. demographic information (section A);
2. perception of the role performed by examining the time spent on each function and personal assessment of the importance of these functions (section B);
3. dimensions of effective tutoring: 40 statements on the activities carried out by the tutor are listed (section C);
4. self-assessment of skills and importance of functions in providing guidance and support to students in the academic field through 15 items (section D);
5. in-depth questions. Three open-ended questions were included to allow for a deeper level of information sharing and analysis. Respondents were asked to discuss what factors influenced their effectiveness as an e-tutor and what were the difficulties that prevented them from being an effective e-tutor, and if they had any other comments on their e-tutoring experience (section E).

In order to meet the objectives (1) and (2) of the research, the working group conducted an analysis of the job descriptions and documents within the University relating to the institutional role of the TOL and the tasks connected to them starting from the results achieved by De Metz & Bezuidenhout [14] based on research conducted by both Collins & Berge [15]: "Seven roles were identified from the literature, namely: administrative, informative, managerial, pastoral, pedagogical, social, and technical" [14].

This questionnaire was translated and adapted into Italian by the research team. The validation process of this translation followed rigorous steps, using statistical analysis.

In this contribution, starting from the profile data, we limit ourselves to discussing the results regarding area B and D.

3 Results

The framework of the e-tutor's functions that we report in the Fig. 1 is what emerges from the verification of these elements within the institutional documents of eCampus, in particular the University Guidelines for tutoring.

Functions	*Descriptive summary*
Administrative	Design an educational programming plan together with the student.
Informative	Provide the student with suggestions.
Managerial	Provide support in the temporal organization of the student's activity.
Guidance	Provide students with information and guidance.
Pedagogical	Ensure the necessary motivational support. Adequately modulate the course of study to the characteristics of each one.
Social	Encourage participation.
Technical	Support the student in secretarial activities.

Fig. 1. Functions of the etutor in eCampus

Following this first analysis, the questionnaire was administered to detect the contact points and the main differences between the tasks described in the official job description of the TOLs and TDs, as well as the practices carried out by them [16]. The research was conducted on the group of TOL and TD based within the University in the academic year 2020/2021. Through the QuestionPro online platform, the group of 220 TOLs and 62 TDs of eCampus was reached, obtaining 133 complete questionnaires from the TOL group (corresponding to 60.4% of the collective) and 42 (corresponding to 67.8%) of the related group of TDs. Among the TOLs the substantial majority is female (76.7%, while only 22.3% is male) and the average age corresponds to 39 years, while among the TDs the percentage of female sex drops to 57, 1% (remaining 42.9% male) and the average age is around 37 years. Almost all TOLs access the role with a three-year degree (67.7%) or a master's degree (23.3%), the remaining 10% of the sample also have a first or second level master (respectively about 4.5% and about 2.3%) or a PhD (2.3%). Among the TDs, the totality of the sample enters the role with at least a master's degree (38.1%) or a research doctorate (40.5%), the remainder has a first or second level master (4.7% respectively) and 16.7%. The sample of TOLs is evenly distributed with respect to the affiliation to the Departments of the University, although there is a slight decrease in the engineering department: 22% holds the role of online tutor for the law department, 21% for psychology, 20% for letters, 18% for economics, while 15% for engineering; the TDs are more present in the cdl belonging to the Psychology department (19 or 45.2% of the TDs), followed by Law and Letters with a total of 8 disciplinary tutors per department (18.6% each), engineering with 5 TDs (11.6%) and Economy with 3 TD (about 7%). As for the practices carried out, TOL and TD show a high degree of attachment to the role and the university institution they represent. In response to the question "How important is the work of e-tutor for you", 68% and 57.1% of the TOL and TD sample assign the maximum value of 5 (on a scale from 1 to 5) and 26, 3% of TOLs Vs 33.3% choose the value of 4, signaling attachment to the role. 65.4% of TDs and 73.8% of TDs state that it is important to represent the University (value 5).

Here are the results obtained regarding the evaluation that roles of TOL and TD require in terms of time. Summing up the results of response modalities 1 and 2 (more time) and 6 and 7 (less time), the results of the TOLs indicate that the highest percentage of respondents (33.8%) classified the administrative and informative role as those which require more time; the technical role (31.6%) and the social role (30.1%) follow. Among the roles that require less time to work at TOLs we find the pedagogical one (36.1%), the social one (30.1%) and the guide (27.1%). Conversely, however, among the TDs it stands out that the role that requires more time is the pedagogical one (40.5%), followed by the leadership role (33.3%). Again for TDs, the roles that require less time are administrative and information (both 33.4%), followed by managerial (33.3%). In particular, the little time dedicated to the social function of the two roles is striking, a function that is one of the main success factors in online learning. In fact, this function is expressed in the creation of a friendly and comfortable social environment in which students feel that learning is possible. Furthermore, e-tutors are the first point of contact for students, especially when students encounter difficulties in their learning process [3]; result that we would have expected more from TOLs.

From the point of view of the importance of the functions (using a scale from 1 to 7 where 1 = more important and 7 = less important), identifying the answers given to modalities 1 and 2 (and modalities 6 and 7 as those considered less important), we note that 31.6% of TOLs believe that the technical function is the most central one, followed by the managerial one (31.6%), as shown in Fig. 2. In line with what was declared to the previous question relating to "time spent", the pedagogical role is the least important for TOLs (36.1%), followed by managerial (33.1%) and Guide (33.1%) roles.

TDs, as shown in Fig. 3, declare that they consider the Pedagogical (47.6%) and Guide (30.9%) role as more important (modalities 1 and 2), while less important (answer modalities 6 and 7)) the managerial (40.4%), administrative (38.1%) and technical (38.1%) roles.

Figure 4 illustrates the gap between the perceived importance within the university for each function and the skills that the e-tutors claim to have mobilized (section D of the questionnaire). These are the results of the importance-performance analysis [17].

The factorial analysis conducted confirmed the 4 factors of De Metz & Bezuidenhout [14] and made it possible to detect the difference between the importance of each function

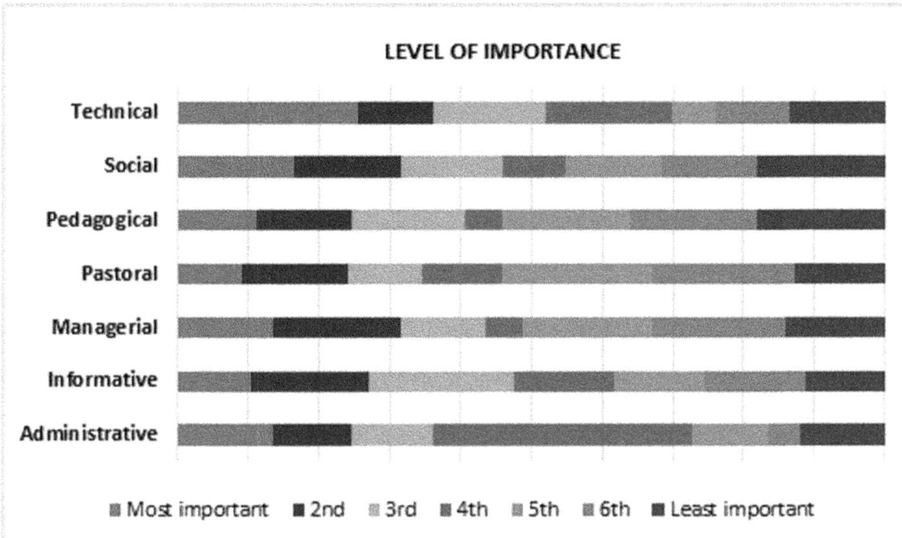

Fig. 2. TOL perceived importance of work roles.

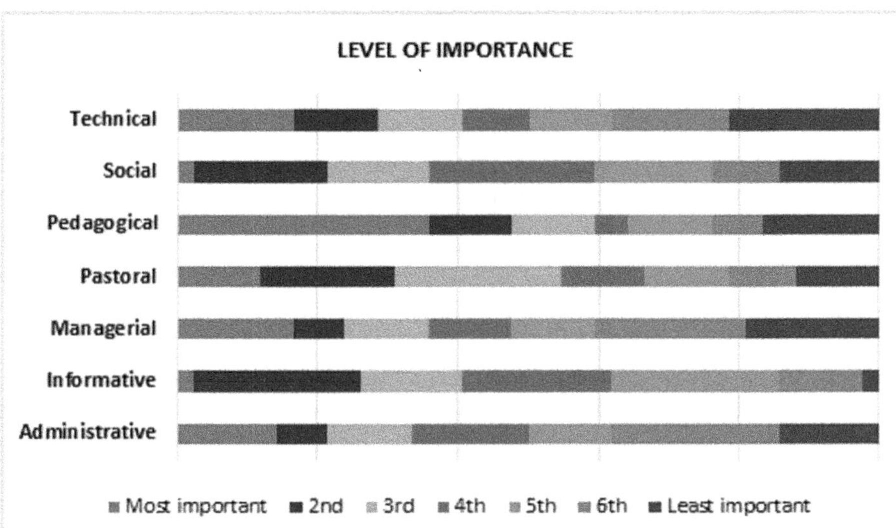

Fig. 3. TD perceived importance of work roles.

for the university and the level of competence perceived by the tutor, as summarized in Fig. 4, distinguishing between the two roles.

Analyzing this figure, it is noted that the TOLs have expressed significant discrepancies between the perceived skills and the functions actually performed. These differences relate in particular to supporting students' reflection on learning activities and outcomes

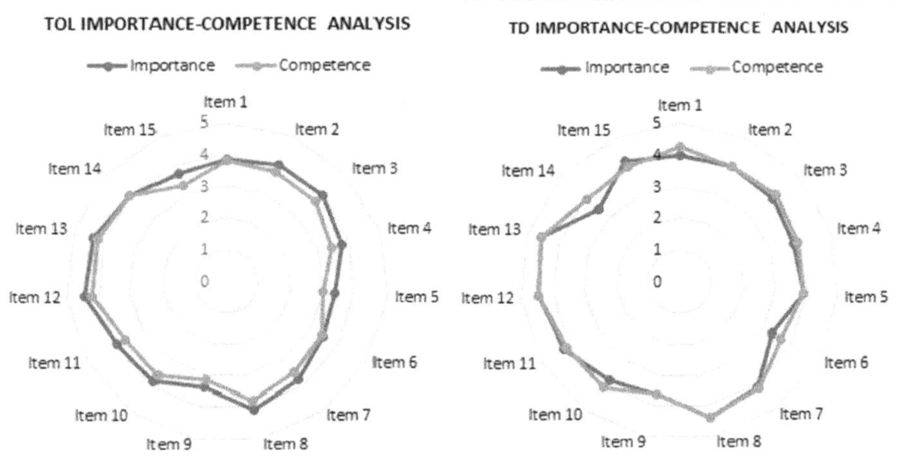

Fig. 4. Roles and skills perceived by e-tutors (TOL and TD).

(item 2), assisting learners in the development of study skills (metacognition) (item 3), making technological choices to improve learning online environment (item 4), the design of useful learning activities (item 5), the preparation of a welcoming online environment (process facilitation) (item 7), the management of communication and the creation of online communities in discussions (item 9), just-in-time identification, localization, development and production as in learning support (item 11) and, finally, the creation of new and relevant knowledge (item 15). TDs, on the other hand, perceive themselves to be more competent than TOLs in all 15 areas, believing that their skills are spent less in the role of accompanying students (item 14, with an average difference of −0.54) and in the facilitation of content (item 1, with an average difference of −0.34).

4 Conclusion

Higher education e-tutors play a key role in facilitating the learning process for students. They provide crucial support to the interaction between students and academic organizations essential to achieve educational success. The main role of the e-tutor is focused on ensuring that the student does not feel isolated and that the distance between students, student and teacher, student and university is bridged. Ideally the e-tutoring system should provide a community space, where students can meet and feel part of the wider academic community. This aspect is essential to minimize the feeling of detachment that is common among students who attend online universities.

In the case examined, the eCampus University, the e-tutors perceive their role as central to the University and see it above all as a role of orientation and facilitation for the students. The key competences of the e-tutors in this context are mainly on the technical infrastructure, on the organization of the university and on the social dimension, important aspects for effectively managing the relationship with students. The role of tutors in this university is not aimed so much at providing specific disciplinary support to students, even if each tutor works mainly on a faculty, in fact they do not necessarily have an academic background in areas relevant to the degree courses they refer to.

Compared to the work of De Metz and Bezuidenhout [14] the technical and information functions are perceived as the more relevant, the pedagogical function appears to be relatively less central in the case examined in this work while in the research cited it occupies the second place for perceived importance. Comparing times, the administrative activities appear to be those to which a greater amount of time is dedicated; in this case the results are in line with the research by De Metz and Bezuidenhout [14] which highlights how tutors devote on average 25% of their time to administrative activities even if they consider them relatively less important than the others.

Overall, the e-tutoring model promoted by the university for TOLs clearly focuses on the transversal dimension linked to the use of technological infrastructures and the organizational and administrative processes of the University. On the other hand, the strictly pedagogical dimension remains in the background, which is the one on which the modeling dimension would find an opportunity for reflection and awareness for the tutors themselves. In fact, it is the TOLs that contribute substantially to the unfolding of the student's training experience in practice, supporting students in structuring the time and learning path. It seems likely that the modeling space could be a space of overlap with the disciplinary tutors but it could become, if well structured, also the space for comparison of the reciprocal practices also articulated on different levels.

References

1. Ferrari, S.: Mediamorfosi dell'e-learning. In Rivoltella P.C., Rossi P.G. (eds.) Tecnologie per l'educazione. Pearson, Milano (2019)
2. Goold, A., Coldwell, J., Craig, A.: An examination of the role of the e-tutor. Australas. J. Educ. Technol. **26**(5), 704–716 (2010)
3. Rivoltella, P.C.:. E-tutor. Profilo, Metodi, Strumenti. Carocci, Roma (2006)
4. Salmon, G.: E-moderating: The Key to Teaching and Learning Online. Psychology Press (2003)
5. Bonaiuti, G. (ed.): E-Learning 2.0. Il futuro dell'apprendimento in rete, tra formale e informale. Erickson, Trento (2006)
6. McPherson, M., Nunes, M.B.: The role of tutors as a integral part of online learning support. Eur. J. Open Dist. E-learn. **7**(1) (2004)
7. Greco, G.: L'apprendimento nell'era della connettività: una riflessione sociologica al confine tra comunicazione ed educazione. In: Scarcelli, C.M., Stella, R. (eds.), Digital literacy e giovani. Strumenti per comprendere, misurare e intervenire (21–31). Franco Angeli, Milano (2017)
8. Denis, B., Watland, P., Pirotte, S., Verday, N.: Roles and competencies of the e-tutor. In: Networked Learning 2004: A Research Based Conference on Networked Learning and Lifelong Learning: Proceedings of the Fourth International Conference, Lancaster, pp. 150–157 (2004)
9. Montero-Fleta, B., Pérez-Sabater, C.: Guiding in tertiary education: a case study on social networking and e-learning platforms. Procedia—Soc. Behav. Sci. **159**, 410–414 (2014)
10. Kim, J.Y.: A study on learners' perceptional typology and relationships among the learner's types, characteristics, and academic achievement in a blended e-Education environment. Comput. Educ. **59**, 304–315 (2012)
11. Ardizzone, P., Rivoltella, P.C.: Didattiche per l'e-Learning. Carocci, Roma (2003)

12. Raviolo, P.: Online higher education teaching practices. In: Proceedings of the 10th International Conference on E-Education, E-Business, E-Management and E-Learning. Association for Computing Machinery, New York, NY, USA, pp. 79–84 (2019)
13. Mirzadeh, S.I., Farajtabar, M., Li, A., Ghasemzadeh, H.: Improved knowledge distillation via teacher assistant: Bridging the gap between student and teacher. arXiv preprint arXiv:1902.03393 (2019)
14. De Metz, N., Bezuidenhout, A.: An importance–competence analysis of the roles and competencies of e-tutors at an open distance learning institution. Australas. J. Educ. Technol. **34**(5) (2018)
15. Collins, M.P., Berge, Z.L.: Moderating online electronic discussion groups. Paper Presented at the American Educational Research Association Conference, Chicago (1997). http://emoderators.com/wp-content/uploads/aera97c.html
16. Creswell, J., Plano Clark, V.: Designing and Conducting Mixed Methods Research, SAGE Publications Inc. (2017)
17. Lovelock, Patterson & Walker: Service marketing. Prentice-Hall, Sydney (1998)

Student's Perception of Online Learning, Teaching, and Assessment in Higher Education

Interpersonal Distance in *CReAP+T Method* in Distance Learning

The Paradigm of Space in Technology-Based Dialogues

Nadia Carlomagno[1(✉)] and Valeria Minghelli[2]

[1] Suor Orsola Benincasa University, 80135 Naples, Italy
nadia.carlomagno@docenti.unisob.na.it
[2] University of Study of Salerno, 84084 Salerno, Italy
vminghelli@unisa.it

Abstract. Research born during the health emergency imposed the remodulation of didactics, repositioning studies inside a new *Umwelt*, which, at a distance, constitutes itself as a spatial and relational environment, strongly influenced by the dialogue through the use of technology. Starting from considerations regarding the constitutive function carried out by the *presence of the body* in the educational relationship it was outlined throughout these months the CReAP+T Method centred on *Corporeality, Creatitvity, Relationship, emotion, Action, Performativity + Technology.* The method is structured on theatrical techniques and performative practices, that in the analogy between theatre and teaching become also learning strategies. A model of performative didactics which places the body in action, as an element capable of sustaining a relationship, even at a distance, through the recourse to the *simplex properties* and *principles* such as of the *separation of functions* and the *creator inhibition* which allow the activation of strategies of *vicariance.*

The exploratory survey aims to investigate around the theme topic of "perception of learning space", connecting the latter to the construction of the relationship in teaching, in order to understand and describe the perception of *interpersonal distance* in the relationship teachers/learners and between learners, in the educational model CReAP+T declined in DLaD.

Keywords: Interpersonal distance · Virtual learning environmemt · Perception · Performative theatrical didactic · Simplexity

Nadia Carlomagno is the main researcher of the project; she designed the project and wrote sections "1. Introduction", "2. Space as a place of interpersonal distance in the teacher-learner dialogue: the 'measure of the relationship'", "2.1. From the framework to the CReAP+T Method", "3. From the CReAP+T Method in DLaD to Methodology", "3.1. CReAP+T Method in DLaD: some aspects", "3.2. Research design and methodology", "3.3. Sample", "3.4. Research question", "5. Conclusion and future perspec-tive", she is also the scientific responsible; Valeria Minghelli is the co-author, she structured with the author the questionnaire and wrote the section "3.5. Investigative tools", "4. Results", "4.1. Discussion".

G. Casalino et al. (Eds.): HELMeTO 2021, CCIS 1542, pp. 199–214, 2022.
https://doi.org/10.1007/978-3-030-96060-5_15

1 Introduction

During the last year, because of the pandemic, even taking into account the scientific knowledge pertaining to the fields of psychopedagogy, neurosciences, as well as Embodied Cognition Science, which reaffirm the centrality and the inseparability of the cognitive, corporal, and emotional dimensions within the learning process, it has been necessary to review and remodulate the constitutive paradigms of didactics, repositioning studies inside a new *Umwelt* [1], which, at a distance, constitutes itself as a spatial, relational and a shared environment, strongly influenced by dialogue through the use of *technology* [2]. Von Uexkull (1993) describes the Umwelt as that *"portion of the world that every species is capable to perceive and in which it can act according to the parameters that are important to it"* [1].

Starting from considerations regarding the constitutive function carried out by the *presence* of the body in the educational relationship [3] and from the assumption that *"culture is not transferred, it is embodied and experienced"* [4], the DLaD model (Didactic Laboratory at a Distance) outlined throughout these months centred on the *CReAP* Method, whose acronym stands for *Corporeality, Creativity, Relationship, emotion, Action, Performativity + Technology,* from now on *CReAP+T,* intends, even though at a distance, to continue to promote significant experiences generating that transformative activity necessary both in didactics and in theatre. Through the design of workshops that return the centrality of embodied action so that *knowing knowledge* becomes *taught knowledge*, and, in turn, *comprehended* [5]. If, on the one hand, the duration of the pandemic has inhibited the return to didactics in presence, on the other it has also extended the experience of didactics through distance learning, both requiring and allowing for greater experimentation and refinement of the strategies implemented in the first phase. This study, in fact, poses itself as a continuation, in its explorative intention, of a previous experience in DLaD centred on CReAP+T in which elements of the constitutive model aimed at empowering, even at a distance, the bodily aware action, responsible and competent of the future teachers, recognizing the performative role of the body as a tool of relation and cognition, also through the dialogue between the body and technologies.

Around this topic, throughout the months, further reflections on the constructs of intersubjective space [6], closeness and *interpersonal distance* [7], have been made. In investigating on the possible interactions at distance, the dialogue with technologies asks teaching staff to assume a *holistic perspective*, regarding the *relationship between technology and education* [8]. Hence observations are not to be restricted merely to digital literacy of teachers and students, rather they should reflect upon the good practices deployed in fostering interactive experiences through the act of creative *deviation* [9], simultaneously systemic and *recursive* [10] regarding the *man-body-machine relationships* [8]. In these months, during workshops held with students and teachers in training at the University Suor Orsola Benincasa of Naples and the University Cattolica del Sacro Cuore of Milan, a model of *performative didactics* which places the *body in action* [4], as an element capable of sustaining a relationship, even at a distance, of performing messages, content and emotions, through the recourse to the *simplex properties* and *principles* such as of the *separation of functions* [11] and the *creator inhibition* [9] which allow the activation of strategies of *vicariance* [12], fostering different *uses and expressions* of the *scenic bios* [13], researching the pre-expressive level, is being faced in a synchronic and diachronic manner.

2 Space as a Place of Interpersonal Distance in the Teacher-Learner Dialogue: The 'Measure of the Relationship'

"L'espace, ce n'est pas seulement une affaire de géomètres et d'architectes. Il est utilisé depuis longtemps pour la mémoire [...] c'est aussi une technique utilisée depuis toujours pour trouver des solutions nouvelles dans les fonctions cognitives" [14]. The brain, in fact, is not limited to receive information, but rather *"il projette sur le monde ses interprétations e ses hyphotèses [...] modifie les relations spatiales"* [14].

Neurophysiologist Alain Berthoz's reflection shows how space not only affects higher cognitive functions such as memory and reasoning, but also highlights the brain's ability to modify space by inventing *"forms that do not exist"* [11]. In the debate between pedagogy and neuroscience, in particular, space is positioned as a determining element of learning experiences, supporting the idea that cognition is born and progresses in the experience of perceiving the environment and the action taking place in it, and "*depends crucially on the kind of experience the body has had the opportunity to live*" [15]. This makes *human educability "a concrete potential which finds its tools precisely in the processes of communication and in the interactive experiential exchanges that guarantee the relationship with the environment and the other individuals"* [16].

In reflecting on the circular relationship between teacher/learner/context, in the light of phenomenological beliefs, the experience of "knowledge" is placed in that "space of encounter", in the *structural coupling* [17] that arises from the interaction between the two poles of the process, *"acquainted and known"* [18] in a given context that guarantees the relationship. An interaction that is structured, as well as in the theatrical artistic experience, *hic et nunc*, in the corporeal and spatial copresence, where it is *"the action to be crucial for perception"* [19].

It is now clear how isolated the bodies have been in the distance imposed by the pandemic situation and how the perception of the "space" of learning has changed significantly: space, as physical one, has become virtual, technological, metaphysical and social. On this basis, the need to understand how, in the distance, we can recreate a generative and co-agent space of empathic processes that can support the teacher-learner and learner-learner relationship and implement the same process of teaching-learning that, even in DLaD has not renounced the intention of constituting itself as a transformative process, aimed at increasing incarnate knowledge and developing skills. Endorsing the concept of the *"tyranny of perception"* [14] that sees the brain creator of worlds starting from "[...] *a body that acts in the world thanks to the flexibility and multiplicity of the mechanisms of manipulation of space"* [11] the idea of space as potential for action is structured, *"broken into areas corresponding to actions that can be performed"* [12] dominated by a perception that also acts in the representation of the muscular sensations of such actions, on the simulation of the sensory-perceptive process.

This is in keeping with Poincaré's thesis, which states that "*locating an object in space simply means representing the movements that would be necessary to reach it. It's not about representing the movements themselves, it's just the muscular sensations that go with them*" [20].

An idea of space definable as a potential space for encounter, action, where the perception of simulated and concrete actions co-inhabits in recalling also emotional memories that allow to imagine and simulate places, spaces, actions and situations, thanks to the action of creative inhibition that *"est aussi un outil essentiel pour nous permettre de faire face au caractére improbable du monde qui nous entoure, par la nécessaire adaptation à ses changements en général imprévisibles"* [9]. The basis of our perception of the world and of ourselves *"It is not only the action, but act; act with its intentionality, its memory of the past, its projection towards the future, the specification of what interests us in the world according to our Umwelt [...] The identity of the self is also a flow between memory autobiographical, phenomenal self-perception at every moment and prediction of the future. One might think brain can build a virtual world, a kind of dream lived by its double, that allows the permanent simulation of the act and the choice of the best solutions or the inhibition of useless acts"* [11]. From this point of view, virtual space has determined the experience of relationships at a distance, structured on the sensory experience. Experience of the senses and of feeling, of the co-presented bodies, where the technological instrument has taken on the connotations, not only of the interface, responsible just for the mediation of communication, but has also itself become a constitutive element of the relationship that coevolves in an *enactive logic* [10]. The subjects are involved in constituting the formative and transformative experience centred on the enhancement of creativity and imagination also through the simulation of the act. The studies around the *"embodied simulation"* [6] have led to the identification of "we-centric" space that welcomes the idea of being *"singular-plural"*, a space that creates community [21]. The mechanisms of mirroring and resonance, which in embodied simulation allow the establishment of a shared manifold, generating that *"intentional consonance [...]"* thanks to which each one feels *"[...] with the other, a relationship of identity and reciprocity"* [22].

In this context, it is the "system of relations" that qualifies and quantifies the event, relativizing "space to time" and ending up by combining, in the human sciences, *"the physical environment to questions rooted in the 'history' in which the event itself takes place"* [23]. Space is not understood as the sphere (real or logical) in which things are arranged, but *"the means by virtue of which the position of things becomes possible. This is equivalent to saying that [...] we must think of it as the universal power of their connections"* [24]. This defines a space of dislocation, which for Foucault is defined by *"proximity relations between points or elements"*, a *third space* [25], as a place of construction and negotiation of structured meanings on proximity perception, even at a distance. As part of his studies on proxemics, anthropologist Hall identified four types of *interpersonal distance* [7], assumed in different ways by subjects within social relationships: the intimate distance involving a physical distance within 50 cm; the personal distance (between 50 and 120 cm); the social distance (120–240 cm); the public distance (over 240 cm).

In this perspective "*a 'perfect proximity' is flanked by the concept of distance, by the use of the gaze, by the tone of the voice, by the sensory perception of heat, noise and smell, physical contact, by non-verbal relations between speakers, body dynamics in interactive contexts"* [23]. In the absence of that physical contact, odors, and bodily dynamics constitutive of the perception of "proximity" in interactive contexts, a *vicarious* and *creative* approach [9, 12] has been strongly sought in the field of DLaD. This could, through a design remodulation, restore the perception of a shared space centred on dialogical and performative ability to establish an empathic educational relationship.

2.1 From the Framework to the CReAP+T Method

Within the DLaD, the director/teacher and actor/learner relationship, both spectators of new performances, was redefined in the light of the repositioning in the "space of distance". Here the bodies, suspended in a limbic dimension, have not taken on monadic connotations inhibiting communication, but have experienced different vicariant, expressive and communicative modes, opening new relational windows, using the principle of deviation and the *function separation property* [11], so that in the inhibition of some of them, others have been strengthened, with the aim of structuring new spatial/temporal and relational coordinates of didactics. As part of the first experiences and research on distance training, carried out in the first lockdown from March to June 2020, in the structuring of the CReAP+T method declined in DLaD, it was possible to investigate every conceivable mode of communicative and perceptive relationship able to elaborate a *surplus of meaning* [26], strengthening the *bodily, conscious, competent and responsible of the future teacher* [27]. A second research implemented during the second lockdown (October 2020-January 2021) investigated, instead, the replicable elements of teaching practices activated and analyzed around the role of *feedback* communication in the teacher/learner relationship, director/actor [27] as *autopoietic loop* tool [28]. This, with the intention of pursuing, in the analogy between theatre and didactics, an idea of *"event"* not intended as a show that is offered to the viewer's gaze but as a *"social game [...] that is produced in the interaction between actors and spectators"* [28], capable of generating a circular relationship.

The embodied and enactive experiential dimension has made it possible to identify, in the feedback and in the performance teaching strategies proper to the model, dialogical and autopoietic, cyclic and recursive features which *"allow students to have not only interpretative skills, but also the ability to activate an argumentative process with the instructor, an open and dynamic process in which the people involved are engaged in mutual alignment"* [29]. On these elements it was possible to generate a shared, *morphogenetic* space [30], capable of extending into the *extended mind* [31], beyond the tangible reality, consisting of an *intersubjective* [6] dimension and emotional variables of the processes of participation and restitution, *empathic tuning, and resonance* [22]. Hence the intention to continue to investigate the theme of the "framed" space in its "metaphysical" and relational dimension in order to understand what were the didactic strategies that would allow the approach of extended "minds" and "bodies" able to continue to "be present" even in the absence of their tangible portion, supporting relational, emotional, mental and cognitive processes.

Artifacts and nature, biology and culture, are co-inhabiting an integrated view of the mental domain (of cognition) *"we are made of complex and changing instruments of 'our own' internal and external tools of thought. We're our best artifacts, and we have always been"* [32].

3 From the CReAP+T Method in DLaD to Methodology

3.1 CReAP+T Method in DLaD: Some Aspects

The CReAP+T Method is an experimental method structured on theatrical performing techniques and practices, on the embodied and enactive experiential dimension that translates the phenomenological concepts of *Leib* [33] into action. It is a dialogic and active method that, declined in the DLaD, acquires a re-thinking that strengthens it and also increases it in the technologic dimension (T) becoming CReAP+T. It is centred on the role of feedback and presence, understood as a *scenic bios and source of energy* [13], as a "sense of being there" in connection with oneself, with the place and others.

Through the practice of acting training, activities based on breathing, eye contact, relationship and individual and group body explorations, one works on the activation of the emotional and bodily awakening, investigating the energetic abilities of the body through the awareness of its own potentialities and expressive and creative instruments, explicit and implicit, that lead to the elevation of the plane of consciousness and to the full self-consciousness and self-awareness and self-determination, elements capable of co-creating a reality in which alienation gives way to resonance and empathy. A holistic process that is activated when one connects to their own creativity, that is to the condition of abandonment, of listening and connection to oneself and others, in the Body-Mind-Heart alignment.

In this sense, performative, interactive and multimodal didactics that favor the embodied cognitive process of *didactic transposition* [5] are implemented. These didactics are centred on formative, performative and transformative activities in a condition of alignment and structural coupling made possible by the triggering of empathic relationships. This process is based on the active listening of a body that generates "living" perceptions [34], proper and specific to a sensitive, present, perceptive and acting body. The different use of the *body in a situation* [4] affects not only the pre-expressive and expressive level of each, but also the perception level of space, able to amplify the energy of the actions and to strengthen their repercussions in the empathic dialogue between the interlocutors and between them and the technologies used. Workshop activities allow, in this sense, the creation of a protected space, *without judgment* [35], where even at a distance, it is possible to stimulate creative processes of knowledge acquisition [36]. Where the teacher becomes the director and the learner the protagonist of their cognitive process through autonomous actions in which each has the opportunity to measure themselves with their own attitudes, with their own creativity, with one's own body in action and to get to know one's own world from personal abilities in sharing with others. Resuming Matteucci's point of view that invites one to engage in *"an experience 'with' the world before an experience 'of' it"* [37]. The CReAP+T Method moves on from the relationship of feeling with the other and with the world promoting continuous solicitation through *autopoetic feedback* [28] activities that involve the student/actor in their multiple possibilities "to be there" with voice, gaze and gestures, with the body and beyond the body.

3.2 Research Design and Metodology

Starting from *art-based research* (ABR) [38] that identifies all those practices which use artistic processes, specifically those inherent to performative practices, as main factors probed also in education [39], the DLaD model centred on CReAP+T affirms a series of elements aimed at outlining the interconnections between director/teacher and actor/student and between all actors. This takes place through dynamics of relation and exchange centered on ever-changing *autopoietic feedback* [28] which assumes strategic value in defining the temperature of the learning environment which determines the experience.

In the systematic application of the model, the focus of the survey has changed, from time to time, with the aim of achieving a comprehensive vision of the model, around which to redefine new awareness of the effectiveness of the strategies.

On this occasion, therefore, the intention was to reflect around the theme of "perception of the learning space" at a distance, connecting the latter to the construction of the teaching relationship, aiming to understand the perception of the learning climate in interaction with the teacher and other students. In particular, reference was made to the paradigm of *interpersonal distances* stated the anthropologist Hall [7].

To improve the didactic model, the basic research and the applied research have followed the *arts-based practices* founded on the paradigm of Anne Brown and Alan Collins' *Design Based Research* (DBR) [8].

Consequently, a two-pronged approach has been adopted: one synchronic, stemming from single workshop experiences, and one diachronic, which frames the reflections considering previous experiences and future ones. The synchronic level intends to pursue the intention that every workshop represents an opportunity to experiment, also in distance learning, the performative use of the body, beginning from the construction of the setting of the *virtual learning environment* and from *actor training* [40] which influences the experience intended as irradiation, intensification of the body as *"some sort of aura"* [41] surrounding the body but not lined up with it, exceeding it and leading one's body to imagine the body [42]. While the diachronic level of the study, through the months and following experimentations of the model, is optimizing the strategies, perfectioning the probe's tools and recalibrating dynamics.

3.3 Sample

The sample of 1071 students surveyed (1038 M; 33 F), represents the students involved in the different training courses using the CReAP+T Method in the DLaD, based on the same methodological and scientific framework. Specifically, these are courses such as: Special pedagogy of integrated group management of the Specialization Course for – Primary School - Support; Playing by learning: creative techniques for theatre animation and communication, and Evaluation in children's education services, all pertaining to the degree in Educational Sciences; Workshop in Education of Movement and Workshop of Planning and Evaluation pertaining, instead, to the degree in Primary Formation Sciences held at the University Suor Orsola Benincasa in Naples, Italy.

3.4 Research Question

This exploratory survey aims to investigate the theme of "learning space perception", connecting the latter to the construction of the teaching relationship, in order to understand and describe the perception of "interpersonal distance" in the teacher/learner relationship and between learners, based on the CReAP+T educational model used in DLaD by trying to:

- better understand what influences the relationship and perception of interpersonal distance in the DLaD learning process;
- obtain relevant information for model implementation and define detection tools.

3.5 Investigative Tools

An exploratory research design has been considered [43] for this survey. A questionnaire consisting of a semi-structured list of 3 items for the collection of personal data (gender, age, type of course attended), 15 items with dichotomic choice, and 6 items with multiple choice by ticking a single answer [44] was submitted to be completed independently by all subjects. The collection of quantitative data has made it possible to collect general information relating to a large number of people, albeit with the inevitable limit of constraining the response opportunities of the respondents: this applies to both dichotomous and multiple-choice questions.

For this reason, open answer questions were also submitted, but these are not subject to any analysis in the present contribution. Especially in this phase of the construction of detection tools, in which the intention is to reflect on what the objects of the investigation itself should be, for the detection of the educational and transformative effectiveness of the CReAP+T Method in its hybrid application (both at a distance and in presence), the analysis of the open questions could allow us to identify recurrent elements in students' statements that could open up new scenarios for reflection that will need to be discussed in the future.

The questionnaire was carried out following the administration of a Pre-test, in which students of similar courses previously held answered with the aim of calibrating the questions, verifying their comprehensibility. The closed-answer questions were aimed at gathering students' opinions useful in answering the first of the research questions. The qualitative level of the survey, which is only anticipated in this work, will aim at a later stage and through the analysis of open-answer questions, to understand the individual and collective dynamics [43] which arise in relation to the perception of relationship and space in a more thorough way, in order to guide the choices of future educational research.

It should be noted that some of the contents under investigation (specifically, the paradigm of interpersonal distance) refer to theoretical contents that were widely treated with students and explained during the compilation phase in a special section preceding the questions. In order to ensure greater clarity in reading and understanding the items and to facilitate subsequent analysis and interpretation of the results, the different items were grouped in the following sections: personal data; learning environment in presence; elements that affect the perception of the distance learning environment; perception of the other and the distance group; empathic climate in DLaD and elements that could determine it; interpersonal distance perception with the camera on and off; elements that influence the perception of distance (number present, camera activation, interaction); self-assessment of the experience in DLaD; perception of space in DLaD. The questionnaire was administered anonymously through the Google Forms digital platform, following the completion of the training courses. An introductory passage informing the subjects about the purposes of the research was provided and the students gave their informed consent before compiling the questionnaire.

4 Results

The quantitative data was collected and processed in an Excel environment and then organized in Table 1, which shows the frequencies of each response expressed using percentages.

4.1 Discussion

See Table 1 above for the discussion of results. The first part of the questionnaire was aimed at understanding whether, for the participating students, the learning environment in presence affects their level of concentration, participation, and how they interact with the teacher and colleagues (IT B 1-2-3-4). Learners reported that the learning environment affects each of the following dimensions respectively: 89% (concentration level), 87,3% (participation), 86,1% (interaction with the teacher) and 88,5% (relationship with colleagues). Therefore, the learning environment, in the data noted, would appear to be a significant variable with considerable influence both in terms of learning and in terms of participation and relationship. In this perspective, the importance of investigating what might be the elements that, at a distance, allow the perception of an environment, characterized as a place that "receives" students and "contains" them in a climate of motivating and stimulating learning, is clear. On the other hand they were asked whether these variables in turn affected their own perception of the learning environment, to understand whether there are elements that, though at a distance, allow students to perceive a space of sharing (IT C 1-2-3). In this regard, 83,2% of the respondents reported that, even at a distance, it is possible "to organize some factors that define a learning environment". Among the factors considered as being able to influence this, the relationship between learners receives positive responses in 79,9% of the answers, while the relationship with the teacher accounts for 84,7% of responses. This would seem to confirm the importance of putting in place strategies to facilitate the relationship in support of effective interaction.

In continuing to investigate the relationship, with reference to the virtual learning environment, the questionnaire asked students whether it was possible to "perceive the other" at a distance (70,3%) and "the totality of the group" (47,9%) and what were the elements capable of determining this possibility (IT D 1-2-3-4): in reference to the perception of the other the interaction was considered influential by 52,8% of learners, the possibility of "seeing the other" is influential for the remaining part.

Table 1. Results

Item	Question	Answer	Perc. %
IT B1	*Do you think the learning environment in presence affects your concentration?*	Yes	89
		No	11
IT B2	*Do you think the learning environment in presence affects your interaction with the teachers?*	Yes	86,1
		No	13,9
IT B3	*Do you think the learning environment in presence affects your level of participation?*	Yes	87,3
		No	12,7
IT B4	*Do you think the learning environment in presence affects your relationship with colleagues?*	Yes	88,5
		No	11,5
IT C1	*Do you think that, at a distance, learners relationships affect your perception of a learning environment?*	Yes	79,9
		No	20,1
IT C2	*Do you think at a distance, it is possible to organize some factors that define a learning environment?*	Yes	83,2
		No	16,8
IT C3	*Do you think that, at a distance, the relationship with the teacher affects your perception of a learning environment?*	Yes	84,7
		No	15,3
IT D1	*Can I perceive the other at a distance?*	Yes	70,3
		No	29,7
IT D2	*Can I perceive, at a distance, the whole group?*	Yes	47,9
		No	52,1

(continued)

Table 1. (*continued*)

Item	Question	Answer	Perc. %
IT D3	*When do I perceive the other?*	When you speak	52,8
		If I cross his gaze	18,8
		If I look at it	28,5
IT D4	*When do I perceive the group better?*	When the webcam is on, and I can see the others	44,4
		When others interact with the teacher independently of the webcam	47,6
		Always anyway	5,7
		Never in any case	2,2
IT E1	*Does DLaD give me a chance to create an empathic climate?*	Yes	76,5
		No	23,5
IT E2	*Developing empathy in virtual classrooms:*	It's possible, but it depends on the teacher's engagement skills	77,1
		It is possible, but depends on the number of people in the group	18,5
		It's impossible	4,4
IT F1	*In the lessons in DLaD, with the camera off, what distance (cf. E. Hall) do you perceive from colleagues?*	Intimate 20–50 cm Personal 50–120 cm Social 120–240 cm Public da 240 cm in su	4,7 12,8 37,6 44,8
IT F2	*In the lessons in DLaD, with the camera on, what distance (cf. E. Hall) do you perceive from colleagues?*	Intimate 20–50 cm Personal 50–120 cm Social 120–240 cm Public da 240 cm in su	7,7 34,8 48,5 9,1
IT G1	*Is the perception of the area (intimate, personal, social, public) related to the number of people who populate the classroom in DLaD?*	Yes	62,8
		No	37,2
IT G2	*Is the perception of the area (intimate, personal, social, public) linked to the activation of the camera?*	Yes	72,5
		No	27,5

(*continued*)

Table 1. (*continued*)

Item	Question	Answer	Perc. %
IT G3	*Is the perception of the area (intimate, personal, social, public) linked to the interaction between teachers and learners and between learners and learners*	Yes	86,9
		No	13,1
IT H1	*Can DLaD be considered a significant experience?*	Yes	93,5
		No	6,5
IT H2	*Can DLaD be considered a transformative experience?*	Yes	90,4
		No	9,6
IT I1	*How would you define space in DLaD?*	Relational	7,5
		Metaphisical	14,3
		Shared	43,8
		Isolated	24,1
		Other	10,3

Even in group perception, the gaze or the "possibility of seeing the other" (44,4%) and the "interaction" in its different forms (47,6%) are indicated as elements that favor this perception.

In the conviction that in learning relationships the perception of the other alone is not enough to determine the "relationship" and subsequent transformative action, at which the teaching performance of the DLaD model aims, it was asked whether even at a distance it was possible to establish or perceive a "empathic climate", in reference to the DLaD experience (IT E 1-2). 76,5% of Students answered that it is possible to establish an empathic climate; 77,1% that this depends on the teacher's ability to "involve" students.

The question about the perception of interpersonal distance [7] was investigated with the webcam off and on (IT F 1-2), in support of the theme of presence promoted by the model: the data relating to personal distance increases significantly when the camera is on, in contrast to the decrease in the perception of public distance.

Specifically, the perception of personal distance goes from 12,8% with the camera off to 34,8% with the camera on, and on the contrary the perception of public distance decreases considerably (44,8% camera off; 9,1% camera on).

Furthermore, with due caution, it is possible to assume that the increase of the perception of personal and intimate distance could be related to the constituent elements of the model and in particular to the recall of presence through the practice of body training in action that has naturally stimulated and influenced the switching on of the webcam and the systematic application of feedback in the empathic relationship in the CReAP+T method by the teacher.

With reference to the perception of interpersonal distance, students were also asked what the elements they considered capable of influencing this perception were (IT G 1-2-3): the "visibility" of the other takes on greater value than the data on the "number of students". In fact, activation of the webcam is crucial for 72,5% of students and the number of students, instead, is crucial for 62,8%. In support of what has been said so far, the perception of "closeness" is placed more in relation to another element, namely the interaction teacher/ learner (86,9%). With the aim of self-evaluation, students were asked whether, even at a distance, it had been possible to live a "significant" and "transformative" educational experience (IT H 1-2): students responded affirmatively in 93,5% and 90,4% of cases, respectively. It appears possible to state that this data, that is only apparently "natural" in an effective "in-presence" educational model, is not so obvious in distance teaching, therefore it is worth continuing in the implementation of the CReAP+T Method, to outline it's most effective constituent elements.

Finally, in reference to the CReAP+T model in DLaD, among the different multiple-choice options present to describe the space in DLaD, students choose the item "relational space" in 7,5% of cases, "metaphysical" in 14,3%, "shared" in 43,8%, despite the physical distance, which shows limits found in 24.1% of students who describe themselves as "isolated".10,3% answered "other", which will be the subject of further analysis in future qualitative data (IT I 1).

To conclude the discussion with reference to a first analysis of quantitative data, it seems that open responses offer research important information about how, even at a distance, the empathic relationship, the interaction/activation of learners, the perception of the other (body language, gaze, tone of voice) are useful elements in triggering a meaningful teaching process based on "a shift from an 'experience-of' to an 'experience-with' which can signify a kind of participatory experience" [37]. It would appear that the results so far in the quantitative analysis could be used to describe an experience which, although has resulted in the abstraction of a virtual learning environment, has also resulted from its *'creative inhibition'*, making new *deviations* [9] possible.

5 Conclusion and Future Perspectives

On the basis of the framework, of the model's progressive structuring and of the reflections that have emerged from subsequent experimentation, it is appropriate to continue investigating what the elements capable of bringing interpersonal distances closer together are, which actions allow the setting to be redefined and reposition the subjects at the centre of the didactic action, reifying, even at a distance, a learning environment that is recognizable as such regarding interpersonal proximity.

The emergency situation, in its continuation, is offering the opportunity to modify those elements of teaching that, over time, have demonstrated their inefficacy in favor of improvements and implementing models that are gradually emerging in different training contexts, including the multiple and different kinds of scientific awareness generated. In this context, the application of the rising CReAP+T Method along with the quality-quantity probe has experimented and investigated the constructs of space in relationships and in interpersonal distance in order to systematize strategies and structure preventive and systemic interventions that will enable future decisions to be guided, particularly in the field of education, as well as in the case of *project-based research* (DBR) [8].

One of the strengths of this method is in its capacity to recognize and assign, even at a distance, a central role to the embodied action of didactics. In this context, didactics assume the characteristics of performative didactics and generate the teacher/student relationship which sees the space for action in its *structural coupling* [17]. A critical element is undoubtedly identifiable in the tools used to collect the data pertaining to the research, which need to be improved and which in the construction *in fieri* aim to identify future indicators for a qualitative-quantitative probe. Such research, in fact, is often configured as a process developing learning environments through subsequent optimizations before developing systematically structured and conducted experimental studies [38]. Referring to the socio-cultural approach according to which *"the focus in educational technology has appropriately turned from artificial intelligence to amplifying the intelligence of teachers and students*" [45], in reflecting on prospects, the conviction that dialogue through technology cannot stop with the end of the global health emergency is inevitably born. There is awareness that virtual devices have demonstrated, like never before, their prosthetic function, able not only to extend bodies but render them open and *dilated* [46] to perception in relation to the capability of our brain/body to navigate inside a virtual simulation. The human brain is a *creator of worlds* [12] and does not limit itself only to simulating reality, it also emulates possible worlds. Moreover, it can be stated that experience has once again confirmed the idea that it is the quality of the relationship between teachers and learners to reposition teaching in presence even at a distance, through active, performative and transformative methodologies, able to generate a learning climate that assumes the characteristics of a shared space resulting from intimate and personal proximity, in the circular relationship between teacher/learners and between learners.

In conclusion, in the light of new approaches, research implies the intention to identify a hybrid model of teaching in combining the relationship between man-body-machine dictated by the emergency, and to aim to derive the dimensions of effectiveness, implementable even in presence, in a blended perspective. A model of teaching based on relationship and participatory and performative dimension of the body, supported by non-linear methods and techniques and practices of theatrical matrix, working on the creation and care of the learning setting, both virtual or real/physical, offers the possibility to consider space not as an external element, data of the objective world which one experiences, but as a way of experiencing which produces forms in structuring the interaction relationship [47]. It is in the places, that is in the lived spaces (in which the emphasis is more on the lived than on the space), *"that the experience of human subjectivity is generated and articulated"* [48]. A place of welcome [49] living in respect of each and every one, where each person can experience their communicative, emotional, cognitive and relational self in the construction of their own sense and form in a holistic way, where *"Living means leaving traces"* [50].

References

1. Von Uexkull, J.: Ambienti animali e ambienti umani. Una passeggiata in mondi sconosciuti e invisibili (1933). Mazzeo, M. (ed.) Quodlibet, Roma 2013. In: Guidi C., Tra mente estesa e plasticità neurale: il linguaggio come "artefatto fondamentale" RIFL/SFL, pp. 129–142 (2017). https://doi.org/10.4396/SFL201710

2. Laurillard, D.: Insegnamento come scienza della progettazione. Costruire modelli pedagogici per apprendere con le tecnologie. Rossi, PG., Rivoltella, P.C. (trad.it). Franco Angeli, Milano (2014)
3. Carlomagno, N., Ciasullo, A., Orefice, C., Frauenfelder, E.: Didactic "Harmonies" in a bioeducational perspective. Educ. Sci. Soc. **4**(1) (2013)
4. Rivoltella, P.C.: Corpi in situ-azione: presupposti neuroscientifici e drammaturgici per una nuova formazione degli insegnanti. In: La professionalità degli insegnanti. La ricerca e le pratiche, pp. 89–99, p. 95. PensaMultimedia, Lecce (2017)
5. Chevallard, Y.: La transposition didactique. Du savoir savant au savoir enseigné. Grenoble (1989)
6. Gallese, V.: Dai neuroni specchio alla consonanza intenzionale. Meccanismi neurofisiologici dell'intersoggettività. Riv. Psicoanalisi **LIII**(1), 197–208 (2007)
7. Hall, E.T.: A system for the notation of proxemics behaviour. Am. Anthropol. **65**, 1003–1026 (1963)
8. Rivoltella, P.C., Rossi, P.G.: Il corpo e la macchina. Tecnologia, cultura, educazione. Morcelliana, Brescia (2019)
9. Berthoz, A.: L'inhibition créatrice, p. 19. Jacob, Parigi (2020)
10. Rossi, P.G.: Didattica enattiva. Complessità, teorie dell'azione, professionalità docente. FrancoAngeli, Milano (2011)
11. Berthoz, A.: La semplessità, p. 92, p. 120. Codice, Torino (2011)
12. Berthoz, A.: Vicariance (La): Le cerveau créateur de mondes. Odile Jacob, p. 47 (2013)
13. Barba, E.: La canoa di carta, Trattato di antropologia teatrale. Mulino, Bologna (1993)
14. Berthoz, A.: Fondements cognitifs de la perception de l'espace. 1st International Congress on Ambiances, Grenoble 2008, pp. 121–132. Grenoble, France (2008). halshs-00836199
15. Iverson, J.M.; Thelen, E.: Hand, mouth and brain. The dynamic emergence of speech and gesture. Journal of Consciousness Studies **6**(11–12), 19–40 (1999). p. 22
16. Frauenfelder, E.: Perché una relazione tra pedagogia e biologia? Sezione Brain Education Cognition. RTH, p. 3 (2018)
17. Maturana, H.R., Varela, F. J.: Autopoiesi e cognizione. La realizzazione del vivente. Marsilio, Venezia (1980). (trad. it. 2001)
18. Proulx, J., Simmt, E.: Enactivism in mathematics education: moving toward a reconceptualization of learning and knowledge. Educ. Sci. Soc. **IV**, 1 (2013)
19. Caruana, F., Borghi, A.: Embodied Cognition: una nuova psicologia. G. Ital. Psicol. **1**, 23–48 (2013)
20. Poincaré, H.: L'espace et la géométrie. Rev. Métaphys. Morale **3**(6), 631–646 (1895). In Einstein, A.: Conceptions scientifiques, p. 29. Flammarion (Ed. originale 1955), Paris (1990)
21. Nancy, J.L.: Essere singolare plurale. Piccola biblioteca Einaudi (2021)
22. Gallese, V., Morelli, U.: Il teatro come metafora del mondo e il teatro nella mente. Castiglioncello (Pi), p. 4 (2011). https://www.ugomorelli.eu/pp/Gallese-Morelli-Teatro-metafora-mondo.pdf
23. Gennari, M.: Pedagogia degli ambienti educativi, p. 22. Armando Editore, Roma (1997)
24. Merleau-Ponty, M.: Phenomenologie de la perception. Gallimard, Paris (1945); ed. it. Fenomenologia della percezione, Mimesis, Milano (2003)
25. Potter, J., McDougall, J.: Digital Media, Culture and Education: Theorising Third Space. Springer, Heidelberg (2017)
26. Varela, F.J.: Ethical Know-How: Action, Wisdom, and Cognition. Stanford University Press, Stanford (1999)
27. Carlomagno, N., Minghelli, V.: Distance teaching as a performative experience. Ital. J. Health Educ. Sports Inclusive Didact. - Anno **5**(2), 187–198 (2021). ISSN 2532-3296 ISBN 978-88-6022-411-8 - aprile – giugno

28. Fischer-Lichte, E.: Estetica del performativo. Una teoria del teatro e dell'arte, p. 13. Carocci Editore, Roma (2014)
29. Rossi, P.G., Pentucci, M., Fedeli, L., Giannandrea, L., Pennazio, V.: From the informative feedback to the generative feedback. Educ. Sci. Soc. **9**(2), 83–107 (2018). p. 91
30. Sheldrake, R.: New Science of Life. 3rd edn. Icon Book (2009)
31. Clark, A., Chalmers, D.J.: The extended mind. Analysis **58**, 10–23 (1998)
32. Clark, A.: Natural Born Cyborgs: Technologies and the Future of Human Intelligence, p. 192. Oxford University Press, Oxford (2004)
33. Husserl, E.: L'idea della Fenomenologia. Il Saggiatore, Milano (1988) (1907)
34. Grotowski, J.: Vers un théâtre pauvre. L'Âge d'Homme, Lausanne (1965)
35. Rogers, C.: La terapia centrata sul cliente. Giunti, Firenze (2013)
36. Dewey J.: Art as experience. TarcherPerigre (2005)
37. Matteucci, G.: Estetica e natura umana. La mente estesa tra percezione, emozione ed espressione. Carocci editore, Roma (2019). In: Iannilli, G.L., Marino, S.: Book Forum on Estetica e natura umana. Questions by Chiodo, S., Dreon, R., Gallagher, S., Griffero, T., Levinson, J., Paolucci, C., Shusterman, R.: Replies by Giovanni Matteucci. Meta research in hermeneutics, phenomenology, and practical philosophy, vol. XII, no. 2, pp. 593–639, p. 599; 610, December 2020
38. McNiff, S.: Art-based research. In: Knowles, J.G., Cole, A.L. (eds.) Handbook of the Arts in Qualitative Research: Perspectives, Methodologies, Examples, and Issues. Sage Publications, Thousand Oaks (2007)
39. Pellerey, M.: Verso una nuova metodologia di ricerca educativa: la ricerca basata su progetti (design-based research). Orientamenti Pedagogici **52**(5), 721–737 (2005)
40. Carlomagno, N.: Le potenzialità didattiche delle arti sceniche. Educ. Sci. Soc. 346–359 (2020). 1/2020 ISSN 2038-9442, ISSNe 2284-015X
41. Jouvet, L.: Les comédien désincarné, p. 47. Flammarion Editeur, Parigi (1954)
42. Nancy, J.L.: Corpo-Teatro (tr. it.) Moscati, A. Cronopio, Napoli (2010)
43. Trinchero, R., Robasto, D.: I mixed methods nella ricerca educativa. Mondadori, Milano (2019)
44. Trinchero, R.: Manuale di ricerca educativa. Franco Angeli, Milano (2002)
45. Dede, C.: The role of digital technologies in deeper learning. Students at the Center: Deeper Learning Research Series. Jobs Future, p. 7 (2014)
46. Barba, E., Savarese, N.: L'arte segreta dell'attore. Dizionario di antropologia teatrale. Edizioni di Pagina, Bari (2011)
47. Simmel, G.: Sociologie. UntersuchungenüberdieFormender Vergesellschaftung. Sociologia. Edizioni Comunità, Torino (2019)
48. Pezzullo: Fenoglio, M.T. (ed.): Andar per luoghi. Natura e vicende del legame con i luoghi, p. 119. Ananke, Torino (2007)
49. Tagliapietra, A.: Lo spazio e il luogo. La memoria ospitale, dal Convegno "Spazi del contemporaneo", Alghero, 29 September–2 October 2005
50. Benjamin, W.: Parigi capitale del XIX secolo (1986). In: Fortini, A. (Trad. it) Temperino, Brescia (2014)

Enhancing Learning in Higher Education Using MOOC: The Experience of the University of Padua

Monica Fedeli[1(✉)], Marica Liotino[1(✉)], Edward W. Taylor[2], and Marianne G. Araneta[3]

[1] University of Padua, Via Beato Pellegrino, 28, 35122 Padua, Italy
monica.fedeli@unipd.it, marica.liotino@phd.unipd.it
[2] Penn State University, 777 West Harrisburg Pike, Middletown, PA 17057, USA
[3] University of Padua, Via Del Padovanino, 9, 35123 Padua, Italy

Abstract. Research on massive online open courses (MOOCs) is growing, but critical points about their use in blended courses are still being investigated and reported. A new MOOC designed on the principles of constructivism was launched on the FutureLearn platform by the University of Padua in October 2020 and was offered as an optional course to 31 students in a master's degree program. A case study methodology allowed the authors to explore its effectiveness in terms of improving participant learning, promoting learner engagement, and assessing learner satisfaction. A variety of data sources were used, and an in-depth study of the learning experiences reported by the students was carried out. Overall, the experience was effective, offering an example of an active and engaging MOOC that overcame challenges previously reported in the literature. Excellent results emerged from its use in the blended course, as it proved to be a valid integration tool for the development of new skills and knowledge in an international online environment; the course has helped open new paths for the use of MOOCs in the academic context.

Keywords: Blended program · Online courses · University · Active learning · Learners' perspective

1 Introduction

Interest in active learning (AL) is becoming relevant to education research, especially regarding adult education [1, 2]. AL has been defined as "instructional activities involving students in doing things and thinking about what they are doing" [3]. It "is the process of engaging learners with the topic and each other where they are talking, doing, and creating, together" [4]; in this way students construct their learning by interacting with the context, accessing higher-order thinking, and delving into their own attitudes and values [4, 5].

The COVID-19 pandemic has destabilized university communities around the world by forcing the sudden replacement of in-person teaching with distance learning [6].

G. Casalino et al. (Eds.): HELMeTO 2021, CCIS 1542, pp. 215–229, 2022.
https://doi.org/10.1007/978-3-030-96060-5_16

Doubts and perplexities have been expressed by many teachers regarding distance teaching [7], which some consider a hostile environment for learner engagement and not always as effective as face-to-face teaching. Indeed, the pedagogical effectiveness of online courses, especially massive open online courses (MOOCs), remains a matter of intense debate among researchers, as we discuss below.

As part of a trend toward distance learning that predates COVID-19, the University of Padua activated a MOOC project in the 2014–2015 academic year with the aims of improving the quality of higher education, "enhancing the university's international presence [...], encouraging the use of different languages" among learners [8], and promoting university-society interaction and lifelong learning. In this context, MOOCs in several areas of study have been realized and delivered; at present, 11 MOOCs are hosted by the FutureLearn platform, 6 by EduOpen, and 14 by Federica.EU[1].

The present study aims to investigate the learning experience of the learners who attended the MOOC "Innovative Teaching: Engaging Adult Learners with Active Learning," with a particular focus on a group of master's degree students who voluntarily participated. This MOOC specifically fosters learning using AL methods and has been developed and hosted by the FutureLearn platform. The level of satisfaction, the engagement, and the learning processes of learners are explored to better understand how a MOOC can improve learning in blended courses.

2 Theoretical Framework

MOOCs "are one of the important outputs of connectivism" [9]; the several generations of MOOCs have a range of connections to the main theories of learning. A first generation of MOOCs that promoted the connectivity and exchange of social networks and the accessibility of online resources [9–12], was succeeded by a second generation in which the organization of activities was determined by teachers, who followed the principles of behaviorism [11, 12]. Later another MOOC model was developed by combining the principles of constructivism and connectivism [11].

MOOCs designed along the principles of constructivism [9, 13–16], offer opportunities for cooperative learning [17] through a collection of activities, such as online forums, group work to carry out projects, case analysis, panel discussions, peer assessment activities, and dedicated spaces for question-and-answer sessions [18–20]. Support agents are usually involved to stimulate collaboration and interaction among participants [12] and to create communities of inquiry [21, 22]. These kinds of MOOCs also attempt to promote AL [1, 3, 4] by supporting learning through ongoing quizzes and real-life learning applications [18]. All these activities are also designed to give prompt feedback to learners [18, 20]. Moreover, they provide a variety of resources with the aim of "addressing diversity of learners" [18]. With the same intention, they allow for integration through group or individual offline activities [20], equip learners with short videos and summary related to the content of the course [12, 20] and analyze learners' behaviors and preferences to create personalized quizzes [12].

[1] Data retrieved in the official page of the University of Padua https://www.unipd.it/mooc, last accessed 2021/04/12.

There has been growing international interest in the use of MOOCs in blended curricula [23–26]. Indeed, MOOCs have been used to harness the potential of blended learning, which has been defined as the "thoughtful integration of classroom face-to-face learning experiences with online learning experiences" [27], combining the mainly online content and activities of the MOOC with face-to-face classroom learning [28]. Prior studies have proposed models to design this integrated setup. Zhang's five models focus mainly on the purpose of MOOCs: (1) learner services for MOOC participants, with MOOCs as part of a service provided by the university; (2) MOOCs as open resources, where MOOCs are used to supplement classroom learning but are not necessarily part of the curriculum or used as integral parts of classes; (3) flipped classrooms, in which the content of a MOOC is used to study at home; (4) challenge courses for MOOCs, with projects used to assess learning previously conducted in a MOOC; and (5) credit transfer from MOOCs, where completion of a MOOC earns extra credit in a given class [29]. On the other hand, the model of Kloos et al. [25] focuses on MOOC delivery rather than purpose [30] and describes six types of experiences: (a) local digital prelude, which usually functions as a preparatory class for freshmen or students who need to fulfill certain prerequisites; (b) flipping the classroom, with students initially working through the MOOC content at home and then reinforcing that learning in class; (c) canned digital teaching with face-to-face tutoring, which functions as reinforcement classes for those students who have failed a semester and work independently on a MOOC aligned with the curriculum but can still consult with the professor instead of having to take a class again; (d) face-to-face and canned teaching, where the material for a MOOC is used to supplement a face-to-face class; (e) face-to-face teaching with remote tutoring, where experts are invited to teach from a distance; and (f) canned digital teaching with remote tutoring, where the MOOC content is supplemented by remote tutoring from a professor.

Along with the spread of MOOCs, research confirming that student retention is one of the most critical aspects of MOOCs is increasing. A little under a decade ago, it was found that only 7%–10% of enrollees typically completed a MOOC course [31, 32]. Therefore, some researchers have sought to identify factors related to course dropout: dissatisfaction with interactions with classmates and educators, inadequacy of course design, presence of challenging assignments, setting deadlines for assessment and missing learning support and scaffolds, use of transmissive teaching methods and lack of interactive and collaborative assignments, difficulty navigating the platform, the inadequacy of quality of teaching materials, and a lack of engagement and motivation [33–37].

Critical issues in the use of MOOCs in hybrid format have also been reported, and there is substantial overlap with those enumerated above. A lack of experiments integrating MOOCs into traditional classrooms has been reported, which contributes to the challenge of synchronizing the two paths of teaching that educators often face [38]. MOOCs are generally teacher-centered and learning outcomes can be compromised in that kind of format [39]. Moreover, some instructors found it challenging to ensure student engagement, satisfaction, and ultimately learning [23]. This concern was confirmed by Atiaja and Proenza, who noted that little "value is placed on participation and/or student's interaction with peers and teachers [... and] the course content is not innovative or interactive in comparison with new technology" [40].

In response to these concerns, greater "levels of student engagement" are considered relevant to successful learning in MOOCs [41]. Moreover, the consequences perceived by learners, such as "knowledge growth, social interaction, compatibility, and affect," and using MOOC positively impact learning [35]. Researchers at the Australian National University examined whether studying through a MOOC integrated with in-person courses was effective. Interviewing students in four popular courses in modern astrophysics, they found that 87% of those enrolled declared that they learned much more than in face-to-face classes [42]. The potential and effectiveness of MOOCs for learning have been confirmed by other researchers, who have found that "students in blended MOOCs in traditional classrooms performed almost equal or slightly better than students in only face-to face class environment" [38].

Within this framework, the MOOC "Innovative Teaching: Engaging Adult Learners with Active Learning" was developed at the University of Padua in 2020.

3 Methodology

The MOOC was designed in line with constructivist principles and proposed as an optional activity in the second year of a master's program in adult and lifelong learning during the 2020–2021 academic year. The MOOC's content was developed by three professors from different universities and hosted on the FutureLearn platform.

The course was launched on October 26th, 2020 and lasted for four weeks. However, active moderation in the course was extended for two more weeks to accommodate latecomers, and the course remained open (without moderation) until May 2021. During the MOOC's initial four-week run, each professor was assigned a week to facilitate the discussion, with an additional member of the team assisting them in moderating comments and feedback. In addition to its educational purpose, the study had the goal of overcoming the challenges found by previous researchers in fostering student engagement in MOOCs by exploring their learning experience. Therefore, the guiding research questions were:

How satisfied were learners with the MOOC, based on their learning experience? To what degree did the MOOC meet their expectations?

How effective was the MOOC in terms of improving participant engagement and learning?

A case study methodology was chosen because it allowed the researchers to narrow the units of analysis so that each had its own structure, was delimited in terms of space, time, and actors, and was characterized by unity and specificity [43]. The researchers attempted to investigate the learning experience of the learners by using a variety of data sources [44], with a specific focus on master's degree students. This was based on Bali's suggestion that it makes more sense to investigate MOOCs individually, as the perceived success of a given MOOC is relative and depends on a wide variety of factors [18]. A multitude of variables occur in the complex environment of a MOOC; therefore, a limited picture is offered when the success of a MOOC is determined only by the achievement of certain standards, such as the run retention index.

The analysis is based on the course's 1067 enrollments, whose characteristics are described in Table 1.

Table 1. Percentages of enrollments by gender, countries, age, and employment status (n. 1067)

Gender		Countries[a]		Age		Employment status	
Male	31%	United Kingdom	21%	18–25	12%	Working full time	45%
Female	69%	Italy	10%	26–35	26%	Working part time	21%
		United States	5%	36–45	25%	Self employed	15%
		Australia	4%	46–55	25%	Full time student	9%
		India	3%	56–65	9%	Looking for work	6%
		Brazil	3%	65+	3%	Retired	2%
		Russia	3%			Unemployed	2%

[a]Only data related to the most frequent countries are reported.

Nearly a quarter (24%) of joiners completed at least half of the steps in the course, and 18% completed 90% or more of them. This last portion of MOOC learners was analyzed more closely, with the opinions of those who completed the course and responded to the final survey (n = 86), including 31 students (26 female, 5 male) in the master's program. It should be noted that in this paper we use the words "learners" or "participants" to refer to all those who attended the MOOC, including the master's students, and the word "students" to refer exclusively to those master's students. As noted above, to answer the research questions, the researchers explored the opinions of the learners, paying particular attention to the students' views. Therefore, the data obtained from the FutureLearn portal, including learners' demographic data, the end-of-course survey, and the activities report were analyzed. In addition, students responded to a critical incident questionnaire (CIQ) at the end of each week [45, 46].

There were three main sources of data:

- a survey provided on the FutureLearn platform and submitted to learners when they completed all the steps of the course. It aimed to collect information on participants' satisfaction and was composed of four closed-ended questions and two open-ended questions.
- activity report, concerning the activities carried out by the learners, which helped the researchers infer their learning progress and interactions.
- a CIQ submitted at the end of each week of activities by the master's students (n = 31) consisting of six open-ended questions that investigated their learning experience and the level of engagement.

Descriptive statistics analyses were conducted on the quantitative data using Excel. Qualitative data were analyzed with the ATLAS.Ti 8 software, a CAQDAS (Computer Assisted Qualitative Data Analysis Software) that supported the text analysis.

4 Results

The study results are reported into the three following sections. First, the results of the final survey, through which the researchers investigated learners' overall satisfaction, are presented. These data answer the first and (partially) the second research questions. In Sect. 4.2, the quantitative data gained from the activity report are described; they were useful for interpreting participants' learning progress and interaction and beginning to zoom in on the student learning experience. Finally, the qualitative analysis of the CIQ completed weekly by students is reported, which paid more attention to the students' perceptions and reflections on their learning experiences. The data in the second and third sections answered the second question posed by the researchers and allowed them to reflect on possible improvements in the MOOC.

4.1 Final Survey Results

This section presents the data collected from the end-of-course survey on FutureLearn. Among learners who completed the course, 86 participants completed the final survey, including master's students.

Almost all respondents indicated they were satisfied, declaring that the course met their expectations (49%) or that it was even better than expected (48%). They also agreed that new knowledge or skills were gained by taking the course (94%), with most acknowledging that they had applied what they had learned (74%) and shared their learning with other people (68%).

Participants used this space to express their appreciation for the course they had just completed and to make suggestions for its improvement. Some indicated approval of the course's format, content, and ability to bring people from different backgrounds into a dialogue, while others emphasized the effectiveness of the course, as these examples indicate: "I think this course is a great opportunity to discover different points of view, to dialogue with other perspectives and people" (learner 1), and "I found this course very useful for my job and feel it will really improve my ability as a teacher" (learner 2). Other participants suggested offering a free certificate for those who could not afford upgrades or using videos from a source other than YouTube because it is restricted in some countries.

4.2 Activity Report

The activity report provided learners demographics and allowed the authors to gain an overview of the course run in terms of learners' progress and interactions. As noted above, not all those who enrolled completed the course; a run retention index of 41.5% was recorded. The number of visitors and the percentages of comments and completion of each step were also taken into account, as shown in Fig. 1. The same graph reveals how the number of visitors to each step gradually decreased before reaching a certain stability in the third and fourth weeks.

As to how students learned during the course, according to data as of March 29, 2021, 180 people posted at least one comment on any of the steps. The number of total comments recorded in the analyzed period was 3.091. As Table 2 indicates, comment

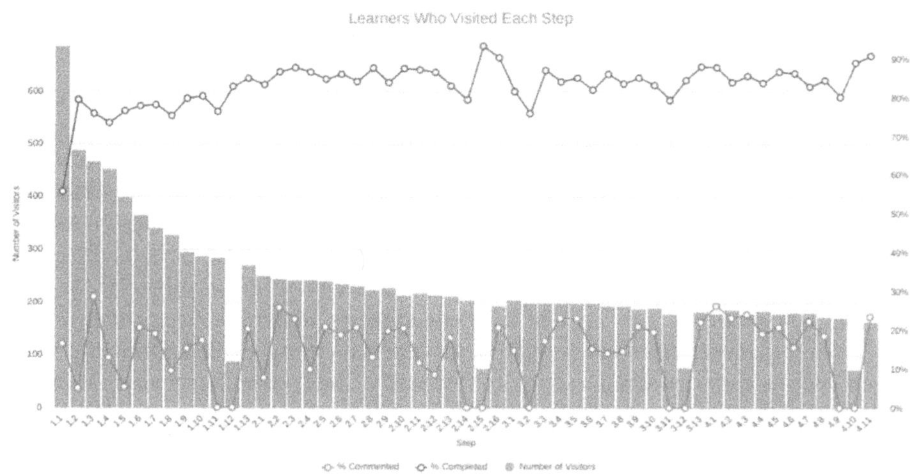

Fig. 1. Number of visitors, percentage of comments, and percentage of completion for each step of the "Innovative Teaching: Engaging Adult Learners with Active Learning" MOOC course.

frequency decreased as the weeks progress, but the average number of comments per learner increased in the second week and stabilized as the number of learners decreased. In other words, while the number of learners visiting the various steps declined from week to week, the average number of steps visited and completed per learner, and the number of comments posted, tended to increase, and then remain constant: this is an indication of the fact that the students who continued into the later weeks of the course were genuinely interested and active. Of course, these numbers become higher when looking at total average counts, since the first week has a heavy influence on per-learner averages.

Table 2. Number of comments and average number of comments per learner for each week of the "Innovative Teaching: Engaging Adult Learners with Active Learning" MOOC course.

Week	1	2	3	4
Comments	988	914	612	577
Average comments per learner	5	11	10	10

Looking in detail at the master's students' activity report reveals that they completed an average of 99% of the steps. Over the four weeks, these students posted a minimum of 26 to a maximum of 96 comments, with an average of about 58 comments per student. Students achieved an average score of 92% on the weekly quizzes over the four weeks, with 75% their lowest overall score, and six students achieved 100%.

4.3 Critical Incident Results

The CIQ collected qualitative data solely on the students' learning experiences.

Before presenting the results, we briefly introduce the instrument. The CIQ is useful for educators to obtain accurate information about students' learning, monitor what was significant for that learning, and adjust their teaching according to the information gathered [45, 46]. In fact, the choice to use this tool was closely linked to the educators' desire to investigate students' opinions more thoroughly for each week of the course and understand which activities were working and which were not. Therefore, at the end of each week, the students were asked to provide six pieces of information: (a) the most engaging moment of the week, (b) the least engaging moment of the week, (c) the most surprising thing during the week, (d) the most important thing learned during the week, (e) the topic students would like to explore more fully, and (f) any further suggestions for improvement. Again, the qualitative data reported below refer to the master's program students and are presented week by week.

First-Week Results. The first week's most engaging activities were reflective, such as identifying personal teaching and learning assumptions. These activities were appreciated because they encouraged students to meet with other learners and develop group activities to reflect on their personal beliefs through case studies and examples of real situations. Another engaging aspect was reading and exchanging written comments with other learners, because it allowed students to gain new perspectives, exchange feedback, and interact with other participants. However, activities related to the teaching perspective inventory (TPI) [47] were less engaging because they required students to imagine teaching situations that most of them had not experienced, which left most students feeling disoriented; they had difficulty understanding the task. One of the most positive aspects for students was the international and interactive nature of the course and, as had already emerged, the possibility of exchanging ideas with other learners. The importance of reflective practices and learning through knowledge sharing were cited as the most important learning experiences of the first week. Students asked that more time be devoted to contextualizing educational philosophy, particularly in online environments, delving into the skills and strategies required of teachers to cope with a variety of situations, and the results of the TPI. Students made a number of interesting suggestions to improve the first-week activities: using more videos and images to summarize content, support learning, and foster involvement and enjoyment; introducing direct chats to foster participants' interaction; and providing alternative activities for non-teacher participants.

Second-Week Results. During this week, most students found the videos related to the interactive lessons very engaging. Others found information about interactive teaching methods excerpted and adapted from Bierema's chapter "Incorporating Active Learning into your Educational Repertoire" interesting [48]. This week's survey results revealed a particularly high level of engagement, with only three students less engaged when they encountered some redundancies. The explanation and connotations of AL surprised students the most, such as the variety and effectiveness of the strategies that can be used to promote it and their wide range of application. They were also surprised by the effectiveness of small changes in traditional lectures to improve learners' engagement (such as question-posing style and changes in tone) and by discovering the important role of experience in the learning process reflecting on bad learning or sharing past experiences. Consistently, the most important learnings involved strategies and methods to foster AL and student engagement, the efficacy of small changes to counteract resistance and deliver a greater impact, and the importance of adapting teaching methods to situational needs. The second-week activities were adequately developed, according to most of the students; however, they would have liked more examples of applications and interactive strategies. Another reported curiosity concerned exploring students' opinions and feelings about different teaching techniques and the consequences of poor teaching on learners. Among the students' suggestions to improve the activities, the use of more videos emerged again; they also suggested considering the time and effort required to develop the tasks, some of which needed more time and were more challenging than the students had expected.

Third-Week Results. Activities that required planning a lesson or course were successful this week. They gave students a chance to approach this type of experience by imagining real situations, comparing themselves to other participants, and reflecting on learner-centered teaching. Again, this week engaged the students most of the time. Some students felt unchallenged by the quizzes, while others felt unprepared to undertake an assessment of their teaching, as they lacked this type of experience. Still others found difficulties using the learning designer tool. Most students faced teaching planning for the first time in the MOOC; therefore, they were surprised by some of its aspects, such as the discovery of useful tips, strategies, and techniques, the need to have time management skills, the effort required to plan even a single lesson, and how important an appropriate opening class is to the overall progress of a course. Students were surprised to discover how useful group discussions with other learners were for their own learning. Therefore, effective, detailed teaching planning, co-constructed and shared with learners and anchored to learning outcomes was the master's students' most important learning experience of the week. Additional information and examples on planning principles, time management, how to improve planning skills, and how to use the learning design tool properly were requested. The presentation of more examples, videos, images, and summary grids were also recommended.

Fourth-Week Results. In the final week, students were engaged and especially enjoyed learning about feedback. In fact, the students recognized feedback as essential for learning and widely usable in different contexts. Second, they appreciated having the opportunity to share assessment practices and strategies. The task on assessment was useful and involved reflection, creativity, and comparison with other participants. As with the first week, the least engaging activities were those that required teaching experience, which involved reflection on and sharing one's teaching practices. Some other students encountered topics they were already familiar with and criticized the length of some of the articles provided, so they identified these moments as less interesting. In addition, in this week, learning through comment sharing was a source of surprise for the students, accompanied by the reflection on assessment and feedback. Features of effective feedback and assessment for learning were the more interesting topics learned, although additional examples about their impact on emotions, promotion of student-educator feedback, authentic assessment, and differences between various types of assessment (i.e., assessment of, as, or for learning) would have been appreciated. The use of more videos and images was suggested for activities in the last week, as were strategies such as case studies, role play, and online meetings. As in the first week, the creation of alternative activities for those without teaching experience was suggested.

5 Discussion and Conclusions

The percentage of learners who completed the MOOC in this case study is higher than percentages considered average in the consulted literature, as it registered a high run retention index. However, as explained in the methodology section, we do not dwell on this single datum; rather, we evaluate the effectiveness of the MOOC based on learners' opinions.

To answer the first research question, almost all learners were satisfied with the MOOC, which exceeded their expectations, according to the data obtained from the final survey. In the same survey, learners reported having acquired new knowledge and skills by attending the MOOC. Specifically, the learnings reported by the students through the CIQ were largely related to the following topics: assessment and feedback, teaching planning, AL strategies, and the importance of learning through knowledge sharing and reflective practices. The scores recorded during the weekly quizzes also confirmed a positive learning experience. Therefore, the intended learning outcomes were successfully achieved, which answers the second research question.

In support of the second question, a digression on students' engagement was helpful; indeed, they stated that they always felt engaged in the MOOC's activities, except when they encountered inexperience in the subject. This was reported mainly in one activity in the first week, which focused on students' identification of their teaching philosophy [47, 49], and another in the fourth week, which required the students to share examples of their teaching strategies using real-world situations. The most engaging activities were those that involved videos, case studies, reflection on real-life situations, knowledge application, discussion, and comparison among learners. The high levels of engagement, learner interaction, and learner retention achieved in this first run of the MOOC provide powerful evidence of the effectiveness of the activities offered by MOOCs built in line with the principles of constructivism and AL discussed in the theoretical framework [18–20]. In fact, there is already evidence in the literature that correlates AL and student satisfaction [1, 50] and that designates AL a preferred learning style among students who have attended other MOOCs [51]. Therefore, the use of these kinds of activities appear to offer a solution to the concerns expressed by Bruff et al. about the difficulty of creating MOOCs that are satisfying and engaging [23]. These indications could be useful to other scholars who want to develop new MOOCs or complement and improve existing MOOCs.

The CIQ has been used by other researchers to explore the MOOC learning experience [52, 53], in the present study it also proved a valuable tool for investigating the surprising aspects of the MOOC as perceived by students: specifically, the possibilities offered to students by the MOOC in addition to the blended course they attended. They were pleasantly surprised not only by the topics covered but also by the opportunity to interact with people from different professional and cultural backgrounds. They enjoyed learning interactively and from the experiences reported by professionals. Indeed, "learning through the experience of others," "learning through group discussion," and "learning about new perspectives through reading the comments of other learners" were all aspects stressed frequently by students in almost every week's CIQ. The 31 master's students from the University of Padua were very active in the discussions, and the overall comment exchange among all learners was good, reaching an average of about 10 comments per learner in the last three weeks, according to the activity report. From this perspective, MOOCs could be a valuable tool to encourage interaction between students from different countries, thus reducing mobility costs, and between students and professionals in an international online environment. Based on what was found in this case, it is not surprising that the educational and attractive character of MOOCs among students, workers between 25 and 40 years old, and retired people from both developed and developing countries has already been stressed [54]. MOOCs thus offer an effective way for universities to open themselves to international society and reach new groups of possible enrollees.

The data collected from the students also allowed the researchers to reflect on possible improvements to the MOOC, and the MOOC's second run has been implemented based on the interests, criticisms, and suggestions collected through the CIQ. Video resources offering further explanation and examples related to TPI and educational philosophy were added to week one; a reading on "small teaching" adaptations that can improve student engagement in online teaching was added to week two; a video tutorial on using the learning designer tool, examples, and a summarizing infographic related to principles for designing effective lessons in line with AL principles were added to week three; one video resource to clarify assessment as, for, and of learning and another with students' opinions on the use of feedback in university contexts were added to week four; and finally, optional resources for deepening the topics covered were added in all weeks.

The studied MOOC, which can be labeled as the second purpose type identified by Zhang [29] and the fourth delivery type according to Kloos et al. [25] classification, offered engaging activities and interesting topics, leaving the floor open to participants to learn in an interactive, cooperative, and active manner and suggesting the appropriateness of constructivist principles for this type of online course just like other emerging approaches for distance learning [55]. The intended learning outcomes were achieved, and the MOOC proved to be a positive resource within the blended program, overcoming the challenges previously reported in the literature and empirically helping to support the findings of other scholars who see MOOCs as an additional and effective resource to traditional courses for cognitive growth, improved performance, and students' engagement and interaction [35, 38, 41, 42]. Improving the MOOC and the tools for collecting learners' opinions about the learning experience is our next step. In fact, among the limitations of the study, it is fair to mention the number of students involved in the research and the general nature of the information collected from the other learners about their opinions. These could be remedied through the implementation of the assessment process and instruments and the longitudinal conduction of the study in subsequent runs. Comparisons with other experiences of this type may be of interest to scholars in the field. International interactions and the dialogue between students and professionals are important aspects that emerged in the research that could be further explored and suggest important advances for university courses.

References

1. Prince, M.: Does active learning work? A review of the research. J. Eng. Educ. **93**(3), 223–231 (2004)
2. Sivan, A., Leung, R.W., Woon, C.C., Kember, D.: An implementation of active learning and its effect on the quality of student learning. Innov. Educ. Train. Int. **37**(4), 381–389 (2000). https://doi.org/10.1080/135580000750052991
3. Bonwell, C.C., Eison, J.A.: Active learning: creating excitement in the classroom. Office of Educational Research and Improvement, Washington, DC (1991). https://files.eric.ed.gov/fulltext/ED336049.pdf
4. Fedeli, M., Bierema, L.L.: Connecting Adult Learning and Knowledge Management. Springer, Cham (2019)
5. Matsushita, K.: An invitation to deep active learning. In: Matsushita, K. (ed.) Deep Active Learning, pp. 15–33. Springer, Singapore (2018). https://doi.org/10.1007/978-981-10-5660-4_2
6. Kaup, S., Jain, R., Shivalli, S., Pandey, S., Kaup, S.: Sustaining academics during COVID-19 pandemic: the role of online teaching-learning. Indian J. Ophthalmol. **68**(6), 1220–1221 (2020). https://dx.doi.org/10.4103%2Fijo.IJO_1241_20
7. Boersma, K.S., Ellington, R.M., Harris, B.N., Malish, J.L., McCarthy, P.C., Manning, L.A.: From panic to pedagogy: using online active learning to promote inclusive instruction in ecology and evolutionary biology courses and beyond. Ecol. Evol. **10**, 12581–12612 (2020)
8. De Notaris, D., Canazza, S., Mariconda, C., Paulon, C.: How to play a MOOC: practices and simulation. Entertain. Comput. **37**,100395 (2021). https://doi.org/10.1016/j.entcom.2020.100395
9. Mattar, J.: Constructivism and connectivism in education technology: active, situated, authentic, experiential, and anchored learning. Revista Iberoamericana de Educación a Distancia **21**(2), 201–217 (2018)
10. McAuley, A., Stewart, B., Siemens, G., Cormier, D.: The MOOC Model for Digital Practice. University of Prince Edward Island, Charlottetown, PE (2010)
11. García-Peñalvo, F.J., Fidalgo-Blanco, Á., Sein-Echaluce, M.L.: An adaptive hybrid MOOC model: disrupting the MOOC concept in higher education. Telemat. Inform. **35**(4), 1018–1030 (2018)
12. Apoki, U.C., Crisan, G.C.: Employing software agents and constructivism to make massive open online courses more student-oriented. In: 11th International Conference on Electronics, Computers and Artificial Intelligence (ECAI), pp. 1–8. IEEE, Piscataway, NJ (2019)
13. Lave, J., Wenger, E.: Situated Learning: Legitimate Peripheral Participation. Cambridge University Press, Cambridge (1991)
14. Wenger, E.: Communities of Practice. Learning, Meaning and Identity. Oxford University Press, Oxford (1998)
15. Peck, K.L., Jonassen, D.H., Wilson, B.G.: Learning with Technology: A Constructivist Perspective. Merrill, Upper Saddle River, NJ (1999)
16. Fox, R.: Constructivism examined. Oxf. Rev. Educ. **27**(1), 23–35 (2001)
17. Johnson, D., Johnson, R., Smith, K.: Active Learning: Cooperation in the College Classroom. Interaction Book Company, Edina, MN (1998)
18. Bali, M.: MOOC pedagogy: gleaning good practice from existing MOOCs. J. Online Learn. Teach. **10**(1), 44–56 (2014)

19. Abeer, W., Miri, B.: Students' preferences and views about learning in a MOOC. Procedia – Soc. Behav. Sci. **152**, 318–323 (2014)
20. Chen, M.: Study of instructional model for information technology fundamental courses under MOOC environment. In: 1st International Conference on Information Technologies in Education and Learning (ICITEL-15), pp. 5–10. Atlantis Press, Dordrecht (2016)
21. Kaul, M., Aksela, M., Wu, X.: Dynamics of the community of inquiry (CoI) within a massive open online course (MOOC) for in-service teachers in environmental education. Educ. Sci. **8**(2), 40–54 (2018)
22. Kovanović, V., et al.: Exploring communities of inquiry in massive open online courses. Comput. Educ. **119**, 44–58 (2018)
23. Bruff, D.O., Fisher, D.H., McEwen, K.E., Smith, B.E.: Wrapping a MOOC: student perceptions of an experiment in blended learning. J. Online Learn. Teach. **9**(2), 187–199 (2013)
24. Rodríguez, M.F., Hernández Correa, J., Pérez-Sanagustín, M., Pertuze, J.A., Alario-Hoyos, C.: A MOOC-based flipped class: lessons learned from the orchestration perspective. In: Delgado Kloos, C., Jermann, P., Pérez-Sanagustín, M., Seaton, D.T., White, Su. (eds.) EMOOCs 2017. LNCS, vol. 10254, pp. 102–112. Springer, Cham (2017). https://doi.org/10.1007/978-3-319-59044-8_12
25. Kloos, C.D., Muñoz-Merino, P.J., Alario-Hoyos, C., Ayres, I.E., Fernández-Panadero, C.: Mixing and blending MOOC technologies with face-to-face pedagogies. In: 2015 IEEE Global Engineering Education Conference (EDUCON), pp. 967–971. IEEE, Piscataway, NJ (2015)
26. Bralić, A., Divjak, B.: Integrating MOOCs in traditionally taught courses: achieving learning outcomes with blended learning. Int. J. Educ. Technol. High. Educ. **15**(1), 1–16 (2018)
27. Garrison, D.R., Kanuka, H.: Blended learning: uncovering its transformative potential in higher education. Internet High. Educ. **7**(2), 95–105 (2004)
28. Eradze, M., Urrutia, M.L., Reda, V., Kerr, R.: Blended learning with MOOCs. In: Calise, M., Kloos, C.D., Reich, J., Ruiperzez-Valente, J.A., Wirsing, M. (eds.) European MOOCs Stakeholders Summit (EMOOCS 2019), pp. 53–58. Springer, Cham (2019). https://doi.org/10.1007/978-3-030-19875-6_7
29. Zhang, Y.: Benefiting from MOOC. In: Herrington, J., Couros, A., Irvine, V. (eds.) Proceedings of EdMedia 2013–World Conference on Educational Multimedia and Technology, pp. 1372–1377. Association for the Advancement of Computing in Education, Waynesville, NC (2013)
30. Pérez-Sanagustín, M., Hilliger, I., Alario-Hoyos, C., Kloos, C.D., Rayyan, S.: H-MOOC framework: reusing MOOCs for hybrid education. J. Comput. High. Educ. **29**(1), 47–64 (2017). https://doi.org/10.1007/s12528-017-9133-5
31. Jordan, K.: Initial trends in enrolment and completion of massive open online courses. Int. Rev. Res. Open Distrib. Learn. **15**(1), 133–160 (2014)
32. Daniel, J.: Making sense of MOOCs: musings in a maze of myth, paradox and possibility. J. Interact. Media Educ. **2012**(3) (2012) https://www-jime.open.ac.uk/articles/10.5334/2012-18/. Accessed 07 Sept 2021
33. Skrypnyk, O., de Vries, P., Hennis, T.: Reconsidering retention in MOOCs: the relevance of formal assessment and pedagogy. In: Proceedings of the 3rd International Conference on European MOOCs Stakeholder Summit, pp. 166–172. OpenupEd, London (2015)
34. De Freitas, S.I., Morgan, J., Gibson, D.: Will MOOCs transform learning and teaching in higher education? Engagement and course retention in online learning provision. Br. J. Edu. Technol. **46**(3), 455–471 (2015)
35. Tamjidyamcholo, A., Gholipour, R., Kazemi, M.A.: Examining the perceived consequences and usage of MOOCs on learning effectiveness. Iran. J. Manag. Stud. **13**(3), 495–525 (2020)

36. Gamage, D., Perera, I., Fernando, S.: Evaluating effectiveness of MOOCs using empirical tools: learners' perspective. In: 10th International Technology Education and Development Conference, Valencia, Spain. https://library.iated.org/view/GAMAGE2016EVA (2016)
37. De Santis, A., Sannicandro, K., Bellini, C., Minerva, T.: Reasons for attending a MOOC: a survey on EduOpen learners. In: EDEN Conference Proceedings, no. 1. pp. 365–373 (2019). https://www.eden-online.org/proc-2485/index.php/PROC/article/download/1732/1440#:~:text=the%20main%20reasons%20for%20registration,users%20place%20greater%20emphasis%20on. Accessed 07 Sept 2021
38. Israel, M.J.: Effectiveness of integrating MOOCs in traditional classrooms for undergraduate students. Int. Rev. Res. Open Distrib. Learn. **16**(5), 102–118 (2015)
39. Yousef, A.M.F.: Effective design of blended MOOC environments in higher education (Doctoral dissertation, RWTH Aachen University). https://publications.rwth-aachen.de/record/479221/files/479221.pdf (2015). Accessed 07 Sept 2021
40. Atiaja, L.A., Proenza, R.: The MOOCs: origin, characterization, principal problems and challenges in higher education. J. e-Learn. Knowl. Soc. **12**(1), 65–76 (2016)
41. Prinsloo, T., Ainslie, A.: A thematic literature review of the implementation of MOOCS-2008 to 2018. In: Proceedings of the 2018 AIS SIGED International Conference on Information Systems Education and Research, Article no. 34 (2018)
42. Francis, P.: 87% of students say they gain as much or more from online courses compared to on-campus courses, edX Blog. https://blog.edx.org/87-students-say-they-gain-much-or-more (2015). Accessed 07 Sept 2021
43. Trinchero, R.: Manuale di ricerca educativa. Franco Angeli, Milan (2002)
44. Yin, R.K., Pinnelli, S.: Lo studio di caso nella ricerca scientifica: progetto e metodi. Armando, Roma (2005)
45. Brookfield, S.D.: Powerful Techniques for Teaching Adults. Jossey-Bass, San Francisco, CA (2013)
46. Brookfield, S.D.: Teaching for Critical Thinking: Tools and Techniques to Help Students Question Their Assumptions. Jossey Bass, San Francisco (2011)
47. Pratt, D.D., Collins, J.B.: Teaching perspectives inventory (TPI), Adult Education Research Conference (2000). https://newprairiepress.org/aerc/2000/papers/68
48. Bierema, L.L.: Incorporating active learning into your educational repertoire. In: Fedeli, M., Bierema, L.L. (eds.) Connecting adult learning and knowledge management: Strategies for learning and change in higher education and organizations, pp. 27–50. Springer, New York (2020). https://doi.org/10.1007/978-3-030-29872-2_2
49. Tisdell, E.J., Taylor, E.W.: Adult education philosophy informs practice. Adult Learn. **11**(2), 6–10 (2000)
50. Hyun, J., Ediger, R., Lee, D.: Students' satisfaction on their learning process in active learning and traditional classrooms. Int. J. Teach. Learn. High. Educ. **29**(1), 108–118 (2017)
51. Hmedna, B., El Mezouary, A., Baz, O.: How does learners' prefer to process information in MOOCs? A data-driven study. Procedia Comput. Sci. **148**, 371–379 (2019)
52. Tzovla, E., Kedraka, K., Karalis, T., Kougiourouki, M., Lavidas, K.: Effectiveness of in-service elementary school teacher professional development MOOC: an experimental research. Contemp. Educ. Technol. **13**(4), ep324 (2021). https://doi.org/10.30935/cedtech/11144
53. Ardavani, S.: How MOOCs can develop teacher cognition: the case of in-service English language teachers. Eur. J. Open Distance E-Learn. (EURODL) **22**(2), 56–71 (2019)

54. Zhenghao, C., Alcorn, B., Christensen, G., Eriksson, N., Koller, D., Emanuel, E.J.: Who's benefiting from MOOCs, and why. Harv. Bus. Rev. (2015). https://hbr.org/2015/09/whos-benefiting-from-moocs-and-why. Accessed 07 Sept 2021
55. Picerno, P., Pecori, R., Raviolo, P., Ducange, P.: Smartphones and exergame controllers as BYOD solutions for the e-tivities of an online sport and exercise sciences university program. In: Burgos, D., et al. (eds.) HELMeTO 2019. CCIS, vol. 1091, pp. 217–227. Springer, Cham (2019). https://doi.org/10.1007/978-3-030-31284-8_17

Faculty Development, Distance Education and Online Learning Systems in Higher Education

Lab-H: A Laboratory to Develop 3D Printable Inclusive Open Educational Resources

Stefano Di Tore[1](✉), Michele Domenico Todino[2], and Lucia Campitiello[1]

[1] University of Salerno, 84084 Fisciano, Italy
{sditore,lcampitiello}@unisa.it
[2] University of Sannio at Benevento, 82100 Benevento, Italy
micheledomenico.todino@unisannio.it

Abstract. This work principally offers selected educational experiences, a set of case studies, about 3D printing skills to support the interchange of Media Education practices between the University of Salerno and educators, generally teachers, of different grades of the school system. Each 3D models is related to a case study, they are on the website ready to be free downloadable, all projects follow an Open Education policy. All of these resources become a set of inclusive open-source resources, ready for a free download, for 3D printers to develop teachers' and students' digital skills. The technologies that can be downloaded from the Lab-H website try to help teachers in their daily activities. Lab-H in collaboration with "G.Rodari" primary school of Perugia tested D-BOX and Ames Room, and it will test soon also Montessori didactical object and a 3D printable robot. D-Box is a 3D printing game to convert a decimal number into a binary number; to realize this it is based on a set of platforms related with powers of 2. The distorted room of Ames based on a well-known test of New Look psychology endorses the perspective-taking skills. Moreover, ASD-robot is designed to increase social skills in children affected by Autism Spectrum Disorder for better recognize emotions through the use of a display that acts as a human face with emoticons images tested in "Collodi" primary school of Pagani (Salerno).

Keywords: Maker culture · Open education · 3D printing · STEM education

1 Introduction

The work offers a set of case studies about 3D printers technology used as support to open educational resources in some Italian schools. In this chapter, the main topic is to describe how 3D printing objects can be realized and supported inclusive didactical activities. As usual, it is significant starting with a literature review contextualised in current researches and challenges in the field and Educational technologies and more in general in the Maker culture. However, a full report of published sources about 3D printing is quite hard task to do, due to the fact that 3D printing could change the world [1] and this technique is used in many fields, such as dentistry [2], surgery, industries and engineering to create prototypes [3]. The short, but very fast, story of 3D printers

G. Casalino et al. (Eds.): HELMeTO 2021, CCIS 1542, pp. 233–247, 2022.
https://doi.org/10.1007/978-3-030-96060-5_17

concerns "humble manufacturing machines that are bursting out of the factory and into schools, kitchens, hospitals, even onto the fashion catwalk" [4], technologies that are charming users all over the world. Outside Italy, it is now almost proven that digital fabrication, in terms of 3D design and printing, "have taken root in school education as curriculum-based and maker-oriented learning activities in multidisciplinary learning modules in elementary school education", moreover, "3D printing activities, learning is centred on the technical skills and the usage of 3D tools" [5]. In other terms, "it is increasingly argued that classroom use of these technologies can re-orientate schools towards forms of skills and knowledge appropriate for contemporary industry, STEM education and Maker culture"[6]. Not only primary school is involved in this process of 3D printing technology introduction but also middle school and high school, where students participate in technology education experiences "in mechanical engineering, applied mathematics, materials processing, basic electronics, robotics, industrial manufacturing, and other STEM-focused areas through the addition of 3D printers"[7]. In 2016, Pier Cesare Rivoltella stated that there are many inclusive education opportunities using 3D printers (such as to print supports for blind people) to be used in everyday teaching, besides, to understand ICT global market trends, it is emblematic that Samsung, after selling its (traditional) printers division to HP for about a billion dollars, is encouraging 3D printing in schools [8]. Starting from this considerations, since 2015 Lab-H at the Department of Humanities, Philosophy, and Education of the University of Salerno, studies solutions about Didactic, Technology, and Inclusion. Starting from the first release of the DISUFFO project [9], Lab-H promotes an Open design approach that concern 3d printing skills, to support the interchange of Media Education practices between university and teachers. Nowadays, due to COVID-19 above all activities are delivered in distance learning, for this reason, Lab-H published 3D models of digital assets files for free under Creative Commons license related to these practices and experience for teachers education. These digital assets related to the following projects: 3D printing Ames Room [10], D-Box [11], Montessori didactical objects and ASD-robot. In other cases Thingverse home page (thingiverse.com) digital assets are downloadable and customizable to promote an open access philosophy. To slice these digital assets are often used Ultimaker Cura (downloadable at ultimaker.com/software/ultimaker-cura), one of the world's most widespread 3D slicing and printing software. In this way, an academic can easily implement lessons, seminar and courses concerning 3D printing for teachers training and teacher's education, starting from an ideal object moving to a.stl files developed an easier workflow that starts with the use of a CAD software and finish with a real 3D printing object (Figs. 1 and 2).

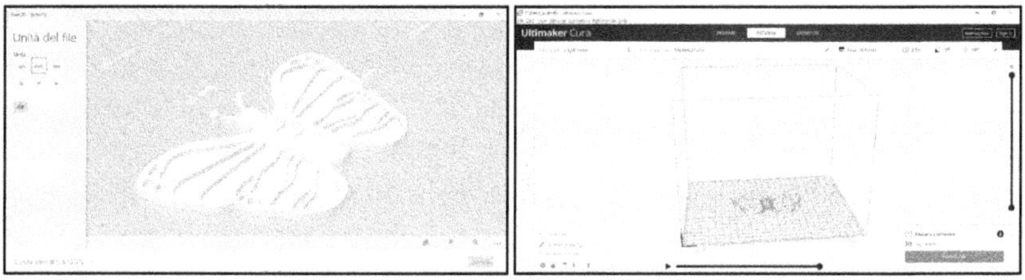

Fig. 1. On the left side a 3D object downloaded from Thingverse, on the right side Ultimaker Cura to slice and print

Fig. 2. A butterfly printed with a ZYYX+, layer 0.15 mm, material PLA

2 Open Educational Resources (OERs) and Open Education Philosophy

Lab-H promotes the exchange of Open Educational Resources (OERs) and follows an Open Education philosophy that allows researchers and school teachers to cooperate downloading materials from Lab-H web site (http://www.labh.it) to produce their own digital assets for a 3D fabrication; in this way, educators and students can download files and they can increase their mastery on 3D making process and it is important to support constant acquisitions following a "Think-Make-Improve" learning process [11]. More in detail, the Italian Ministry of Education really advises promoting these practices in each school by Media Educators. From an institutional point of view, the Italian Ministry of Education really advises promoting these practices in each school by Media Educators and this role is covered by a special professional figure called *Animatore Digitale* defined by action #28 of PNSD (*Piano Nazionale per la Scuola Digitale*) i.e. the National plan for digital school [12]. Lab-H attitude is to follow the idea that is possible to learn through games, i.e. using a ludic approach, to the teaching-learning process [13–18] introducing new digital and technological teaching tools to support didactical activities and produce benefits on students that can learn through new inducements and motivations offered by the use of new technology (in this specific case 3D printing) that can arouse their curiosity. In addition, with new digital assets hopefully could be proposed specific lessons for support different learning styles in a theoretical framework that draws to Gardner's theory of multiple intelligences [19]. The main works of Lab-H available on-line (links are provided beloved in this work) are ideated to be an Open Educational Resource in line with *Cape Town Open Education Declaration* [20] thus digital assets produced are "freely shared through open licences which facilitate use, revision, translation, improvement and sharing by anyone. Resources [are] published in formats that facilitate both use and editing, and that accommodate a diversity of technical platforms [and] also be available in formats that are accessible to people with disabilities and people who do not yet have access to the Internet", this strategy represents "more than just the right thing to do" united with an Open Education policy "constitute a wise investment in teaching and learning for the 21st century. They will make it possible to redirect funds from expensive textbooks towards better learning. They will help teachers excel in their work and provide new opportunities for visibility and global impact. They will accelerate innovation in teaching. They will give more control over learning to the learners themselves" [20].

3 An Easier 3D Printing Workflow for Teachers Training

For teachers, who are not computer experts, it is useful to have a guideline for 3D printing. Printing in 3d is not something very well known in practices because almost no one has a 3D printer at home. This print process needs some ICT skills and it is not so easy such as a paper's printer that everyone has been using for years. The 3D printer is not so easy to install and configure, it has no easy drivers to download and configure on the contrary it needs specific software, more than once, in a specific workflow. But all teachers understand the didactic opportunity offered by 3D printing to customized or create their own objects for educational porpoise to be used in their lessons. This paragraph is describing a short guideline that summarized in short points how to make a printed version of a 3D object.

1) The physical plate calibration: (to be done at each print) often, when a 3D printer is new or after a big number of objects produced, it is possible that the plate of the 3D printer is positioned incorrectly; in this case, the plate must be adjusted to let the plastic come out from the extruder but this plastic material must be deposited on the plate, but without crushing it; this substance must be slightly lower than the thickness of the space between the extruder and the plate. Moreover, the user must be remembered that the plate is made of aluminium (metal that expands with heat, if it is possible is better to change the plate with a glass one and not aluminium because it is flatter), so if the user wanted to calibrate it accurately who prints must first heat the plate to its operating temperature that about is 55 °C (this process takes place usually from the menu screen) and this temperature depends by the 3D printer model and it is shown in its data sheet [21]. To test if this calibration is well done the user must provide an A4 sheet and verify if this paper can pass between the extruder and the plate. To calibrate all there are usually for or more screws, one in each corner of the plate. The user raises the sheet to the height of the edge, without hire it blocked between the plate and the extruder. In a recursive way, the user can define the right position the each of the four corners using the plate's screws (Fig. 3).

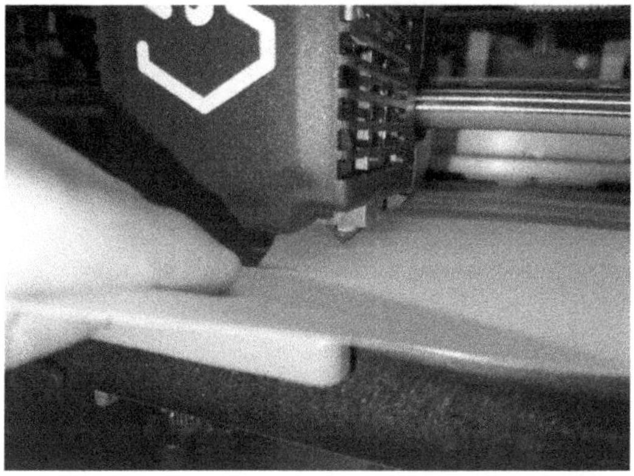

Fig. 3. A4 sheet to verify the distance between the extruder and the plate

2) The physical choice of material: the best solution for a teacher is to promote a biodegradable material for the 3D printing process. In this case, Polylactic acid (PLA) is a natural alternative to polyethylene and it is based on a filament of bio-sourced photopolymer obtained from corn starch EN 13432 standards [22], this material is not toxic and it is in line with Agenda 2030 guidelines and it Sustainable Development Goals. However, sometimes for well-motivated didactical reasons, it is important to use other kinds of materials that must be flexible or carbon fibre-filled, metal filled, wood-filled [23], bamboo-fitted, brass-fitted, PLA-silk (a filament that is not done with real silk but so called due to its brightness), photochromic filament, thermochromic filament, and much more useful for many didactical uses to realize specific object such as, just to give an educational example, the reproduction of ancient coins of artefacts for history didactics. Besides, it is possible in specific ceramic 3D printing to use a fluid-dense material to emulate earthenware glazed or unglazed no vitreous pottery. Moreover, similar to marble or stone filaments [24, 25] are available in the ICT market stores. In specific cases, with a particular kind of 3D printer, it is possible to print also foods, noble metals, etc. [26].
3) The physical load of the filament and the initialization of x-y-z axes position: the user must cut the filament at 45degrees, to better enter inside the bulge that transports it to the extruder (motor), which has usually only one wheel, in which the filament will be inserted; through the 3D printer menu moves it to initialize 3D Cartesian axes position fixes x = 0 and y = 0 and moving z by plus 1 mm (or less if it is possible, it depend from the minimum z step of the 3D printer model) (Fig. 4).

Fig. 4. The filament cut at 45°

4) Printer settings and customization of the GCODE: before starting a 3D printing process, a user must be used a program called slicer, which, convert a digital asset in its GCODE file containing commands in G-Code the most commonly used computer numerical control programming language adopted by 3D printer's company (GCODE derived from Computer Numerical Control (CNC) machine industry standards, it is called EIA RS-274-D standard and it was writed in 1979). This file gives commands to the printer, to print one layer after another to produce the object. Free software is a good solution to convert.stl files in GCODE files is Ultimaker Cura has a big database of 3D printer models and gives the opportunities to set many properties to customize the printing process.
5) Prepare the filaments for printing: usually through the 3D printer menu, on its display, a user can preheat the printer process to insert a filament at the right temperature, often 185 °C (this depend, it is necessary to check on the product data sheet); at this point, a user can insert the filament inside; at the meantime, the plate temperature must be about 50 °C (read on data-sheet the exact temperature); the printer moves axes 0.1 mm, once some filament has come out, the printer is ready to print. At this point, the material reaches 200 °C (always check the temperature on the data-sheet for each kind of model) and the printing process begins, it will last approximately hours to finish it depends on the 3D printer model and the physical dimension of the object.
6) Modification of the spatula: a user must know that to take the finished object from the plate it is important to use a sharp spatula to be able to remove the printed object from the plate, to avoid breaking this plate, it is necessary to bind the corners of the spatula from an iron one or buy a plastic spatula produced for 3D printer. Furthermore, to minimize the glue effect between the object and the plate there are 2 methods: insert on the base of the scotch for 3D printer or a paper masking tape, or use a hair spray on the plate (Fig. 5).

Fig. 5. A spatula with rounded corners, scotch for 3D printer and hair spray can be useful for the 3D printing process to avoid the glue effect between that plate and the base of a printed object

7) Print upgrades: for each kind of 3D printer model, there are lots of 3D objects designed for it to upgrade and optimize the 3D printing process, it could be useful to search on Google by the name of printer used, to print objects that could be useful to customized and improve it [27].

4 Lab-H Main Projects: A Set of Inclusive Open-Source Resources for 3D Printers to Develop Teachers' and Students' Digital Skills

Lab-H projects on-line are four, as already said they are Open Educational Resources freely shared through Creative Commons licence Resources are published as.stl files, accessible to everybody in the world, just digital divide could be the real problem. All projects follow an Open Education policy and not only.stl files are given to the users but also a full paper that describes how to use objects in a teaching-learning process. Until now, Lab-H main 3D printer's projects are described as beloved.

1) The distorted room of Ames based on a well-known test of New Look psychology, which endorses the perspective-taking skills. The main object of this experiment is a strange room that was built to be print in 3D, the key aim of this device is to decline some perceptual biases both in teachers and students and prove that every person world's interpretation is altered and it depends on the phenomenon perspective-taking knowledge [28]; In this workout, with the care of an educator who leads students, it is possible to understand that the room of Ames contains an optical illusion because it is observed with just one eye through a peephole. Therefore, at the end of the experience, the teacher emphasizes that often the observed reality is different from the truth (Fig. 6).

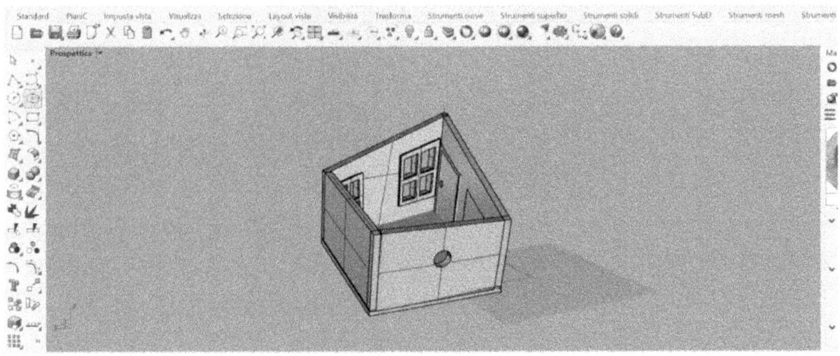

Fig. 6. The distorted room of Ames 3D printed project

2) D-Box is a 3D printing game to convert a decimal number into a binary number, to realize this, it offers a configuration of a set of platform based on the powers of 2 [11]. D-BOX connects some disciplines: mathematic, information technologies and media education; it provides a way to show how mathematic is essential and necessary to the modern digital world. This game is based on two concepts already studied in the fifth grade of primary school: 1) mathematical operations knowledge (computing) 2) recognizing geometric figures [29]. The teacher gives a number of marbles to the student that has to place on platforms in a proper way to give back a digital number composed just with 0 or 1 digit (Fig. 7).

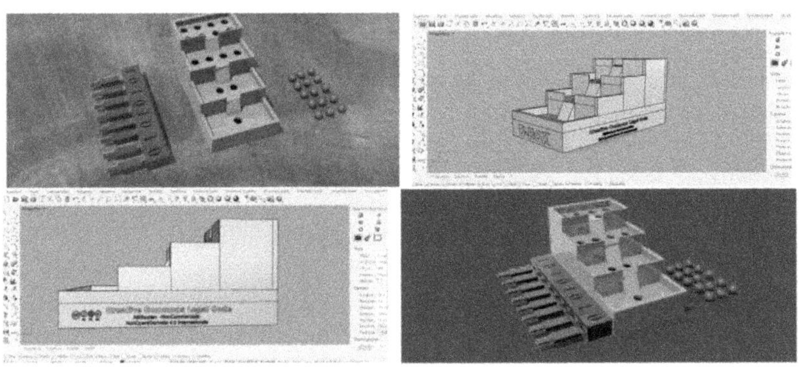

Fig. 7. D-BOX 3D model ready to be printed

3) The 3D models of Montessori didactical objects, it is well known that Maria Montessori didactics are supported by educational material to support practical life equipment; sensory material; language equipment and mathematics materials plus other objects to supports other disciplines such as science, botany and geography, music

and art [30]. Starting from 2021, Lab-H decides to produce.stl files of these materials and released them for free under creative commons licence. Another use that can be made of these files is to insert them in a 3D graphic engine, for example, Unity3D, and use them to "decorate" virtual worlds and augmented reality. More in details augmented reality has been, in last years, central in some studies concerning inclusive education and practices that involve, without distinction or discrimination, the whole students [31]. More in details, a didactic approach that focuses at the same time "on the use of technology" and on the "educational contexts" try to aim learners' development especially in the "case of special educational needs" starting "from the assumption that technological tools tend to be able to cope with the complexity of learning difficulties" [32] due to a disability or a disorder and students, helped by technologies can find a vicariant mode [28] to learn in their own way thus promote inclusive technologies is a part of promoting inclusive practices at school [33] (Fig. 8).

Fig. 8. The 3D models of Montessori didactical objects (objects can be used to teach both Italian and English alphabet. Koala for letter K, moreover, T as the first letter of *Torta*, or Cake in English, B as the first letter of Bowling, in a previous figure Butterfly, *Farfalla*, can be used for letter F in Italian of B in English)

4) ASD-robot is designed to increase social skills in children affected by Autism Spectrum Disorder to better recognize emotions through the use of a display that acts as a human face with emoticons images. The first prototype of this robot was drowned by Rhinoceros and printed with a Prusa MK3S 3D printer. A Rhinoceros file, ready to be downloaded, allows a researcher, an educator or a therapist to customize each part of the robot, in order to adapt it in terms of inclusive use of these technologies. Usually, to use properly this robot is better to create a team that must be composed of three specialists: an ICT expert (to customize hardware and software), a researcher (to collect and analyze data), and a therapist (to drive human-machine interactions) (Fig. 9).

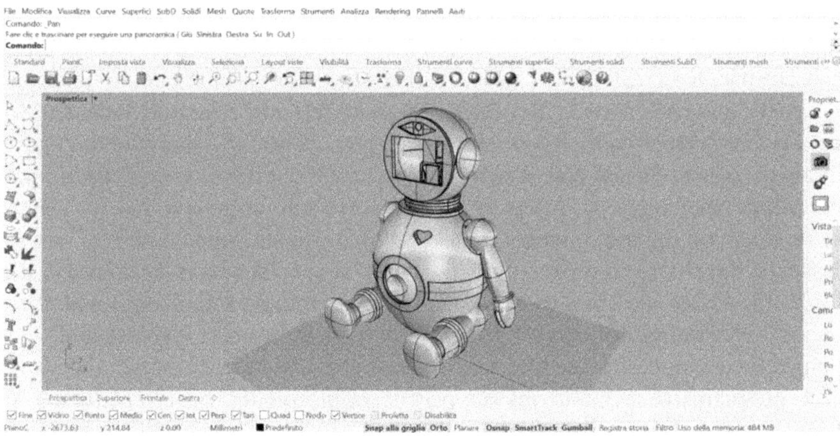

Fig. 9. ASD-robot

5 B-BOX and Ames Room Tests at "G.Rodari" Primary School of Perugia

These Open Education resources perform, hopefully, a stimulating contribution to 3D printing projects in Italian schools. Usually, the Minister of Education intends to promote the adoption of innovative teaching methodologies by schools, with particular reference to digital teaching and STEAM disciplines (Science, Technology, Engineering, Arts and Mathematics), inspired by students' leadership, active learning and cooperative, to relational well-being, in line with the "Skills and Contents" area of the National Plan for the digital school (30 April 2021, n. 147) and many schools buy 3D printer but, unfortunately, often they are "parked" in a laboratory because there is no project to follow and/or adequate training of the teaching staff. The impact of the solutions developed by Lab-H would help this staff in order to improve the digital skills of teachers and students. This impact will be better highlighted with some data. Lab-H in collaboration with "G.Rodari" primary school of Perugia tested D-BOX and Ames Room in this academic year 2020–21, and it will test also Montessori didactical object in the next academic year 2021–22. About D-BOX, usually to convert decimal number into binary number an easy algorithm is this: 1) divide the decimal number by two; 2) write the integer quotient to be used int next iteration; 3) write the remainder that is the binary digit; 4) repeat until the quotient is equal to zero. Vice versa (the reverse algorithm), to convert a binary number (such as a four bit number Bit_3 Bit_2 Bit_1 Bit_0) in its decimal number must be add binary digits Bit_n times their power of 2. This procedure is quite hard for students that are some gaps in mathematical or students less motivated to activate mathematical intelligence, in terms of Gardner's theory of multiple intelligences [19]. Students (15 students composed by 12 males, 3 females), not helping by teacher, in classroom: 1) converted number 16 and 81.3% answered correctly; 2) converted number 15 and 68.8% answered correctly; 3) converted number 10 and 68.8% answered correctly. The playful approach of D-BOX was compared with the traditional approach (of the algorithm proposed above) in students of a fifth class where they were studying the powers of two. They starting using D-BOX and then they used traditional method. Fifteen students, the same of before, was asked, by the school teacher already trained about D-BOX, to convert number 4 all students answered exactly (100% correct answers). Then, the students converted number 7 (which requires more attention because it is not an even number or a power of two), 87.5% answered correctly. Then, the students converted number 2 (which is a simple question but it can be misleading) and 93.8% of the students answered correctly. Finally, they converted number 25 (assuming an additional platform with 16 grooves to verify the ability to extend the numbering) and 93.8% of the students answered correctly. To verify the students' ability to think about the concept of zero (essential for continuing their mathematical studies after primary school), students had to convert the number 0 into its binary equivalent (to do this, students had to leave all platforms empty) and 100% of the children answered correctly. To test and verify students learning they converted a binary number in its decimal equivalent. Numbers were: Bit_5 Bit_4 Bit_3 Bit_2 Bit_1 Bit_0 (with six bits). The students converted the binary number 001112 into decimal, 81.3% of the pupils answered correctly and 87.5% of the pupils converted 00001 correctly. After that they used the traditional method to convert decimal number into binary numbers alone, they converted: 1) 23 and 100% answered correctly; 2) 21 and 93.8% answered correctly; 3) 20 and 68.8% answered correctly. Comparing data, and taken into account that they convert alone with no help from their teacher is quite motivating the improvement regarding the conversion from decimal in binary numbers but there are still in students some problems regarding the concept of zero (Fig. 10).

Fig. 10. D-BOX tested at "G.Rodari" primary school in Perugia

Still, in the same school, and with the same teacher, Ames' room was used by the same students. The children observed the room from inside the buttonhole and 64.3% were "victims" of the illusory effect. In other words, they believed that the two pawns (teacher used two little plastic cakes) inside the room were of different heights. Through a Google Form, which the children filled out in class with their smartphones, some questions were asked. Google Form was mainly used for two reasons: 1) leave students free to respond without fear of the teacher's judgment (it was an anonymous form); 2) use the smartphone for educational purposes. Just one student understands by himself that the room was a "trick". The first question was: If you made a mistake, what mistake did you make the first time you looked inside Ames' room? student 1 "I said the room was curved but then I realized it was an optical illusion"; student 2 "The first time I got the shape of the room wrong because I said it was rectangular; student 3 "I thought it was rectangular"; student 4 "I was wrong about the shape and size of the objects"; student 5 it understood the optical illusion at first glance; student 6 "I thought the room was square or rectangular but it wasn't"; student 7 "I thought the two cakes were the same"; student 8 "I was wrong about how tall the cakes were"; student 9 "I thought it was square"; student 10 "I have mistaken the proportion of the objects and also the shape of the room"; student 11 "the two objects seemed to be one larger and one smaller instead they were the same"; student 12 "I thought they were different but they were the same"; student 13 "I had said that the two objects were different in size, but then I discovered that they were the same"; student 14 " I said the room was round but it was actually square" (Fig. 11).

Fig. 11. Ames Room used in classroom at the "G.Rodari" primary school in Perugia

After having tested Ames's room in the classroom, the teacher had each child build their own Ames room. Not having a 3D printer at school, the children built one out of cardboard. Students created their own room in Ames just before the Christmas holidays and during the holiday period; they had an enjoyable task: showing the Ames room to their relatives and friends. They must act as "researchers" at home. They must count how many people discovered the truth about Ames room at the glace and teach them the illusion if they didn't get it by themselves (Fig. 12).

Fig. 12. Ames Room tested at home by students of "G.Rodari" primary school in Perugia

Thus, the second question was: If you had tried your Ames room at home, what happened? Did your family members and friends find at once the optical illusion? Student 1 "Yes but at the end"; student 2 "no, they didn't understand it the first time"; student 3 "I questioned my brother and sister and they said the two objects were with the same dimensions"; student 4 "I interviewed my father and he answered all questions well except about the shape of the room"; student 5 "yes"; student 6 "the people I showed the room to quickly discovered it was an optical illusion"; student 7 "no, they didn't find out"; student 8 "they thought the room was round and the objects of different sizes"; student 9 "no"; student 10 "no"; student 11 "yes"; student 12 "they couldn't see it"; student 12 "I showed to six people the Ames room, all of them to the same typical mistake"; student 13 "Initially no but then they realized it"; two students did not do this homework. The thirteen students, who made this experimentation, were very proud and satisfied of themselves that people (relatives and friends), generally older than themselves, had made the same mistake as themselves, they were satisfied with having shown the optical illusion and declared, as the teacher had done them, that they have to be careful about what you observe: you can fall into errors and prejudices and in their own way they have learned a little lesson on the concept of change of perspective that is the basis of empathy [34].

6 ASD-Robot Test in "Collodi" Primary School of Pagani

ASD-robot aims to provide support for therapists, this robot must be a low-priced system and easily customizable for them. More in detail, the system is quite cheap, all technologies are realized using standard components (such as Arduino) easy to be found on Amazon or, obviously, on MePA (Mercato elettronico della Pubblica Amministrazione). This robot is easily customizable by everybody who has proper digital skills learned in a teachers' education ICT course, for example (consider that to achieve these skills there are many courses offered by the MIUR itself on the S.O.F.I.A. for trainee teachers). Anyways, although is better to have a team to use ASD-Robot, as already said, to customize an ASD-robot hardware or software component, a teacher or a therapist often just needs to search on YouTube videos to find a proper video about 3D printing or Arduino. ASD-robot was tested in "Collodi" primary school in Pagani (Salerno, Italy); the experimentation is part of a doctoral thesis, it was conducted on a 9-year-old child. A team was created by a teacher, a therapist and a PhD student. All of them were present during the child experience with the robot. The observed student uses the robot during morning school breaks. The trial lasted two months, it was done in 2019 (before the health emergency lockdown), it was done about 2/3 times per week. The child was enthusiastic about interacting with the robot, he likes technology and he played with ASD-robot whenever he could (i.e. whenever the team gave him the robot during the breaks). Clearly, saying that the robot is patient is a rhetorical form to say that a robotic system cannot be "bored" because it is artificial while a therapist could be bored by a cyclical form of the teaching-learning process that creates "infinite" loops as sometimes happened during their activities. Hopefully, nobody wants that a child with ASD leaves alone with a robot, the point is to alternate, in a profitable way, therapist and artificial robotic system to better-optimized didactics activities.

7 Conclusions

This work mainly presents some educational experiences about 3D printing skills to support the interchange of Media Education practices between University of Salerno and educators, generally teachers, of different grades of the school system. The technologies that can be downloaded from the Lab-H website try to help teachers in their daily activities. The teacher should read the information provided on the website relating to the objects or contact the researchers to better used the downloadable material. Lab-H continuously monitors all activities, realizes questionnaires and gives support all the time.

Acknowledgements. As already assert, Lab-H in collaboration with "G.Rodari" primary school of Perugia tested D-BOX and Ames Room, and it will test soon also Montessori didactical objects. These experimentations were possible thanks to Roberta Bertellini, School Principal, and Giovanna Nunzia Parisi, the teacher that tested these technologies with students. A final consideration: the 3D models are on the website ready to be free downloadable, all projects follow an Open Education policy, regardless to establish contact with their inventors thus each object will have an "its own life" but the creators always will give support to all those who need technical, didactic or pedagogical guide, advice or support. Future projects and new 3D objects will extend the set of objects presented in this work. They will be related to robotics for children and Digital Assets to improve digital skills for both teachers and students to better understand algorithms [34], such as D-BOX, to produce assistive technologies such as ASD-robot and to improve perspective-taking skills such as Ames room.

References

1. Campbell, T., Williams, C., Ivanova, O., Garrett, B.: Could 3D printing change the world. Technologies, Potential, and Implications of Additive Manufacturing. Atlantic Council, Washington, DC (2011)
2. Dawood, A., Marti, B.M., Sauret-Jackson, V., Darwood, A.: 3D printing in dentistry. Br. Dent. J. **219**(11), 521–529 (2015)
3. Schubert, C., Van Langeveld, M.C., Donoso, L.A.: Innovations in 3D printing: a 3D overview from optics to organs. Br. J. Ophthalmol. **98**(2), 159–161 (2014)
4. Lipson, H., Kurman, M.: Fabricated: The New World of 3D Printing. Wiley, Hoboken (2013)
5. Leinonen, T., Virnes, M., Hietala, I., Brinck, J.: 3D printing in the wild: adopting digital fabrication in elementary school education. Int. J. Art Design Educ. **39**(3), 600–615 (2020)
6. Nemorin, S., Selwyn, N.: Making the best of it? Exploring the realities of 3D printing in school. Res. Pap. Educ. **32**(5), 578–595 (2017)
7. Lacey, G.: 3D printing brings designs to life. Tech Dir. **70**(2), 17 (2010)
8. Polli, A.: Samsung ed Energy Group portano le stampanti 3D nelle scuole italiane (2016). https://www.replicatore.it/la-scuola-si-fa-ancor-piu-interessante/
9. Di Tore, S., Todino, M. D., Sibilio, M.: Disuffo: design, prototipazione e sviluppo di un robot didattico open-source. Form@re **19**(1), 106–116 (2019)
10. Todino, M.D., Campitiello, L., Di Tore, S.: Come la stampa 3D della Stanza di Ames può favorire il cambio di prospettiva visuo-spaziale nei discenti e nei docenti. Italian J. Special Educ. Incl. **8**(2), 169–189 (2020)

11. Todino, M.-D., Campitiello, L., Di Tore, S.: D-BOX: binary code, Knowledge representation in the digital age, and how to teach it using a game in primary school. Form@re - Open Journal per la formazione in rete **20**(3), 86–102 (2020)
12. Todino, M.D.: La complessità dell'interazione uomo-macchina. Aracne, Roma (2018)
13. INDIRE: Maker@scuola Stampanti 3D nella scuola dell'infanzia (2017)
14. PNSD, Ambito Formazione e accompagnamento, Azione #28, Animatori Digitali. https://www.istruzione.it/scuola_digitale/prog-animatori-digitali.shtml. Accessed 20 Mar 2021
15. Rieber, L.-P.: Seriously considering play: designing interactive learning environments based on the blending of microworlds, simulations, and games. Educ. Tech. Res. Dev. **44**(2), 43–58 (1996). https://doi.org/10.1007/BF02300540
16. Whitton, N.: Learning with Digital Games: A Practical Guide to Engaging Students in Higher Education. Routledge, London-New York (2009)
17. Benigno, V., Chiorri, C., Tavella, M.: Giochi di Pensiero e Abilità di Ragionamento: il Progetto Logivali. Formazione, Innovazione e Tecnologie, 305–322 (2010)
18. Di Tore, S., Aiello, P., Di Tore, P.-A., Sibilio, M.: Exergames as teaching tools: new forms of human machine interaction. Acad. J. Interdiscip. Stud. **1**(2), 165 (2012)
19. Gardner, H.: Formae mentis. Saggio sulla pluralità della intelligenza. Feltrinelli, Milano (2002)
20. The Cape Town Open Education Declaration. https://www.capetowndeclaration.org/read-the-declaration. Accessed 20 Mar 2021
21. Common Prusa3D manual (3D printing handbook online). https://www.electronicsdatasheets.com/datasheet/Original%20Prusa%20i3%20MK3%20user%20manual.pdf. Accessed 20 Mar 2021
22. EN 13432 certified bioplastics performance in industrial composting by European Bioplastics Private Company (Germany). https://docs.european-bioplastics.org/publications/bp/EUBP_BP_En_13432.pdf. Accessed 20 Mar 2021
23. Ultimate 3D Printing Materials Guide by Slimplify3D website. https://www.simplify3d.com/support/materials-guide. Accessed 20 Mar 2021
24. Marble PLA: Marble Filament Brands Compared by all3dp.com website. https://all3dp.com/2/marble-pla-marble-filament-brands-compared. Accessed 20 Mar 2021
25. Architectural Marble 3D Printing Filament, Marble-solid 3D Printing with Monumental by TreeD. Or was it rock-solid? By treedfilaments.com website. https://treedfilaments.com/3d-printing-filaments/architectural-marble. Accessed 20 Mar 2021
26. Guida ai Materiali per la stampa 3D – dalle Plastiche ai Metalli all'Alimentare, by stampa3dstore.com website. https://www.stampa3dstore.com/guida-ai-materiali-per-la-stampa-3d-dalle-plastiche-ai-metalli-allalimentare. Accessed 20 Mar 2021
27. Top Ten Upgrades for your 3D Printer by matterhackers.com website. https://www.matterhackers.com/articles/top-ten-upgrades-for-your-3d-printer. Accessed 20 Mar 2021
28. Berthoz, A.: La vicarianza. Il nostro cervello creatore di mondi. Codice, Torino (2015)
29. Castoldi, M., Sbaragli, S.: Matematica e contesti di vita. Che cosa vuol dire essere competenti in matematica alla scuola primaria? La vita scolastica. **6**(74) 8–10 (2020)
30. http://www.lesvoyellescolorees.com/didactic-materials
31. Cottini, L., Pascoletti, S., Zanon, F.: Realtà aumentata e didattica inclusiva. La vita scolastica **7**(74), 26–27 (2020)
32. Aiello, P., Di Gennaro, D.C., Palumbo, C., Zollo, I., Sibilio, M.: Inclusion and universal design for learning in Italian schools. Int. J. Digit. Liter. Digit. Comp. (IJDLDC) **5**(2), 59–68 (2014)
33. Booth, T., Ainscow, M., Black-Hawkins, K., Vaughan, M., Shaw, L.: Index for inclusion. Develop. Learn. Participation Schools (2002)
34. Grasso, N.: Algoritmi: manipolare significati. Tanti modi di operare. La vita scolastica. **4**(75), 62–63 (2020)

Planning the "New Normality" to Address the Pandemic in Higher Education: Blended Scenarios at the Catholic University of the Sacred Heart

Serena Triacca(✉), Federica Pelizzari, Flavia Scott, and Pier Cesare Rivoltella

Catholic University of the Sacred Heart, Milan, Italy
{serena.triacca,federica.pelizzari,flavia.scott,
piercesare.rivoltella}@unicatt.it

Abstract. Since the early spring 2020, universities had to accept the impact of the first wave of Covid-19 disease and manage the emergency: students and teachers experienced a massive shift from traditional face-to-face education to online education. This new situation has been more properly defined "emergency remote teaching". Catholic University of Sacred Heart has guaranteed the regular course of study to all the students. The contribution intends to present the *#eCatt plan* for the academic year 2020/21: it provides for a blended solution which moves on four scenarios, two in synchronous and two in asynchronous modes of learning (Dual mode, Online interactive lecture, Talking head, Voice-over presentation). To accompany the faculty to lesson design, self-training modules have been developed. In addition, weekly webinars have been planned and proposed, focusing on the scenarios, available technological solutions and educational tools. Data collection aims to provide a quantitative overview of the access to the online courses, participation in training sessions, adoption of synchronous and asynchronous solutions, focusing on teaching practices in synchronous sessions.

Keywords: Higher education · Blended learning · Faculty development · Synchronous mode · Asynchronous mode

1 Introduction

1.1 Online Teaching

Since the early spring 2020, Italian schools and universities – in line with what was happening worldwide – suffered the impact of the first wave of Covid-19 disease and

---

This article has been developed jointly by the authors. Serena Triacca wrote the sections 1.2 Blended learning scenarios: the #eCatt plan, 2. Method, 4. Discussion. Federica Pelizzari wrote the sections 1.1 Online teaching, 3.2. Digitally Augmented Education (Blackboard course), 3.3. Synchronous lessons analysis. Flavia Scott wrote the section 3.1. DidaTec Corner (Blackboard course). Pier Cesare Rivoltella wrote the section 5. Conclusions.

G. Casalino et al. (Eds.): HELMeTO 2021, CCIS 1542, pp. 248–263, 2022.
https://doi.org/10.1007/978-3-030-96060-5_18

managed the emergency [1]: students and teachers experienced in fact an unexpected, rapid and massive shift from traditional face-to-face education to online education [2].

This new situation has been more properly defined "emergency remote teaching". Unlike the learning paths planned from the beginning to be online, emergency distance teaching is a temporary transition of the provision of education to an alternative mode of delivery due to crisis circumstances. It involves the use of completely remote teaching solutions that would otherwise be provided in presence and that will return to that format once the crisis has subsided [3].

The pandemic has actually led to rethink and redesign the teaching, trying to find flexible and creative solutions that could adapt to rapid and sudden changes [4]. The main objective of teaching is to enable students to be the protagonists of their own learning path; in this perspective, the shift to online education can allow the flexibility of teaching and learning anywhere and anytime, but the rapidity at which this transition to online education has been expected is clearly unprecedented [5].

The concept of classroom needs to be revised and no longer considered as a physical place but as a learning environment, in which one or more systems interact for a common purpose: learning [6]. In this sense, the teacher interacts with different "classrooms", defined in a pragmatic sense as different scenarios for teaching action, on the basis of descriptors of situations (setting), actions (strategies) and didactic (teaching typology) [7] (see Table 1). The five scenarios can be thought of both as a context - a course could be completely face-to-face or completely online - and as different dimensions of a training path to be combined.

Table 1. The five classrooms of teaching [7]

Scenario	Situation	Actions	Didactic
Presence	Physical Classroom	Exposition	For contents
Teledidactic	Integrated Classroom	Mediation	For problems
Online course	Third Classroom	Management	Self-learning
Virtual Group	Fourth Classroom	Communication	Collaborative
Community	Fifth Classroom	Participation	Community of practice

Furthermore, it is possible to refer to the model of the four teaching methods [8], based on five variables: learning to be promoted, method of teaching activity (active/transmissive), setting (face-to-face/online), temporality of teaching (synchronous/asynchronous) and sociality (individual/groups) (see Table 2). Since settings and learning to promote, it is possible to understand which strategies are most suitable to obtain the desired results.

Within this framework, the design activity, especially in distance learning, should consider three fundamental dimensions [9]:

- the architectural dimension: the planning of the teaching actions, the choice of methods and tools and the design of the student's activities;
- the ergonomic dimension: the didactic transposition, in particular with regard to cognitive load, didactic mediators and formatting;

Table 2. Model of the four teaching methods [8]

	Didactic transmission	Individual teaching	Group teaching	Informal teaching
Synchronous face-to-face	Lessons	Modelling Apprenticeship Problem solving	Tutorial Case study Brainstorming Project work Problem solving Role playing Jigsaw	
Online synchronous	Videoconference	Simulations	Web seminar Brainstorming	
Online asynchronous	Hypertexts Drill and practice Learning Object	Problem solving Role playing Serious games	Discussions Case study Project work Problem solving Role playing Jigsaw	Information retrieval Discussions
Learning	Acquiring Remembering	Experiencing Discovering Solving	Collaborating Cooperating Doing together	Participating Deepening Personalizing

– the process dimension: the evaluation and management of teaching and learning time, as well as aspects related to communication management and its moderation.

1.2 Blended Learning Scenarios: The #eCatt Plan[1]

Catholic University of Sacred Heart has ensured regular teaching activities to all the students of the 12 faculties of the 5 campuses for the entire duration of the first phase of the health emergency linked to Covid-19[2].

[1] The *#eCatt plan* is the result of a strategic alliance of skills between the University Quality Presidium, iLab (Center for Innovation in educational technologies), CREMIT (Research Center on Media Education, Innovation and Technology), the Faculties, Rector's Delegate for Teaching and the Commission of the Academic Senate in charge of this. Federico Rajola is the Director of iLab, Flavia Scott is the Program Manager of iLab and the working group is composed by Marco Bertin, Enrica Bolognese, Chiara Rizzi, Elena Tassalini, Luigi Scazzola and Elsa Zoffi. Pier Cesare Rivoltella is the Director of CREMIT and the working group is composed by Sara Lo Jacono, Federica Pelizzari and Serena Triacca.

[2] From 24th February to 30th May 2020, thanks to Blackboard platform, the University's Learning Management System, 1877 teachers carried out a total of 37419 distance learning lessons (26564 recorded video-lectures and 10855 live lectures on Collaborate Ultra). Likewise, exams and graduation sessions have not been rescheduled and took place regularly through Microsoft Teams. 6775 exams took place from 18th March to 23rd June. Starting from 11st March to 23rd June, 525 graduation commissions were regularly held.

To allow class attendance for the academic year 2020/21, the *#eCatt plan* was fine-tuned[3]: it provides for a blended solution [10, 11] which moves on four scenarios, two in synchronous and two in asynchronous modes of learning [12, 13] (see Fig. 1). These scenarios can be combined to create content-rich, integrated and interactive courses for planning the "new normality", with the aim to guarantee the quality of the teaching-learning in the different phases of the pandemic emergency:

- Dual mode: the teacher and a group of students are in an equipped classroom that allows to reach other students remotely connected. Real time audio-video communication, chatting, breakout sessions, contents, applications and whiteboard sharing are made possible by an online video conferencing tool (Blackboard Collaborate Ultra) [7, 14]. Lessons can be post-produced with the VCMS Panopto and published on the Blackboard course;
- Online interactive lecture: the teacher gives a synchronous lesson - in a university equipped classroom or at home - using an online video conferencing tool (Blackboard Collaborate Ultra). In both cases, students follow the lesson remotely. Collaborate ensures real-time audio-video communication, chatting, breakout sessions, content, applications and whiteboard sharing [7]. Lessons can be post-produced with the VCMS Panopto and published on the Blackboard course;
- Talking head: the teacher records and edits the lesson in advance, using different formats (talking head with or without slides, whiteboard, text overlay, object or green screen) and publishes it on the Blackboard course to allow students to view it. Captions, slides and interactive elements can be included in the content using a VCMS as Panopto [15];
- Voice-over presentation: the teacher records a content in advance, using different formats (voice-over narration, pencast writing, screencast, animation, podcast) and publishes it on the Blackboard course [15].

To support faculty development and accompany the teachers in their lesson design, four self-training modules have been developed and implemented in the Blackboard course *Digitally Augmented Education*. Moreover, an overview on the scenarios was provided, with a focus on the tools and teaching formats with the regard to the six learning types (acquisition, investigation, discussion, collaboration, practice, production) [16].

Free interactive weekly webinars have been delivered, focusing on the scenarios, on available technological solutions (Blackboard, Collaborate, Panopto) and educational tools (such as forum, wiki, assignment).

Furthermore, the possibility of tests and simulations in the classroom with the whole set of functionalities of dual mode scenario have been provided.

---

[3] In Internet, URL: https://www.unicatt.it/ecatt. For the implementation of the plan, whose philosophy is *"Everything possible in presence, everything necessary remotely"*, Catholic University has invested financial resources for an amount of 3.5 million euros which, in addition to the one million euros initially conferred for the *Agostino Gemelli Fund* to support students, includes investments for digital teaching made possible also by the requalification of the 500 classrooms of the Catholic University.

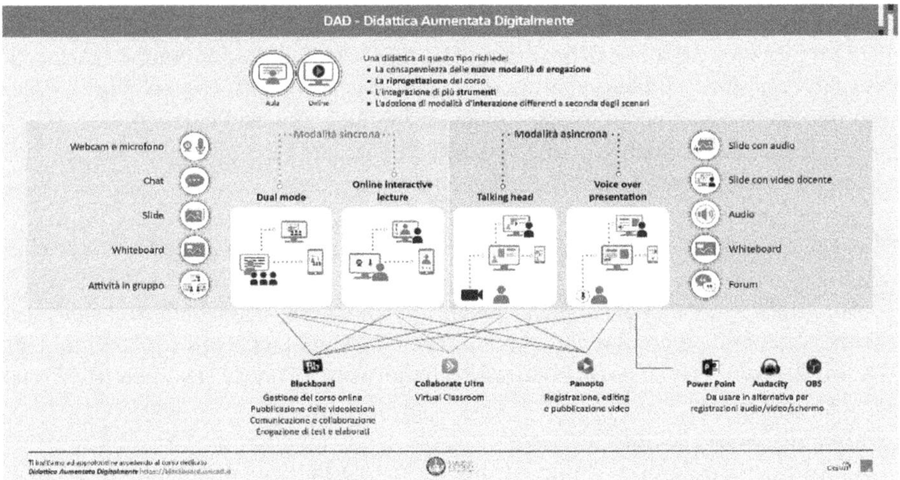

Fig. 1. The four pillars of the *#eCatt plan*

2 Method

To provide a quantitative overview of the different actions related to the *#eCatt plan*, data collection focused on:

- access to the Blackboard courses *DidaTec Corner* and *Digitally Augmented Education* and the actual use of learning contents by teachers (sources: Blackboard course report from July 2020 to May 2021; document analysis);
- training sessions delivered and participation (sources: Blackboard Collaborate Ultra report from March 2020 to May 2021; document analysis);
- adoption of the synchronous and asynchronous scenarios during the academic year 2020/21 (sources: Blackboard Collaborate Ultra data mining from September 2020 to May 2021).

In addition, a sample of 40 recorded synchronous sessions (20 I term sessions; 20 II term sessions) was analyzed in order to focus on the teaching practices. A simple random sampling procedure was adopted [17][4]. The analysis grid [18] included the following sections:

- general information: course, Faculty, campus, scenario, duration, number of connected students, number of recording views;
- description of the session structure in three main teaching phases (start, development, conclusion);

[4] The original database included sessions delivered from September 2020 to May 2021 in all campuses and faculties, but many strings - due to technical problems - did not contain all the references to courses (ID, course name, Faculty). For this reason, the sample does not contain an equitable distribution of all the faculties.

- technical quality of the video and audio transmission;
- teaching formats;
- interaction.

A descriptive analysis has been carried out on the different items.

The preliminary analysis of the session structure has been carried out by attributing to each teaching phase a design level (basic, intermediate, advanced), since the presence or absence of the elements characterizing the phases (see Table 3).

Table 3. Elements of the teaching phases

Start	Development	Conclusion
Welcome of participants Sharing of netiquette, agenda, objectives Recap of the past lesson(s) Warm up	Sub-phases in which transmissive moments alternate with interactive ones; individual activities, in couples or small groups	Summary Brief preview of the next lesson Eventual assignments (e-tivities or readings) Final greetings

3 Results

3.1 *DidaTec Corner* (Blackboard Course)

The Blackboard course *DidaTec Corner* was released in March 2019. It has been redesigned from an existing one implemented since 2012, which included several face-to-face training meetings, reflections on educational technologies and their application in different disciplines, case studies and testimonials [19].

The course as currently conceived has a dual purpose: delivering weekly webinars about the blended scenarios, Blackboard tools and more generally to technologies and their use in teaching and offering in-depth contents on these issues. 8579 users were enrolled, including teaching staff (professors, teaching assistants, tutors), doctoral students and technical-administrative staff.

The course is structured in the following areas (see Fig. 2):

- Announcements: news about the course;
- Join the webinar: link to the weekly webinars;
- Archive of webinar recordings: playlists of webinars delivered from March 2020 to May 2021;
- Live lectures: insights into the two scenarios proposed for live teaching (Dual mode and Online interactive lecture) and guidance on the use of Blackboard Collaborate Ultra;
- Recorded lessons: detailed overview of the main tools for the asynchronous scenarios (Talking head, Voice over presentation);

- Assessment/Exams: guides for managing the continuous and final assessment with Blackboard tools (test, assignment) and proctoring system (Respondus Lockdown Browser);
- Tools for online interaction: the section is dedicated to the deepening of interaction tools in Blackboard (news, e-mail, discussion board, virtual workgroups);
- Blackboard basics: video-tutorial and handbooks about designing and managing online courses;
- FAQs: answers to Frequently Asked Questions.

Each section contains a road map of the key-concepts and several folders with video and textual contents.

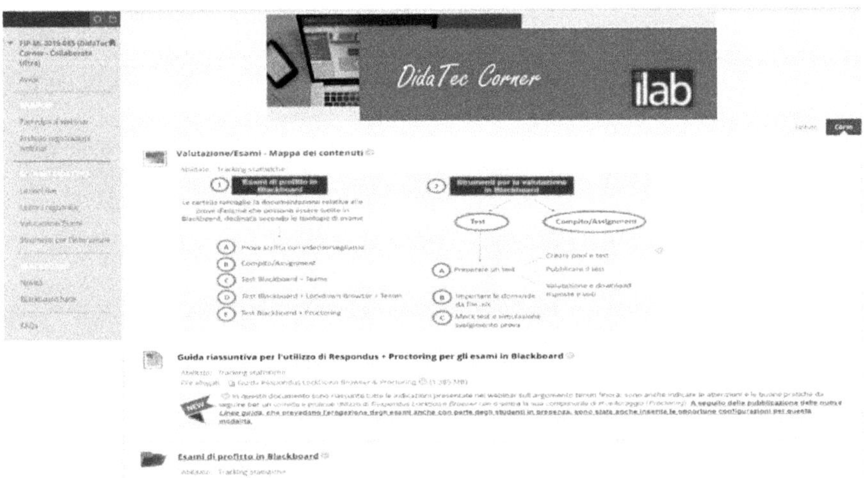

Fig. 2. *DidaTec Corner* Blackboard course

42% of the teaching staff had access to the course. The most clicked and viewed materials in the course, from 1st July 2020 to 31st May 2021, are the section of assessment management (31%), tools for live lessons (Blackboard Collaborate Ultra) (20%), vademecum for recording, editing and publishing a video lesson with Panopto (18%) and webinars recordings (18%).

The 91 weekly webinars provided from March 2020 to May 2021 have an average duration of 75 min and the average number of participants per session is 64, with a peak of 245 participants at the beginning of the first semester of the a.y. 2020/21. The topic was how to manage a Dual mode lesson with Blackboard Collaborate Ultra. However, the highest turnout was in March and April 2020, at the beginning of the emergency phase of the COVID-19 pandemic. As can be seen in Fig. 3, different themes were covered. In particular, a large percentage of webinars focused on assessment tools (designing pool of questions, tests, assignments; using Respondus Lockdown Browser), due to the need to continue the regular examination sessions from March 2020 onwards.

As further support for the use of Panopto for recording and editing video-lessons and Microsoft Teams, the platform chosen by the University for oral exams from the summer 2020 session, a free-flow service has been made available for teachers, which allows them to get daily personalized help with troubleshooting.

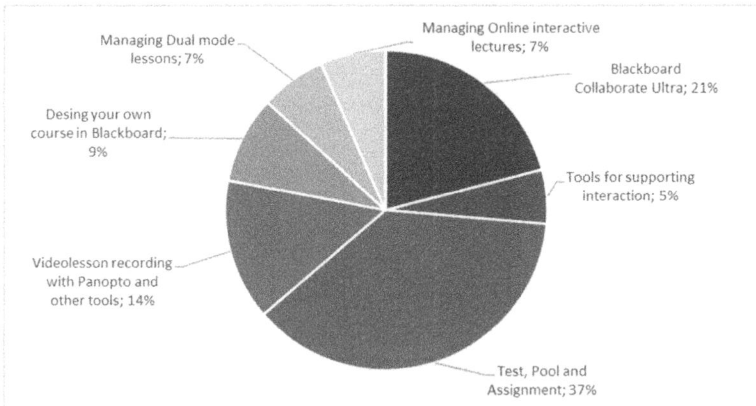

Fig. 3. Percentage distribution of webinars delivered in the course *DidaTec Corner*

3.2 *Digitally Augmented Education* (Blackboard Course)

As mentioned earlier, to promote the approach of digitally augmented education and guide the adoption of the four teaching scenarios for the a.y. 2020/21, a new Blackboard course has been developed. The online environment has been officially released in July 2020 (see Fig. 4). 6065 users were enrolled, including teaching staff (professors, teaching assistants, tutors), doctoral students and technical-administrative staff.

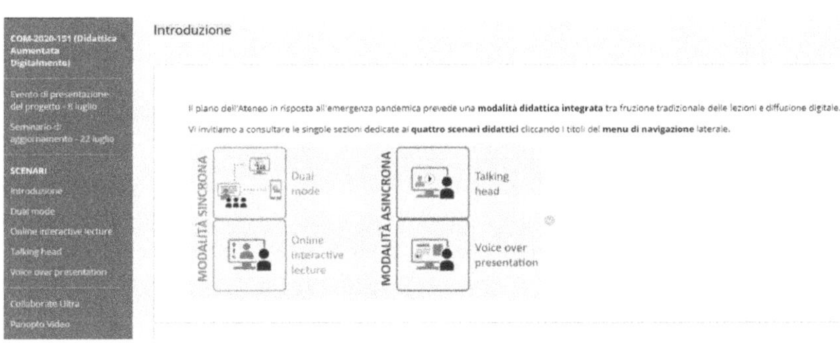

Fig. 4. *Digitally Augmented Education* Blackboard course

The first areas of the menu collect the main materials of the project:

- recording of webinar *#eCatt and the Digitally Augmented Education project* and slideshows;

- recording of webinar for Deans and Degree Course Coordinators about the provisions of classroom lessons for the new academic year (access planning, app for class attendance, upgrading technological infrastructure) and an overview on the four teaching scenarios, with a focus on the tools and teaching formats with reference the six learning types [16] (see Fig. 5).

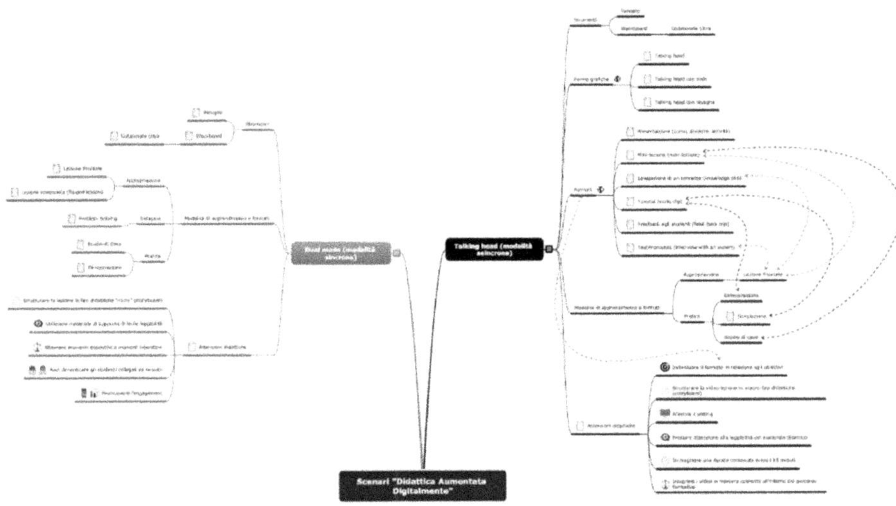

Fig. 5. Detail of the map of the synchronous and asynchronous teaching scenarios

The core of the course consists of four self-teaching modules, one for each scenario (Dual mode, Online interactive lecture, Talking head, Voice-over presentation), to allow teachers to learn the basics of each of them independently and facilitate them to lesson planning process. Each scenario includes:

- an interactive educational content: the objects, with a navigable index, have a common structure that provides an introduction about the four teaching scenarios, a brief presentation of the scenario, design tips, good practices, examples, a theoretical framework and a bibliography. In addition, downloadable tools - such as storyboard templates, checklist, lists of apps for promoting interaction, presentation design tips - were added. To support the understanding of key-terms, both at an educational and technical level, a glossary was implemented[5]. A voiceover explains the contents, while short texts, icons and customized graphics appear on the screen (see Fig. 6);
- an infographic: a graphic summary with a concise definition of the scenario, the tools needed, suggestion on possible teaching formats;
- a technical sheet: description of the flow of activities and technical steps required to manage lessons with the available tools;

[5] The modules, developed with Articulate Storyline, were designed by a team of iLab and CREMIT experts. The Dual Mode module was designed as a prototype: the larger working group feedbacks were functional to orient the production of the other contents.

– a printable document: transcription of the full text.

Fig. 6. Screenshot of the learning object about the Dual mode scenario

59% of the teaching staff had access to the online environment. Considering all the contents of the Blackboard course, 60% of the users' activity is related to the project presentation materials; the remaining 40% focuses on the educational contents.

Figure 7 shows the percentage distribution of accesses to the four scenarios: from 1st July 2020 to 31st May 2021, the most clicked and viewed scenario is, as expected, Dual mode, most probably due to the novelty of the solution proposed at the Catholic University.

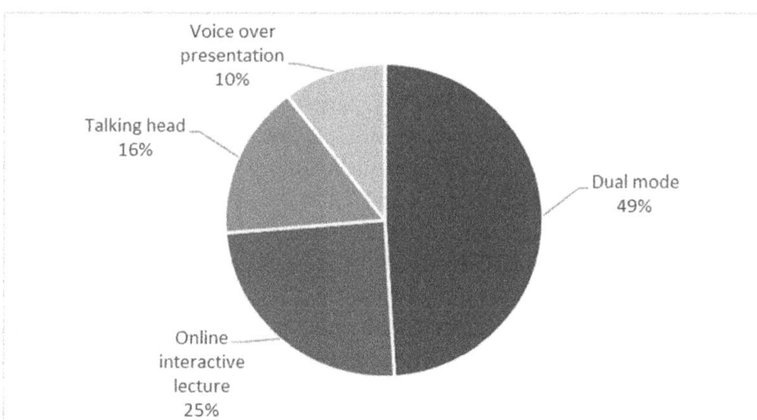

Fig. 7. Percentage distribution of accesses to the materials of the four scenarios

3.3 Synchronous Lessons Analysis

Before dwelling on the analysis carried out on a sample of synchronous sessions, Table 4 offers a quantitative overview of the synchronous and asynchronous lessons delivered during the academic year 2020/21.

Table 4. Overview of the synchronous and asynchronous lessons delivered in the a.y. 2020/21

Faculties	Synchronous lessons		Asynchronous lessons	
	I term	II term	I term	II term
Economics	5248	5287	333	118
Economics and Law	1717	1901	106	110
Law	1641	1809	21	58
Literature and Philosophy	2408	3340	1487	752
Medicine and Surgery	7551	9743	383	356
Psychology	1786	1726	34	24
Agriculture, food and environmental sciences	2048	1945	200	245
Banking, Finance and Insurance Sciences	1460	1124	62	35
Education	3979	4602	572	340
Linguistic Sciences and Foreign Literatures	8477	8708	428	421
Mathematical, Physical and Natural Sciences	489	468	130	103
Political and Social Sciences	4321	3491	332	176
Total	41125	44144	4088	2738

From 7th September 2020 to 4th June 2021, 5087 teachers of the 12 Faculties of all the campuses (Brescia, Milano, Piacenza-Cremona, Roma) had made a total of 92095 lessons (45213 in the I term, 46882 in the II term): 6826 video-lessons, recorded and uploaded to Blackboard and 85269 synchronous lessons with Collaborate Ultra[6].

The analysis of the recordings of the synchronous sessions was carried out on a sample of 40 lessons, 20 in the first term and 20 in the second term. 15 were delivered in Dual Mode and 25 in Online Interactive Lecture mode. Almost half of the sessions observed lasted between 20 and 60 min (48%), 30% between 60 and 90 min, 15% lasted between 90 and 180 min.

In most of the sessions, the quality of the video transmission was excellent (55%); in 43% of cases, the quality was not detectable as in the recording the teacher never

[6] In addition to what was done within the 12 Faculties, we report the data regarding the educational offer of the Theology Courses, the Higher Institute of Religious Sciences and the University Language Service (SeLdA): from 7th September 2020 to 4th June 2021, 181 teachers had made a total of 4084 lessons: 372 video-lessons, recorded and uploaded to Blackboard and 3712 synchronous lessons with Collaborate Ultra.

appears on webcam. The audio quality was excellent in 88% of them, thus allowing a fluid listening of the lectures.

Regarding the structure of the lessons, we identified three main phases (start, development, conclusion). The phases were tagged in basic, intermediate, advanced level because of the presence or absence of the described elements characterizing the phases. As seen in Fig. 8, teachers stress different moments of the lecture in different ways. Nearly 70% of the conclusions and one half of the beginnings have been described as "basic" relying on the featured elements. The "advanced" indicator reaches a value above 30% only for the development part of the lecture, while stays below 20% for the other phases.

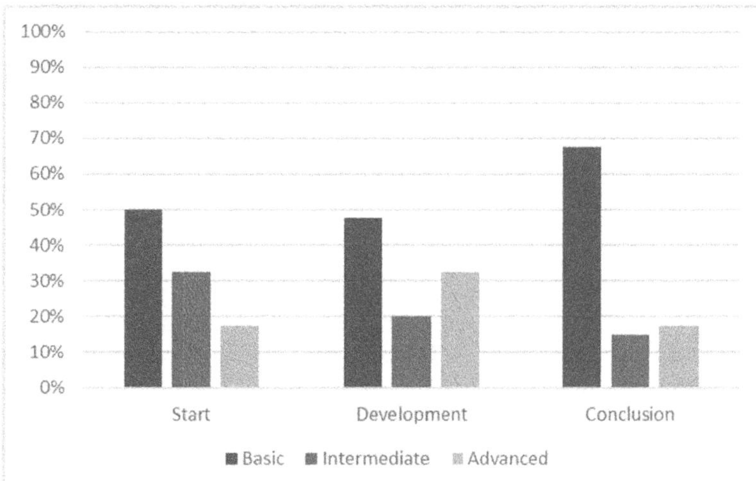

Fig. 8. Phases of the lessons distributed by level

Observing the teaching formats adopted [20], we discover that 64% of teachers choose frontal lectures, 16% asked students to do exercises and 13% propose guided exercises.

93% of teachers used teaching aids: in 71% of the sessions, they used software to support oral presentation (Power Point, Word, Excel,...), only 14% used Blackboard Collaborate Ultra tools (screen sharing, whiteboard, pool, breakout groups) and 14% used other visual resources as videos and websites.

Regarding to presentations, it is possible to observe that the choice of the font and the contrast background-text allowed the full readability (71%; 64%). It should be noted, however, that 50% do not use semantic markers on key-elements (bold, italics, colours etc.) and only 18% of presentations contained the agenda. Finally, it can be observed that 50% of the presentations use images, orally commented by the teacher; images had short written captions or keywords in only 25% of the cases.

The prevailing degree of interaction between students and teacher is rather low, considering that in 33% of the sessions no interactions are recorded and in 18% students are not explicitly encouraged to ask questions, but when they do, the teacher answers them. In almost a quarter of the sessions (23%), there is a meaningful communicative exchange between students and teachers, both verbally and in written form. The most populated chat session collected 147 messages; in 13 sessions no chat message and audio interaction were recorded.

Finally, it can be noted that in the cases in which students asked questions spontaneously (54%), the teacher was asked for clarification on sentences or small parts of the topics covered (48%), examples (19%) and explanations about continuous assessment and final exams (23%).

4 Discussion

The proposed data bring to a reflection on three main aspects of teaching to focus on: lesson planning, utilization of teaching aids and teacher training.

Analyzing the recordings, we realize that 64% of sessions used frontal lectures and in 33% of the sessions no interactions were recorded, neither solicited nor spontaneously. What distinguishes a video-lesson from a synchronous lesson is the possibility of interacting, stimulating the sharing of ideas, hypotheses, questions. The most interactive sessions are that of the language teaching (Arabic, French, English, Russian, German), psychology courses and traineeship, which strongly solicit the participation of students, configuring as "protected spaces" in which to learn from mistakes and misconceptions thanks to the guidance of the teacher.

In a recent systematic review of meta-analyses that synthetized the variables associated with student achievement in higher education, it is highlighted that teachers with the highest performing students invest time and effort in designing the microstructure of their courses, set clear learning objectives and use feedback practices. Of the 105 variables identified, the preparation of the course by the teacher is the third for effect size [21]. Given the synchronous lessons analyzed, a suggestion for teachers could be to structure lessons in well-defined phases [22], which perform specific functions and may involve the use of different tools, for example shared boards and Student Response Systems (SRS) to stimulate participation. It can be seen that 30% of the analyzed structures of sessions are totally "basic" and 15% totally "advanced". In the first case, agenda, objectives and netiquette of the lesson are not shared with the students; the lesson is not structured in well-defined moments alternating lecturing, interactions, individual and group activities; in the end, there is no space for a summary of the highlights or a brief preview of the next lesson. The main limitation of the analysis is linked to the fact that it was carried out on the recordings and not directly observing the lesson or reading the lesson plans (if present); this means that some elements may have been omitted before the start and after the stop of the recording.

Regarding the utilization of the teaching aids, its importance is emphasized for favoring the anchoring of the attention of the students, something that in 50% of the analyzed cases has been made. Unfortunately, the importance of this has often been underestimated, although several authors have supported positive effects on students [23] and on teachers [24]. In addition, providing visual aids (synthetic slides, graphic organizers, blackboard on which to write also collaboratively, short videos etc.) supports the anchoring of concepts, especially if combined with the explanation of the teacher [25].

In the end, some considerations about the online access to the Blackboard courses: on the total number of enrolled teachers, 42% and 59% accessed respectively to *Digitally Augmented Education* and *DidaTec Corner* courses; teachers seem very interested - and may be worried - in technical aspects, those on which they perhaps feel less capable. This could also imply a lack of didactic culture and of an overall vision of student's learning. Instead, it would be useful for teachers to learn in a more systematic way how to approach a digital augmented class and how to manage computer mediated communication in order to promote effective exchanges [26].

5 Conclusions

Future studies and actions in Catholic University could consider the following elements:

- faculty development: in order to guarantee systematic training for in service and newly hired teachers, it may be necessary to invest on development of Digital Literacy and educational culture [27]. Technical training should be complementary to methodological training, with targeted coaching actions aimed at supporting teachers in designing the courses (from syllabus to lesson plan), which in perspective could be increasingly blended, and in moderation of synchronous and asynchronous communication;
- new specialized figures to support the interactions in Dual mode scenario: as the main difficulty is managing face-to-face and online classrooms simultaneously [28, 29] and the adoption of Dual mode for the academic year 2021/22, it could be strategic to invest on technical and methodological training of tutors who can act as facilitators of communication between the master classroom and slave classrooms. The tutor is in fact considered as a crucial figure in blended learning courses, both for students and for teachers [30]. The presence of an e-moderator would allow, on the one hand, to lighten the teacher and, on the other, to promote more effective communication exchanges between the classrooms, in an increasingly inclusive and interactive logic [31].

References

1. Agasisti, T., Soncin, M.: Higher education in troubled times: on the impact of Covid-19 in Italy. Stud. High. Educ. **46**(1), 86–95 (2021)
2. Limone, P., Toto, G.A., Sansone, N. (eds.): Didattica universitaria a distanza. Tra emergenze e futuro. Progedit, Bari (2020)
3. Hodges, C., Moore, S., Lockee, B., Trust, T., Bond, A.: The difference between emergency remote teaching and online learning (2020). https://tinyurl.com/95dkb3x8. Accessed 01 Sept 2021
4. König, J., Jäger-Biela, D.J., Glutsch, N.: Adapting to online teaching during COVID-19 school closure: teacher education and teacher competence effects among early career teachers in Germany. Eur. J. Teach. Educ. **43**(4), 608–622 (2020)
5. Zimmerman, J.: Coronavirus and the Great Online-Learning Experiment (2020). https://tinyurl.com/3hy4pbrz. Accessed 01 Sept 2021

6. Basque, J., Doré, S.: Le concept d'environnement d'apprentissage informatisé. J. Dist. Educ. **13**(19), 40–56 (1998)
7. Ardizzone, P., Rivoltella, P.C.: Didattiche per l'e-learning. Metodi e strumenti per l'innovazione dell'insegnamento universitario. Carocci, Roma (2003)
8. Garavaglia, A.: Didattica online. Dai modelli alle tecniche. Unicopli, Milano (2011)
9. Rivoltella, P.C. (ed.): Apprendere a distanza. Teorie e metodi. Raffaello Cortina, Milano (2021)
10. Garrison, D.R., Kanuka, H.: Blended learning: uncovering its transformative potential in higher education. Internet High. Educ. **7**(2), 95–105 (2004)
11. Garrison, D.R., Vaughan, N.: Blended learning in higher education. Framework, principles and guidelines. Jossey-Bass, San Francisco (2008)
12. Sistek-Chandler, C.M. (ed.): Exploring Online Learning Through Synchronous and Asynchronous Instructional Methods. IGI Global, Hershey (2019)
13. Watts, L.: Synchronous and asynchronous communication in distance learning: a review of the literature. Q. Rev. Dist. Educ. **17**(1), 23–32 (2016)
14. Cain, W., Henriksen, D.: Pedagogy and situational creativity in synchronous hybrid learning: descriptions of three models. In: McBride, R., Searson, M. (eds.) Proceedings of Society for Information Technology & Teacher Education International Conference, pp. 291–297. Association for the Advancement of Computing in Education (AACE), Chesapeake (2013)
15. Hansch, A., Hillers, L., McConachie, K., Newman, C., Schildhauer, T., Schmidt, P.: Video and online learning: Critical reflections and findings from the field. SSRN, HIIG Discussion Paper Series No. 2015-02 (2015)
16. Laurillard, D.: Teaching as A Design Science Building Pedagogical Patterns for Learning and Technology. Routledge, London (2012)
17. Viganò, R.: Pedagogia e sperimentazione: Metodi e strumenti per la ricerca educativa. Vita & Pensiero, Milano (2002)
18. Rivoltella, P.C. (ed.): E-tutor. Profilo, metodi, strumenti. Carocci, Roma (2006)
19. Rizzi, C., Bolognese, E.: Il DidaTec Corner per i docenti universitari. L'evoluzione di un'iniziativa di formazione all'uso delle tecnologie didattiche. https://tinyurl.com/ep6fd8uf. Accessed 01 Sept 2021
20. Bonaiuti, G.: Le strategie didattiche. Carocci, Roma (2014)
21. Schneider, M., Preckel, F.: Variables associated with achievement in higher education: a systematic review of meta-analyses. Psychol. Bull. **143**(6), 565–600 (2017)
22. Mishra, R.C.: Lesson Planning. APH Publishing Corporation, New Delhi (2009)
23. Crook, C.: Rendere più interattivi i materiali ipertestuali per la lezione universitaria: le reazioni degli studenti. TD, **5**(1), 34–34 (1997)
24. Castaldo, U., Mezzalama, M., Venuto, E.: Multicanalità e e-learning: nuovi scenari tecnologici e didattici. In: Atti convegno nazionale Didamatica 2013 "Tecnologie e metodi per la didattica del futuro", pp. 359–368. AICA (2013)
25. Paivio, A.: Dual coding theory: retrospect and current status. Canadian J. Psychol./Revue canadienne de psychologie **45**(3), 255–287 (1991)
26. Felisatti, E., Serbati, A.: Apprendere per imparare: formazione e sviluppo professionale dei docenti universitari. Un progetto innovativo dell'Università di Padova. Italian J. Educ. Res. **14**, 323–340 (2015)
27. Rivoltella, P.C., Rossi, P.G. (eds.): L'agire didattico. Manuale per L'insegnante. La Scuola, Brescia (2017)
28. White, C.P., Ramirez, R., Smith, J.G., Plonowski, L.: Simultaneous delivery of a face-to-face course to on-campus and remote off-campus students. TechTrends **54**(4), 34–40 (2010)
29. Bower, M., Dalgarno, B., Kennedy, G.E., Lee, M., Kenney, J.: Design and implementation factors in blended synchronous learning environments: outcomes from a cross-case analysis. Comput. Educ. **86**, 1–17 (2015)

30. Triacca, S., Bodega, D., Rivoltella, P.C.: Blended solution and Higher Education. The case of the Catholic University: e-tutoring for personalization. Educ. Sci. Soc. **9**(2), 198–210 (2019)
31. Salmon, G.: E-moderating: The Key to Teaching and Learning Online. Routledge, New York (2011)

Virtual Patient Education Scenarios: Exploratory Step in the Study of Obesity Prevention Through Telemedicine

Loredana Perla(✉) and Stefania Massaro

University of Bari Aldo Moro, Bari, Italy
{loredana.perla,stefania.massaro}@uniba.it

Abstract. Within the current AI-based and patient-centered e-health framework aimed at developing accessible and resilient health systems, the paper presents a project addressing obesity prevention and healthy lifestyles education through Telemedicine transdisciplinary research. The goal is the development of a holistic and sustainable approach to health literacy within the new digital ecosystem, empowering patients and rethinking active citizenship education with aims of well-being, quality of life and equity. Purpose is education to be responsive to current healthcare innovations implementing patients' learning experience and promoting the idea of change as learning rather than adaptation. We present an exploratory research involving 357 students attending degree courses in Education and Training Sciences and Primary Education Sciences of the University of Bari and of the Mediterranea University of Reggio Calabria aimed at investigating the social impact of obesity and students' engagement with health technologies in terms of reliability, learning and use of data. The first results highlighted showed urgent need to build more inclusive schools and universities and new needs of citizenship addressing active participation in new digital health systems, from everyday wearables to telemedicine sensors.

Keywords: Telemedicine · Health education · Digital health literacy

1 Telemedicine and the New Digital Healthcare Ecosystem

Current change in population health needs, with constant ageing processes and chronic or 'non-communicable diseases' (heart disease, stroke, cancer and diabetes) progression, is promoting local assistance and technological innovation, shifting healthcare from the hospital to the territory and showing the need of a redesign of the services network [1]. The World Health Organization Global Strategy on Digital Health 2020–2025 promotes healthy lives and wellbeing for everyone, asking member states for digital health initiatives integrating financial, organizational, human and technological resources. Telemedicine is part of this rapidly developing *digital health ecosystem* by applying information and communication technologies to the healthcare system. The evolution of ICT in the health system has so designed an innovative model of "electronic health" (E-health) based on the information conveyed by new digital platforms, to support health system and management.

G. Casalino et al. (Eds.): HELMeTO 2021, CCIS 1542, pp. 264–277, 2022.
https://doi.org/10.1007/978-3-030-96060-5_19

According to international indications defining health as biopsychosocial well-being [2], educational research is urged to ensure its participation in the governance of telemedicine innovations and work in a transdisciplinary perspective on the patient experience [3]. This means education research can employ its humanistic knowledge to design new relational organizational models, being the healthcare efficacy related to innovative and inclusive models centred on citizens. Areas of relevance in the applicability of Telemedicine projects must indeed be referred to cost containment and clinical efficiency, but also to patient satisfaction processes concerning participation, well-being and independence [4].

The perspective highlighted is that of the overall strategy for chronic disease management is shifting from a system that reacts to a sudden and unplanned event, to a system that empowers the patient to actively care for his disease and treatment regimen. It means building a human-based digital medicine connecting artificial intelligence-based innovations in healthcare to a *person-centred approach,* moving beyond the traditional paternalistic and prescriptive one. Patient centredness is actually becoming a widely used, even if poorly understood concept in medical practice, commonly understood for what it is not-technology centred, doctor centred, hospital centred, disease centred [5]. In patient-centred medicine the evidence-based bio-medical model of clinical trials is linked to the bio-psycho-social model, with attention to the meanings that the disease has for the patient, his needs and his insight to remove barriers to diagnosis and treatment.

In this background the single individual assumes different relevance and roles [6]:

- he is a *person*, bearing dignity and respect,
- he is a *citizen* with rights relating health and duties
- he is a *patient* when directly involved in the care processes.

This means engaging education in building a renewed citizenship for patients and citizens in the transforming contexts of health promotion and healthcare delivery and addressing the challenge of creating a new health governance taking into account digital innovation together with citizen and patient empowerment. The health system becomes e-health, provided that the active role of the patient/citizen in the health system is redefined and it generates quality of life outputs as satisfaction, well-being and personal happiness. The effectiveness of the ongoing e-health system is based in fact on the ability to integrate digital health innovation with inclusive trainings of *patient empowerment* and construction of *health literacy* as capacity to access information and use it effectively [7].

2 Towards Co-participation Strategies: Patient Empowerment and Digital Health Literacy

Empowerment is a widely accepted concept in health-related disciplines and is confirmed as one of the strategic elements for the management of health systems: participation, responsibility and citizens' sense of belonging indeed favors the sustainability of the system [8]. Over the past few years, citizen empowerment has been receiving growing attention from health institutions: different experiences implemented by national and international health organizations are helping to create a "new culture" towards the participation of citizens in health processes and services. Empowerment - based approaches are highlighted in literature as training methodologies with educational objectives linked to the development of *psychosocial skills*, *experiential learning* activities and the definition of an *inclusive patient-doctor relationship* [9].

As Anderson [10] recalls, empowerment is a process that the patient continually redefines and perfects through the development of autonomy, responsibility and cooperation and the progressive awareness of his own health needs and of the strategies connected to therapeutic pathways. Studies on barriers and facilitators in Telemedicine underline experiences of patient empowerment as a facilitator of patient satisfaction and the effectiveness of interventions [11].

According to Rappaport [12] empowerment is a mechanism that allows people, organizations and communities to increase the ability to control their own lives. There is no univocal definition of the concept of patient empowerment: it is a multidimensional concept that involves the difficulty of a one-sided approach on a theoretical level and the operational complexity of political choices and socio-health planning. Zimmerman [13] defines the three fundamental components of empowerment: control, critical awareness and participation. Control refers to the perceived or actual ability to influence decisions that affect one's existence; critical awareness consists in understanding the functioning of power structures and decision-making processes, how the factors involved and the resources mobilized are influenced; participation is about knowing how to work together with others to obtain the desired and shared results. There emerges a profile of the "new patient/user" as a citizen:

- *informed* - knows all the necessary information relating to his health needs, the most effective pathways to reach them and the resources available to satisfy them;
- *cooperative* - consciously adheres to health indications, implementing good compliance with health professionals;
- *active* - knows how to be a protagonist on the public stage;
- *reflective* - reflects on his own path, evaluates options and makes appropriate decisions;
- *competent* - has developed skills and abilities and moves in the healthcare environment with good knowledge and flexibility;
- *empowered* - full aware of himself and of his context as a person who understands and chooses.

In order to strengthen the concept of empowerment, the World Health Organization [7] overcomes the border of health literacy referring to "social and cognitive skills that determine the motivation and ability of individuals to obtain access, understand and use information in order to promote and maintain a good state of health". The connection between health literacy and health outcomes includes access and utilization of healthcare services, patient/provider interaction and self-care [14]. Health literacy thus becomes a tool for promoting health education not limited to the transmission of information but aiming at developing skills to retrieve information, evaluate reliability, use it to exercise control over health determinants and make informed, conscious and optimal choices on health. From a traditional definition connected to the basic concept of literacy, empowerment becomes the foundation of a modern citizenship [15].

The new telemedicine applications in the e-health field today support *digital health literacy* as an extension of health literacy in the digital context as "the ability to seek, find, understand, and appraise health information from electronic sources and apply the knowledge gained to preventing, addressing or solving a health problem" [16]. In the context of post covid society the World Health Organization recommendations are increasingly paying attention to digital health literacy as artificial intelligence and machine learning, virtual and augmented reality, etc. offer opportunity to actively participate in one's own health and in the doctor-patient communication: the citizen-empowerment-model translates into an investment in digital skills and *data literacy*, focusing on the ability to access and share data and learning online. Online learning can be accomplished in a variety of ways (e.g. through online tutorials, computer-supported col laborative learning or computer simulations), and keys to success include focusing on a perceived need, careful planning, clear communication, and the creation of a sense of community [17].

Through the application of learning management system platforms in telemedicine, the health system has become linked to the world of digital training, borrowing infrastructure and organizational logic: the learning management system platforms allow personalized treatment plans, remote monitoring of vital parameters, television and re mote assistance services, up to sharing collaboration between professionals, remotely monitored. Furthermore, the use of LMS platforms in healthcare allows doctors to share information with homecare personnel or family caregivers improving the process effectiveness.

3 Telemedicine and Virtual Patient Education: The Transdisciplinary Study

Growing attention is gaining worldwide the theme of obesity prevention and treatment. Overweight and obesity are defined as abnormal or excessive fat accumulation. As World Health Organization databases report, from 1975 to 2016, the prevalence of overweight or obese children and adolescents aged 5–19 years increased more than four-fold from 4% to 18% globally. Once considered a problem only in high-income countries, overweight and obesity are now on the rise in low- and middle-income countries, particularly in urban settings. Childhood obesity is associated with premature death and disability in adulthood. Obesity also represents an illness with psychological correlates (unsatisfactory body image, depressive and anxious symptoms, eating disorders, low self-esteem) and prejudice and social and media stigmatization of people with obesity are frequently reported (bullying, weight bias, fat shaming). Its multietiology, including individual, family and socio-cultural factors, make prevention difficult.

The 'WHO Global Strategy on Diet, Physical Activity and Health 2004' calls upon all stakeholders to take action to improve diets and physical activity patterns at population level. The 2030 Agenda for Sustainable Development recognizes NCDs as a ma jor challenge for sustainable development. As part of the Agenda, heads of state and government committed by 2030 to reduce premature mortality from NCDs through prevention and treatment (SDG target 3.4). The World Health Assembly welcomed the report of the Commission on Ending Childhood Obesity (2016) to address the obesogenic environment and critical periods in the life course to tackle childhood obesity. The idea on focusing on obesity gained concern in particular after the covid-19 pandemic when evidence showed that excess weight is a highly significant predictor for covid-19 complications, other respiratory viral infections are aggravated by this condition and there are lower response to vaccines for covid-19 and influenza of subjects with obesity.

International organizations [18] at present focus on integrated model of obesity prevention and promotion of healthy behaviors according to systems-based approach (health-education-food): this means creating an equitable, comprehensive and person-centred approach calling into question education in its capacity building.

In the presented framework, within the Citel Interdepartmental Research Centre in Telemedicine at University of Bari[1], we are implementing a project to understand the transition processes towards obesity through a transdisciplinary perspective. Fields of research as medicine, biomedicine, pharmacy, computer science and education are connecting to develop innovative approaches for community well-being, enhancing:

- multidisciplinary research approaches
- strong support of digital technology and AI tools
- community-based engagement in preventive practices

Connecting different research areas, the Citel centre represents a junction between the academic and the industrial world responding to the digital evolution of traditional, while health emerges at societal level as a complex problem and not only medicine's domain. The current covid-19 scenario has actually reactivated attention to the emergence of complex problems, defined by investing reality without being interpretable through the perspective of single disciplines, rather appealing to transdisciplinary research-based interventions.

The '*E-health education and wellbeing* Citel Research Unit' (coordinated by professor L. Perla) has been involved to connect socio-humanistic and medical disciplines and to develop a salutogenic model of analysis as a viable paradigm for health promo tion and quality of life objectives [19].

Purpose of the study with the Citel research centre are:

- improve patients management in prevention and surveillance phases with artificial intelligence-based *phenotypic avatars* or *dual twins* (see Fig. 1) developed by a national network of research infrastructures working on obesity. This means experimenting, within a research network, advanced AI-based applications of telemedicine in the framework of the current avatar-based medicine: the avatars combine different kinds of patient data gathered for clinical diagnostics allowing personalized medicine and clinical simulations, therefore are now to be tested in the study of the correlations between childhood obesity and high-impact diseases in adults (fatty liver/nash, obstructive sleep apnoea syndrome, hypertension, diabetes, chronic kidney disease, increased cardio-vascular risk);

[1] www.citelmedicina.it.

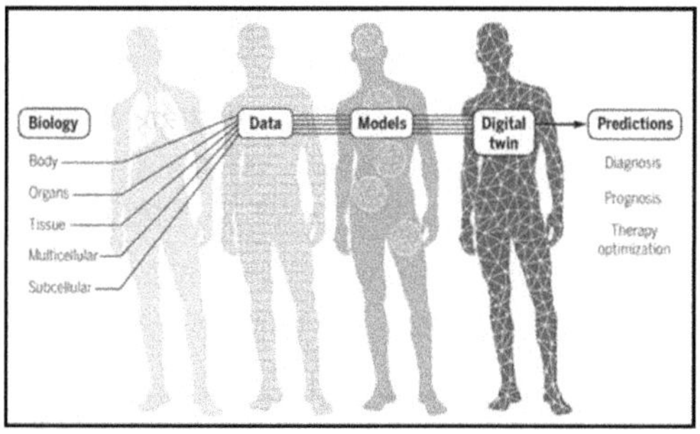

Fig. 1. Avatar-based predictive modelling (source: https://tectales.com/bio-tech-it/digital-twins-for-more-persoalized-medicine.html)

- development of an *empowerment-based educational model* to promote healthy lifestyles education with gamification activities and inclusive trainings. The education intervention addresses obesity with the involvement and engagement of patients and families in long-term behavior changes, using gamification dynamics to trigger changes concerning the person's identity and moving beyond the adherence to the treatment, with purpose of social inclusion.

Objectives of the study are:

- experiment avatar-based clinical protocols for the diagnosis, treatment and educational therapy of children with severe overweight or obesity through digital platform integrated by artificial neural networks, decision support systems and advanced sensors;
- design social robot coaching activities and gamified applications within 'health-aware food recommender systems' [20] and 'e-health conversational system' [21] as applications meant to develop empathic and personalized interaction with patients
- carry out data collection operations to develop an evidence-based knowledge derived from the medical and clinical investigation and define guidelines and best practices (e.g. on diet, physical activity, etc.) to be integrated into a *citizen's health education model* and a *therapeutic patient education model*

Educational key challenge of the study is therefore to promote life-long learning for health and wellbeing, in particular:

- working on the design of a new transdisciplinary paradigm, "Virtual Patient Education" (see Fig. 2), in the emerging context of telemedicine applications: moving from the traditional patient education (defined as "an individualized, systematic, structured process to assess and impart knowledge or develop a skill in order to effect achange in health related behaviors" [22]) the aim is to improve clinical indicators together with *patient knowledge, quality of life, self-care and ability to manage digital healthcare* within online learning systems and virtual learning environments;

- developing a healthy lifestyle competency model and health literacy promotion in primary prevention contexts
- connecting an evidence-based health approach with an ermeneutical work on narratives, for a narrative-based health promotion within a salutogenic perspective, that is a scholarly orientation focusing attention on the origins of health, rather than the origins of disease.

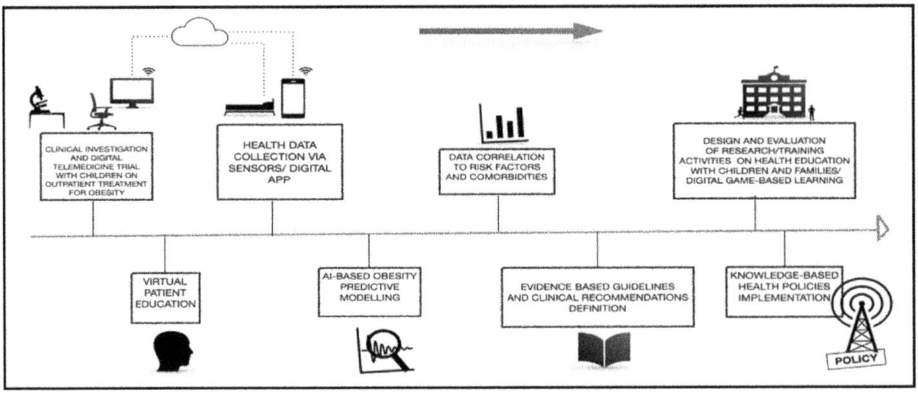

Fig. 2. Virtual patient education designed within the Citel obesity prevention project.

As narrative approaches to health education have emerged over the past decade as potentially powerful tools for promoting positive health behavior changes, research methodologies at present to be investigated are:

- narrative-based medicine, enhancing the patient's history as a fundamental tool for understanding the disease and construction of an effective patient-doctor communication, allowing the possibility of personalization and co-construction of the diagnostic, therapeutic and rehabilitative path and the construction of a therapeutic alliance [23]. The disease path becomes a path of care and empowerment beyond the idea of support, in a training perspective that reconceptualizes health care by focusing attention on patient, complexifying his judgment and promoting change management in clinical situations [24].
- digital narrative medicine: guided path through the application of a narrative digital diary complementary to the episode diary - created with a platform and useful for collecting information that contributes to diagnosis, treatment and therapeutic adherence. Digital narrative medicine is a web and mobile tool that the therapeutic team offers to the patient to tell his story, through a guided narrative path. The platform can be used by health professionals, scientific companies, hospital departments.
- educational accompaniment through targeted toolkits: interview conducted with narrative skills; semi-structured narrative interviews; story sharing intervention (SSI); reflective writing; vicar narrator; video interviews;

- training and use of digital technologies, with an adaptation from the "Digital Competence Framework for Citizens with eight proficiency levels and examples of use-DigComp" Joint Research Center (JRC) of the European Commission, as a tool to improve citizens' digital competence and reference point for initiatives aimed at de veloping digital competence at European level. Areas of expertise concerned: Information and data literacy/Communication and collaboration/Digital content creation/Security/Problem solving.

4 An Exploratory Research

The survey presented aimed to explore perceptions, experiences and beliefs of 357 students attending degree courses in Education and Training Sciences and Primary Education Sciences at University of Bari (Italy) and at Mediterranea University of Reggio Calabria (Italy) on theme of obesity, eating disorders, educational strategies for prevention and treatment and youngster engagement in new digital health applications.

The involvement of students in a collaborative research and the setting of a multi-actor approach, with new and open processes of interactions, was intended to constitute an experience of activation, strengthening social transformation and social innovation, understood as a different - better and more sustainable - use of resources, and therefore social capital [25].

Research questions that guided the research were:

- *What kind of representations do students have about obesity and eating disorders?*
- *On which dimensions is based their knowledge concerning nutrition and health?*
- *What are their perceptions regarding the design of an education for healthy life-styles?*
- *What kind of involvement are they developing with the new digital health technologies? What knowledge they derive it from? What is the impact of the new digital apps on their health practices?*

The data were collected through:

- the administration of a questionnaire consisting of 31 questions with both open and closed answers;
- the task of writing an episode evoked by the word 'obesity' personally or indirectly experienced.

The activities were preceded by viewing a short solicitation video. The activated laboratory followed the protocol setting of EduLabo [26]. Indeed narrative writing allows the researcher to explore the meanings conveyed by the biographical reconstruction. In its ability to re-signify and at the same time address juvenile disorder, writing can also integrate clinical protocols as a tool of a 'narrative medicine' capable of bringing together biomedical and biographical dimensions and transform the history of the disease into a history of care, with tools such as the digital diary [27]. At the end of the workshop a debriefing was conducted with questions having an explanatory, reflective and metacognitive function.

357 students (242 UNIBA; 115 from UNIRC) answered the questionnaire. The data were analyzed in aggregate form. The analysis was conducted by dividing the analysis of the 11 closed-ended items (using descriptive statistical techniques) and that of the 20 open-ended questions (by means of qualitative data analysis and content exploration criteria through computational analysis according to Queries functions[2]). 99% of respondents state that they have heard of the problem of obesity or eating disorders and 98% consider obesity a relevant topic. With regard to the channels of access to information relating to the issue of obesity and eating disorders, the analysis shows the prevalence of informal channels compared to formal channels, as shown by the highest co-occurrences (Table 1):

Table 1. Word Frequency Query with 30 minimum length

Word	Count
Television	128
Social	106
Internet	72
School	63
Media	48
Books	38
Social networks	37
University	31

221 out of 357 respondents (62%) stated that the topic of health education was addressed at school or during their studies, but many specify in a superficial, not in-depth way or in informal discussions. Among the causes attributed to the condition of over-weight or obesity in children, most (N = 203; 57%) consider psychological ones (insecurity, frailty) as priority, followed by sociocultural ones (family income, cultural background; N = 42; 12%). It is interesting to note the representations on the impact of the variables 'age' and 'gender' on the problem of eating disorders: if there is agreement on considering the gender variable (male/female) to be of little relevance (78% replied negatively), as regards age, the population is divided, as 53% answered affirmatively and 47% negatively. 59% believe that healthy food is generally accessible to everyone and that healthy habits to promote with children are physical activity (96%), hours of night sleep (38%) and time spent on displays (e.g. no longer than one hour).

[2] Query functions are methods of exploration and display using graphs or diagrams according to precise selection criteria, such as the calculation of the most frequent words, called Word Frequency. For the analysis of the open answers, the NVivo computational linguistic analysis software was used in the Word Frequency function.

There emerged also:

- accessibility to healthy food only for 42.6% of students;
- critical connection recognized by students between intervention on obesity and environmental sustainability (84.4%)
- important consequences of childhood obesity in terms of discrimination and prejudice (weight bias and bullying at school and at work)
- Students' personal appropriation of nutritional and healthy lifestyles principles, but difficulties in gathering ideas for educators and teachers trainings: courses, semi-nars, training and meetings with nutritionists are generally proposed by students as activities suitable for teachers and educators.

School emerges as the main context for health education that must necessarily involve families, to convey the basic principles of a healthy lifestyle to be articulated in: healthy nutrition (characterized above all by the absence of excessively processed foods) - physical activity - hours of sleep and control of the time spent on the displays. The theme of the emergence of a prevention aimed at adolescents emerges, as it must bring to light their frailties and help to comparing oneself with similar stories, while game-based activities stands out as indispensable didactic mediators for children, to grasp the information of a healthy diet, but in an active, relational and collaborative dimension, that therefore can become meaningful. The game appears in the answers in many of its manifestations: in the form of motor play to promote physical activity, cooking competitions to learn preparation of healthy foods, and also as story-telling on the subject. Game-based learning is also evidenced for adults, with an indication in some cases of game-based learning designed to convey information in the manner of informal learning of "serious" content. The answers compiled show a wide range of indications for activities involving adults in the obesity problem (mainly attributable to sports, social initiatives, courses) including elderly people, with reference to activities that do not require physical activity but motivational strategies, at the centre of an idea of active ageing.

The last section of the questionnaire was built with questions aimed at grasping the involvement and impact of the new digital health applications on the lifestyles of the generation involved in the research, to detect their access and impact in terms of learning and practices about health. As adolescents are digital frontrunners and early adopters of technology, digital health interventions and gamification appear the most practical modality for healthy behavior change interventions. Engagement with digital health interventions is an important mediating factor to improve dietary behaviors and prevent and manage obesity in adolescents. Despite the rapid growth in digital health interventions, effective engagement with adolescents can be considered a pertinent issue [28].

In the last section questions asked were:

- *Do you use digital devices or apps to stimulate and/or monitor physical activity or food (eg. Wearable devices for controlling or stimulating physical activity or apps to guide food choices)? If so, which ones?*

- *Do you think that these digital technologies (e.g. smartwatches, pedometers, bracelets with sensors, etc.) can generate real forms of knowledge in those who use them about their physical condition?*
- *Do you think that obesity prevention interventions can be implemented through Telemedicine platforms?*
- *How do you think digital can currently contribute to supporting the issue of obesity prevention? (e.g. online counseling, devices such as pedometer or Applewatch, digital apps to guide food consumption, etc.*

About half of the target of respondents (42%) uses digital devices or apps to stimulate and/or monitor physical or food activity, among which are mentioned in particular the Pedometer (N = 45), App to monitor physical activity (N = 17), the Smartwatch (N = 9) and a variety of applications to monitor calories, weight control, training. As many as 71% believe that digital technologies (e.g. smartwatches, pedometers, bracelets with sensors, etc.) can generate real forms of knowledge about one's own physical condition and open to a wide range of solutions to improve health and prevent eating disorders, from online counseling to digital apps to personalize food consumption and provide healthy suggestions. They are seen as a tool to support motivation and provide just-in-time adaptation, showing good reliability for accessing health information, but at the same time feared as can create addiction in more emotional subjects, too dependent on the information actually built by media, social media and informal communication channels.

Students believe that digital can help support the issue of obesity prevention as 'digital devices and apps can help regulate and monitor a certain lifestyle', 'they are more practical as they are more Smart', 'they can guide food consumption', 'they give an idea of what you take and what you burn', 'they provide continuous feedback useful to stimulate attention on the subject', 'they often arrive where people they do not arrive and often much more quickly', 'they disclose the benefits of a correct diet and the risks that lead to obesity', 'allow independent control' (only some fragments of the textual corpus are reported, postponing the detailed categorical analysis of the open answers in an extended descriptive contribution of the research). Only 15% have heard of telemedicine, most seen as the possibility of intercepting patients who are unwilling to have a direct relationship with the doctor.

5 Conclusions

The data analysis enquiring relationships between knowledge, learning and digital health innovations across different social contexts and citizen's engagement is currently in progress and further development of the study is expected also in other Education degree courses [29]. The intent is to obtain a database that can offer useful interpretative support in the interdisciplinary work started with Citel University of Bari Research Centre and infer some central topics in the project design, developing a critical understanding of the social impact of digital health technologies and engaging education with the complexities of this embodied learning.

This is means constructing a pedagogical mediation on this new digital health perspective, mainly based on interacting strategies of personalization and just-in-time ad aptation [28], meant as:

- broadening a deeper understanding of the transformative potential of digital health on young people's identities,
- exploring how young people engage with digital health technologies as shaped by socio-cultural context and background,
- identifying disparities and their connections with other sources (parents, family members, teachers/education system, healthcare professionals, friends etc.).

Many of these technologies are now being promoted by schools, but for these opportunities to be realised, existing research must better understand the contexts within which digital health is used and address some of the emerging ethical questions [30].

Asking how young people are negotiating their own health through mobile apps [30] we have involved future teachers and educators in digital health promotion with the aim to move further to primary, secondary and tertiary prevention contexts: we can so address major gaps in a patient education to be designed and co-designed in new digital environments, deconstructing and reconstructing the patient's experience with technologies and his proactive role in building his own knowledge on the disease.

The aim is also to demonstrate, in fields with a strong bio-medical-informatics connotation, the important role that knowledge and educational practices can play within a scenario that will revolutionize the approach to care. Educational developers in higher education have currently strong responsibility in providing students and citizens with knowledge and skills to engage on an informed basis in a rapidly changing society, addressing the challenges and responsibility of this institution to respond to the societal issues of access and equity and restore the traditional vision of a democratic and knowledge-based society [31].

References

1. Temesgen, Z.M., et al.: Health care after the COVID-19 pandemic and the influence of telemedicine. Mayo Clin. Proc. **95**(9S), 66–68 (2020)
2. International Health Education Conference: Health for all by year 2000. Health Educ. J. **41**(3), 79–80 (1982)
3. Eze, N.D., Mateus, C., Cravo Oliveira Hashiguchi, T.: Telemedicine in the OECD: an umbrella review of clinical and cost-effectiveness, patient experience and implementation. PLoS One **15**(8) (2000)
4. Koch, S.: Improving quality of life through eHealth. The patient perspective. Stud. Health Technol. Inform. **180**, 25–29 (2012)
5. Stewart, M.: Towards a global definition of patient centred care. BMJ (Clin. Res. Ed.) **322**(7284), 444–445 (2001)
6. Laverack, G.: Health Promotion Practice: Power and Empowerment. Sage, London (2004)
7. World Health Organization. Division of Health Promotion, Education, and Communication. Health promotion glossary. World Health Organization (1998)

8. Chang, L.C., Li, I.C., Liu, C.H.: A study of the empowerment process for cancer patients using Freire's dialogical interviewing. J. Nurs. Res. **12**(1), 41–50 (2004)
9. Aujoulat, I., d'Hoore, W., Deccache, A.: Patient empowerment in theory and practice: polysemy or cacophony? Patient Educ. Couns. **66**(1), 13–20 (2007)
10. Anderson, B., Anderson, R.M., Funnell, M.M.: The Art of Empowerment: Stories and Strategies for Diabetes Educators. American Diabetes Association, Alexandria (2000)
11. Almathami, H., Win, K.T., Vlahu-Gjorgievska, E.: Barriers and facilitators that influence telemedicine-based, real-time, online consultation at patients' homes: systematic literature review. J. Med. Internet Res. **22**(2) (2020)
12. Rappaport, J.: In praise of paradoxe. A social policy of empowerment over prevention. Am. J.Commun. Psychol. **9**, 11–26 (1981)
13. Zimmerman, M.A.: Empowerment theory: psychological, organizational and community levels of analysis. In: Rappaport, J., Seidman, E. (eds.) Handbook of Community Psychology, pp. 43–63. Kluwer Academic/Plenum Publishers, New York (2000)
14. Conard, S.: Best practices in digital health literacy. Int. J. Cardiol. **1**(292), 277–279 (2019)
15. Kickbusch, I., Maag, D.: Lo sviluppo della Health Literacy nelle moderne società della salute. In: Ingrosso, M. (ed.) Fra reti e relazioni: percorsi nella comunicazione della salute, Salute e società, VI (1), pp. 185–200. FrancoAngeli, Milano (2007)
16. World Health Organization. WHO Guidelines: recommendations on digital interventions for health system strengthening (2019)
17. Steinert, Y. (ed.): Faculty Development in the Health Professions. A Focus on Research and Practice, Innovation and Change in Professional Education. Springer, Dordrecht (2014). https://doi.org/10.1007/978-94-007-7612-8
18. World Obesity Federation, COVID-19 and Obesity: The 2021 Atlas. The cost of not addressing the global obesity crisis, London (2021)
19. Antonovsky, A.: The salutogenic model as a theory to guide health promotion. Health Promot. Int. **11**(1), 11–18 (1996)
20. Ricci, F., Rokach, L., Shapira, B. (eds.): Recommender Systems Handbook. Springer, Boston (2015). https://doi.org/10.1007/978-1-4899-7637-6
21. Rönnberg, S.: Persuasive Chatbot Conversations: Towards a Personalized User Experience (2020). http://liu.diva-portal.org/smash/get/diva2:1439036/FULLTEXT01.pdf
22. Paterick, T.E., Patel, N., Tajik, A.J., Chandrasekaran, K.: Improving health outcomes through patient education and partnerships with patients. Proc. (Baylor Univ. Med. Center) **30**(1), 112–113 (2017)
23. Giarelli, G.: Storie di cura. Medicina narrativa e medicina delle evidenze: l'integrazione possibile. FrancoAngeli, Milano (2005)
24. Shapiro, J.: Narrative medicine and narrative writing. Fam. Med. **44**(5), 309–311 (2012)
25. Bezzi, M.: Ricerca e innovazione aperta, partecipativa e responsabile: un glossario. Znodo (2020). https://doi.org/10.5281/zenodo.4454630
26. Perla, L., Agrati, L.S.: Training the design skills based on the Agire educativo paradigm. The laboratories at the Sciences of Education Degree courses (L19). Form@re - Open Journal Per La Formazione in Rete **20**(2), 145–168 (2020)
27. Charon, R.: Narrative Medicine: Honoring the Stories of Illness. Oxford University Press, Oxford (2006)
28. Partridge, S.R., Redfern, J.: Strategies to engage adolescents in digital health interventions for obesity prevention and management. Healthcare (Basel, Switzerland) **6**(3), 70 (2018)

29. Massaro, S., Perla, L.: Studio esplorativo sulla prevenzione e cura dell'obesità attraverso la telemedicina: orizzonti transdisciplinari del lavoro educativo. In: Ricerca e Didattica per promuovere intelligenza comprensione e partecipazione. Atti del X Convegno della SIRD 9–10 aprile 2021, pp. 635–642 (2021)
30. Rich, E., Miah, A.: Understanding digital health as public pedagogy: a critical framework. Societies **4**, 296–315 (2014)
31. Valimaa, J., Hoffman, D.: Knowledge Society Discourse and Higher Education. Springer, New York (2008)

Distance Learning and Digital Scholarship: New Challenges for Faculty Development

Viviana Vinci[1(✉)] and Alessia Scarinci[2]

[1] Mediterranea University of Reggio Calabria, Reggio Calabria, Italy
viviana.vinci@unirc.it
[2] University of Bari Aldo Moro, Bari, Italy
alessia.scarinci@uniba.it

Abstract. The professional development of university teachers is a policy priority of Higher Education on a global scale. Teaching and Learning Centers have been built at international level and they provide validation and valorization of academics' competences developed through training. The need for research processes and innovation in teaching methods has become even more pressing with the 2020 pandemic emergency. In that circumstance, all universities were forced to improvise and hybridize teaching with digital tools. The traditional scholarship of teaching and learning of the university has thus been transformed into a field of experimentation of practices. The research specifically investigates the experience of Distance Learning (DL), defining the construct, to bring out the changes in teaching practice, paying particular attention to didactic mediation and evaluation, two areas considered foundational and emblematic in teaching-learning action. Through the administration of an online questionnaire to which 721 teachers responded, we highlight the metamorphoses involved in mediation and evaluation. The findings highlighted the need to support teachers' digital training to develop a new type of sophisticated knowledge and the ability to transform disciplinary content into digitalized disciplinary content.

Keywords: Distance education · Didactic mediation · Faculty development

1 Academics' Professional Development

The professional development of university teachers is a policy priority of Higher Education on a global scale, and a strategic driver for the improvement of student learning [1]. The reform inspired by the Bologna process has led to institutional changes in the way of organizing teaching: to harmonise higher education systems in the European area in order to achieve a common understanding not so much of curricula as of course structures; to promote the development of teaching skills and develop monitoring and evaluation strategies [2] to ensure that adequate levels of teaching quality and student service are achieved. Sorcinelli [3] identified a constellation of issues that coalesced around three primary challenges and forces of change: the changing professoriate (facing a growing array of changing roles and responsibilities that will require them to

G. Casalino et al. (Eds.): HELMeTO 2021, CCIS 1542, pp. 278–290, 2022.
https://doi.org/10.1007/978-3-030-96060-5_20

engage in ongoing professional growth: expanding faculty roles, finding balance, needs of new faculty), the changing nature of the student body (increasing multiculturalism and diversity, the challenges of the underprepared student), the changing nature of teaching, learning, and scholarship (emphasizing learner-centered teaching, integrating technology into teaching and learning, emphasizing assessment of student learning outcomes, expanding definitions of scholarship, building interdisciplinary collaborations).

As early as 2013, the European Commission recommended that European universities 'care for' the pedagogical training of teachers along the lines determined by ENQA [2]. The intent is to recognize and certify the pedagogical competences of academics in designing, delivering and assessing learning [4–10]. In recent decades, Teaching and Learning Centers have been built at international level and they provide validation and valorization of academics' competences developed through training [5, 11]. Two issues are highlighted in the report Modernisation of Higher Education in Europe: Academic Staff [12]. The first concerns the lack of initiatives aimed at the lifelong professional development of professors (which, if present, remain isolated and episodic). The second regards the lack of activities targeted at PhDs and young researchers. Universities are called to respond to new challenges: the heterogeneity of students and the need to promote their 'hard' as well as 'soft' skills; the reorganization of courses to ensure greater coherence with the emerging professions; the rethinking of teaching, considering technologies has no longer simple tools for the transmission of knowledge, but opportunity to improve the students' learning outcomes offering a higher level of personalization, adaptive and flexible learning [13] and to organize, in an alternative way, curricular activities normally carried out in presence, such as internships, stages or workshops [14]. Technologies are 'amplifiers' of learning spaces and opportunities for learner-centered strategies, that can ensure greater accessibility of learning environments and resources [15].

The Italian higher education system has appeared, for many years, reluctant and unable to develop effective policies for change, within a highly centralised system, in which the opportunities for training and professional development of staff have been for decades nil or, mostly, characterised by "fragmented" approaches [16]. Several delays are confirmed on this regard for the Italian case: the rate of graduates remains the lowest in Europe; the number of dropouts is among the highest; unemployment among graduates reaches 25%, thus showing a mismatch between market offer and demand.

After the phase of reorganization of the educational paths and the one related to the introduction of evaluation strategies for quality assurance (ANVUR), the Italian path to the Bologna process now requires promoting teaching and learning practice.

In the absence of a national university policy, many Italian universities – also driven by Faculty Development actions carried out at the international level [17] – have been experimenting for less than a decade from-below training programs (for new faculty or those already in service) aimed at improving the quality of university teaching. These experiences are emerging in individual universities [10, 18] and they still lack visibility, recognition and national coordination. Moreover, there is a lack of models for assessing the outcomes of training – as intended from the perspective of assessment and feedback for learning [19] – capable of monitoring the impacts of faculty development initiatives and enhancing the plurality of training experiences, which run the risk of fragmentation and compartmentalization. Only very recently, also in Italy, has the importance of supporting teaching professionalism and the development of innovative teaching methodologies assumed a central role at a regulatory level which emphasise the valorisation of the relationship between teaching and research and identify a path that starts from the identification of criteria for "good teaching"[1] – and in research: pioneering, in this direction, is the PRODID project, born on the initiative of Ettore Felisatti at the University of Padua [20] and subsequently implemented by the network of Italian universities (Bari, Camerino, Catania, Florence, Foggia, Genoa, Turin) constituting the Italian Association for the promotion and development of didactics, learning and teaching in universities (initiatives shared on the occasion of the conference held in Bari on 28 June 2017 - ASDUNI Network, 2017 - and of the conference Faculty development and enhancement of the teaching skills of university teachers held in Genoa on 23–24 May 2019).

2 From COVID-19 Pandemic to Digital Scholarship

The logic of the network and the opportunities offered by contemporary communication tools represent disruptive technologies that have changed the classic formats of communication and are transforming the sphere of academic research and teaching activities. The digital transformations underway for several years in the university context have particularly affected the management aspects of the university's organization by improving and simplifying processes and activities. Technologies also offer new and different opportunities in terms of improvements in teaching and learning actions [21].

The changes brought about by technological innovation, especially from the point of view of educational practice, have often encountered resistance, leading to a strong contrast between what happens at the administrative and organizational level and the use of digital tools at the didactic level [22]. In fact, despite the various government initiatives aimed at strengthening the infrastructures and the technological equipment required to be able to face the transformations implemented by technological innovation, in terms of the digitization of the teaching and learning process, an investment in training is necessary of teachers [21]. The teacher must, in fact, be able to combine professional, pedagogical, relational and technological skills and be able to evaluate the most suitable technological tools to be used in the various areas and in the construction of a virtual space for the delivery of contents and the management of interaction with students [23].

The pandemic crisis caused an acceleration of this internal and external digitization process and represented a strong break with traditional university teaching.

As pointed out by the European University Association (EUA) [24] the health emergency has challenged higher education institutions in many new and unexpected ways, particularly in relation to learning and digitally enhanced teaching [25]. The World Health Organization declared the COVID-19 outbreak as a pandemic on May 11, 2020. As a result, governments had issued directives that imposed the compulsory suspension of the attendance of degree courses, including the Italian government (D.P.C.M. of 9 March).

[1] The characteristics of didactics enunciated by the QUARC_doctor guidelines are: the centrality of the student; didactic innovation and learning methodologies; ICT; monitoring and evaluation of learning; internationalisation; lifelong/lifewide learning and employability.

This rapid transition from distance learning in the presence forced teachers to adapt their teaching action in a distance learning context, and placed students in a position to use tools for which they were not adequately prepared [26]. It has also led to the use of educational technologies, already existing but too little considered as a possible added value to teaching, for the provision of courses that, in the absence of a critical situation, would have been given face to face [27, 28].

Unlike the planned online teaching and learning experiences, the experience derived from the pandemic crisis was implemented without an appropriate preliminary design, bringing out the various problems and deficiencies both in the organizational, infrastructural and in the teaching and digital skills of teachers and of the students [21]. It was not a question of making a transition from presence to an online teaching/learning mode because this, in order to be effective and have a positive impact on the quality of education and learning, requires a good planning of experiences and a capacity for planning teaching and learning by the teacher [23, 28, 29]. Instead, we speak of emergency remote teaching, as suggested by Hodges et al. [28], in which planning, planning and above all the possibility of choice are lacking and whose goal is to offer and guarantee all students "temporary access to education and teaching aids" [28].

As Perla, Scarinci and Amati [30] underline, the pandemic has confronted teachers with the need to redesign their teaching action, considering technologies no longer simple tools for the transmission of knowledge: teaching is redefined as mediated action to high hybridization potential. Online learning cannot be seen as a mere, extemporaneous transposition of teaching in the presence [31], as it can change not only the space-time organization, favoring greater flexibility, but also relational dynamics and social interaction, which often require different teaching approaches and skills [28].

Beyond the didactic and organizational difficulties initially encountered, the emergency situation also proved to be a precious opportunity to rethink the forms of mediation in distance learning through technology, in an adaptive and flexible learning perspective [32], that is, able to offer wider choices and with a higher level of customization for students.

The network, in this phase, has not only offered a new context for learning without traditional spatial and temporal limits but has also been a "network" in an educational metaphorical sense since it has offered a space, a constructivist-type learning environment for sharing and building knowledge, safeguarding students' right to study [33]. Each student had a "personal" didactic experience: mediation was forcibly re-invented and rewritten through the web within a common space [34] in which experiences and emotions connected to the imprisonment induced by the prescriptions were also inserted sanitary.

If on the one hand, therefore, this state of emergency has introduced a new and destabilizing element in the academic world, making the planning and intentionality of distance learning disappear, on the other hand it has constituted a push that has accelerated a process of change of the training offer in place for several years but which has often found resistance [35, 36]. A change that involves different figures (teachers, students, administrators, technicians) and involves a series of adaptations and rethinking from the point of view of teaching and the training environment that becomes digital space. A change that pushes us to reflect on the need for high-quality professional development, for advancement in the field of digital scholarship, for support for teachers' professionalism and for the development of teaching skills aimed at improving learning of students [37].

A survey is presented aimed at exploring the experience that Italian university professors have achieved in the reconversion phase due to the Covid-19 health emergency, focusing in particular on the optional forms of educational mediation and remote educational evaluation in the period of sanitary emergency.

3 Method

The research specifically investigates the experience of DL, defining the construct, to bring out the changes in teaching practice, paying particular attention to didactic mediation and evaluation, two areas considered foundational and emblematic in teaching-learning action. Through the analysis of the metamorphoses taking place in teaching and evaluation practices, we intend to initiate an initial reflection on the impact that they can induce to deeply rethink university teaching in a 'hybrid' direction [30] (also in the return to normality of resumption of classroom teaching), on the quality of student learning, on the innovation of university teaching and on the highly specialized skills required of the teacher: the ultimate aim, in fact, is to trace - also following impact assessments and further studies of a longitudinal-comparative nature in programming - of the possible trajectories for the professional development of the university teacher.

Through the administration of an online questionnaire to which 721 teachers responded, we highlight the metamorphoses involved in mediation and evaluation. The research comes within the ASDUNI association and was carried out by an inter-university working group[2]. In particular, the following objects of the 'mediation' and 'evaluation' didactic dimensions were investigated:

- DL procedures implemented in the experience, instruments used (in the past/the present/future), media used, the quality of communication with students, student engagement, differentiated teaching methods for students with Special Educational Needs, the relationship between DL and disciplinary knowledge, positive and negative aspects of DL, redesign mode of operations in the situation;
- online assessment, tests and assessment methods used (in the past/present/in the future), moments of the assessment in DL, function of the assessment, feed-back, difference between assessment in presence and remote online assessment, remote online assessment, concerns and/or difficulty in a remote online assessment, training needs in terms of valuation.

The research was conducted in accordance with the ethical and anonymity rules in compliance with the EU General Data Protection Regulation no. 679/2016 and of Legislative Decree no. 196/2003 "Personal data protection code" (amended by Legislative Decree no. 101 of 10.08.2018).

[2] The working group consists of researchers/professors from four universities: L. Perla, E. Felisatti, V. Grion, L.S. Agrati, R. Gallelli, A. Serbati, V. Vinci, I. Amati, R. Bonelli.

As regards the data collection tool, a Computer Assisted Web Interviewing (CAWI) questionnaire was proposed, consisting of 29 closed-ended questions and 11 open-ended questions. The questionnaire was sent to all Italian universities. Some partial results of the investigation are returned. The required compilation time was 15 min.

For both the investigated dimensions - didactic mediation and evaluation - it was decided to insert some questions structured in such a way as to offer, to the responding teacher, the possibility of providing information on past, present and future practices (ie: Which tools has used in the past/currently uses in the DL/and do you think you will use in the future? You can choose multiple response options using the modalities referring to both the past, the present and the future): this choice was determined by the desire to go further the comparative analysis between the practices implemented in the Covid-19 emergency and those carried out in the past, to also understand the wishes of the teachers, therefore the practices considered effective and to be implemented in the future. These questions are functional above all to understand, in a perspective direction, the training needs of teachers towards which to structure professional development paths.

4 Data Analysis

The data were analyzed in aggregate form. They analyzed 721 compilations in total, dividing the analysis of item 29 closed questions (via statesmen-ca descriptive techniques) and that of the open-ended questions (by means of qualitative analysis criteria of the data). 721 university teachers took part in the survey, divided almost equally between male teachers (N = 370; 51%) and female teachers (N = 351; 49%). The age of respondents is distributed with a prevalence of people aged between 41–50 years (31%) and between 51 and 60 years (37%).

As regards the CUN areas of the teachers, the most represented is area 11 "Historical, philosophical, pedagogical and psychological sciences" (147 teachers), the least represented area is area 04 "Earth sciences" (14 teachers). 40% of the respondents are Associate Professor, 25% Researcher, 20% Full Professor, 15% on contract. With regard to regional distribution, the area of Northern Italy and the South and Islands are equally represented, each with 43% of teachers out of the total; the area of central Italy is lower (14%). 39% of the respondents belong to a "large university", with a number of students between 20,000 and 40,000. With regard to the context and organizational analysis, it emerged that in the majority of cases (86%) there are support technicians and that almost all of the collective (91%) received useful information to undertake the DL [37]. As many as 64% of the respondents, however, declared that they did not have the opportunity to participate in technological training activities; while 74% of the respondents declared that they had carried out exclusively face-to-face teaching, before the epidemiological emergency phase; only 136 teachers out of 721 declare that they have integrated some moments online. The section of the questionnaire relating to "didactic mediation" was structured in order to: analyze the practices declared by the teacher in the DL experience, more specifically the procedures used, the tools, the multimedia contents and the differentiated methods implemented for students with Special Educational Needs; make explicit the representations of teachers about distance learning, its positive and negative aspects, its role in changing the relationship with knowledge, the perceived quality of communication with students, the possibilities of future redesign of teaching activities in DL [37].

As regards the analysis of the practices declared by the teacher, it is possible to highlight some findings worthy of interest. The implemented procedures seem to show a tendency towards critical and participatory activities, such as the presentation of content in the form of demonstrations or explanations (57%) and the presentation of content in the form of demonstrations or explanations that involve a response or product from the students (24%); very low percentages related to lectures accompanied by slides or recorded lessons. 60% of the respondents declared that the multimedia contents used in the DL in the emergency period were mainly taken from pre-existing material and adapted; 37% declare that they have used ad hoc materials (Fig. 1 and 2).

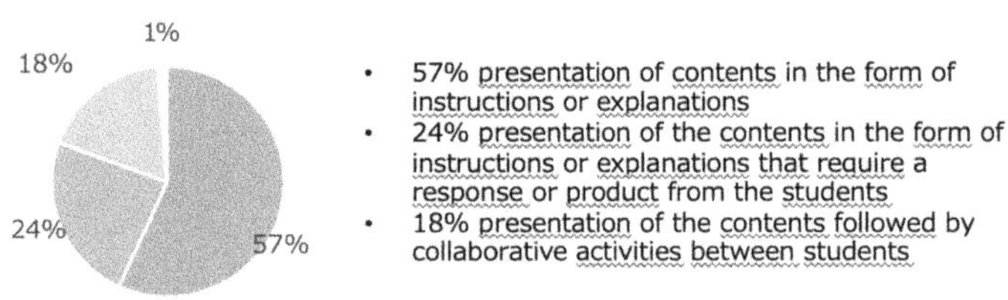

Fig. 1. 2.1 What procedures have you currently implemented in your predominantly DL experience?

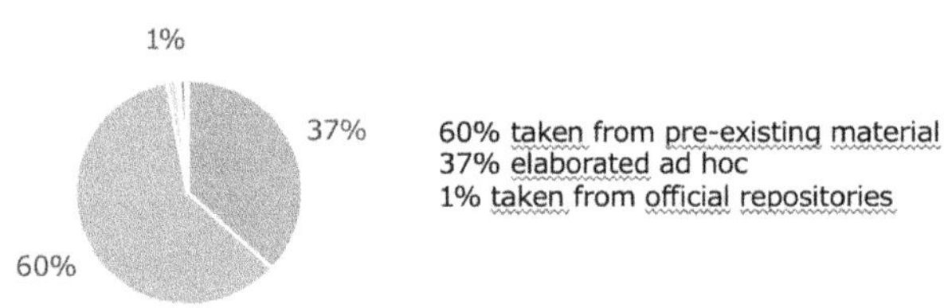

Fig. 2. 2.3 The multimedia contents used in the DL in this immediate period are mainly:

With reference to the specific tools of didactic mediation, a first data worthy of attention concerns the difference between the past (in which many optional teaching tools have never been used by teachers), present (in which a good percentage of teachers declare to use different didactic tools in DL) and future (in which there is the will to use some tools in particular), with a gradual increase of interest in their use. Suffice it to think, in this regard, that more than 60% of responding teachers (445 out of 716, 5 n.r.) believe that they will use distance learning also in the future.

More specifically, as regards the present, the didactic tools most used in DL are audio-video recordings (49%, n = 350); web conference lessons with skype, zoom, webinar (76%, n = 544); discussion and collaboration environments such as web forums, blogs and wikis, which allow brief interventions by the students (32%, n = 232); software for information processing such as PowerPoint, Excel, Word etc. (60%, n = 433). As for the future, there is the will to use some tools, in particular: Social Networks (17%, n = 124), Demonstrations or additional explanations present in the faq (19%, n = 134); Structured and individual activities, such as reports, exercises, case studies, problem solving, web quests, projects, production of artifacts, simulations (29%, n = 208); activity in web forum with demonstration or operational suggestions on how to solve a problem (20%, n = 141). At the pedagogical-didactic level, another interesting result recorded concerns the activities - in addition to the use of the lesson - towards which the teachers direct the students' commitment: this was mainly aimed at the use and analysis of teaching material (47%) while little space was dedicated to product development by students at home (24%), problem solving (21%) and self-assessment (8%) (as shown in Fig. 3). This shows a certain criticality with respect to the assessment activities in the DL, which was also confirmed by the questions in the section relating to the assessment [37].

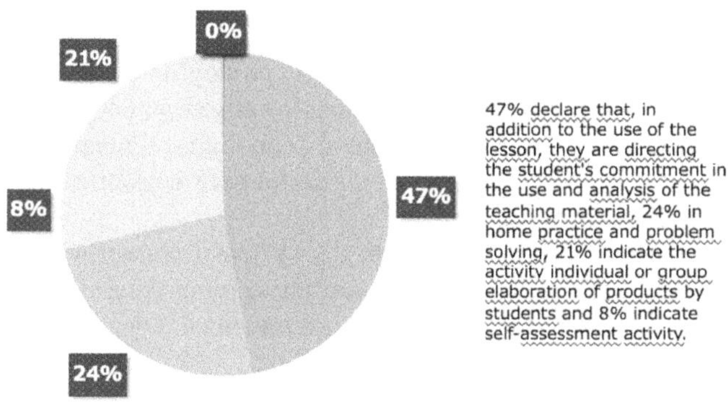

Fig. 3. 2.5 With respect to which of the following activities, in addition to the use of the lesson, is the student's commitment addressing?

From the analysis of the data it emerges that inclusive practices, together with those of promoting student self-assessment, seem to represent the "weak points" of distance learning mediation, perhaps even those on which a stronger training investment is required. Evaluation is experienced as a problematic moment and largely characterized by traditional practices. Even in the emergency situation, which could push teachers to find alternative and innovative solutions, the evaluation practices remained mainly anchored to a summative and certification vision. However, it should be noted that a small minority of teachers have been induced to explore new evaluation possibilities, which, even in the face of a generalized resistance to change, appear to be considered promising, given that the data show the greater intention to implement them in the future, compared to what has been done in the past and achieved in the present moment [37].

With respect to the representations that teachers have of the DL, it emerged that, as regards its functions, many teachers recognize the merit of having contributed to improving the professionalism of teachers (33%, n = 237); a lower percentage (22%, n = 159) believe that DL increases communication interactions between students and between students and teachers; only about 1/7 of the interviewees (101 out of 716, 5 n.r.) instead consider the DL as a tool that makes students' learning more effective. As for the quality of communication with students, the answers show a positive picture: for 43% of the interviewees it is good/fair; for 16% effectiveness; 10% excellent/excellent; for 8% it is difficult and for 5% not very interactive. 51% of respondents stated that their relationship with the knowledge taught has been changed by the use of the DL (24% see no change). The declared change concerns the modality of communication with a tendency to a greater clarity of presentation, a care in the preparation of the didactic material and a simplification of the contents [37].

5 Discussion and Conclusion

The health emergency has pushed, as already highlighted, the university to a spatial, instrumental and methodological reorganization, as well as to a redefinition of the roles of teachers who have had to redesign their own distance teaching quickly and in many cases without adequate technical and methodological support [21, 28, 38]. The results obtained from the survey conducted on didactic mediation and on the timely evaluation of COVID-19, is not limited to providing a simple photograph of the existing, but aims further, to understand the possible implications of development and the implications for the future hybrid mediation and therefore also on digital scholarship processes. It is necessary that the technological achievements no longer "demonized" become part of a didactic action on the part of the teacher.

University management must focus on the system for improving the digital and methodological skills of teachers as they are the driving force that can lead to full innovation. Technologies, in fact, "alone cannot transform educational paradigms, the way of teaching and learning" [21].

It is therefore necessary to involve the teacher in faculty development processes that enhance community approaches, experiential dimensions, active involvement and reflective learning, in order to support a constant review of professional representations and practices. This is made possible by the active involvement of teachers in planned faculty development actions activated by training institutions aimed at acquiring the necessary methodological and digital skills and having effective tools for quality teaching and improving student learning outcomes [21, 38].

Therefore, contexts of analysis, reflection and re-elaboration of didactic models and professional action are needed, to be brought into the system. In this regard, already in 2010 Yvonne Steinert pointed out that the faculty development activities can move along two dimensions: from individual (independent) experiences to group (collective) learning, and from informal approaches to more formal ones [39] (Fig. 4).

As shown in the figure above, according to Steinert [39], it is possible to synthesize and collect the Faculty Development actions by arranging them according to two main axes representing the context/type of learning and the type of program proposed: an axis which ideally sees at its extremes exclusively individual forms of learning and exclusively group forms of learning; an axis which sees at its extremes exclusively formal activities and exclusively informal activities.

By crossing the two axes in a Cartesian way, it will be possible to define the activities of Faculty Development and propose the following classification:

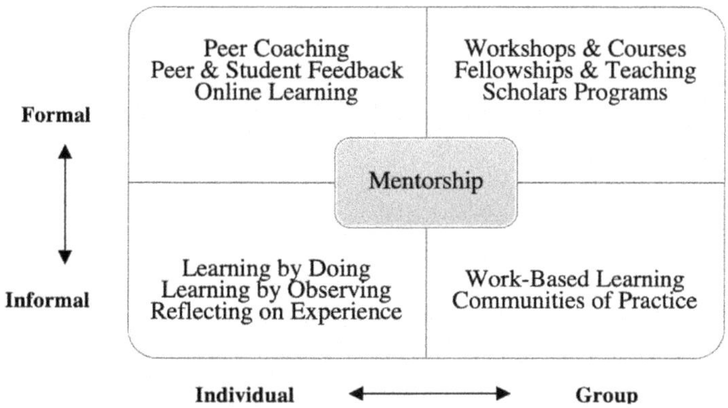

Fig. 4. Faculty Development Approach Source: Steinert, 2010 (adapted)

- formal activities based on individual learning: online learning, peer training, feedback from students; formal activities based on group learning: workshops and seminars, fellowships, longitudinal training programs;
- informal learning activities based on individual learning: reflective activities, learning from observation, learning by doing;
- informal activities based on group learning: work-based learning, communities of practice.

At the intersection of the two axes, it is possible to define a final type of activity: mentorship, which can be both formal and informal, and which can be defined as both personal and group-based, since each personal improvement strategy benefits from the support or comparison that a mentor can provide to the individual. With reference to the research carried out, Steinert's classification suggests the opportunity - whether individual/group or formal/informal actions - to activate support actions ('mentorship') capable of promoting the achievement of central objectives for the improvement of university teaching: reflective practices, specific teaching skills, reorganization of curricula, creation of communities of practice and forms of inter-institutional exchange.

The research results also make it possible to critically problematize didactic mediation in the context of higher university education in a direction of revision of the ways in which the teacher chooses, uses and transforms disciplinary contents into digitalized disciplinary contents [40].

In conclusion, the research offers interesting opportunities for understanding and deepening the distance teaching action, both in didactic mediation and in evaluation. At present, it seems very urgent to channel the result of the lived experience towards a profound renewal of teaching which, fully welcoming the perspective of the active centrality of the student, prepares a new professionalism of the teacher capable of guiding teaching 'with' it is beyond the same DL.

In this regard, some possible actions to be taken in the near future with respect to didactic mediation and evaluation could concern:

1. the didactic transposition of the knowledge taught in terms of countertransposition [41] or of an environment that generates knowledge and practices strongly linked with topical contents (the "knowledge of life", soft skills);
2. the construction of a different perception of the educational "space" by the students and the teacher
3. the transition to hybrid teaching through mediatization work by mediators to compensate for the "excessive tension" induced by the student's experiential experience: "containment" through artefacts and more structured forms of accompaniment;
4. reflection on the use of traditional assessment practices in the DL, to introduce more authentic and supportive assessment approaches at the service of student learning;
5. the initiation of experiences that aim at an evaluative partnership with the student, giving him the leadership and autonomy necessary to allow him to achieve self-evaluation and self-management skills in his own learning processes.

These actions can be implemented starting from an organizational and professional rethinking of the teacher, placing the emphasis on improving training processes and teaching innovation. Universities and their governing bodies are therefore prompted to question themselves on the actions and possible lines of action to be adopted "aimed at strengthening the teaching-learning skills of teachers" [42].

It is therefore necessary now to work on the planning of initial and in-service training courses for university teachers so that they can be prepared to face the continuous transformations of the context, of the student body, and of the teaching-learning activity. Paths that must aim not only at the training/integration of professional, pedagogical, relational and technological skills but above all to make teachers able to adapt the disciplinary contents to the different needs of students in terms of personalization (according to the sophisticated knowledge framework) [40].

References

1. Saroyan, A., Amundsen, C.: Rethinking Higher Education: From a Course Design Workshop to a Faculty Development Framework. Stylus Publishing, Sterling (2004)
2. ENQA: European standards and guidelines for internal quality assurance within higher education institutions. ENQA, Helsinki (2007)
3. Sorcinelli, M.D.: Faculty development: the challenge going forward. Peer Rev. **9**(4), 4–8 (2007)
4. Biggs, J., Tang, C.: Teaching for Quality Learning at University. Open University Press/McGraw Hill, Buckingham (2007)
5. Felisatti, E., Serbati, A.: Preparare alla professionalità docente e innovare la didattica universitaria. FrancoAngeli, Milano (2017)
6. Perla, L.: Formare il docente alla didattica universitaria: il cantiere dell'innovazione. In: Michelini, M. (ed.) Riflessioni sull'innovazione didattica universitaria, pp. 79–88. Forum, Udine (2018)

7. Perla, L., Vinci, V.: Dall'analisi dei bisogni formativi dei docenti universitari all'organizzazione del Teaching Learning Laboratory: la ricerca PRODID presso l'Università di Bari. Educ. Sci. Soc. **2**, 120–140 (2018)
8. Perla, L., Vinci, V.: TLL (Teaching Learning Laboratory) e formazione dialettica dei docenti universitari alla didattica: primi passi verso la certificazione della competenza pedagogica in Uniba. Lifelong Lifewide Learn. **15**(32), 68–88 (2018)
9. Perla, L., Vinci, V.: Didattica, riconoscimento professionale e innovazione in Università. FrancoAngeli, Milano (2021)
10. Perla, L., Vinci, V.: Modellistiche co-epistemologiche per la formazione del docente universitario: il progetto Prodid Uniba. Excellence and Innovation in Teaching and Learning, Special Issue, pp. 11–30 (2021)
11. EC: High Level Group on the Modernisation of Higher Education. Report to the European Commission on Improving the quality of teaching and learning in Europe's higher education institutions. Publications Office of the European Union, Luxembourg (2013)
12. EC: Modernisation of Higher Education in Europe: Academic Staff. Publications Office of the European Union, Luxembourg (2017)
13. Li, K.C., Wong, B.Y.Y.: Revisiting the definitions and implementation of flexible learning. In: Li, K.C., Yuen, K.S., Wong, B.T.M. (eds.) Innovations in Open and Flexible Education. EIS, pp. 3–13. Springer, Singapore (2018). https://doi.org/10.1007/978-981-10-7995-5_1
14. Agrati, L.S., Vinci, V.: Virtual internship as mediatized experience. The educator's training during COVID19 emergency. In: Agrati, L.S., et al. (eds.) HELMeTO 2020. CCIS, vol. 1344, pp. 170–183. Springer, Cham (2021). https://doi.org/10.1007/978-3-030-67435-9_14
15. Huang, R.H., et al.: Handbook on Facilitating Flexible Learning During Educational Disruption. The Chinese Experience in Maintaining Undisrupted Learning in COVID-19 Outbreak. Smart Learning Institute of Beijing Normal University, Beijing (2020)
16. McCaffery, P.: The Higher Education Manager's Handbook. Effective Leadership and Management in Universities and Colleges, 3rd edn. Routledge, London and New York (2019)
17. Sorcinelli, M.D., Austin, A., Eddy, P., Beach, A.: Creating the Future of Faculty Development. Jossey-Bass, San Francisco (2006)
18. Lotti, A., Lampugnani, P. (eds.): Faculty Development e valorizzazione delle competenze didattiche dei docenti nelle università italiane, GUP Genova University Press, Genova (2020)
19. Grion, V., Serbati, A., Nicol, D., Tino, C.: Ripensare la teoria della valutazione e dell'apprendimento all' università: un modello per implementare pratiche di peer review. Giornale Italiano della Ricerca Educativa **X**(19), 209–229 (2017)
20. Felisatti, E., Serbati, A.: Apprendere per imparare: formazione e sviluppo professionale dei docenti universitari. Un progetto innovativo dell'Università di Padova. Giornale Italiano della Ricerca Educativa **14**, VIII, 323–339 (2015)
21. Dipace, A., Scarinci, A.: Formazione metodologica, tecnologie didattiche ed esperienze nella promozione delle competenze di insegnamento e apprendimento. In: Excellence and Innovation in Learning and Teaching, vol. Special issue, pp. 95–111 (2021)
22. Tømte, C.E., Fossland, T., Aamodt, P.O., Degn, L.: Digitalisation in higher education: mapping institutional approaches for teaching and learning. Qual. High. Educ. **25**(1), 98–114 (2019)
23. Barberà Gregori, E., Badia Gargantè, A.: El uso educativo de las aulas virtuales emergentes en la educación superior. Revista de Universidady Sociedad del Conocimiento (RUSC), vol. 2, no. 2. UOC (2005)
24. Estermann, T., et al.: The impact of the Covid-19 crisis on university funding in Europe. Lessons learnt from the 2008 global financial crisis. EUA, Switzerland (2020)
25. Vinci, V.: Didattica digitale in Università: luci, ombre, prospettive. Giornale italiano di educazione alla salute, sport e didattica inclusiva **4**, 103–110 (2021)

26. Lederman, D.: Will shift to remote teaching be boon or bane for inline learning? Inside Higher Ed., 18 March 2020
27. Eradze, M., Dipace, A., Limone, P.: Hybrid flexible learning with MOOCs: a proposal to reconceptualize the COVID19 emergency beyond the crisis. In: Proceedings of 2020 IEEE Learning with MOOCS, Guatemala, vol. 2020 (2020)
28. Hodges, C., Moore, S., Lockee, B., Trust, T., Bond, A.: The difference between emergency remote teaching and online learning. Educ. Rev. **27** (2020)
29. Aguilera-Hermida, A.P.: College students' use and acceptance of emergency online learning due to COVID-19. Int. J. Educ. Res. Open (2020)
30. Perla, L., Scarinci, A., Amati, I.: Metamorphosis of space into digital scholarship. A research on hybrid mediation in a university context. In: Agrati, L.S., et al. (eds.) HELMeTO 2020. CCIS, vol. 1344, pp. 226–239. Springer, Cham (2021). https://doi.org/10.1007/978-3-030-67435-9_18
31. European Distance Education Network – EDEN: Connecting through Educational Technology to produce effective learning environments. EDEN 2019 Annual Conference, Bruges, Belgium (2019)
32. Huang, R., Tlili, H., Chang, T., Zhang, X., Nascimbeni, N., Burgos, D.: Disrupted classes, undisrupted learning during COVID- 19 outbreak in China: application of open educational practices and resources. Smart Learn. Environ. **7**, 19 (2020)
33. Calvani, A., Rotta, M.: Fare formazione in Internet: manuale di didattica online, Erickson, Trento (2000)
34. Cope, B., Kalantzis, M.: New Learning: Elements of a Science of Education. Cambridge University Press, Cambridge (2008)
35. Speck, M.: The change process in a school learning community. Sch. Commun. J. **6**(1), 69–79 (1996)
36. Mishra, L., Gupta, T., Shree, A.: Online teaching-learning in higher education during lockdown period of COVID-19 pandemic. Int. J. Educ. Res. Open (2020)
37. Perla, L., et al.: Oltre l'era Covid-19: dall'emergenza alle prospettive di sviluppo professionale. Excellence Innov. Teach. Learn. **2**, 18–37 (2021)
38. Scarinci, A., Dipace, A.: Formazione pedagogica per l'insegnamento: il nuovo profilo professionale del docente universitario. In: Dipace, A., Tamborra, V.I.V. (a cura di): Insegnare in università - metodi e strumenti per una didattica efficace, Franco Angeli, Milano (2019)
39. Steinert, Y.: Becoming a better teacher: from intuition to intent. In: Ende, J. (ed.) Theory and Practice of Teaching Medicine, pp. 73–93. American College of Physicians, Philadelphia (2010)
40. Perla, L., Agrati, L.S., Vinci, V.: The 'Sophisticated' knowledge of e-Teacher. Re-shape digital resources for online courses. In: Burgos, D., et al. (eds.) Higher Education Learning Methodologies and Technologies Online, HELMeTO 2019, pp. 3–17. Springer, Cham (2019). https://doi.org/10.1007/978-3-030-31284-8_1
41. Frisch, M.: La contre-transposition/Counter-transposition. Internal seminar, Programme Erasmus+, Université Aldo Moro, Bari, June 2018, Italy, Bari ⟨hal-02104645⟩ (2018)
42. ANVUR: Linee di indirizzo per lo sviluppo professionale del docente e strategie di valutazione della didattica in Università (2018). https://www.anvur.it/wp-content/uploads/2018/05/lineeguidaquarcdocente15032018.pdf

Developing the Novice Teacher Evaluation Competence: The Challenge of Online Training

Laura Sara Agrati[1(✉)], Svetlana Karkina[2], Roza Valeeva[2], and Marco Lazzari[1]

[1] University of Bergamo, Bergamo, Italy
{laurasara.agrati,marco.lazzari}@unibg.it
[2] Kazan Federal University, Kazan, Russia

Abstract. This study aims at describing how the provision of teaching in the evaluation area was adapted online during the emergency period due to the COVID-19 pandemic, at two universities – University of Bergamo (Italy) and Federal University of Kazan (Russia). The questions of investigation are: 1. what evaluation concepts and key principles do student teachers possess? 2. Have student teachers been able to design assessment tools? 3. Did the online adaptation of the courses have a relation with knowledge and skills of student teachers?

The triangulation of methods in adult distance learning has been the methodological basis of the study. Referring to the Kirkpatrick model, adapted to the e-learning criteria, attention was focused on level of student's learnings – *knowledge* (1) and *ability* (2) - with reference to two courses involved.

The analysis highlighted that the adaptation of university training courses for future teachers, in the area of evaluation, had in general a considerable impact. The instructional articulation and the offer of multiple online resources by the university courses involved had mainly a relation on the student teacher's skills (2): the high average to the assessment tools infers the preparation and commitment of students by the means of online resources. The effect on knowledge (1), on the other hand, was diversified: greater on operational and didactic aspects, less on conceptual and personal aspects - where personal beliefs and sometimes misconceptions prevail. Further in-depth analysis will detect the impact of each resource on the skills trained.

Keywords: Teacher evaluation competences · Adaptation of university courses · Cross-cultural study

1 Introduction - Training of Teachers' Evaluation Competences

School evaluation is a process that appreciates many aspects of educational intervention: the effectiveness of systems and types of interventions, learnings in terms of outcomes, etc. [1–4]. It is also a professional activity that each teacher must carry out in order to continually review and improve students' learning [5, 6]. Over the years, teacher training in evaluation is becoming an object of increasing interest for decision-makers [5, 7], and, although considered a problematic area [8], stimulated research interest in two directions: on the methods of providing initial and in-service training (contents,

G. Casalino et al. (Eds.): HELMeTO 2021, CCIS 1542, pp. 291–305, 2022.
https://doi.org/10.1007/978-3-030-96060-5_21

teaching strategies, etc.), on the causes of the ineffectiveness of training and professional development courses for evaluation [9]. Research has provided, above all, sufficient elements to define a series of foundational dimensions for an accurate and valid use of evaluation by teachers [10], as well as, focalized topics for teacher training in evaluation (see Table 1 [11]), in order to recover the found gaps.

Table 1. Topics for professional development programs in evaluation. Adapt.: [11]

Topics	Focus
Assessment terminology and concepts	The terminology, concepts and key principles teachers, inspectors, in-service providers and teacher educator should understand
The role of assessment in learning and teaching	The implications of the phrase *assessment is integral to teaching and learning* for classroom practice. Distinguishing between assessment *of* learning and assessment *for* learning
Planning assessment	The importance of identifying key learning outcomes across the different subject areas and matching them to assessment methods/tools
Assessment during the teaching and learning process	The nature, potential and conduct of formative assessment including provision for appropriate feedback. Assessment approaches that can be integrated with ongoing teaching and learning to improve achievement
Paper-and-pencil assessments of achievement	The role of teacher made tests and external assessments of achievement in teaching and learning. Planning, constructing and administering tests; using test data
Performance assessments	Using hands-on tasks to assess and improve learning processes
Standardized testing of academic achievement	Interpreting standardized test results. The role of standardized testing in teaching and learning
Interpreting assessment information	Making judgements about the quality of pupil work across the curriculum. Identifying standards of work at different achievement levels
Grading	Issues and challenges when grading, making grading procedures explicit, report card writing

The evaluative competence of teachers, defined differently in the research literature [12, 13] consists, among others, in to be able to design tests, to use assessment instruments constructed by others, to make decision based on evidences, to report the achievements, to choose appropriate method and know the philosophy of evaluation. Such evaluative competences have been inserted, above all, in the broader background of teacher professionalism [14], and explained by the incidence of conceptions, representations, personal beliefs on evaluation [15], that develop during the teacher's career [13] - Fig. 1 - and which are strongly linked to basic knowledge concerning the discipline, teaching knowledge of the discipline, assessment methods, grading methods, forms of feedback, self-assessment and peer evaluation as well as the ethics of evaluation.

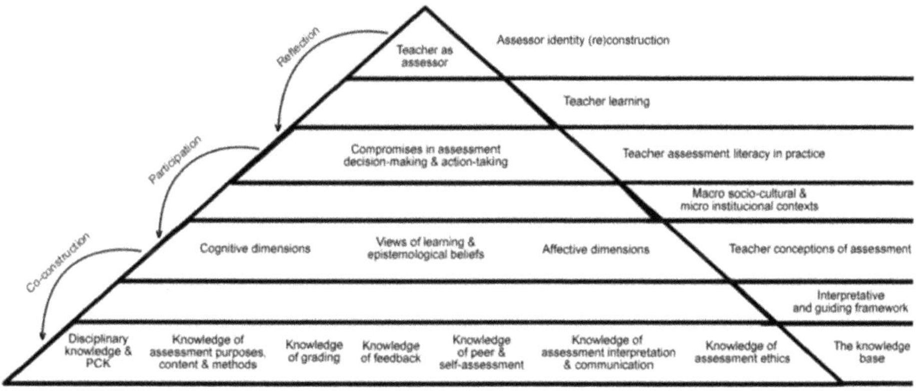

Fig. 1. Teacher Assessment Literacy in Practice. Retrieved: [13, p. 19].

Some studies have investigated the initial teacher training curricula, in order to know how the foundations for the construction of teachers' evaluation competences are laid (which dimension is preferred, what type of guaranteed knowledge, etc.) [16, 17]. The ways in which specific evaluation skills are exercised in the university environment - in relation to which other disciplines, through which instructive methods (lectures, seminars, laboratories, etc.), through which tools for assessment and evaluation - was also investigated [18]. This has also favored the comparison between the universities of different countries that train teachers as it provides a base of meanings, as well as a common language that allows for the cross-cultural dialogue [16, 19].

2 Objectives, Question of Investigation – Student Teacher Knowledge and Ability

The basic training of prospective teachers in evaluation is often carried out in a theoretical way, detached as much from daily practice as from standards identified [16], although it represents a priority, given the link it has with the improvement of schools and students' learning. The general purpose of the study is to offer useful results to research on teacher training in evaluation, in terms of initial training provided at the university.

The current historical situation has made it necessary to investigate an unforeseeable aspect: the adaptation that the study courses have undergone following the pandemic due to COVID-19 [20, 21]. Since the second semester of 2020 many degree courses had to guarantee online methods consistent with the expected outgoing skills; those specifically aimed at the formation of professional profiles have experimented with new e-learning design solutions to make students exercise in experiential practices (internships, practical exercises, laboratories) no longer feasible face-to-face but to be performed remotely. Such urgent situation and the online reconversion experiences of many professionalizing degree courses animate the debate on higher education today and direct the interest of scholars on theoretical aspects (training e-learning environment) and practical (the preparation of functional e-tivities for specific skills). For this reason, it is now necessary to focus the research attention on how the skills that define evaluation competences have been taught online - in a 'hybrid' mode, which guarantees activities in presence or at a distance [22, 23] or in e-learning environments, through specific resources [24–26] and e-tivity [27].

With reference to some specific topics [11 - see Table 1] of the training curriculum ('assessment terminology and concepts' and 'paper-and-pencil assessments of achievement'), assumed as assessment skill, the study aimed, particularly, at describing how the provision of teaching in the assessment area was adapted online during the emergency period due to the COVID-19 pandemic. Descriptive and investigative questions are:

- *what evaluation concepts and key principles do student teachers possess?*
- *have student teachers been able to design assessment tools?*
- *did the online adaptation of the courses have relation with knowledge and skills of student teachers?*

3 Context and Method – A Cross-Cultural Study

A comparative and cross-cultural study of 2 university courses (University of Bergamo, Italy; Federal University of Kazan, Russia) in the area of evaluation, belonging to degree courses aimed at the initial training of future primary and secondary school teachers, was carried out (Table 2). The study involved n. 312 students – n. 62 primary student teachers, n. 182 secondary student teachers; it was made in the February-March 2021 period.

A comparative design, in the perspective of the educational knowledge [28], through a cross-cultural approach [29, 30], has been adopted. Since the study focused on assessment skill as 'assessment terminology and concepts' and 'paper-and-pencil assessments of achievement' (see Table 1), in order to conduct the cross-cultural investigation, in the first phase of pre-data collection conceptual and functional equivalences have been defined [31]. The aim was to know and establish possible relationships, regarding the concepts of evaluation and evaluation skills of teachers, between the Italian and Russian contexts.

In the Russian tradition, the concept of evaluation literacy is generally defined as a component in a set of competencies acquired during the educational process. Among other competencies researchers define the evaluation competence as a "test-quality assurance and self-control" or "control and diagnostic" and is clearly distinguished as an independent category [32]. This competence researchers feature as a significant technological component in a teacher's professional activity which allows a teacher to make correct decisions in various pedagogical situations. Russian researchers define competence in the pedagogical evaluation as the ability to evaluate the students' achievements

Table 2. Degree and university courses involved.

Universities	Degree courses	Courses	Year, semester	N. of students
Bergamo	Primary Teacher Education	Issue and technique of assessment	2020/21, 2nd	120
Kazan Federal	Music Teacher Education	Workshop on the professional educational methods	2020/21, 2nd	164
	Professional Teacher Education	Workshop on the professional educational methods	2020/21, 2nd	371
	Additional teacher education and English	Modern tools for evaluating learning outcomes	2020/21, 2nd	105

based on their personal characteristics, including self-assessment and self-control. In order to support this process, a teacher as a facilitator need to provide psychological comfort for the student to demonstrate the efficacy of control and evaluation activities. In determining assessment competence, researchers distinguish it's several types.

1. The analytical and evaluative competence as a valuable component of personal development featured as a set of specific knowledge about criteria educational results based on the key competencies, and skills for assessing educational achievements, using a variety of pedagogical tools, different types of assessment scales [33]. Among the criteria of this competence, the researchers point out skills in information search, data assessment, and classification, analysis, application in the course of a comprehensive analysis of pedagogical, socio-economic, and cultural processes and educational environment, development of educational activity indicators for the independent assessment system. For the evaluation competence improvement researchers offer to develop the self-reflection, communication skills, tolerant attitude in pedagogical activity, empathic behavior of a teacher, pedagogical ethics [33].
2. The next type of evaluation competence is defined as the formative evaluation which allows increasing the students' motivation to learning in general and to plan ways for achievement educational results [34]. The implementation of this type is based on common methods such as tests, surveys, projects, but aimed at the determination of each student's individual achievements, and does not have a comparative function of the training results. The competence used as feedback allows clarifying the educational level in order to provide students' effective learning, as well as to correct the curriculum or the course content, for the purpose to improve it.
3. Another type of evaluation competence is defined as a summative evaluation which means the determination of students' knowledge, corresponds to any learning indicators, and demonstrates the actual students' training level [34]. Summative evaluation is carried out often by independent experts, representatives of official organizations, based on the regulatory documents and the state assessment scale. The results of this

evaluation are strictly recorded in state-issued documents (class journals, certificates, report cards, personal files of students), determined by local acts of the educational institution.

Despite all researchers agree that evaluation competence is based on the ability to evaluate learning results according to the objective criteria, some of them emphasize the specific feature of this process for some subjects in the cultural field. Such disciplines as Music, Fine arts, Choreography, and Physical training include personal evaluation as a crucial component that establishes the main result as unique rather than similar to each other [35]. The evaluation of creative activity results needs in keeping the balance between objective criteria and personal achievements that reflect the personality, artistic skills features, mastery.

The evaluation practices in the Italian school are multiple and linked to different procedures and purposes:

- *diagnostic* evaluation (initial) - to know the initial level of a student in a given field, at the beginning of the school, annual or cycle path, through tests or observation sheets - and *summative* evaluation (final) - as a synthesis of the periodic checks (*in itinere*), through various devices (written assignments, oral questions, group achievements, objective tests, informal activities), useful for expressing the final grade in the official documentation;
- certification assessments, through objective tests, established by the school or standardized at an international level [36], with function of social accountability;
- evaluation of knowledge (declarative and procedural - what the student knows or can do) [37] and skills (dispositions and attitudes to use knowledge and skills learned in new situations [38].

The Italian teacher is asked to master these procedures and tools, for this reason, as noted by Viganò [39], 'the evaluation competence is a professional dimension qualifying the teacher, capable of obtaining information on the learning and development of the student for the purpose to regulate didactic action' [40, 41].

Italian educational research has produced little of systematic on teacher training in evaluation also due to the 'regulatory jungle' [42] establishing phases, deadlines, verification methods and types of devices, often in continuous definition - see ministerial order n. 172/2020 for primary school.

From the survey and organizational point of view, an enormous effort is being made to try to bring together the practices of daily evaluation (of students' learning and behavior) with the evaluation processes of the entire system (with quality management function) [43–45]. From the exclusive attention to the objectivity of the information collected, importance has been given to the intertwining of cultural, ideological, social and psychological aspects often implicitly connected to evaluation practices [22, 46].

A comparative table depicts a global mapping of online resources used to convert specific instructional modalities and to support targeted evaluation skills (interactive webinars, discussion forums, recorded video lectures) (Table 3).

Table 3. Adaptation of courses in online mode.

University	Instructional modalities	On-line resources
Bergamo	a. introductory lesson b. provision of examples c. individual and group work d. final task	a. a-synchronous lesson b. pdf files c. interactive seminar + chat/forum d. assessment tool loaded on platform
Kazan Federal	a. introductory lesson b. provision of examples c. individual and group work d. final task	e. synchronous lesson f. e-sources g. interactive seminar + chat/forum h. assessment tool loaded on platform

3.1 Data Collection and Data Analysis

The triangulation of methods in adult distance learning has been the methodological basis of the study. Referring to the Kirkpatrick model, adapted to the e-learning criteria [47], attention was focused on level of student's learnings – *knowledge* (1) and *ability* (2) - with reference to two courses involved.

The teacher students' knowledge (1) were detected by 'ad hoc' questionnaire, administered online through the platform at the end of the course. It was structured in 4 close-ended items (see Table 3 and 4), which provided quantitative data.

After clarifying the term 'evaluation' on a cross-cultural level, Vertecchi [37] and Galliani [4] were taken as a reference in order to elaborate the alternative answers, respectively, to item nn. 2 and 4. The questionnaire focused attention on those relating to the evaluation definition (*question 1*: value, judging, classifying), the relation evaluation/assessing (*question 2*: specific case, different plan), the objects of school assessment (*question 3*: verifying students' knowledge and skills, evaluate competences, assessing learnings), the learning outcomes and processes (*question 4*: assessing student outcomes, assessing teaching processes).

The students' ability (2) was inferred from the assessment tools, designed and uploaded to the platform at the end of the course. Three 'criteria of relevance' have been identified for the analysis - *validity*, *consistency*, *clarity* [48][1]. Each criterion was assessed by a two-point scale 'satisfied vs. dissatisfied' in relation to the key feature of each of them. On the basis of these criteria three levels have been established: level 3 = satisfaction of three criteria; level 2 = satisfaction of two criteria, etc.

The quantitative data analysis process was carried out in two phases [49]:

- descriptive analysis of the answers to the questionnaire (*knowledge*), which provided the mean and standard deviation (Table 5);
- cross-analysis between those answers and the average rating of the assessment tools developed by students at the end of the course (*ability*) (Table 6).

[1] *Validity* - tool capable of soliciting performances directly related to the learning objectives; *Consistency* - between the expected performance and the key competence of the task; *Clarity*- linguistic clarity of the requested task.

Table 4. Items nn. 1–4 of 'ad hoc' questionnaire.

Question	1. Evaluation is the determination of: *(complete the following sentence)*	2. Assessing is: *(complete the following sentence)*	3. Which of the following statements do I agree with? It is possible …	4. The evaluation carried out at school concerns: *(complete the following sentence)*
Focus	Evaluation function	Difference between evaluation and assessing	Objects of the school assessment	Learning outcomes and processes
Response alternatives	- value - value for the purposes of a judgment - value for the purposes of a judgment to obtain a classification - other	- a specific case in the evaluation process - a different plan then evaluation - other	- to verify and evaluate both knowledge and skills and competences - to verify both knowledge and skills and competences - to verify both knowledge and skills	- student learning outcomes - student learning and learning processes - student learning and teaching processes

4 Results

Table 5 shows a substantial homogeneity and specific differences between Bergamo and Kazan, as regards the student teachers' knowledge (1).

Homogeneity is found with respect to the questions n. 2 and n. 3. Student teachers from Bergamo and Kazan consider assessment as a specific case of evaluation (48,4%, 50,0%) and knowledge, skills and competences of students as objects of school assessment (43,5%, 58,8%). Homogeneity is also given by the high variability indices, in general, both in Bergamo ($\sigma = 1{,}78$) and in Kazan ($\sigma = 1{,}93$). Furthermore, the variability is lower in both universities ($\sigma = 0{,}68$; $\sigma = 0{,}50$) compared to question n. 2, relating to the difference between evaluation and assessment.

With regard to the evaluation knowledge of student teachers, the most evident differences concern instead: the evaluation function (question 1) - judgment prevails (37.1%) in Bergamo, classification (48.9%) in Kazan; learning outcomes and processes (question 4) - the evaluation of teaching processes prevails (46.8%) in Bergamo, while the evaluation of student outcomes (58.2%) in Kazan.

The data relating the teacher students' ability are shown in Table 6. The table shows the average grade obtained by students in the development of the assessment tools. The general average grade - from 0 to 3 - was 2.54 with the satisfaction of the reliability criterion (40.3%). The average grade in Bergamo was 2.61, with a low dispersion index

Table 5. Answers to teacher students' knowledge questionnaire (1).

N. students Question	Tot n. 312 m = 6,83/σ = 1,90	Bergamo n. 62 m = 7,27/σ = 1,78	Kazan Federal n. 182 m = 6,68/σ = 1,93
1 Value Judging Classifying Other	m = 2,01/σ = 1,01 24,7% 24,4% **39,7%** 11,2%	m = 1,87/σ = 1,03 16,1% **37,1%** 32,3% 14,5%	m = 2,06/σ = 1,00 33,0% 13,2% **48,9%** 4,9%
2 Specific case Different plane Other	m = 1,43/σ = 0,56 **56,4%** 40,7% 2,9%	m = 1,22/σ = 0,68 **48,4%** 37,1% 14,5%	m = 1,50/σ = 0,50 **50,0%** 50,0% 0,0%
3 Verifying learnings/competence Eval. competences Ass. learnings Other	m = 1,58/σ = 0,87 **50,0%** 11,5% 36,9% 1,6%	m = 1,98/σ = 0,93 **43,5%** 14,5% (41,9% 0,0%	m = 1,45/σ = 0,81 **58,8%** 11,5% 26,9% 2,7%
4 Ass. students' outcomes Eval. learnings processes Eval. teaching processes Others	m = 1,80/σ = 0,90 **45,5%** 21,3% 30,7% 2,5%	m = 2,19/σ = 0,95 8,1% 35,5% **46,8%** 9,7%	m = 1,67/σ = 0,85 **58,2%** 16,5% 25,3% 0,0%

Table 6. Average rating of assessment tools developed by teacher students (2).

Assessment tools	Tot. n. 233 m = 2,54/σ = 0,33	Bergamo n. 81 m = 2,61/σ = 0,30	Kazan Federal n. 152 m = 2,33/σ = 0,39
Validity	29,1%	**35,7%**	25,9%
Consistency	**40,3%**	**34,6%**	**36,0%**
Clarity	30,4%	29,7%	**38,0%**

(0.30) and the satisfaction of the criteria of validity (35.7%) and reliability (34.6%). The average grade in reference to Kazan was 2.33, with a low index of dispersion (0.39) and the fulfillment of the criteria of coherence and reliability. The results obtained allow us to answer the research questions.

Question n. 1 - what evaluation concepts and key principles do student teachers possess? Student teachers involved:

- recognize evaluation, in general, the function of classifying things, events, objects, etc. This concept is more evident in the student teachers of Kazan, less so in those of Bergamo;
- consider the assessment a specific case of evaluation;
- recognize students' knowledge, skills and competences as objects of school evaluation, both in Bergamo and in Kazan.

Student teachers in Kazan consider the evaluation carried out at school as mainly focused on student learning outcomes, hand on learning processes; on the other hand, the Bergamo student teachers consider the evaluation carried out at school to be more relevant to the teaching processes as a whole.

Question n. 2 - have student teachers been able to design assessment tools?

The student teachers involved were able to design good assessment tools that responded to criteria of reliability in general, and also of validity, in Bergamo, and coherence, in Kazan.

Question n. 3 - did the online adaptation of the courses have a relation with knowledge and skills of student teachers?

The study highlighted that the adaptation of university training courses for future teachers, in evaluation area, had a general relation. The instructional articulation and the offer of multiple online resources by the university courses involved (see Table 3) had mainly a relation on the student teacher's skills (2): the high average to the assessment tools infers the preparation and commitment of students by the means of online resources. All the students demonstrated skills in the design of assessment tools according to the teachers' instructions and using computers with access to the Internet. The instructions for the designing of assessment tools were covered by the content of each course which was delivered to students in an online way. So, in the design of these tools students showed the knowledge in the studied field. Despite this, the online adaptation of the courses in relation to knowledge (1), was diversified: greater on operational and didactic aspects, less on conceptual and personal aspects - where personal beliefs and sometimes misconceptions prevail. Further in-depth analysis will detect the impact of each resource on trained skills.

5 Discussion

The evaluation on a conceptual level includes many aspects of educational intervention such as students' motivation, initial level diagnostic, learning outcomes, and educational process in general [2, 3]. The future teachers who mustered evaluative literacy should demonstrate the ability to students' strength and skills diagnoses, the didactics definition according to educational needs and purposes, bridging learning advantages and social requirements, evaluation subject contents as well as teacher interventions effectiveness.

The definition of evaluation covered various aspects include knowledge, skills, and attitudes in assessment activities. Despite this, necessary to point the gap between general and specifically teaching knowledge: although at a general level ideas of classification evaluation prevail, at the didactic level there is an awareness of the close relationship between evaluation of learning and evaluation of teaching.

The essential tendency in pedagogical education is to include all aspects of school teacher work in the evaluation explanation as an open idea that required the design of a new course for future teachers. Table 1 demonstrates the structure of the course including all specific topics for preparing a teacher for future school work, while topic number four points the educational process in general. The focus on dialog among scholars will offer the clarification of the meanings of evaluation terminology in comparison with the teaching and learning process evaluation as it whole.

In order to improve students' skills to design assessment tools the specific topic was developed. Studying the approach to identify key learning outcomes across the different subject areas and matching them to assessment methods or tools allows students to create the set for assessment reflected educational purposes for a school subject.

Despite the study where experimental results confirmed the effectiveness of online resources for the students' preparation and commitment to developing assessment tools in general, the adaptation of online courses demonstrated variable effects on the student teachers' knowledge and skills. Students have favored procedural knowledge included designing and implementing evaluation tools more than theoretical knowledge consists of definition of evaluation, function of evaluation at school.

The online format provides opportunities for improvement computer-based skills [24] due to the specific interaction between a teacher and students through home electronic gadgets. The availability of personal computers allows to prioritize procedural knowledge, offering special tasks in development evaluation tools, when students learn new applications, and improve their ability to use them in the most proper way. At the same time, the gap in face-to-face interaction complicates for teacher the feedback about conceptual and personal aspects. Providing the theory of an evaluation a teacher meets difficulties in discussing the information with students or using active learning methods for explanations based on students' personal interaction and command work. Perhaps the implementation of the hybrid forms of future teacher education which combined online and face-to-face work will allow bridging the gap between procedural and theoretical knowledge delivering by teachers.

6 Conclusions

The study contributes the experience of online adaptation of the course content in the field of future teachers' evaluation competence during the emergency period due to the COVID-19 pandemic. The research was aimed to offer useful results on teacher training in evaluation in terms of initial training provided at the university. The investigation was based on a comparative and cross-cultural study of two university courses (University of Bergamo, Italy; Federal University of Kazan, Russia) in the area of evaluation, belonging to degree courses aimed at the initial training of future primary and secondary school teachers was carried out. The methodology of the study was based on the triangulation of methods in adult distance learning and adapted to the e-learning criteria of the Kirkpatrick model allowing to focus on the level of student's learnings knowledge and ability, which were covered by both courses content. The impact of the adaptation of university training courses for future teachers in the area of the evaluation was analyzed in the aspects following the objectives of the study and promoted the conclusions:

1. The future teacher online training of evaluation competence carries challenges for universities and study courses. The research data let us state the diversity approach in recognizing evaluation, which can be focused on the function of classifying things, events, objects, etc., demonstrated by student teachers of Kazan, or paying attention to other aims, like in Bergamo. Besides were established, that courses in training evaluation competence in both countries Italy and Russia cover the same content in the issues of the definition of assessment as a specific case of evaluation, and recognization of students' knowledge, skills, and competencies as objects of school evaluation. The deep gap in the courses of two Universities content was found in the point of learning outcomes and processes. Student teachers in Kazan consider the evaluation carried out at school as mainly focused on student learning outcomes, hand on learning processes, while the Bergamo student teachers consider the evaluation carried out at school to be more relevant to the teaching processes as a whole. The comparison of the experience let us point the trend in redesigning courses in order to bridge the gap in the development of evaluation competence. Following the trend will provide the knowledge for linking the specific terms in the evaluation of the teaching and learning process.
2. Using the online resources foster the student teachers' ability to design assessment tools. Students in both Universities involved in the online training process demonstrated mentioned skills. The designed tools were assessed by a set of criteria including reliability, which reached good level in general, as well as by criterion of validity, bigger in Bergamo, coherence, that featured students' works in Kazan more. Besides, the designing of the assessment tools based on computers simplified the mastering of modern technologies, including special applications that delivered usefulness to academic purposes.
3. From the specific evaluation competencies perspective, the implementation of teacher training courses in an online environment demonstrated relation to knowledge and skills of student teachers. The instructional articulation and the offer of multiple online resources by the university courses involved promoted student teachers' skills in designing the assessment tools, including the preparation and commitment of students by the means of online resources. The analysis of students' works showed the adherence to teachers' instructions and requirements, as well as the appropriate quality of all designed tools. The practical tasks were based on the content of the courses that students studied in an online way and reflected the correlation. The online adaptation of the courses discovered diversity: the operational and didactic students' skills prevailed in comparison with their abilities to focus on conceptual and personal issues in designing assessment tools. Despite, were concluded, that the pedagogically oriented organization of online resources, linked to specific knowledge and skills, within the path - be it online or hybrid, could be implemented for the initial training of teachers, beyond the COVID emergency, and perhaps also used for in-service training.

7 Limitations

The research work demonstrated the relation of the adaptation of the online course to the student teachers' knowledge and skills. Despite this fact, in the study, some limitations appeared due to the specific features of the learning environment. So, the measuring of educational results by using pre-and post-test was not organized because of the unpredictable shifting of the educational process in the case of emergency from face-to-face to online way but was included in the proposal of future researches in order to establish the effectiveness of developed resources, as well as the impact of each of them on trained skills.

References

1. OECD. Education at a Glance 2015: OECD Indicators. OECD Publishing (2015). https://doi.org/10.1787/eag-2015-en
2. Love, A.J.: Understanding approaches to evaluation. In: Peterson, P., Baker, E., McGaw, B. (eds.) International Encyclopedia of Education, 3rd edn., vol. 3, pp. 798–807. Elsevier Ltd., Oxford (2010)
3. Ainscow, M., Beresford, J., Harris, A., Hopkins, D., Southworth, G.: Creating the Conditions for School Improvement: A Handbook of Staff Development Activities, 2nd edn. Routledge, London (2012)
4. Galliani, L.: (a cura di). L'agire valutativo. Manuale per docenti e formatori. La Scuola, Brescia (2015)
5. OECD. Teachers matter Teachers Matter: Attracting, Developing and Retaining Effective Teachers (2005). https://www.oecd.org/education/school/34990905.pdf
6. Andrade, H., Heritage, M.: Using Formative Assessment to Enhance Learning, Achievement, and Academic Self-regulation. Routledge, London (2018)
7. Black, P., Wiliam, D.: Inside the Black Box: Raising Standards through Classroom Assessment. King's College, London (1998)
8. La Marca, P.: Assessment literacy: building capacity for improving student learning. Paper Presented at the Council of Chief State School Officers (CCSSO) Annual Conference on Large-Scale Assessment, San Francisco, CA (2006)
9. Pastore, S.: Saper (ben) valutare. Repertori, modelli e istanze formative per l'assessment literacy degli insegnanti. Milano: Mondadori (2020)
10. Brookhart, S.: Educational assessment knowledge and skills for teachers. Educ. Meas. Issues Pract. **30**(1), 3–12 (2011)
11. O'Leary, M.: Towards an agenda for professional development in assessment. J. In-Serv. Educ. **34**(1), 109–114 (2008)
12. Popham, J.: Why assessment illiteracy is professional suicide. Educ. Leadersh. **62**(1), 82–83 (2004)
13. Xu, Y., Brown, G.: Teacher assessment literacy in practice: a reconceptualization. Teach. Teach. Educ. **58**, 149–162 (2016)
14. Willis, J., Adie, L., Klenowski, V.: Conceptualizing teachers' assessment literacies in an era of curriculum and assessment reform. Aust. Educ. Res. **40**(2), 241–256 (2013)
15. Münster, W., Schneider, C., Bodensohn, R.: Student teachers' appraisal of the importance of assessment in teacher education and self-reports on the development of assessment competence. Assess. Educ.: Principles Policy Pract. **24**(2), 127–146 (2017)
16. DeLuca, C., Klinger, D.A., Searle, M., Shulha, L.M.: Developing a curriculum for assessment education. Assess. Matt. **2**, 20–42 (2010)
17. Ogan-Bekiroglu, F., Suzuk, E.: Pre-service teachers' assessment literacy and its implementation into practice. Curric. J. **25**, 344–371 (2014)
18. DeLuca, C., Volante, L.: Assessment for learning in teacher education programs: navigating the juxtaposition of theory and praxis. J. Int. Soc. Teach. Educ. **20**(1), 19–31 (2016)

19. De Luca, C., Schneider, Ch., Pozas, M., Coombs, A.: Exploring the Structure and Foundations of Assessment Literacy: A Cross-cultural Comparison of German and Canadian Student Teachers. ECER 2018 (2018). https://eera-ecer.de/ecer-programmes/conference/23/contribution/43815
20. Gaebel, M., Zhang, T., Stoeber, H., Morrisroe, A.: Digitally enhanced learning and teaching in European higher education institutions. European University Association absl (2021). https://eua.eu/downloads/publications/digihe%20new%20version.pdf
21. EUA, 2020 – European Higher education in the COVID-19 crisis. https://eua.eu/downloads/publications/briefing_european%20higher%20education%20in%20the%20covid-19%20crisis.pdf
22. Perla, L.: Valutare per valorizzare. La documentazione per il miglioramento di scuola, insegnanti, studenti. La Scuola, Brescia (2020)
23. Allen, E., Seaman, J., Poulin, R., Straut, T.T.: Online report card: tracking online education in the United States. Babson Survey Research Group and Quahog Research Group, Needham (2016)
24. Vai, M., Sosulski, K.: Essentials of Online Course Design, II Routledge, London (2015)
25. Read, M.F., Morel, G.M., Butcher, T., Jensen, A.E., Lang, J.M.: Developing TPACK understanding through experiential faculty development. In: Niess, M.L., Gillow-Wiles, H., Angeli, C. (eds.) Handbook of Research on TPACK in the Digital Age, pp. 224–256 (2019)
26. Poulin, R., Straut, T.: WCET distance education enrollment report 2016. WICHE Cooperative for Educational Technologies (2016). http://wcet.wiche.edu/initiatives/research/WCET-Distance-Education-Enrollment-Report-2016
27. Salmon, G.: E-tivities: A Key to Active Online Learning. Routledge, London (2002)
28. Kazamias, A.M.: On educational knowledge – a neglected theme in comparative education. I. In: Cowen, R., Kazamias, A.M. (eds.) International Handbook of Comparative Education, vol. 1, pp. 803–813. Springer, Heidelberg (2009)
29. Alexander, R.: Dichotomous pedagogies and the promise of cross-cultural comparison. In: Lauder, H., Brown, Ph., Dillabough, J.-A., Halsey, A.H. (eds.) Education, Globalization and Social Change. Oxford University Press, Oxford (2006)
30. Birkeland, A.: Cross cultural comparative education – fortifying preconceptions or transformation of knowledge? Policy Futures Educ. **14**(1), 77–91 (2016)
31. Malhotra, N.K., Agarwal, J., Peterson, M.: Methodological issues in cross cultural marketing research. Int. Mark. Rev. **13**(5), 7–43 (1996)
32. Sizintseva, E.: About the teacher's assessment competence. Almanac Mod. Sci. Educ. **5**(48), 134–136 (2011)
33. Michajlyuk, L.: Analytical and evaluative competence in the structure of a teacher's professional activity. People Educ. **2**(55), 149–153 (2018)
34. Vladimirova, L.: Development of evaluation competence teachers as a pedagogical problem. Sci. Sch. **3**, 93–99 (2020)
35. Bystritskaya, E., Alenina, A., Labazova, A., Antonova, V.: Theoretical and methodological foundations of the process of forming the evaluation competence of the future teacher of the disciplines of the general cultural cycle. Phys. Educ. Phys. Cult. **12**(117), 89–91 (2020)
36. Corsini, C.: La validità di contenuto delle prove INVALSI di comprensione della lettura. Giornale Italiano della Ricerca Educativa **VI**(10), 46–61 (2013)
37. Vertecchi, B.: Manuale della valutazione: analisi degli apprendimenti e dei contesti. FrancoAngeli, Milano (2003)
38. Castoldi, M.: Valutare a scuola. Carocci, Roma (2012)
39. Viganò, R.: Quality and the teaching profession: assessment as a resource. EDETANIA **52**, 269–285 (2017)
40. Maccario, D.: Valutare per promuovere il successo scolastico. Educ. Sci. Soc. **2**, 56–68 (2011)

41. Damiano, E.: L'insegnante. Identificazione di una professione. La Scuola, Brescia (2004)
42. Dutto, M.: Acqua alle funi. Per una ripartenza della scuola italiana. Vita e Pensiero, Milano (2013)
43. Viganò, R.: Educational research between practices and institutional policies. Ital. J. Educ. Res. **16**, 71–84 (2016)
44. Landri, P.: Governing by standards: the fabrication of austerity in the Italian educational system. Educ. Inq. **5**(1), 1–17 (2014)
45. Grion, V., Restiglian, E.: Valutare nella scuola e nei contesti educativi. CLEUP, Padova (2020)
46. Palumbo, M., Pandolfini, V.: Valutare per migliorare tra retorica e ricerca. RIV: Rassegna Italiana di Valutazione **60**, 85–101 (2014)
47. Hamtini, T.M.: Evaluating e-learning programs: an adaptation of Kirkpatrick's model to accommodate e-learning environments. J. Comput. Sci. **4**(8), 693–698 (2008)
48. De Ketele, J.-M., Gerard, F.-M.: La validation des épreuves d'évaluation selon l'approche par les compétences. Mesure et évaluation en education **28**(2), 1–26 (2005)
49. Salkind, N.J.: Encyclopedia or Research Design. SAGE, London (2010)

E-Learning and Disciplinary Teaching: Issues and Innovations in Contemporary Higher Education

Narrative Learning and Transformative Practices in Higher Distance Education

Antonella De Blasio(✉) and Fiorella Vinci

Università eCampus, Novedrate, Italy
{antonella.deblasio,fiorella.vinci}@uniecampus.it

Abstract. This study investigates the relationship between e-learning and disciplinary teaching through the magnifying lens of narration, understood as a cognitive tool for learning. Applied in a digital environment, narrative learning is particularly effective because it favours a kind of transformative learning able to create Communities of inquiry where the knowledge is constructed through critical reflection and shared with others.

The contribution is divided in two parts. The first part explores the ways in which e-learning, thanks to a renewed methodological awareness, can reshape the university disciplinary teaching by fostering the development of new interdisciplinary relationships. In the second part, an empirical research on the use of narrative as a teaching tool in e-learning activities such as Virtual Labs and e-Portfolio exercises is presented.

Keywords: Narrative learning · eLearning · Distance education · Disciplinary teaching · Transformative learning · Cognitive-constructivist perspective

1 Introduction

The concept of disciplinary teaching appears fruitful in the analysis of the recent transformations of the university ecosystem not only for the historical-sociological resonances it evokes, but also from an epistemological point of view. In fact, it seems extremely appropriate in the identification of a perspective of analysis of the transformations of the university that does not propose the dichotomy between structuralist and cognitive traditions, but seeks to bring the two traditions into dialogue [1]. In particular, a reflection on didactics seems useful since it allows the connection between two distinct levels of analysis: that of academic contexts, with their institutional transformations, and the techno-cultural one, with the impact of major transformations – such as those related to the digital revolution – on individual disciplinary traditions and university learning.

Starting from some reflections on how e-learning could help to change disciplinary teaching, this study aims to propose an investigation of the cognitive-constructivist theoretical perspective and to present exploratory empirical research based on narrative learning.

The thesis guiding the research stems from the idea that narrative learning may constitute a specific type of reflective learning that seems particularly suitable in an

G. Casalino et al. (Eds.): HELMeTO 2021, CCIS 1542, pp. 309–320, 2022.
https://doi.org/10.1007/978-3-030-96060-5_22

e-learning environment and seems to foster transformative learning. The latter favors the active involvement of both students and teachers through the creation of a didactic aiming at critical understanding.

The study is divided into two parts. The first is devoted to an analysis of the methodological innovation introduced by the e-learning and a theoretical analysis of the contribution that narrative learning can make to disciplinary teaching. The second part is dedicated to the presentation of an empirical research based on the introduction of narrative as a teaching tool in an e-learning environment and to an analysis of its effects.

These effects were derived from the e-activies (Virtual Lab and ePortfolio) of two distinct telematics university courses, on the basis of student performance and disciplinary teaching.

2 Disciplinary Teaching and E-learning

The major changes that e-learning causes on disciplinary teaching in universities seem to have a methodological impulse. The clarification of the methodological issue seems relevant both in reference to the phenomenology of innovation and in relation to its analysis and the epistemological meanings it conveys. The methodenstreit, vector of the e-learning if applied to disciplinary didactics, reveals a specific pragmatic-analytical value. On the one hand, it offers fundamental instructions on the consequences of technological innovation on didactics, and on the other hand, it brings to light the epistemological challenges intrinsic in the subject of disciplinary didactics.

The use of digital tools does not only seem to activate a reflection on the didactic effectiveness of the tool itself within the individual disciplines, but also a reflection on the curricular effectiveness of the teaching of the individual discipline with respect to a specialised but necessarily multidisciplinary training. It also seems to operate not only vertically, like within the relationship between disciplinary teaching and individual teacher, but also horizontally, fostering relationships between multiple interdisciplinary fields of knowledge.

Drawing on Morin's [2] idea of the primacy of analysis and separation over interconnection and synthesis in the organization of knowledge and its teaching, which is widespread in Western societies, it could be argued that e-learning can help to bring out the limits of such a primacy while pointing to the social dynamics of change.

The analysis on the impact of e-learning on disciplinary didactics, combining technological innovation to didactic action, conveys firstly a specific theoretical legacy: it reveals the fruitfulness of a cognitive-constructivist perspective of analysis. According to Vygotskij and Lurija [3], as Glaserfield points out to rediscover the roots of constructivism [4], this perspective highlights in particular the functions of technology in the social innovation. The technological tools not only change the ways through which the individuals live in the world, but above all, the way through which they can vary their relation with their history, modifying the knowledge they have of the world and the possibility to transmit it. The attention that constructivism turns to technology is very interesting because it is far from reproducing a preconstructed world in which individuals find themselves acting passively. Instead, it contributes to bring out the active role of individuals in modifying their social relations by changing the meanings that they attribute themselves to their actions. In this perspective, technology takes on value in understanding the social as it helps to generate new relational logics [5]. As Boudon [6] underlines, the social change often does not derive from a predefined individual plan, but from the cognitive and normative mechanisms that individuals constantly activate in their daily lives.

Dubar [7] helps to specify this perspective of analysis, applying it to professional contexts and emphasizing that the actions of subjects who share work roles, contributing to the creation of a defined work environment, is a professional action conditioned by the previous meanings attributed to their professional experiences. At the same time, it is remodeled thanks to cognitive and normative adjustments emerging from the social relations established in the professional environment [8].

This specific professional action appears as a reflexive didactic action [9, 10] if it is promoted in particular by the e-learning mode. First of all, the introduction of online or blended courses in a university degree course raises methodological questions on the use of the most suitable tools for transmitting certain disciplinary contents. The teacher's choice of the most suitable tool for achieving certain teaching goals, especially when the tool is digital and its use is usually uncertain, is a reflexive choice with a specific social logic. This choice, instead of strengthening the elitist and traditionally hierarchical character of academic disciplinary knowledge, leads the teacher towards what Habermas [11] has called inclusive communicative action. New learning frames appear: the search for the relationship with the other, colleague and/or student, it's not just a response to a physical need produced by the distance course, but takes the form of a social reorganization that contributes to redefine the disciplinary communities [12]. In this way, the common sense of disciplinary belonging, its collective plausibility, and its effectiveness are modified. The online educational environment exposes subjects to greater degrees of uncertainty compared to those required by a face-to-face teaching situation, giving rise to common needs for digital literacy, new interdisciplinary plausibility of didactic action. E-learning favours, among the actors involved in the teaching experience, the circulation of a daily reflexivity on the educational solutions adopted.

The reflexivity conveyed by e-learning outlines a reflexive action which, in disciplinary training, decentralizes the predominant function of the teacher to promote the discovery of a relational teaching environment. Within this environment, meanings are co-constructed not only in the presence of others, but with others and for others.

According to Donati [13], such a relational logic is attentional; in this environment the others become significant, and allow the subject to reinvent his own subjectivity and also the relationship that the subject has with his own disciplinary knowledge, its objectives, its forms of expression. The attentional relationship lives on logics and behavioural manners based on the eventual discovery of the other, on the possibility that with the other, with his differences, we can experience a common human condition. This kind of reflexivity establishes a specific form of connection between the motivations of the actors involved and the expressions of their actions, but above all it makes explicit the constitutive practical tension of didactic action, leading to the search for suitable teaching methods and practices.

3 Narrative Learning

Among the teaching methods defined as innovative, narration occupies a relevant position for its power to make interdisciplinary relationships explicit and thus reshape disciplinary teaching.

The relationship between narrative form and learning has been investigated by scholars belonging to different disciplinary fields, such as cognitive sciences, neuroscience, pedagogical sciences [14–17].

Since the origin of humankind, the human being shares stories, feeds on narratives. In other words, narrative is an anthropological, social, cultural constant, which manifests itself identically in time and space. Humans have always been attracted to stories and this incessant need for *life narratives*, of plausible fictions or fantastic tales can be explained by considering narratives as an essential element of life at trans-temporal level [18].

The scholar Gottschall [19], who is interested in evolutionary theory and fiction, moving between biology, psychology, neuroscience and literature, points out that narrative represents an evolutionary advantage for the human species, a stage that allows a development in the construction of the human community.

As already intuited by the American psychologist Bruner [20], narrative thinking is the main cognitive device through which individuals organize experience and social exchanges. According to Bruner, narration is the first interpretative and cognitive device that the human being, as a socio-culturally situated subject, makes use of in his life experience. Furthermore, he explains that from an early age, we develop our language skills in such a way that we are able to participate in conversations with our parents and peers, engaging narratively in the storytelling practices that are ubiquitous in our social contexts and physical environments.

The importance Bruner [21] ascribes to narration leads him to state that it is also a field of investigation in education and especially in learning psychology. He theorizes the existence of a narrative thinking, based on the criterion of verisimilitude and which has the characteristics of a story, through which it is possible to restore consistency and give meaning to personal events. Narrative is thus the cognitive mode par excellence because it is not only an afterwards reconstruction of experience but also provides the formats and patterns of experience itself, and is thus fundamental in the construction of meaning. In today's academic world, storytelling is gaining renewed attention from practitioners and academics across a variety of disciplines, as it expands into the formal pedagogy of education [22].

Scholars have showcased the relevance of storytelling in education. It allows to emotionally engage students with learning objectives and strengthen their comprehension and capacity to learn [23, 24].

Literature is full of examples in which stories are used effectively within a group to teach various disciplines, from scientific ones [25] to artistic ones [26]. Just to give an example, in Business Schools and many training programs, educational practices which use life stories and educational biographies are increasingly being adopted.

Several studies show that the introduction of narrative elements and interactive storytelling is also effective in web-based learning platforms, as it can foster student engagement and help develop their critical thinking. As highlighted by Clark and Rossiter [27], narrative learning must be understood in a dual sense:

- as a chance to fostering learning through stories
- and conceptualization learning as a narrative process.

In the analysis of the effects of narrative learning on disciplinary teaching in a web-based university context, the combination of these two concepts appears particularly relevant.

This study points out the possibility that narrative learning constitutes a communicative frame suitable for enhancing the constructivist dimension of learning [28]. According to a constructivist framework «learning is a process of sense-making, of adding and synthesizing new information within existing knowledge structures» [29].

Moreover, in the educational setting, students do not acquire knowledge passively, since they make connections with their previous experiences and knowledge, they are instead encouraged by the teacher to cooperative learning in which tasks and contents are based on real and contextual problems. Knowledge is thus acquired through experience. In this perspective, the teacher is not the one who transmits information, but the one who facilitates learning.

When a student listens to a story, the vocabulary areas of the brain are not the only one activated, but also the sensory areas of the cortex, as the topic gets activated through a story [30]. The stories and its characters are able to involve students and provide a structure for remembering concepts and creating vivid mental images [31].

According to Mar and Oatley [32] the brain experiences the story in the same way it would as if the events were actually happening to the listener. In addition, stories foster empathy and allow us to understand the thoughts and feelings of others [33].

Storytelling is able to combine the different levels involved in learning by being both a support strategy and a cognitive construct [34, 35]. Being a teaching technique, narrative learning stresses helping students making connections with their experience and knowledge, showing how to construct knowledge for themselves. In this way narrative learning could be analyzed as a transformative learning able to create Communities of inquiry where the knowledge is constructed through critical reflection and shared with others.

The Community of inquiry framework assumes that learning takes place in a community of individuals with a common goal of constructing knowledge through critical and participatory reflection. The Community of inquiry model suggests that certain collaborative interactions create a "presence at distance", which facilitates the emergence of a new educational experience [36], which reshapes the distance between subjects and roles.

The use of storytelling as a learning tool has been fostered by the emergence in the last two decades of the reflective paradigm in education, according to which the goal is not the acquisition of knowledge, but the understanding and development of competence. In this respect, narrative learning can promote transformative learning, which is in contrast to the more common process of assimilative learning, based on the fact that learners simply acquire new information that can easily fit into their pre-existing knowledge structures. In transformative learning the subject expands his/her consciousness by questioning about their own, beliefs, assumptions, and perspective on their purpose. For all these reasons students are thus more motivated, independent, rational, collaborative and empathetic.

This kind of change can help to reshape disciplinary communities, fostering a dual and complementary innovative mechanism. First of all, the change can make disciplinary boundaries more elastic, for instance by promoting collaboration between teachers of different disciplines in the design of university courses. Secondly, the change can concern the transformation of the relationships between teachers and learners. Indeed, it may eradicate the traditionally hierarchical character of such relationships by enhancing the contribution that learners can make to teachers both in adapting teaching methods and in promoting disciplinary contexts in which students play an active role.

4 The Empirical Research

4.1 Research Design

After having reflected on the importance of narrative in life, especially for humans and for the field of education, we will now focus on the ways in which narrative can be used effectively as a learning tool. For this purpose, we will draw on our own experiences as teachers and in addition we have developed an experimental research study. We followed an action research model in which the researcher is directly involved in educational practice also as a teacher [37].

The empirical research was designed as an exploratory one, which does not inspect a defined research hypothesis and does not use a representative population sample, but reconstructs a teaching act in order to highlight its transformative mechanisms. The research arose from the need to understand the effects of using narration in an e-learning environment in the teaching of two specific disciplines.

To this purpose, two experimental teaching situations, carried out in two different courses of study at the eCampus telematic university, were initially identified: the Virtual Labs organized for the course in Text Analysis Methodologies (Literature, Art, Music and Performing Arts course of the Faculty of Arts at eCampus University based in Como) and the exercises that students upload onto their ePortfolio for the course in Sociology of Economic Processes (Science of Communication course of the Faculty of Law based in Como). At a later stage, the two teaching situations were analysed as two case studies from a methodological point of view. The Virtual Labs and the exercises are two online non-compulsory supplementary teaching activities.

The research was carried out between January and June 2021 and involved 56 students in the case of the Virtual Labs and 120 students in the case of the e-Portfolio exercises.

The dynamics of the didactic situation were reconstructed by comparing the specificities of the analyzed situation with a similar didactic situation in the previous academic year, in which narrative learning was not used.

In the identification of research variables:

a) for what concerns the Virtual Labs we have considered as research variables the disciplinary performance of the students involved in the Virtual Lab based on narrative learning. We have measured this performance by evaluating the final exam grade which was compared with the disciplinary performance of students who followed the same activity in the previous year without the application of narrative learning;
b) for the ePortfolio exercises we have considered as research variables:

1) the number of students who chose to carry out the exercise on a topic using a typical narrative learning methodology, such as life stories, compared with the number of students who chose to carry out the exercise on another topic during the same period;
2) the marks assigned to exercises using narrative learning compared to those not using it;
3) the marks achieved in the final examination of the students who did the exercises on the topic using life stories compared to the performance of the students who did not choose that topic.

4.2 Virtual Labs: Storytelling Activities and Outcomes

Virtual Labs are series of technical-practical meetings in which teachers can explore particular topics in depth, accompanied by practical exercises. These are learning environments that allow students to explore concepts and theories together with the teacher.

In particular, the workshops held for the Text Analysis Methodology course are aimed at acquiring the basic terms and concepts of narratology and want to enable students to recognize and analyze the main narrative structures and techniques used in communication, with particular reference to literature.

In the relevant period, four examination sessions were held and, before each examination session, four 1-h Virtual Labs were organized, for a total of twelve meetings. Each meeting was attended by 10 to 14 students for a total of 56 students.

One of the activities proposed during the workshops concerns, for example, the concept of focalization developed by the literary theorist Gerard Genette [38]. 'Focalization' concerns the analysis of some point of view in a narrative text. Genette distinguishes three types or degrees of focalization: zero, internal and external. A text is zero-focalized if and only if the narrator says more than any of the characters already knows. The narrator is then omniscient and outside the story, he moves freely in time and space, inside and outside the characters' minds, and is often not materialized by any physical presence. A text is internally focalized if and only if in it the reader receives only information about what a specific character believes, pretends to believe, thinks, hopes, fears, and so on. A text is externally focalized if and only if the narrator says less than the character already knows.

There are different types of exercises:

- the first consist in writing a story and reading it aloud, letting the students choose the most suitable point of view;
- the second exercise asks students to think of a novel they know and indicate which point of view is used;
- the third exercise asks them to retell one of the shared stories by changing the point of view.

Students are asked to share their story or example, and also to listen and learn from each other's stories. It is recommended to held this with small groups of people for better results.

Storytelling devices in the educational field assume a particular relevance when the aim is to identify previously ignored features in relation to already known elements. Students are required to adopt a critical learning method that connects theoretical skills and empirical analysis and thus develop independent thinking.

The completed exercises help the student to acquire a technical language. They usually spend time, in the initial stages of introduction to new material, exploring the appropriate use of language and specific or technical terms.

Within the Virtual Labs it was also important to provide formative feedback on the shared learning, expounding the appropriateness of the examples to the task. It is useful for the feedback to focus on the appropriateness of the examples chosen and on the inclusion of sufficient and appropriate details. Formative feedback is also useful in providing opportunities for students to explore other ways in which theory can be related to or developed from experience.

The disciplinary performance, as measured by the final exam grade of students who participated in the Virtual Labs during the reporting period, is higher (average 23.5) than that of students who participated in the same months last year in the webinars, where narrative learning was not used (average 22.8). Participation in the Virtual Lab did not result in any marks being added to the final exam grade.

4.3 ePortfolio Exercises: Life Stories and Their Didactic Effects

The exercises that students submit in their e-Portfolios are a form of interactive teaching used in many e-learning courses. During the exercises, students work on a number of topics proposed to them by the professors and relating to specific subject areas. They submit to their personal e-learning platform known as the student's e-Portfolio where the professor reviews the work and provides the student with feedback, assessing in particular the student's internalization of the course content and his or her degree of personal reworking of it.

The exercises submitted to teachers via ePortfolio are relevant to this study as they not only constitute a type of interactive teaching but also present the building blocks of reflective teaching. These elements include the feedback that the teacher gives to the student, which in some cases leads him or her to rework the exercise sent.

By acknowledging the interactive dimension of the exercises delivered via ePortfolio, this research analyzed how the constitutive reflexivity of these e-tivities changes if the exercise makes use of narration as a teaching tool.

The professor of the Sociology of Economic Processes course has included, as one of the many topics proposed to the students, the presentation and commentary of a second-level research study carried out by using life stories.

The purpose of the research concerns the choice of young farmers enrolled in the national Coldiretti (the largest association representing and assisting Italian agriculture) to become agricultural entrepreneurs and is examined through their autobiographical stories. The aim of this experiment was to understand the effects of using autobiographical stories in the teaching of a specific discipline such as economic sociology.

The teacher wanted to observe the effects on student's participation and performance when a specific topic, such as self-entrepreneurship, was introduced through a narrative method.

The analysis of the first results strikes the teacher-researcher for the following evidence. In the period under consideration, out of 120 exercises delivered in the students' e-Portfolio, 78 students chose to analyse the text based on the life stories out of five different themes proposed. The analysis reveals a second piece of evidence: all the exercises were rated higher than the others.

The teacher can give the exercises a score ranging from 0 to 3. The variability of the score depends above all on the degree of completeness, critical interpretation and ability to exemplify that the exercise reveals. The average rating for the exercises presented using life stories is 2.6, the rating for all other exercises is an average of 1.9. The highest score of the exercises based on life stories depends on a specific argumentative structure; 60 of the 78 exercises in fact present the research according to a dialogical scheme, i.e. the students intersperse the presentation and reconstruction of the stories of the various subjects who wrote the stories with autobiographical accounts, as if the life story learned and told again questioned their own biographical experience, prompting the students to tell in turn their professional stories and, frequently, those of their families. Finally, there is a third element of analysis that emerges from the comparison of the exercises involving the research on self-entrepreneurship carried out by means of the life stories with all other exercises handed in during the same time period: the disciplinary performance measured by the final exam grade of the students who carried out the exercise presenting the research on life stories is higher. Their performance is 24.2 compared to 22.6 for the other students who chose other texts to analyse. This element seems to be connected to the previous one and specifically concerns the didactics of the discipline. All students commenting on the research on self-entrepreneurship, in fact, understand and explain effectively, also with examples, an abstract concept that is fundamental in the teaching of economic sociology, such as that of complex rationality. Students who present other topics and research equally related to complex rationality find it more difficult to trace back from the empirical topic to its conceptualization. Why do more than half of the students out of five proposed topics choose to illustrate a research conducted through life stories?

Due to the exploratory nature of the research, rather than providing definite answers to this question, it allows us to formulate hypotheses that may be useful for further research. A first observation relates to the superior evaluation and recurrence of the dialogical structure of text-based exercises on life stories. The life stories learned in an e-learning environment do not only attract and involve the student in the learning process, but also activate cognitive reframing, give the possibility to reinterpret the original story and, above all, transmit conditions of similarity-differentiation. They do not arouse so much identification but rather personal contributions, critical reinterpretations of the themes learnt.

4.4 Research Discussion Outcomes

The superior performance of the students who participated in the Virtual Lab and carried out the exercises is very significant from a didactic-disciplinary point of view as it reveals that narrative learning develops commitment, involvement and a desire to deepen the discipline, facilitates interconnections between different themes of the course, and, above all, encourages processes of conceptual abstraction. The students involved in these didactic activities, in fact, have developed the ability to connect the different themes and concepts exposed in the course and to elaborate interdisciplinary links. Concepts as invariable forms of knowledge, as illustrated by Simmel [39], lend themselves not only to multiple disciplinary declinations, but also to the transmission of their specific disciplinary meanings, thus promoting the possibility of interdisciplinary analysis and knowledge.

Elements of narrative and storytelling are effective in enhancing the experiential dimension of online education [40] and to align on principles of learner-centeredness and agency [41]. The students achieve greater ability to organize course content. So, the authors are confident that the adopted strategies had a positive impact on learners' experience.

In an e-learning environment, learning a subject matter through narratives attracts students, as if storytelling manages to redefine the learning environment not only by making the topics more comprehensible but almost by giving the environment a new physicality, unprecedented communicative possibilities and autonomous participation in the learning situation.

However, in order to better evaluate the results of such an approach in terms of learning outcomes and learners' experience, an extension of the assessment strategies within the program's learning environment, is also required.

5 Conclusions

In recent decades, societies, and with them disciplinary specializations, have undergone extraordinary transformations, real metamorphoses [42] that have concerned the formation of knowledge but also its transmission and learning.

This contribution proposes a theoretical reflection, starting from an approach that wants to analyse some structural variables – related to the organization of e-learning with regard to disciplinary teaching – from a cognitivist perspective.

The first part explores the ways in which e-learning, thanks to a renewed methodological awareness, can reshape the university disciplinary teaching by fostering the development of new interdisciplinary relationships. In the second part of this paper, an empirical research on the use of narrative as a teaching tool in e-learning activities such as Virtual Labs and e-Portfolios is presented. This section highlights the consequences that a didactic method such as narrative learning – increasingly adopted in web-based learning environments – could have on university disciplinary teaching.

As the two case studies considered demonstrate, in e-learning and disciplinary learning, such narrative learning is effective because it creates a participatory and educationally effective learning environment. In particular the study found that students involved in the Virtual Lab based on narrative learning and the students who did the exercises on the topic using life stories tend to earn better grades.

Although the results of this studies provide compelling evidence, we are aware of the fact that our research may have limitations. One of these concerns the fact that it involves a relatively small sample to be considered representative and moreover, it involves only students who have chosen to carry out non-obligatory supplementary teaching activities, thus students who tend to be more motivated. However, it is possible to affirm that storytelling is a valuable tool for learning, especially during this period of intense social isolation, and can be used in different ways to facilitate learning in higher education contexts. Narrative learning seems particularly effective in transforming disciplinary teaching. This kind of change can help reshaping teaching communities by fostering interdisciplinary dialogue and changing the shared meaning of disciplinary knowledge.

Author Contributions. Although this article is the result of a common reflection, Introduction and Sects. 2, 4.3 and 4.4 are attributable to Fiorella Vinci, while Sects. 3, 4.1, 4.2 and Conclusions are attributable to Antonella De Blasio.

References

1. Berthelot, J.M.: Epistémologie des sciences sociales. PUF, Paris (2001)
2. Morin, E.: La testa ben fatta. Raffaello Cortina Editori, Milano (2000)
3. Vygotskij, L., Lurija, A.: Etjuudy po istorii provedenija. Obezjana, prinitiv, rebënok, Gosizdat, Mosca-Leningrado (1930); trad. it. La scimmia, l'uomo primitivo, il bambino. Studi sulla storia del comportamento, Mimesis Edizioni, Milano (2020)
4. von Glasersfeld, E.: Radical Constructivism: A Way of Knowing and Learning. The Falmer Press, London and Washington (1995); trad. it. Il costruttivismo radicale. Una via per conoscere ed apprendere. Odradek, Roma (2016)
5. Olson, M.: La logique de l'action collective. PUF, Paris (1978)
6. Boudon, R.: Social mechanisms without black boxes. In: Hedström, P., Swedberg, R. (eds.) Social Mechanisms. An Analytical Approach to Social Theory, pp. 172–203. Cambridge University Press, Cambridge (1998)
7. Dubar, C.: La socializzazione. Come si costruisce l'identità sociale. Il Mulino, Bologna (2004)
8. Rivoltella, P.C., Rossi, P.: L'agire Didattico. Editrice La Scuola, Brescia (2012)
9. Mortari, L.: Apprendere dall'esperienza. Il pensare riflessivo nella Formazione. Carocci, Roma (2003)
10. Ardizzone, P., Rivoltella, P.C.: Media e tecnologie per la didattica. Vita e Pensiero, Milano (2007)
11. Habermas, J.: Theorie des kommunikativen Handelns, vol. 1: Handlungsrationalität und gesellschaftliche Rationalisierung Frankfurt a.M; trad. it. La teoria dell'agire comunicativo, vol. 1. Razionalità nell'azione e razionalizzazione sociale. Bologna, Il Mulino (1986)
12. Rivoltella, P.C.: Comunità tecnologiche. La scuola, Brescia (2017)
13. Donati, P.P.: Sociologia della riflessività. Come si entra nel dopo-moderno, Bologna, Il Mulino (2011)
14. Minsky, M.: The Society of Mind. Simon & Schuster, New York (1985)
15. Schank, R.C.: Tell Me a Story: Narrative and Intelligence. Northwestern University Press, Evanston (1995)
16. Ryan, M.-L.: Narratology and cognitive science: a problematic relation. Style **44**(4), 469–495 (2010)
17. Armstrong, P.B.: Neuroscience, narrative, and narratology. Poetics Today **40**(3), 395–428 (2019)
18. Calabrese, S.: La fiction e la vita. Letteratura, benessere e salute. Mimesis, Milano (2017)
19. Gottschall, J.: The Storytelling Animal: How Stories Make Us Human. Houghton Mifflin Harcourt, Boston (2012)

20. Bruner, J.: The narrative construction of reality. Crit. Inq. **18**, 1–21 (1991)
21. Bruner, J.: The Culture of Education. Harvard University Press, Cambridge (1996)
22. Hamstra, C.: Complexity storytelling: the science of complexity within the art of communication. Emergence: Complex. Organ. **19**, 1–6 (2017)
23. Woodhouse, H.: Storytelling in university education: emotion, teachable moments, and the value of life. J. Educ. Thought (JET)/Revue De La Pensée Éducative **45**(3), 211–238 (2011)
24. Jarrett, K.: Developing the art of storytelling as a pedagogical tool for academics: Articles from the 2018 University of Brighton Learning and Teaching Conference, Brighton, UK (2019)
25. Horton, H.: Teaching science through story. J. Aust. Sci. Teach. Assoc. **59**(3), 38–47 (2013)
26. Zander, M.J.: Tell me a story: the power of narrative in the practice of teaching art. Stud. Art Educ.: A J. Issues Res. Art Educ. **48**(2), 189–203 (2013)
27. Clark, M., Rossiter, M.: Narrative learning in adulthood. New Dir. Adult Continuing Educ. **119**, 61–70 (2008)
28. Ehrlich, D., Ehrlich, J., Haberyan, A.: Storytelling in a first-year seminar. InSight: A J. Sch. Teach. **15**, 105–121 (2020)
29. Arlidge, J.: Constructivism: is anyone making meaning in New Zealand adult and vocational education? New Zealand J. Adult Learn. **28**(1), 34 (2000)
30. Chow, H.M., Mar, R.A., Xu, Y., Liu, S., Wagage, S., Braun, A.R.: Embodied comprehension of stories: interactions between language regions and modality specific neural systems. J. Cogn. Neurosci. **26**(2), 279–295 (2014)
31. Green, M.C.: Storytelling in teaching. Observer - Assoc. Psychol. Sci. **17**(4), 37–39 (2004)
32. Mar, R., Oatley, K.: The function of fiction is the abstraction and simulation of social experience. Perspect. Psychol. Sci. **3**(3), 173–192 (2008)
33. Zak, P.J.: Why inspiring stories make us react: the neuroscience of narrative. In: Cerebrum: The Dana Forum on Brain Science, p. 2 (2015)
34. Cherry, W.R., Jr.: The importance of story and storytelling in the classroom. Knowl. Quest **46**(2), 50–55 (2017)
35. van Rensburg, G.H., Botma, Y., Heyns, T., Coetzee, I.M.: Creative strategies to support student learning through reflection. South Afr. J. High. Educ. **32**(6), 604–618 (2018)
36. Garrison, D.R., Vaughan, N.D.: Blended Learning in Higher Education: Framework, Principles, and Guidelines. Jossey-Bass (2008)
37. Lipari, D., Scaratti, G.: Comunità di pratica. In: Quaglino, G.P. (ed.) Formazione. I metodi. Raffaello Cortina Editore, Milano, pp. 207–232 (2014)
38. Genette, G.: Figueres III. Seuil, Paris (1972)
39. Simmel, G.: Das Problem der historischen Zeit. Reuther und Reichard, Berlin (2016); tr. fr. Les problèmes de la philosophie de l'histoire. Une étude d'épistemologie. PUF, Paris (1987)
40. Lindgren, R., McDaniel, R.: Transforming online learning through narrative and student agency. Educ. Technol. Soc. **15**(4), 344–355 (2012)
41. Carver, R., King, R., Hannum, W., Fowler, B.: Toward a model of experiential e-learning. MERLOT J. Online Learn. Teach. **3**(3), 247–256 (2007)
42. Beck, U.: The Metamorphosis of the World. Polity Press, Cambridge (2016)

Challenges in Mathematics Learning at the University: An Activity to Motivate Students and Promote Self-awareness

Alessandro Iannella[1(✉)], Paola Morando[1], and Maria Luisa Spreafico[2]

[1] DISAA, Università degli Studi di Milano, Via Celoria 2, 20133 Milan, Italy
{alessandro.iannella,paola.morando}@unimi.it
[2] DISMA, Politecnico di Torino, Corso Duca degli Abruzzi 24, 10129 Turin, Italy
maria.spreafico@polito.it

Abstract. Math anxiety is always just around the corner. At the university, it makes students continuously postpone the Calculus exam, leading them into a vicious circle of low confidence and poor performance. To get out of this situation, students need to be motivated and involved. They also need to master metacognitive strategies that can support their learning process. In this paper, we present a digital activity entitled *Advent Calendar*, focused on storytelling and proposed through the logic of spacing. The aim is to increase students' motivation and self-awareness, but also to obtain learning analytics useful to monitor progress and solve any possible weaknesses with appropriate feedback. The activity was proposed using the tools offered by the Learning Management System (LMS) Moodle. It was tested in three university courses at two Italian universities, the University of Milan and the Polytechnic University of Turin, with students' active participation. This participation had a high impact on the results of the final examination. Feedback demonstrated positive feelings and good results in the motivation process, while the analytics showed a continuous approach to the study of mathematics.

Keywords: Teaching mathematics · Learning strategies · Educational technology

1 Introduction

The main purpose of general scientific degrees' Calculus courses is to introduce students to the scientific method of analysis, providing a suitable language and useful skills in order to effectively face other disciplinary courses. Unfortunately, this does not happen frequently. Many students see the Calculus exam as a stumbling block and try to postpone it as much as possible. This negative mindset can quickly turn into a cycle of low confidence, lower motivation, and poor performance [1, 2]. Math anxiety is always just around the corner [3]. The impact of the COVID-19 pandemic on education, with the distinctive rise of e-learning and digital platforms, has added to this emotional stress and forced teachers to quickly develop new teaching strategies.

G. Casalino et al. (Eds.): HELMeTO 2021, CCIS 1542, pp. 321–332, 2022.
https://doi.org/10.1007/978-3-030-96060-5_23

In this framework, designing preliminary actions aimed at fostering students' motivation and self-awareness is an essential challenge. Literature shows that students with higher learning motivation "achieve significantly higher test scores, enjoy learning more, have more positive self-concepts, make greater use of deep learning strategies and engage to a greater extent in autonomous self-regulated learning" [4; see also 5, 6].

Storytelling can support motivation. Its application to mathematics gives a concrete form and a familiar connotation to abstract concepts, involving emotions and imagination at the same time. "A story tends to have more depth than a simple example" [7]. Several authors have investigated the benefits of storytelling as a powerful medium for teaching and learning mathematics [8–10]. A narrative scenario downplays disciplinary topics and leads students to tackle challenging problems that they would seldom face in a more serious context. Stories and their characters can involve students and provide a structure for remembering concepts, and creating vivid mental images [7, 11]. Bruner underlined that "many scientific and mathematical hypotheses start their lives as little stories or metaphors" [12].

Metacognition can strengthen students' self-awareness. It is essential to focus on the ways in which students manage their study, teaching them appropriate strategies to monitor their own learning. One of the most effective metacognitive control strategies is *spacing*. Spacing consists of spreading out study time across a sufficiently long period in order to produce a more long-lasting learning [13]. It requires planning, however, and students are often unable to do that.

In a digital environment, learning analytics are essential. Tools provided by Learning Management Systems (LMS)—such as Canva, Moodle and Blackboard—make it easy to track students' progress. Teachers can provide global or individual feedback and act promptly on any potential weaknesses. In addition, they can monitor students' participation in the course activities, especially if it is delivered entirely online. In the university context, learning analytics are a powerful resource in view of the final exam.

This paper describes the *Advent Calendar*, a non-conventional digital learning activity designed to work on motivation and awareness (see *Activity Design & Implementation*). We present its features (see *Activity Features*), we provide some examples (see *Unwrapping the Gifts*), and we comment on the results of a pilot test (see *Results*).

2 Activity Design and Implementation

The *Advent Calendar* activity is inspired by the logic of the special calendar used to count the days until Christmas. It combines storytelling and spacing. Every day, students carry out a Christmas-themed mathematical exercise: Santa Claus, the elves and the reindeer are facing problems that can be solved by exploiting suitable mathematics tools introduced during a Calculus' course.

The activity can be carried out using Moodle assignments, along with a Google Drawings file. Google Drawings makes it possible to create an interactive image of the Advent Calendar, which can be embedded in a Moodle page (see Fig. 1). Each gift box is linked to the page of a single exercise hosted inside a Moodle assignment[1]. The Moodle assignment's *restrict access* feature can be used in order to allow students to enter and submit their exercise only on the corresponding day[2]. The first student who submits the correct solution is awarded with his/her name on the corresponding calendar's gift box.

Fig. 1. The *Advent Calendar* activity inside a Moodle page. Each gift box is linked to an exercise.

In order to make the activity effective, it is crucial to give students personalised feedback on their answers or to publish a complete solution to compare with. Moodle assignments provide teachers with a wide range of combinable feedback, such as global or between-the-lines comments, evaluation rubrics, scoring scales or offline gradesheets[3]. In addition, students' submission offers ongoing assessment information that can help them make instructional decisions. For example, teachers can identify and resolve possible weaknesses or track the developing proficiency levels of the individual student in view of the final assessment.

The activity can also be gamified using a system of rewards with the aim of fostering participation and involvement. Students obtain a score for every correct exercise completed within the required time frame. The score distribution starts from 100 for the first exercise submitted and decreases by one for subsequent uploads. This decision aims to

---

[1] Teachers can also use H5P to create an interactive Advent Calendar. H5P is a free, content authoring plugin that can be integrated with Moodle (see https://h5p.org/content-types/advent-calendar, https://moodle.org/plugins/mod_hvp).

[2] Teachers can use the *restrict access* feature to edit the availability of any Moodle's activity or course section according to certain conditions such as dates, groups, grades or activities completion (see https://docs.moodle.org/311/en/Restrict_access).

[3] See https://docs.moodle.org/311/en/Assignment_settings#Feedback_types, https://docs.moodle.org/311/en/Assignment_settings#Grade.

stimulate spacing and to promote regular participation rather than rewarding speed of delivery.

At the end of the activity, a forum can be opened in order to invite students to send Christmas greetings to their colleagues using a mathematical language. It may be useful to stimulate students' participation and curiosity by allowing them to view their colleagues' greetings only after they have sent their own. The Moodle forum type called Q&A enables this dynamic: students need to post before viewing other student's postings[4] (see Fig. 2).

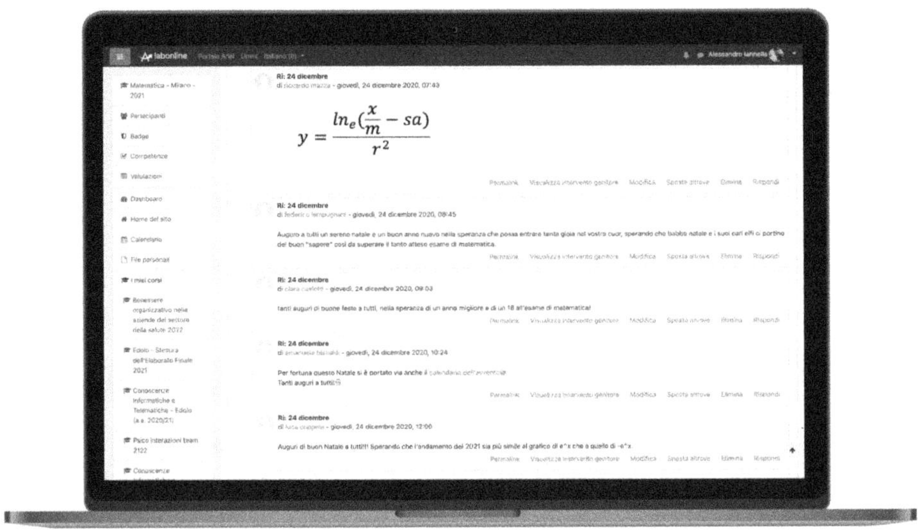

Fig. 2. The Q&A forum where students posted their wishes in mathematical language.

We proposed the *Advent Calendar* in the courses of *Mathematics* at the Polytechnic University of Turin (Degree in Architecture) and at the University of Milan (Degree in Agricultural Sciences and Technologies; Degree in Improvement and Protection of Mountain Environments) during the first semester of the academic year 2020–2021 (see *Results*). Due to the "easy-going" nature of the activity, the final score didn't contribute to the final exam's grade. However, we decided to reward students who sent at least one exercise by sending them a certificate of participation (see Fig. 3). In addition, following the gamification approach, the student with the highest score has been appointed *Mathematical Elf*, the second placed *Deputy Math Elf* and the third one *Second Deputy Math Elf*.

[4] See https://docs.moodle.org/311/en/Using_Forum#Which_forum_do_I_need.3F.

Fig. 3. Certificate given to the students who participated in the activity.

3 Activity Features

The teacher plays a key role in the proposed activity. S/he works on the emotional level, improving students' positive feelings, e.g. exploiting the Christmas spirit or stimulating competition. But s/he also works on the learning level, offering feedback and monitoring students.

From a methodological perspective, the *Advent Calendar* contains the two strategies mentioned above: storytelling in the case of the scenario, and spacing for the fruition modes. In terms of timing, the decision to open the submissions of each exercise at midnight turned out to be very effective. We noticed that many students waited until midnight to do the exercises immediately. The atmosphere was that of a real competition.

From a disciplinary perspective, there are some important aspects that allow us to reflect on the effectiveness of the experience. First of all, we think that the exercises should not be of increasing difficulty.

In fact, the surprise effect is very effective in encouraging students to open the gift box and have a look at the exercise every day, regardless of their ability to solve the previous day's exercise. Furthermore, to keep students engaged, the level of difficulty of each exercise must be chosen very carefully. Exercises that are too difficult or time-consuming risk discouraging students, while problems that are too simple are not challenging enough to stimulate reasoning and competition. A good solution taking both of these needs into account is to replace standard calculus exercises with authentic exercises, which require not only mathematical skills but also problem-solving abilities.

With regard to the review of the exercises, we believe that teachers can proceed in several ways, either by providing personalised feedback or by publishing the solved exercise. We tried both methods, without finding any particular differences (see *Results*). In one course, we published solutions after the deadline of every activity, uploading the file on Moodle. Only students who had submitted the exercise were allowed to see the corresponding solution and most common mistakes were also reported and discussed. In the other two courses, we provided customised feedback, without publishing the solution.

The advantages of mixing didactic methodologies and digital tools through the *Advent Calendar* can be explored answering these research questions (see *Results*):

1. *Does the Advent Calendar promote positive emotions in Math learning?*
2. *Does the Advent Calendar improve each student's learning experience?*
3. *Is gamification effective in supporting spacing? Does it stimulate students to carry out the exercises day by day and accurately?*
4. *Does the participation in the proposed activities have a positive impact on the final exam?*

In order to answer these questions, we used the following parameters:

- students' feedback, measured via the comments posted in the forum and the e-mails sent to the teachers;
- students' reactions to the correction of an exercise, as evidenced by asking for further clarification and/or by repeating it;
- the analytics related to the participation to the activity, on an overall and student-centered level, with particular reference to persistence;
- the comparison between participation to the activity and the results of the final exam.

4 Unwrapping the Gifts

In order to better explain the activity, we provide some example exercises that appeared in the *Advent Calendar*.

1. *To accurately hang the light decorations, two pairs of elves place Santa's house in a reference system. If the first pair of elves hang the lights following a straight line from point A (5;0;4) to B (0;6;7) and the second pair from C (1;0;8) to D (3;5;0), will the wires touch each other? Use GeoGebra to check and demonstrate the solution* (see Fig. 4).

   The math purpose of this question is to revise the equation of straight lines in three-dimensional space and their intersections. The possibility of integrating a GeoGebra content in a Moodle assignment—through embedding or a specific plug-in[5]—allows students to check their computations (using CAS calculator) and provides a three dimensional representation of the problem improving their mathematical spatial visualization ability (using the 3D calculator).
2. *It's Christmas Eve and the elves Hildur, Hrólfur and Eyjólf are very busy wrapping the last few presents. Until now, they packed 24 gifts in all, but Hrólfur and Hildur together packed twice as many as Eyjólf did, and Hildur and Eyjólf together packed 2 more than Hrólfur did. How many presents did each elf prepare? Use Geogebra to provide a geometrical interpretation and representation of the problem.*

[5] See https://moodle.org/plugins/assignsubmission_geogebra.

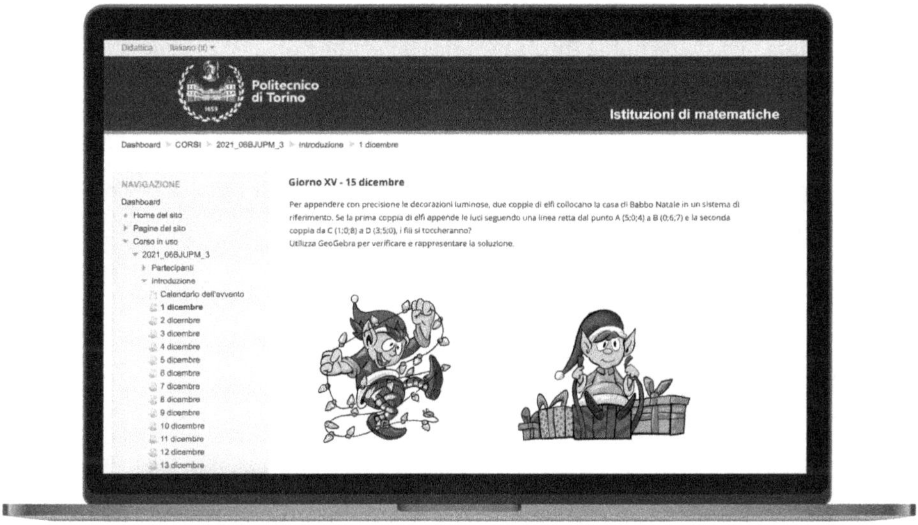

Fig. 4. Exercise 1 inside a Moodle assignment. Pictures by Nicola Spreafico.

The math content of this problem is very similar to the one of Exercise 1. In this case, instead of assigning a standard problem on the intersection of straight lines in 3D, we challenge the student to find the equations through an appropriate modeling of a real situation. Once the student has found the three equations, s/he has to use Geogebra to compare the algebraic and geometric representations of the problem.

3. *To surprise Santa Claus the elves are planning a ski slope. Following the suggestion of the Mathematical Elf they decided to build it following the graph of the function* $y = 10x\exp(-x/k)$ *when* $x \in [2, 8]$*. Indeed, the Mathematical Elf had given some further indications on how to choose the value of k, but the Elves often get distracted when it comes to mathematics and they only remember that k had to be a positive number. Can you help them choose a value of* $k > 0$ *so that the ski slope is all downhill? You can use GeoGebra to find or to check your solution.*

This is a non-standard and quite challenging question, requiring an open mind and a problem-solving approach to be tackled. In fact, the problem does not have a unique solution and can be faced in at least two different ways. The first possibility is to solve the problem analytically, computing the derivative of the function and studying its sign on the interval [2, 8] depending on the parameter *k*. In this case, after finding for which values of *k* the graphic of the function has a downhill slope for $x \in [2, 8]$, students can check the correctness of their solutions by drawing with GeoGebra the functions corresponding to the selected value of *k*. On the other hand, students with a more practical and less analytical inclination can approach the problem by drawing the family of functions depending on the parameter *k* using a slider in GeoGebra. In this way, visualizing the change of the slope of the function when *k* changes, they can easily find the solution experimentally, without performing any computation. In this case, we discussed pros and cons of the two approaches during the following lessons. In particular the analytic approach is more effective in finding the whole range of values of k, while the experimental one gives an immediate idea of how the shape of the function varies depending on k. We think that the use of dynamic softwares such as Geogebra can be very useful for carrying out a parametric problem such as this one (see Fig. 5).

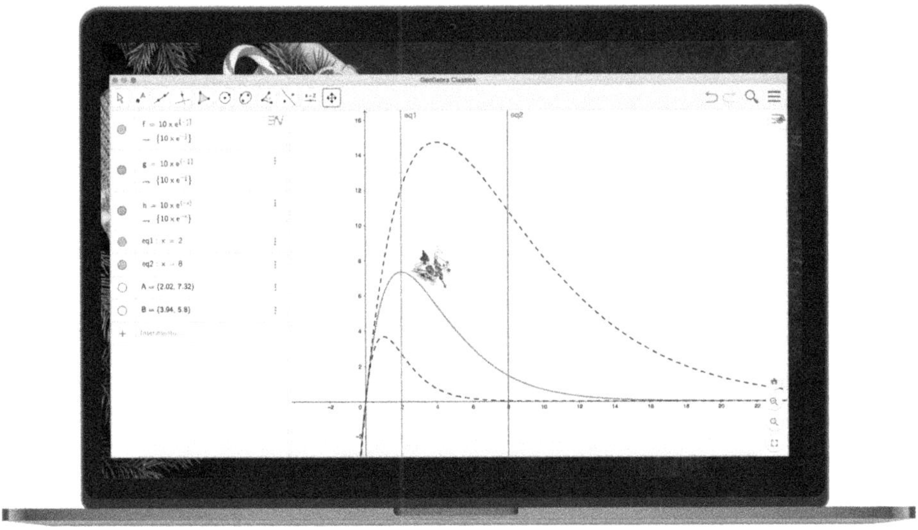

Fig. 5. Solution to Exercise 3. Graph made using Geogebra.

4. *The graph shows the trend in the number of letters and emails received from Santa Claus in the period 2010–2019. Use a spreadsheet to calculate the mean and standard deviation of the number of letters and emails considering the whole period* (see Fig. 6).

   In this case students have to collect data reading the graph and insert them in a spreadsheet. Once again, students worked in two different ways: someone built the formulas for the mean and the standard deviation into the worksheet step by step, while others made direct use of Google Sheets' or Microsoft Excel's statistical functions.

5 Results

Our pilot test of the *Advent Calendar* activity had 121 participants. This is about half of the students enrolled in the three university courses in which we proposed it. Despite the apparent "naive" scenario, the broad participation demonstrated that they got involved in the activity. We answer the research questions below (see *Activity Features*).

1. *Does the Advent Calendar promote positive emotions in Math learning?*

Many students posted funny and positive messages in the Moodle forum opened at the end of the activity, showing how it stimulated their imagination and contributed to their reconciliation with Mathematics. We present some of these posts. Even if some of

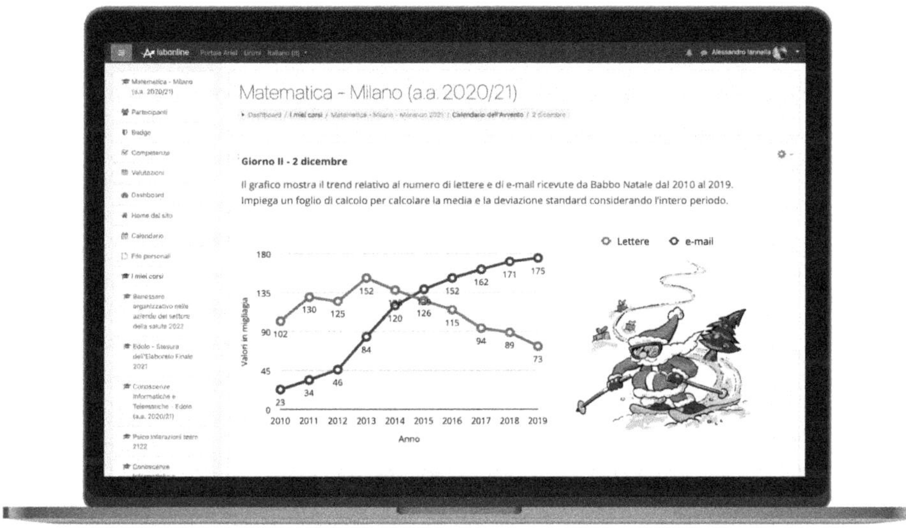

Fig. 6. Exercise 4 inside a Moodle assignment. Pictures by Nicola Spreafico.

them are not mathematically correct, they highlight the good emotion that the activity sparkled in the participants:

(a) "Merry Christmas to all! Hoping that the 2021 trend is more similar to the graph of e^x than to that of $-e^x$";
(b) "For a Christmas in which nostalgia for normality tends to $+\infty$, I wish everyone an indeterminate form that can only be solved through so much joy and the hope of being able to return, very soon, to hug your loved ones again! Greetings to all!";
(c) "I hope that the new year is represented for everyone by the function f (New Year) = hope + $(\text{joy})^2$ and that this can always be strictly increasing for [(January, 1, 2021) <= (month, day, 2021) <= (December, 31, 2021)]";
(d) "Even if the holidays are over, my New Year's greetings for all of you are equal to infinity. I would like to understand if my intervention can be positive, calculating Lim $x \to 0$ of holidays for wishes (0 times infinity) = I. F. I use asymptotic estimates for e^x when $x \to 0$ and I find that e^x is equivalent to $1 + x = 1$, so 0 times 1 = 0…I don't like it!! So I calculate Lim $x \to +$ infinity of holidays for wishes (+infinity times + infinity) = + infinity → yes, yes, I like it!!!".

Moreover, some students sent to the teachers emails sharing their positive feelings about the *Advent Calendar* experience:

(e) "I am finding this initiative very funny and above all very useful for reviewing some concepts of past topics. Finally, I congratulate her on the imagination with which she manages to create these exercises, they are truly incredible!";
(f) "This *Advent Calendar* is a beautiful idea, it had never been proposed to me";
(g) "Thank you for your dedication, thank you for the way you invented these games, thank you for teaching with all the passion in the world".

The engagement of the students is also confirmed by the fact that they played along, providing the answers to the questions in the Christmas spirit (for example: the elves wrap 19 gifts; the Snurf bear wins because its limit is greater; Santa Claus will pass by Marta's house…).

2. *Does the Advent Calendar improve each student's learning experience?*

The activity improved the overall student's learning experience. In fact, a problem-solving approach encourages students to believe in their ability to think mathematically and gives them the tools to apply their mathematical knowledge to solve hypothetical and real-world problems. When solving problems students are exploring mathematics throughout an authentic task instead of an abstract one. This helps them to make sense of mathematical ideas. Moreover, students were invited to use softwares, such as GeoGebra and spreadsheets, in order to explore the problems, to better visualise 3D situations, to check guesses and to find original solution strategies. Another reason that made the *Advent Calendar* experience effective in improving student's learning experience was the presence of a day-by-day feedback on students' activities. As we mentioned above (see *Activity Features*), we provide feedback in two different ways. Both the strategies turned out to be quite effective, since they made students struggle to solve the exercises and test ideas. Furthermore, personalised feedback highlighted a variety of mistakes and made it possible to suggest different approaches to solve the problem. In this way, the activity follows the logic of the *flipped classroom* [14], encouraging students to ask questions during lessons and to actively interact amongst them and with the teacher. It is worth noting also that a certain number of students viewed the exercise without then submitting it. Sometimes they were not able to solve the exercise, while other times they solved it only after the deadline, asking for suggestions or explanations by e-mail or during the following lesson. The day-by-day feedback on the level of understanding of the different topics allows teachers to suggest review activities for specific students, using Microsoft Teams' breakout rooms[6] or Moodle groups[7].

3. *Is gamification effective in supporting spacing? Does it stimulate students to carry out the exercises day by day and accurately?*

Students grasped the spirit of the challenge: 48% of them submitted at least half of the proposed exercises and 28% submitted at least 75% of them. We were surprised that several students submitted their solutions shortly after midnight, obviously waiting awake for the new exercise. Considering that the exercises were also solved during the weekends and taking into account students' access to the Moodle course, the activity demonstrated a good spread of the study across a sufficiently long period of time (*spacing*) for at least 60 students. The Christmas scenario and the logic of gamification certainly played a crucial role, but we also think that students understood the underlying seriousness of the activity. The feedback from the last lesson and the enthusiasm shown during the awarding of diplomas demonstrated that they appreciated its value in improving mathematical skills and in disseminating the importance of distributing learning and practice over time.

---

6 See https://support.microsoft.com/en-us/office/use-breakout-rooms-in-teams-meetings-7de1f48a-da07-466c-a5ab-4ebace28e461.

7 See https://docs.moodle.org/311/en/Groups.

4. *Does the participation in the proposed activities have a positive impact on the final exam?*

Students involved in the activity passed the exam during the first available session with a success rate 15% higher than the class rate. In the Architecture course, 80% of the participants passed the exams during the first session with respect to a mean of 65% success. In the two Agriculture courses, 65% of the participants passed the exams during the first session with respect to the mean of 49% success. In all the courses the medium mark of the participants was 27.5/30, while the medium mark of the students who didn't attend the activity was 23.7/30. These results may suggest that the activity had a positive impact on the final exam, although it is possible that only the most interested or skilled students participated. To confirm the effectiveness of the project, it would be necessary to compare the data with those of a control sample. It is also interesting to remark that most of the students which have been awarded with the maximum grade (30 e lode) participated in the activity—10/12 in the Architecture course and 11/12 in the two Agriculture courses.

6 Conclusions

Calculus course students generally experience a decline in interest and participation, probably due both to disaffection and to the growing complexity of the new subjects. Since Calculus courses are cumulative and require an active learning approach, it is very important to find strategies to keep students involved so that they do not fall behind as the teacher moves on. In this framework, the *Advent Calendar* activity provided an effective review tool, encouraging students to spread out study time across a sufficiently long period of time and to develop their problem-solving strategies.

The success of the activity can be quite surprising in an academic Calculus course because students usually just struggle to pass the exam. However, in this case students turned out to be very open minded and confident in their teachers. In addition, the activity was very useful to play down the subject, to revise previous topics throughout the daily assignments, and to bring students to a satisfactory level of understanding.

This positive attitude suggests that this kind of alternative teaching strategies are welcomed by students and deserve to be proposed again in the coming years, regardless of the online, blended, or face-to-face learning.

The activity can be replicated for different subjects and at different moments of the year, allowing a very effective review experience before the final exam. There are several scenarios into which exercises can be deployed in order to defuse the topics, enhance active participation and provide an unexpected creative side even to apparently hard subjects.

References

1. Ashcraft, M.H.: Math anxiety: personal, educational, and cognitive consequences. Curr. Dir. Psychol. Sci. **11**(5), 181–185 (2002)
2. Lithner, J.: University mathematics students' learning difficulties. Educ. Inq. **2**(2), 289–303 (2011)

3. Bjälkebring, P.: Math anxiety at the university: what forms of teaching and learning statistics in higher education can help students with math anxiety? Front. Educ. **4**(30), 1–30 (2019)
4. Brandenberger, C.C., Hagenauer, G., Hascher, T.: Promoting students' self-determined motivation in maths: results of a 1-year classroom intervention. Eur. J. Psychol. Educ. **33**(2), 295–317 (2018)
5. Gottfried, A.E., Marcoulides, G.A., Gottfried, A.W., Oliver, P.H.: Longitudinal pathways from maths intrinsic motivation and achievement to maths course accomplishments and educational attainment. J. Res. Educ. Effect. **6**(1), 68–92 (2013)
6. Pekrun, R., vom Hofe, R., Blum, W., Frenzel, A.C., Goetz, T., Wartha, S.: Development of mathematical competencies in adolescence. The PALMA longitudinal study. In: Prenzel, M. (ed.) Studies on the Educational Quality of Schools. The Final Report on the DFG Priority Programme, pp. 17–37. Waxmann (2007)
7. Green, M.C.: Storytelling in teaching. Observer **17**(4), 37–39 (2004)
8. Albano, G., Pierri, A.: Digital storytelling in mathematics: a competence-based methodology. J. Ambient Intell. Humaniz. Comput. **8**(2), 301–312 (2017)
9. Casey, B., Kersh, J.E., Mercer Young, J.: Storytelling sagas: an effective medium for teaching early childhood mathematics. Early Child. Res. Q. **19**(1), 167–172 (2004)
10. Schiro, M., Lawson, D.: Oral Storytelling and Mathematics. Pedagogical and Multicultural Perspectives. SAGE Publications, Thousand Oaks (2004)
11. Green, M.C., Brock, T.C.: The role of transportation in the persuasiveness of public narratives. J. Pers. Soc. Psychol. **79**(5), 401–421 (2000)
12. Bruner, J.S.: Actual Minds, Possible Worlds. Harvard University Press, Cambridge (1986)
13. Weinstein, Y., Sumeracki, M., Caviglioli, O.: Understanding How We Learn. A Visual Guide. Routledge, Abingdon-on-Thames (2018)
14. Bergmann, J., Sams, A.: Flip Your Classroom. Reach Every Student in Every Class Every Day. ASCD, Alexandria (2012)

The Digitalization of Engineering Curricula: Defining the Categories that Preserve Constructive Alignment

Eleonora Boffa[1(✉)], Francesco Lupi[2], Michele Lanzetta[2], and Antonio Maffei[1]

[1] Department of Production Engineering, KTH Royal Institute of Technology, 114 28 Stockholm, Sweden
{boffa,maffei}@kth.se

[2] Department of Civil and Industrial Engineering, University of Pisa, 56122 Pisa, Italy
francesco.lupi@phd.unipi.it, lanzetta@unipi.it

Abstract. The COVID-19 pandemic has significantly changed the education domain boosting its digitalization. A pedagogical shift from live to virtual teaching, learning, and assessment activities is the primary outcome of this transition. This work analyses two courses included in the Industrial Engineering program offered in two prominent European higher education institutions. The Constructive Alignment (CA) approach is the baseline of this work and is used to analyze how the Teaching and Learning Activities (TLAs) and the Assessment Tasks (ATs) of the selected courses are adjusted to maintain alignment with the Intended Learning Outcomes (ILOs) defined before the Digital Transition (DT). The main contribution is the definition of the relevant categories, i.e., *Technology, Interaction, and Time*, to guide the DT in engineering and beyond by maintaining the alignment on ILO-TLA-AT.

Keywords: Digitalization · Distance learning · Engineering · Constructive alignment

1 Introduction

Scientific publications discussing online/distance learning have significantly increased throughout the last decade [1]. The COVID-19 pandemic represented an unexpected condition that significantly changed people's lifestyle along with the education domain boosting even further its digitalization, mostly at higher levels [2]. Distance learning is facilitating a pedagogical shift from live to virtual [3] as well as the adoption of digital technologies in education [4]. Therefore, online learning is becoming more popular as it may partially replace on-campus education [3]. In this new digital scenario, the change in teaching methodology will involve several thoughts and preparation [4,5]. The focus is now on the engagement of students, the instructor's role, and course design [1]. As for the course design, teachers have been challenged to comply with the Constructive

G. Casalino et al. (Eds.): HELMeTO 2021, CCIS 1542, pp. 333–346, 2022.
https://doi.org/10.1007/978-3-030-96060-5_24

Alignment (CA) approach [6] which has become a dominant design pattern in education. The forced and the short notice digitalization of education due to the COVID-19 pandemic has challenged educators in designing Teaching and Learning Activities (TLAs) and Assessment Tasks (ATs) that would maintain the Intended Learning Outcomes (ILOs) - TLAs - ATs alignment established before digitalization. As argued by [7], teachers have made adjustments to their assessment approaches but still ensuring that the students have achieved the same ILOs. In terms of new teaching approaches, access to the same on-site course content is a priority.

In view of the above, this paper assesses two courses (i.e., *Scientific methodology* - SM - and *Manufacturing processes* - MP) selected from the Industrial Engineering study program offered in two prominent European higher education institutions (i.e., *KTH Royal Institute of Technology* and *University of Pisa* [8]). The CA approach is the baseline of this work and is used to analyse how the TLAs and ATs of the selected courses are adjusted to maintain alignment with the ILOs defined before the digital transition (DT). The main contribution is defining a set of categories to guide the DT in engineering and beyond by maintaining the alignment on ILO-TLA-AT (Fig. 1).

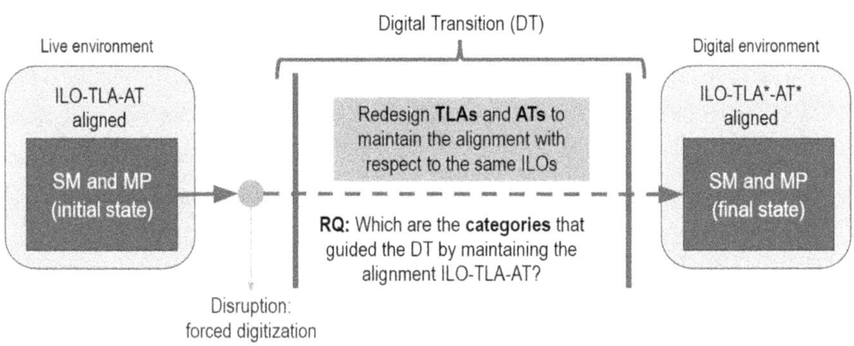

Fig. 1. Graphical representation of the definition of the Research Question (RQ) in the presented context. The star * indicates the redesigned TLA and AT after the DT.

2 Theoretical Background

Teachers have been facing many challenges in course design. Among others, it is worth mentioning: mapping the course onto the study programs, ensuring that the course is consistent, and focusing on what the student does. Regarding this last challenge, the design approach called CA underpins the learners-centered courses. In particular, the CA is a design approach for outcome-based teaching and learning [6] based on two principles:

I. ***The constructivist approach to learning:*** the fundamental assumption is the centrality of the student in the learning process. Learning is an active process in which student constructs their knowledge [9] by bringing a combination of previous knowledge, assumptions, motives, and intentions [10]. This is called *accommodation* process of generating new knowledge, where the student re-frame pre-existing knowledge based on new ones [11]. Therefore, the process of learning focuses on what the student does [12] rather than what the teachers do. Recently, this constructivist approach has become dominant in the education domain.

II. ***The designing of an aligned curriculum:*** three are the basic concepts of an aligned curriculum:
   - the **ILO**. The learners are provided with a set of clearly specified learning goals, i.e., the ILOs. These are expressed from the students' perspective, identifying (1) a *verb*, i.e., it reflects the educational goal and related level of understanding required, (2) a *content*, i.e., the focal concept within the discipline, and (3) a *context*, i.e., the domain in which the content is studied.
   - the **TLA**. Suitable TLAs are designed to engage the students and lead them to achieve the ILOs, by activating the verb conveyed in the ILOs. Each TLA may address a specific ILO.
   - the **AT**. It is created to test the learners and give them feedback. The AT needs to reflect how well the material has to be learned. This is specified by the level of understanding which embeds the complexity required. The level of complexity can be described with the SOLO (Structure of Observed Learning Outcomes) taxonomy [13] that consists of five levels: pre-structural, uni-structural, multi-structural, relational, and extended abstract (Fig. 2). This taxonomy provides a measure of the quality of assimilation [13] which is useful to design effective assessment.

   The alignment ILO-TLA-AT is realised with "action" verbs specified in the ILO that create a common link among the three elements [12]. These "action" verbs are selected looking at the modified Bloom taxonomy (Fig. 3) [14].
   The taxonomy presents a classification of the learning objectives based on six different types of knowledge: remembering, understanding, applying, analyzing, evaluating, and creating. At each level, the taxonomy associates a set of verbs that activate the abilities necessary for a specific learning goal. For instance, remembering which demands for merely recalling facts and basic concepts is associated with verbs such as define or list; analyse which implies drawing connections among ideas is associated with verbs such as compare or examine.

Summarising, the CA can contribute to designing a learning approach that emphasises the students and promotes a deep approach to learning.

3 Experiment

The *Scientific methodology* course from Production Engineering at KTH (The Royal Institute of Technology) Sweden, and the *Manufacturing processes* course

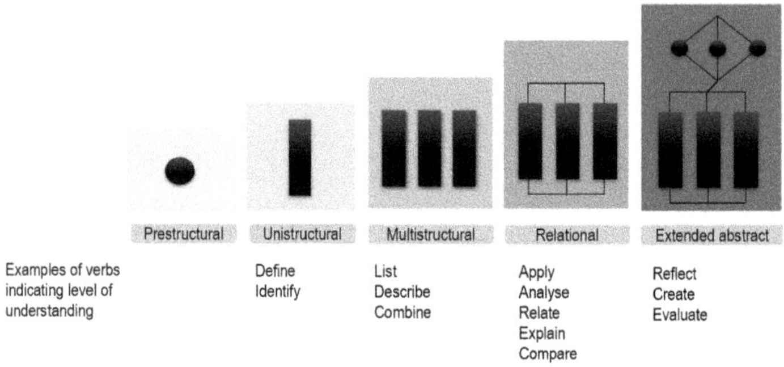

Fig. 2. The SOLO taxonomy, adapted from [13]

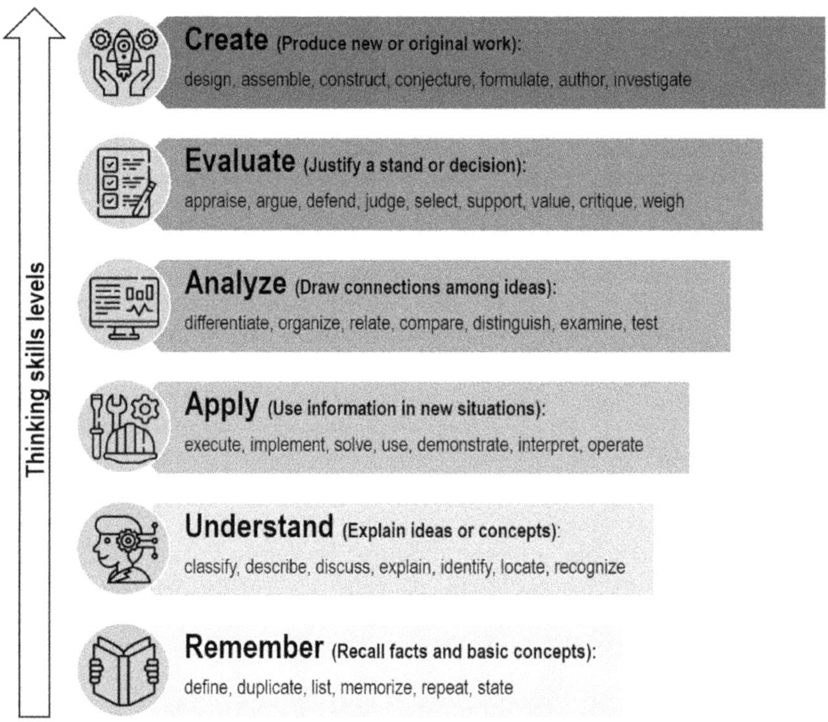

Fig. 3. The Bloom taxonomy, adapted from [14]

from the program of Management and Industrial Engineering at the University of Pisa Italy, are considered for the analysis.

Section 3.1 provides an overview of the two selected courses analysed and their ILOs, TLAs and ATs. These courses represent the input data of the experiment conducted on the whole methodology. Section 3.2 presents the methodology adopted to investigate the main changes that occurred during the DT.

3.1 Description of the Courses (ILO-TLA-AT)

Scientific Methodology Course: It aims at teaching the students how to design, perform and document personal research work. The activities are tailored to industrial and production engineering students who can use the knowledge and skills acquired hereby for their final thesis project. After completing the course with a passing grade, the student should be able to:

- ILO1. **Define** and **discuss** the nature of the research in relation to the two main domains: scientific methodology and engineering design, outlining their importance and use in the context of production engineering.
- ILO2. **Present** and **discuss** the evolution of thoughts from several aspects of the scientific domain such as definition, nature and progress of knowledge.
- ILO3. **Analyse** a scientific text and review the research question, the method and the conclusions.
- ILO4. **Structure**, carry out and document a research endeavour.
- ILO5. **Discuss** the origin of the scientific method as a result of the evolution of the human approach to the main philosophical problems, emphasizing the sociological and economic problems.
- ILO6. **Gather** information and elaborate a strategy to qualify and defend an opinion on a controversial topic, and **analyse** and **summarize** the following debate.

Manufacturing Processes Course: It aims to provide knowledge on the main metalworking processes, starting from the recovery of metal scraps, their transformation into finished or semi-finished products, the optimization of the process parameters and the resulting quality of the product. After completing the course with a passing grade the student should be able to:

- ILO1. **Define** the main materials and **explain** their mechanical and thermo-physical behaviour resulting from conventional manufacturing processes.
- ILO2. **Describe**, **model** and **define** the main conventional manufacturing processes (machining, casting, forming and welding).
- ILO3. **Present** and **discuss** the macro and microgeometrical metrology methods and techniques for the quality assessment of the resulting parts.
- ILO4. **Compare** and **select** conventional machining processes, machines specifications and configuration, production strategy, tools, fixtures and process parameters to manufacture a part, starting from a given mechanical drawing and its possible modifications to prevent defects, improve the mechanical properties and reduce costs.
- ILO5. **Develop** a technical report including process plan, process simulation and costing analysis for a given mechanical part.

The ILOs defined for each course are an important input to define TLAs and ATs. TLAs and ATs are designed taking as a reference the Bloom taxonomy (Fig. 3), and are summarised in Tables 1 and 2 respectively for *Scientific methodology* and *Manufacturing processes.*

Table 1. The digital TLAs and ATs of the course *Scientific methodology* from Production Engineering at KTH (Sweden).

ILOs	TLAs	ATs
ILO1	**TLA1.1** Lectures: Present the scientific methodology and engineering design in a production context	**AT1.1** Final examination: Answer questions regarding the scientific methodology and engineering design
	TLA1.2 Class work: Encourage discussion on the presented methodology and engineering design	**AT1.2** Group work: Discuss in groups on methodology and engineering design
	TLA1.3 Guest seminars: Present the scientific methodology and engineering design in a production context. Encourage discussion on the presented methodology and engineering design	**AT1.3** Written reflections: Write a report on the seminars content and reflect about the main message of the seminars
ILO2	**TLA2.1** Lectures: Present the different aspects of the scientific domain	**AT2.1** Final examination: Answer questions regarding the different aspects of the scientific domain
	TLA2.2 Class work: Encourage discussion on the different aspects of the scientific domain	**AT2.2** Group work: Discuss in group on the different aspects of the scientific domain
ILO3	**TLA3.1** Lectures: Explain the general principles of scientific writing and guidelines for the analysis of a scientific text	**AT3.1** Group work: Report the analysis and the critics of the formal structures and the layout of the contents of a scientific text
	TLA3.2 Homework: Analysis of a scientific text and critically assess each section of the text	**AT3.2** Group work: Report the analysis and the critics of the formal structures and the layout of the contents of a scientific text
ILO4	**TLA4.1** Lecture: Explain how to structure, carry out and organize a research endeavour	**AT4.1** Oral presentation: group presentation in front of the class that summarises the work
	TLA4.2 Homework: Collect and structure information on the proposed topics. Prepare a oral presentation	**AT4.2** Oral presentation: group presentation in front of the class that summarises the work
ILO5	**TLA5.1** Lectures: Present the main philosophical problems	**AT5.1** Final examination: Answer questions regarding the main philosophical problems
	TLA5.2 Class work: Encourage discussion on the presented philosophical problems	**AT5.2** Group work: Discuss in group the philosophical problems
ILO6	**TLA6.1** Lecture: Present how to plan and execute all the activities related with a debate	**AT6.1** Group work: the groups plan and debate on the proposed topics following the activities presented
	TLA6.2 Homework: Collect and structure information on the proposed debate topics. Prepare a oral presentation	**AT6.2** Oral presentation: group presentation in front of the class that summarises the result of the debate

Table 2. The digital TLAs and ATs of the course *Manufacturing processes* from the program of Management and Industrial Engineering at University of Pisa (Italy). Final exams are carried out in seven tests during the year after the class is ended.

ILOs	TLAs	ATs
ILO1	**TLA1** Lectures: Present the structure of matter and transformations, properties and test methods, metal alloys and phase diagrams, standard terminology, notions of continuum mechanics properties of materials	**AT1** Oral examination: Answer questions regarding main material presented
ILO2	**TLA2.1** Lectures: Present the main metalworking processes, the beyond mathematical models, the tools used, the manual and automatic machines and the equipment	**AT2.1** Written essay/quiz: Answer theoretical questions regarding the main manufacturing processes presented
	TLA2.2 Lab demonstrations: Present manufacturing process via practical demonstration at the manufacturing lab's machines	**AT2.2** Numerical exercise: Develop a process plan (process operations, parameters ad specifications) for a given part
ILO3	**TLA3.1** Lectures: Present methodology, tools and machines for micro and macro geometric measurements, characterization of the artifacts (tolerances), via manual or automatic way	**AT3.1** Oral examination: Answer theoretical questions regarding quality control and metrology
	TLA3.2 Lab demonstrations: Present quality control machines and tools via practical demonstration at the metrology lab	**AT3.2** Written essay/quiz: Answer theoretical questions regarding the main quality control approaches presented
ILO4	**TLA4** Lectures: Provide examples of manufacturing processes, machines, parameters, and material selection in a real case study via multi-criteria generation and selection	**AT4** Info graphic: Query, discuss with peers, and produce info graphic to explain, describe and visualize the main criteria in the selection process
ILO5	**TLA5.1** Seminars: Set project work groups, explaining timing, tools, and expected outcome via a case study	**AT5.1** Project work: Provide a technical report including process plan, simulation, verification, cost analysis on the selected mechanical part
	TLA5.2 Class work: Encourage discussion on the use of collaborative tools for remote collaboration during the project group activity	**AT5.2** Discussion: Listed, query and discuss with peers and professor

3.2 Methodology

This section describes the inductive method developed to identify the categories that may be accounted for during the transition to digital education, ensuring alignment with ILO-TLA-AT.

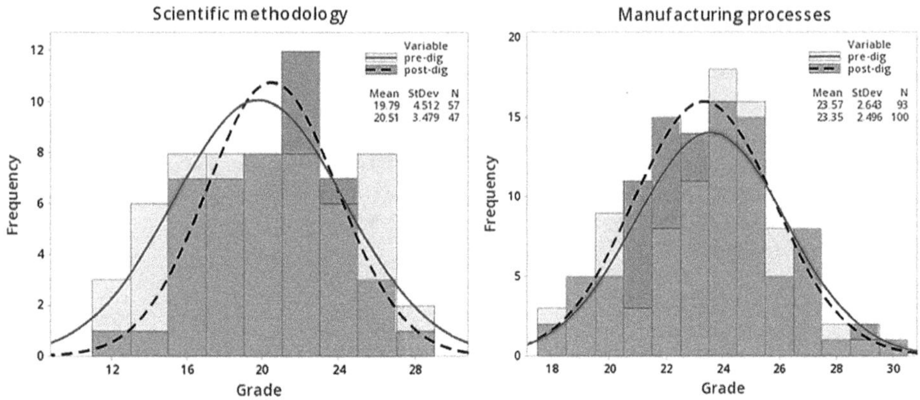

Fig. 4. The final grade's distributions for both *Scientific methodology* and *Manufacturing processes* course before (2019) and after (2020) digitalization of TLA and AT. The number of students are: 57 and 47 before and after digitalization respectively for *Scientific methodology*; 93 and 100 before and after digitalization respectively for *Manufacturing processes.* Please note that the grade scale adopted in the two courses is different. The *Scientific methodology* adopts letter grades that have been converted into numerical grades for the sake of comparability. The numerical grades range from 28 (maximum) to 12 (minimum pass grade). The *Manufacturing processes* course adopts numerical grades where 30 is the maximum and 18 is the minimum pass grade.

A crucial aspect must be clarified before presenting the methodology steps. The two courses have proved to guarantee the ILO-TLA-AT alignment even after the forced DT due to the COVID-19 pandemic. In particular, as shown in Fig. 4, the Gaussian grade's distributions of the *Scientific methodology* and *Manufacturing processes* display similar trends: the mean and standard deviations show a low deviation before and after the DT. As for the mean values, the deviations is around +3,5% for *Scientific methodology*, and –0,9% for *Manufacturing processes.* As for the standard deviation both values decreased of around 22% for *Scientific methodology* and 5,5% for *Manufacturing processes* meaning the distributions of grades are less scattered. From the above, the students have proven to equally perform at the final assessment. Their performances were almost unaffected or even increased by the context and format changes. Therefore, the digital TLAs and ATs were designed coherently with the ILOs preserving the alignment ILO-TLA-AT. The two case studies can be thus considered for the application of the following method.

The main adopted steps of the method are listed below:

1. For each course, all the DTs in teaching, learning, and assessment have been collected using a top-down generation approach. This approach covers all the transitions using the TLA and AT classes and its related sub-classes, i.e., lectures, guest seminars, homework, consultation hours, class work, practical lectures, remote examination, essay reports, and class presentation. The

Table 3. The digital TLAs and ATs designed to ensure the alignment ILO-TLA-AT of the course *Scientific methodology*. The aspects of the digital TLAs and ATs are highlighted in bold and correspond to the sub-categories abstracted to the *Technology, Interaction and Time* (TIT) categories.

TLAs			ATs
Lecture/Guest seminar	Homework	Class work	Remote examination/Essay report/Class presentation
– The **"screen sharing"** of **video conferencing tools** enables **equal visualization** for the students that follow the slides from their own **screen** – Teachers and students connect to the lecture **right on time** – **Live** lectures are **recorded** and published. The videos can be watched at any time and re-watched if something was not clear in the first place – Use of digital **white board**. The computer screen becomes the new board for the teachers thanks to the touch screen technology – Lack of **student's feedback** during the lecture and **connection** with the teachers. The teachers cannot perceive as well as monitor the degree of attention, leading to lack of control	– **Video conferencing tools** allow group work in a virtual setting. This needs more coordination among the group members – **Collaborative tools** (e.g., google docs and presentation) for **co-creation** and **sharing** – **Feedback** from peers on a slower pace. No physical interaction in class for quick update. There is no physical interaction in class for quick update	– The **"breakout rooms"** of **video conferencing tools** splits the students in groups for discussion. This is a **synchronous** method useful during lecture to make students reflect in groups) – An **"online discussion"** is set on the **learning management system** as an **asynchronous** method for students to provide short reflections on a topic related to the lecture given – A "**one-minute paper**"[a] activity where students post their answer in the chat	– The **Video conferencing tools** creates **virtual rooms** for monitoring students creating a virtual room for being in the exam – Questions were open mic or posted on the **chat** – **Learning management system** used to publish the exam tasks and to upload essays and reports – New exam format to avoid cheating: a short initial **quiz** with multiple choice questions is proposed to the students; a series of open book questions are presented as essays

[a] A one-minute paper is a common technique designed to get rapid feedback on whether the teacher's main idea is correctly perceived by the students. In the basic format, students have 60 s to briefly write down on paper anonymous responses to provided questions that reflect a certain aspect of the today's lecture. For instance, students may be asked to highlight the most important points learned during that lecture. The teacher collects the responses and assesses them.

Table 4. The digital TLAs and ATs designed to ensure alignment ILO-TLA-AT of the course *Manufacturing Processes*. Highlighted in bold are the aspects of the digital TLAs and ATs that correspond to the sub-categories abstracted to the *Technology, Interaction and Time* (TIT) categories. The average passing rate is 30–40% at each test, about 50–70 students attend, consequently quiz is selected to reduce instructors' load and because it is very difficult prevent cheating in online essays and numerical tests.

TLAs			ATs
Lecture	Homework/Consultation hours	Class work/Practical lectures	Remote examination/Report/Class presentation
– **Video conferencing tools** causes the **lack of student's feedback** and connection with the teachers that cannot control them easily – **Pre-recorded video** allows students to **customize** the learning process and facilitate numerous activities in the use of the pc at home (visualization, hardware, software, power, etc.) – Easy access at home to visualization, hardware, software, charge power, etc. – **Remote virtual laboratory**[a] using a simple **action cam** that allows a machining process customized experience **"remote piloting"**	– **Video conferencing tools** trigger virtual consultation hours, overcoming logistics and time issues. The live consultation hours make logistics and time issues for students preventing them from taking the opportunity to discuss with the teachers – Increased attendance and **opportunities** of **discussion** with the teacher	– **Virtual team** for homework is a practical experience of project management in the context of remote working. It imposes the communication of the members as well as a formal definition of the task – **Collaborative tools** become a standard in the current skills that a "smart worker" should satisfy	– The high number of participants (100+) requires a **time-framed quiz**. The quiz generation is a **quite time consuming** for professors (but necessary) task – The oral examination is divided into two sections: the **class work presentation** and the theoretical questions; a final report of the project work is uploaded to the **learning management system**

[a] https://www.youtube.com/channel/UCMOdP5P7Q4lbYDZ7x2Bow1g

details are presented in Table 3 for the *Scientific methodology* course and Table 4 for the *Manufacturing processes* course.
2. For each sub-class, the related DTs have been organised in structured lists. Duplicates have been removed, and similar observations have been grouped.
3. Common patterns in the DTs have been identified in these structured lists and further investigated to group them into relevant categories. These categories have been labeled for semantic association as *Technology, Interaction and Time* (TIT).

As a result, *Technology, Interaction and Time* (TIT) are the main relevant categories that need to be considered during the transition to digital education. These categories cover the whole space of the DTs in education and they will ensure ILO-TLA-AT alignment.

4 Results

This work is based on practical experience in re-designing TLAs and ATs in a distance education environment. In particular, the *Scientific methodology* and the *Manufacturing processes* courses are analysed focusing on the TLAs and ATs designed to maintain the alignment with the ILOs. The analysis of the courses identifies the TIT categories and the corresponding sub-categories, namely the aspects of TLA and AT observed for each TIT category. In more details,

- *Technology category* includes the digital technologies involved in TLA and AT. These technologies are introduced to enhance the student learning experience in a distance environment and facilitate the achievement of the ILO. The technology becomes the mean to deliver the lecture, the laboratory or the assignments. The sub-categories identified are: Forum, Action cam, Video conferencing tools, Cloud-based tools, Digital white board, Learning management system.
- *Interaction category* considers the engagement of the learners in the online courses. The level of interaction between teacher-student or student-student, communication and participation, and community building are mainly investigated. Teachers and students needed time to adjust to distance learning, e.g., how to use and exploit the features of digital technologies to facilitate and enhance interaction. In more detail, these technologies created new ways of how interaction happens for both teachers-students and student-student (e.g., through a camera or a chat). The identified sub-categories are: Feedback, Networking, Socialization, Level of student engagement, Level of interaction among peers and teacher-student, Live interaction with chat and with "remote piloting".
- *Time category* refers to how the time dedicated to teaching has been spent with asynchronous and live activities. It has been observed that time may be managed in a more flexible way with the digital version of the course due to the mix of asynchronous and live activities. Sub-categories identified are: Asynchronous and live activities, Time dedicated to teaching, Punctuality.

5 Discussion

The analysis of the two courses has led to the same conclusions in all three categories. The following paragraphs summarise the most relevant observations.

- *Technology category:* digitalization has introduced new digital technologies in education that created new ways of how teaching and learning happen. Digital technologies have improved the student experience of teaching. In particular, the video-conferencing tool has specific features, such as screen sharing, that allow each student to follow the lecture and what the teacher displays from their screen. The combination of video-conferencing tools and action cams is used to stream practical laboratories. Therefore, the students can virtually attend the laboratory sessions that otherwise would not have been possible. The use of digital technologies has also brought a sense of equity in different ways. There is now equal visualization in the virtual classroom by connecting personal laptops to live lectures: the slides are more visible independently of where the student sits. Students do not have to share the limited IT resources available in the computer labs to perform their exercises with other students. Using their laptops allows each student to try out the activities themselves instead of passively following what other group mates do. Moreover, all the previously mentioned technologies highly impact the two remaining categories (cf., following two paragraphs). To conclude this overview, it is worth noting that the only identified drawback of these technology tools is that some disadvantaged students cannot use such power.
- *Interaction category:* communication and interaction between teacher-student and student-student are key challenges. Firstly, it is important to notice that digital technologies allow interaction to happen. In detail, the above mentioned technologies create the interaction platform and tools used by teachers and students. Secondly, virtual interaction has increased the attendees' anonymity (e.g., teachers see the students as black squares on the screen when using video conferencing tools). This anonymity is considered an advantage from the students' perspective (e.g., during consultation hours more students take the opportunities to listen to the discussion or clarify their doubts privately in the chat with peers). As another opportunity to increase the interaction, students are positive about forum-like activities, i.e., online discussion, set on the learning management system. Students can share their thoughts and discuss with others. As a drawback, student engagement during live lectures can drop. For instance, most of the students tend to listen passively to the lecture without asking questions and teachers find it challenging to monitor the degree of attention of the audience.
- *Time category:* the digital technologies allow deciding whether the activity in focus would be asynchronous or live, impacting time management. For instance, students can access the course content via pre-recorded video (asynchronous): lectures, seminars, and laboratories are available "on-demand". This has increased flexibility in managing time. The learning process is now more independent of time. However, the educators dedicate more time and

effort to teach due to a lack of experience in distance learning technologies. This results in stress and increased workload for the educators.

To conclude, this work has focused on two courses that are considered antithetical, meaning that they are characterised by dissimilar content. One course focused on how to perform, design, and document a research endeavor. The other one focused on how to design and optimize specific manufacturing processes and related parameters. The dissimilarity of the courses marked two ways of coping with the DT. However, the analysis has shown similar aspects in dealing with the DT that converged in the TIT categories. Future research may enrich and improve the current work by considering a broader set of courses. This further information may refine or extend the already identified TIT categories.

6 Conclusions

The CA introduces a feedback loop between *what* and *how* the teacher wants to teach. The resulting course design is more resilient and can successfully overcome unpredictable events such as the demand for online teaching.

The forced digitalization of education due to the above mentioned pandemic has challenged constructively aligned courses. Educators had to think about new ways of performing TLAs and ATs to preserve the ILO-TLA-AT alignment established before the DT.

This work proposes the TIT categories as the main relevant dimensions to consider in TLAs and ATs' re-design process. The proposed categories must be considered as guidelines to be followed during the top-down exploration of different domains.

The abstraction process adopted in the methodology allows transposing specific engineering instances to a set of general variables that may be considered as a reference point also in different disciplines. However, further research and additional case studies are needed to validate the proposed categories.

References

1. Martin, F., Sun, T., Westine, C.D.: A systematic review of research on online teaching and learning from 2009 to 2018. Comput. Educ. **159**, 104009 (2020)
2. Crawford, J., et al.: COVID-19: 20 countries' higher education intra-period digital pedagogy responses. J. Appl. Learn. Teach. **3**(1), 1–20 (2020)
3. Mishra, L., Gupta, T., Shree, A.: Online teaching-learning in higher education during lockdown period of COVID-19 pandemic. Int. J. Educ. Res. Open **1**, 100012 (2020)
4. Aute, K.B.: Tools for digitalized/online teaching in the wake of pandemic COVID-19 lockdown: an overview **IX**(IV) (2020)
5. Lupi, F., Lanzetta, M.: A novel approach for cooperative scientific literature search and socialization. In: Higher Education Learning Methodologies and Technologies Online. Springer (2022). https://doi.org/10.1007/978-3-030-96060-5_3
6. Biggs, J.B.: Teaching for Quality Learning at University: What the Student Does. McGraw-Hill Education, New York (2011)

7. Müller, A.M., Goh, C., Lim, L.Z., Gao, X.: Covid-19 emergency eLearning and beyond: experiences and perspectives of university educators. Educ. Sci. **11**(1), 19 (2021)
8. Lupi, F., et al.: Toward a sustainable educational engineer archetype through industry 4.0. Comput. Ind. **134**, 103543 (2022)
9. Jones, M.G., Brader-Araje, L.: The impact of constructivism on education: language, discourse, and meaning. Am. Commun. J. **5**(3), 1–10 (2002)
10. Biggs, J.: Enhancing teaching through constructive alignment. High. Educ. **32**(3), 347–364 (1996)
11. Piaget, J.: The Construction of Reality in the Child, vol. 82. Routledge, Abingdon (2013)
12. Biggs, J.: Constructive alignment in university teaching. HERDSA Rev. High. Educ. **1**, 5–22 (2014)
13. Biggs, J.B., Collis, K.F.: Evaluating the Quality of Learning: the SOLO Taxonomy (Structure of the Observed Learning Outcome). Academic Press, Cambridge (1982)
14. Anderson, L.W., Krathwohl, D.R.: A taxonomy for learning, teaching, and assessing: A revision of Bloom's taxonomy of educational objectives. Longman (2001)

From an Emergency Dad to New Forms of Blended Learning via Effective Methodologies to Design, Deliver and Evaluate Learning

Service Learning and Virtual-Service Learning Experiences in Upper Secondary School: Methodologies and Instruments for Lifelong Learning

Stefania Chipa, Chiara Giunti, Patrizia Lotti(✉), and Lorenza Orlandini

Department of Innovation INDIRE, Firenze, Italy
{s.chipa,c.giunti,p.lotti,l.orlandini}@indire.it

Abstract. Several and continuing technological, economic and social changes have occurred in the last decades, making the labor market more complex, as well as the relation with education, training and professional development. The opening of the educational institutions and their cooperation with the territory to solve problems and promote a sustainable development make careers and curriculum counselling easier in a more and more complex world, particularly in working environment. This research aims at establishing a connection between LifeComp framework and Service Learning by analyzing some experiences carried out in the upper secondary schools with this pedagogic approach in the context of Paths for transversal skills and guidance.

Keywords: Orientation · e-Service Learning · Distance learning

1 Introduction

Rapid changes in technology, markets and related employment opportunities have exponentially increased during the last decades. OECD, the World Bank, and a range of EU agencies carried out all the career guidance reviews due to the need for citizens to be well equipped with skills to manage the complex and non-linear transitions that mark contemporary education, training and working. In particular, the Report of European Lifelong Guidance Policy Network focused on improving the efficiency and effectiveness of education, training and labor market through its contribution to reduce dropout, prevent skill mismatches and boost productivity and it encourages the promotion of both

This paper is the product of a common reflection of the authors. Concernig different parts, Patrizia Lotti is author of paragraph 1, Lorenza Orlandini of paragraph 2, Chiara Giunti of paragraph 3, 3.1, 4 and 4.1, Stefania Chipa 4.2, Chiara Giunti e Patrizia Lotti are authors of paragraph 5.
The guidelines for PCTO are included in the Law No. 145 of 30 December 2018 and recommend Service Learning as one of the methods to guide the choice of the schools in carrying out these activities www.miur.gov.it/web/guest/-/linee-guida-dei-percorsi-per-le-compe-tenze-trasversali-e-per-l-orientamento.

G. Casalino et al. (Eds.): HELMeTO 2021, CCIS 1542, pp. 349–363, 2022.
https://doi.org/10.1007/978-3-030-96060-5_25

social and economic goals as a crucial dimension of lifelong learning. To improve the Career Management Skills (CMS), one of the three key points is its "*embedded in the national curriculum in schools as well as in higher education settings, within a broader lifelong learning framework including the acquisition of CMS by adults within or outside the workforce.*"[1]

Furthermore, in 2017 the *Communication On a renewed EU agenda for higher education* addresses four to give a new direction to EU support for higher education breaking down barriers between higher education and the rest of society[2]. In addition, the final report of the Advisory Group on Social Dimension issued the principles and guidelines to strengthen the social dimension of higher education in the European Higher Education Area (EHEA)[3].

In the same decades, pedagogic researches wondered about the link between excellence and social responsibility. One for all, Gardner's group in Harvard University and his *Good Work project* manage to valorize the three Es of Excellence, Engagement, Ethics [1] by means of the Service Learning (SL) experiences [2]. SL is an approach named and defined in different ways around the world and here we chose that of the European Observatory of Service-Learning in Higher Education (Eoslhe).

Service-learning (sometimes referred to as community based or community engaged learning) is an innovative pedagogical approach that integrates meaningful community service or engagement into the curriculum and offers students' academic credit for the learning that derives from active engagement within the community and work on a real-world problem. Reflection and experiential learning strategies underpin the learning process, and the service is linked to the academic discipline. It brings together students, academics and the community whereby all become teaching resources, problem solvers and partners. In addition to enhancing academic and real-world learning, the overall purpose of is to instill in students a sense of civic engagement and responsibility and work towards positive social change within society[4].

Gardner's interests include how it happens that people come to use their excellence or their potential for "good", considering that any human capacity can be used for "ill" as well as for "good". Therefore, with the Good Work Project he links his research about developing excellence with those of ethic and engagement [1]. Ethical consideration

[1] Lifelong Guidance Policies: Work in Progress. A report on the work of the European Lifelong Guidance Policy Network 2008-10, p. 30 www.elgpn.eu/publications/browse-by-lan-guage/english/european-lifelong-guidance-policies-work-in-progress.-a-report-on-the-work-of-the-european-lifelong-guidance-policy-network-2009201310/.

[2] Communication from the Commission to the European Parliament, the Council, the European Economic and Social Committee and the Committee of the Regions "On a renewed EU agenda for higher education" Brussels, 30.5.2017 COM(2017) 247 final, p. 7 https://eur-lex.eu-ropa.eu/legal-content/EN/TXT/PDF/?uri=CELEX:52017DC0247&from=EN.

[3] EHEA Roma 3030, Advisory Group 1 on Social Dimension. Final Report. p. 26 https://ehea2020rome.it/storage/uploads/0479534b-a889-4fd9-9d15-64b49e6ee768/AG1_Social_Dimension_Final_Report.pdf.

[4] Definition of the European Observatory of Service-Learning in Higher Education:www.eoslhe.eu/what-we-do/.

covered around both the SL approach and the Good Work project. The research focused also on how the participation in a good SL project could increase chances and practices for the large number of individuals giving them the opportunities and the experiences for reflection (thinking-skills) they need to become "good" workers, committed to work, and to the broader society [2].

In this rationale, we chose the LifeComp framework to analyze the experience of Service Leaning developed by three upper secondary schools of the Educational Avantgarde *(Avanguardie educative*-AE). AE[5] is a cultural movement founded to collect the most significant experiences of organizational and educational innovation in Italian schools and encourage transformation of the traditional lecture-based school model. With the aim of supporting an innovation process that has come out of bottom-up reasoning, INDIRE (National Institute for Documentation, Innovation and Educational Research) and 22 founder member schools (advanced schools) have written a Manifesto based on 7 pillars that inspired the "Gallery of 12 Ideas": experiences of innovation re-elaborated by researchers based on experience gained in certain Italian schools which, some time ago, began to gradually change the organization, school time and space for teaching in ways that would encourage pupils to take an active role in teaching-learning processes.

The experiences of the upper secondary schools analyzed in this paper refer to one of these innovation ideas: "Inside/outside the school – Service Learning".

2 Re-read Service Learning Through the LifeComp Framework

The LifeComp framework regards "Personal, Social and Learning to Learn" as a set of competences applying to all spheres of life that can be acquired through formal, informal and non-formal education and can help citizens to thrive in the 21st Century [3].

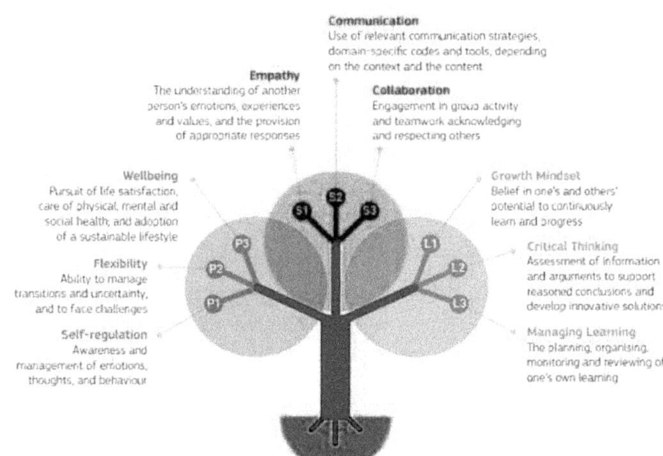

Fig. 1. LifeComp at a glance

[5] http://avanguardieeducative.indire.it/.

The LifeComp framework has nine competences with three descriptors each (Fig. 1). It can be used as a basis for the development of curricula and learning activities, fostering personal and social development, as well as learning to learn. The competences of Life-Comp framework highlights the parallelism with the purposes of SL. This comparison has been made by comparing the results of the research in the reference literature. The results of this survey are briefly shown in Table 1.

Table 1. Comparison between LifeComp and Service Learning purposes.

Area	Competences	Service Learning
Personal	*Self-regulation*	SL promotes experiential learning. The experience is a powerful contributing force to the development of people's self-efficacy; self-regulation encompasses both cognitive skills and social skills [4]
	Flexibility	SL contributes to form an individual as citizen of the world who can interact with the cultural values of everyone and who is willing to put his or her professional competences at service of the society, in order to make it thrive and improve constantly [5]
	Well-being	SL educational experiences foster school well-being and improve learning outcomes [6]
Social	*Empathy*	SL has positive effects on prosocial behavior, acceptance of diversity, development of ethics and strengthening of elements linked to resilience. It stimulates a major capability of empathy and readiness to help others [7]
	Communication	SL activities «help to weave the possible interconnections that link both cognitive and emotional sphere, ethics and ability to organize, initiative and communication skills» [8]
	Collaboration	SL allows to arrange good learning experiences that provide contexts where one can develop the ability to think, feeling and act with competence in the world, cooperating with others [9]
Learning to learn	*Growth mindset*	SL helps to develop and learn social themes [10–12]
	Critical thinking	Critical thinking is the element of SL that causes, deepens and records learning [13]
	Managing learning	SL helps students to choose their course of study or professional career, improving their educational curriculum and the opportunities to find a job after University [14]

In the pandemic context due to Covid-19, SL has turned into e-Service Learning or Virtual-Service Learning [15, 16], allowing the lessons to continue in distance learning or integrated digital teaching mode, and strengthening the expected competences by integrating with Life Comp framework.

3 Research Methodology, Instruments and Actors Involved

The findings we discussed in this paper are based on three case studies [17] of three upper secondary schools selected on the basis of two main criteria. The first one: all of them were secondary schools with a SL pedagogic approach in the context of of Paths for transversal skills and guidance (*Percorsi per le Competenze Trasversali e l'Orientamento* - PCTO[6]) following the five main steps of SL approach [18]: Motivation, Analysis, Preparation and planning, Action, Demonstration and Evaluation. The second one: schools belong to the Avanguardie educative Movement.

The sample included schools located in northern, central and south Italy areas. The selected schools implemented different SL approaches, always in the framework of PCTO.

The General High School "Attilio Bertolucci" in Parma, specializing in sciences and music, has implemented a SL environmental process and engaged students from two classes, third grade (about 40 pupils aged 16) of the sciences specializing path.

The upper secondary school "Sandro Pertini" in Alatri (Frosinone) adapted his SL project to the context of Covid19 pondemic. In particular, the Technical High School provided a tax advisory "service" for citizens that has turned into a telematics way (about 50 students engaged, aged 17–19, from "economic sector" branch of study). More, in this new pandemic context the school produced a sanitizing solution for hands in the laboratory (about 24 students, aged 18–19, engaged from "chemistry, materials and biotechnologies" and "environmental biotechnologies" branch of study).

The upper secondary school "Europa" in Pomigliano d'Arco (Napoli) has set up a Distance Public Relation Office for the inhabitants of the town of Casalnuovo di Napoli. This experience engaged students of the third, fourth and fifth classes from Vocational and Tecncinal High School and in particular from "community online commercial services", "tourism" and "graphics and communications" branch of study (totaling six classes, about 150 pupils aged 16–19)[7].

---

[6] The guidelines for PCTO are included in the Law No. 145 of 30 December 2018 and recommend Service Learning as one of the methods to guide the choice of the schools in carrying out these activities www.miur.gov.it/web/guest/-/linee-guida-dei-percorsi-per-le-competenze-trasversali-e-per-l-orientamento.

[7] More details about the organization of General, Technical and Vocational High School in Italy are available on the Euridyce chapter online "Secondary and Post-Secondary Non-Tertiary Educational" at the link https://eacea.ec.europa.eu/national-policies/eurydice/content/secondary-and-post-secondary-non-tertiary-education-26_en.

Qualitative data collection procedures have been used in order to describe the concrete experiences taken during the 2017/18 school year and from March 2020 to July 2020 during distance teaching in sanitary emergency.

3.1 Research Instruments

In-depth case-study visits were made to each of the three upper secondary schools towards March 2018 and February 2020. Later, the research has been going on with virtual meetings.

During in-schools meetings and virtual meetings, semi-structured interviews [19–21] has been undertaken with school leaders and members of teaching staff who had been involved in the SL programs. Interviews were recorded and transcribed by four researchers. Data have been collected also through collecting public documents, such as "Three-year educational offer plan" (Piano Triennale dell'Offerta Formativa - PTOF) and Self-evaluation report (Rapporto di Autovalutazione - RAV), and through a narrative inquiry methodology-based form [22], filled by the school leader and his teaching staff, aimed at bringing out the "didactic implicit" [23].

These tools have been designed around the LifeComp conceptual framework and aim at analyzing how SL and e-SL experiences can influence the development of competences pertaining to personal, social and learning to learn area. Face-to-face and virtual semi-structured interviews were conducted with a flexible set of pre-determined questions aimed at bringing out the connection between SL experiences and the three connected competence areas and the nine competences that makeup LifeComp. Here below is the conceptual scheme which has guided the interviews (Table 2).

Allowing the participants engaged in the educational practice to be the narrators of their own school story, the narrative approach, allowing the participants engaged in the educational practice to be the narrators of their own school story, actives meta-reflection processes, brings to light interesting reflections on how and why [20, 23].

The narrative form is organized around two sections (Table 3): the first has the purpose to describe the general aspects of the SL experience; the second has the purpose to bring to light the key elements of the experience (goals, stages and processes, community partners, achievements).

Table 2. Semi-structured interviews: conceptual scheme basing on LifeComp framework

Area	Competences	Examples of questions
Personal	*Self-regulation*	Did the SL experience develop students' self-efficacy (identification of personal strengths) and self-regulation (management of emotions, thoughts and behavior, for example stress response)' (*Give an example*)
	Flexibility	Did SL experience contribute to develop students' ability to manage transitions, to adapt to new situations (adapt to change), to deal with uncertainty and to face challenges? (*Give an example*) Did SL experience contribute to develop students' capacity to consider multiple aspects on a specific topic and to understand, negotiate, and weigh up different points of view by understanding that there is no single strategy or behavior, which will always lead to positive out- comes? (*Give an example*) Did SL experience contribute to form an individual who is able to interact with the cultural values of everyone and is willing to put his or her professional competences at service of the society, in order to make it thrive and improve constantly? (*Give an example*)
	Well-being	Did the SL experiences improve students' physical, cognitive and emotional well-being? (*Give an example*) Did the SL experiences improve students' social wellbeing by cultivating their empathy, caring for others and adopting altruistic behaviors, while devoting time to building interpersonal affective relationships, seeking help when needed and offering support to others in need? (*Give an example*)
	Empathy	Did the SL experiences develop students' ability to be aware of other people's emotions and values by recognizing others' feelings and reading nonverbal cues? (*Give an example*) Did the SL experiences develop students' ability to understand others and to reduce personal distress when confronted with others' feelings) (*Give an example*)

(*continued*)

Table 2. (*continued*)

Area	Competences	Examples of questions
Social	*Communication*	Did the SL experiences improve students' use of communication strategies (verbal strategies, non-verbal strategies, and visuals strategies), domain-specific codes and tools (text, email, smartphones, web conferencing, group messaging, and social networks) depending on the context and content? (*Give an example*) Did the SL experiences develop students' ability to manage interactions and conversations in different socio-cultural contexts and domain-specific situations? Did the SL experiences develop students' ability to make safe, responsible and ethical use of social media? (*Give an example*)
	Collaboration	Did the SL experiences develop students' ability to engage in group activity and teamwork acknowledging and respecting others by constructing respectful interaction with people who are perceived to have different cultural affiliations, beliefs, opinions or practices from one-self)? (*Give an example*) Did the SL experiences develop students' capacity to co-participate in collective activities and ventures, and to embolden others to collaborate, deploying collective agency, pooling their knowledge, competences and resources, so that a common goal may be accomplished? (*Give an example*)
	Growth mind-set	Did the SL experiences develop students' curiosity and desire to understand complex topics or problems, and intellectually explore a wide variety of things? (*Give an example*) Did the SL experiences develop students' ability to deal with setbacks, failure and negative feedback and learn from it? (*Give an example*)
Learning to learn	*Critical thinking*	Did the SL experiences develop students' ability to deal with misinformation and willing to fact-check a piece of information and evaluate the credibility of a source? (*Give an example*) Did the SL experiences develop students' capacity to compare, analyze, assess, and synthesize data, information, ideas, and media messages in order to draw logical conclusions and to test the robustness of arguments and thoughts to identify possible biases? (*Give an example*) Did the SL experiences develop students' creativity skill to generate outcomes that are both original and of value, to re-evaluate problems considering different variables and to take sensible risks? (*Give an example*)

(*continued*)

Table 2. (*continued*)

Area	Competences	Examples of questions
	Managing learning	Did the SL experiences develop students' ability to direct their learning, set goals, motivate themselves and apply appropriate strategies to achieve their goals (self-regulation skill)? (*Give an example*) Did the SL experiences develop students' ability to improve their comprehension of the learning processes, by recognizing that learning activities in different domains are similar, and therefore the same strategy can be transferred and applied across different areas? (*Give an example*)

Table 3. The narrative form

General information	Data on experience
Name of the school	
Title of the project/experience	
Classes, students and teachers involved	
Disciplines involved	
Period of development	[Describes the school's features and give information on the educational, geographic and social characteristics of the school]
School context	
Brief description of the project and activities	**Narrative inputs**
SL goals	The social issue addressed is ....and target audience is ... The learning objectives are ...
Stages and processes	The reasons why conducting this project are ... The problem is ....its real impact on the community is... The students are motivated to develop this experience by... The community is motivated to participate by ... The weakest aspects of the project are ... The weakest aspects of the project are ... [Describe your SL/e-SL project referring to the traditional SL design scheme at five steps (1. Motivation; 2. Diagnosis; 3. Concept and Planning; 4. Execution; 5. Closing) and three transversal processes (1. Reflection; 2. Documentation and communication; 3 Evaluation)]
Relations with the community around the schools	Local partners who have participated actively in the development of the project are ... [Describe some of your interactions with families, territory, local authorities, etc. focusing on communication strategies, participation and financial support]
Achievements	The experience achieved the following service goals ... The experience achieved the following learning goals ... [Describe other achievements that may have occurred]

4 Outcomes

4.1 The Narrative Inquiry Methodology-Based Form

Narrative approach analysis revealed interesting aspects of different SL experiences of the three schools. In this paragraph some SL Projects will be briefly described high-lighting the most important features. They had been emphasized by participants' reflection activities.

The General High School "Attilio Bertolucci" specialized in sciences and music is located in Parma, northern Italy, which counts about 1.000 students. 40 students aged 16, from two third grade classes of the sciences specializing path have been involved in "We Lab & We Map", a SL environmental project during the 2017/18 school year. This secondary school coordinated an environmental SL experience aiming at analysis of the characteristics of the water collected from rivers and streams around Parma. It set up a network of 30 secondary schools and partners. Two researchers from Parma University supported students collecting and analyzing water. A bank foundation, together with a start-up company and a Fab-Lab provided a mobile laboratory for sample collection and a database shared. The project started from investigating local environmental issues that highlighted the necessity of monitoring the quality of the water and sharing the outcome with the citizenship (service), while improving students' scientific and citizenship skills (learning). The students, supported by teachers and University researchers, collected the samples water, analyzed them through the mobile laboratory offered by the start-up company and the Fab-Lab and shared data with the other secondary schools through the database. Students' assessment covered both purposes: service and learning, and took place in relation to the planned competences using dedicated tools (i.e.: observational grids, competences assessment grids).

The Technical High School "Sandro Pertini" and the Technical and Vocational High School "Europa" are two secondary schools composed of several study programs of Technical and Professional plans. The first, "Sandro Pertini" High School, is located in Alatri (Frosinone), a town in central Italy, and hosts about 700 students. The second, "Europa" High School, is a secondary school located in Pomigliano d'Arco (Napoli), in south of Italy with about 1.400 students. In both SL activities started during face-to-face phase and went on during distance learning, due to the lockdown caused by the 2020/2021 Covid-19 pandemic.

Concerning the "Sandro Pertini" High School we presented two project that are part of "Pertini MultiService", a framework in which SL is a key part of the curriculum. The first project that we presented – "Desk of the citizen" (Sportello del Cittadino) – is a tax advisory service provided to the local citizens by 50 students, aged 17–19, from two classes (one fourth grade class and one fifth grade class) of the "economic sector" branch of technical study. This experience, started during the 2017/18 school year, has turned into a telematic service. The project is currently ongoing. The "Desk of citizen" responded to a real need of the local community who needed service in the preparation of personal tax computation. Students, supported by teachers, were trained in the use operating functions of tax preparation software and in income tax laws. A physical desk has been set in the school hallway and students' service time has been scheduled. During the 2019/20 school year the requests increase, due to Governmental Decree "Care Italy

(Cura Italia) and its tax refunds. Moreover, Covid-19 pandemic forced the school to turn the tax advisory service into a telematic service. The collaboration among teachers and students was possible thanks to Google Meet, a content-sharing platform already in use in the school. The communication between students and local community was realized via email. Students who participate in SL project have increased their account and finance competences, data analysis and report preparation, also improved their interpersonal communication skills and their problem-solving skills (learning). At the same time, they benefited the community by filling a lack of financial skills in local community (service).

The second SL project – "Purell-chemical" (Amuchimico) – went on during the lockdown caused by Covid-19 pandemic and it is currently ongoing. The project engaged 24 students, aged 18–19, from three classes of the "chemistry, materials and biotechnologies" and "environmental biotechnologies" branch of technical study. During the lockdown, owing to the lack of high-quality sanitizing solutions in the local community, students produced in the lab an alcohol-based hand sanitizer, the "Purell-chemical". They realized the product using the OMS guidelines and approved method. Approved and validated by an efficacy test, the hand sanitizer was delivered on demand, to other schools, municipalities, farms, police offices and even the emergency department of the local hospital. Through the Purell-chemical project, students have increased their chemical competencies (learning) and, at the same time, they have strengthened bonds between school and local community by contributing to deal with a public health emergency (service).

Finally, the upper secondary school ISIS "Europa" realized a Distance Public Relation Office in Casalnuovo di Napoli, the "Europa Community Service". This experience started with face-to-face activities during the 2017/18 school year, and it is currently ongoing in distance learning mode. The "Europa Community Service" engaged students of the third, fourth and fifth classes from "community online commercial services", "tourism" and "graphics and communications" branch of Vocational and Technical studies (totalling six classes, about 130 pupils aged 16–19). During the 2017/18 school year, High School "Europa" set up a Public Relation Office in Palace "Salerno-Lancellotti" (Casalnuovo-Napoli) to offer a local service for the inhabitants of the town of Casalnuovo of Napoli. The "Europa Community Service" has met the needs to simplify the relation between the citizens and the Public Administration by offering a new channel of information and service to local community and by facilitating the use of the online services. Starting in February 2020, at the same time as COVID-19 pandemic, the "Europa Community Service" had to become a telematic service. The Distance Public Relation Office can be reached by the link https://www.europacommunityservice.it/; and citizens access the service through a chatbot. The collaboration between teachers and students, and among students, was only online, thanks to Zoom Meetings and to Edmodo, a content-sharing platform already in use in the school. The "Europa Community Service" combined classroom learning goals (the development of: creative and business competences, communication and interpersonal skills) and community service (simplify the relation between the citizens and the Public Administration) in a way that enhances and benefits both students and the community.

4.2 The Semi-structured Interviews

The semi-structured interviews analysis revealed interesting aspects of the three different SL approaches related to LifeComp skill indicators. The main findings are presented in this paragraph.

Each interview has been transcribed; all the texts have been analyzed through the content analysis methodology in order to bring out the unit of meaning [21] corresponding to LifeComp skill indicators. The interpretative process [24] (Sameraro 2011), described below, aims at understanding the added value of the SL projects in terms of developing personal, social and learning to learn skills. The outcomes of the interviews have shown that SL projects have the identity features of holding together a knowledge approach and a soft-skills development. An approach to disciplines conceived as models for the study of reality with, at the same time, the maturation of the transversal skills that are necessary to thrive citizens in the 21st Century.

The SL project "We Lab & We Map" realized by the General High School specializing in sciences and music "Attilio Bertolucci" has especially contributed to the development of the learning to learn area, "having significantly increased the students' awareness of the effects of globalization and the motivation to deepen the sustainable development and environmental issues" (Head Teacher2). Students felt the responsibility of giving the local institutions strategic data used to set their environmental policies; working in groups, sharing contents, constructing respectful interactions with their mates in order to give the community the best possible result have contributed to increase their social area skills. On-field experience have also contributed to the growth of the personal area, helping students to identify their strengths and weaknesses in order to put her or himself at the service of the group. Regarding the wellbeing indicator (personal area) teachers found students much more engaged; "the relation between us and the students has significantly improved: we had the opportunity to understand better their social and emotional skills, their attitudes and their talents. We had the opportunity to set up more personalized teaching strategies" (Teacher4).

With regards to the Technical High School "Sandro Pertini" SL projects' "Desk of the citizen" (Sportello del Cittadino) and "Purell-chemical" (Amuchimico) the answers to the questions related to the Personal area have shown that students have acquired the awareness that the commitment of everyone is important for resolving the problems of the community: "the needs analysis led the students to imagine viable solutions. Implementing them has shown that everyone's commitment is essential to solve problems and trigger changes. They realized that even the more complex issues, for example the climate change, can be faced if each individual take actions instead of talking about only problem and not the solution" (Teacher1). With regards to the social area, the SL projects increased the sense of feeling part of the community: "Preliminary meetings with local actors to identify the main problems allowed students to fully understand the emergencies of the place in which they live and feel part of the community" (Head Teacher1). In addition, the communication and collaboration skills increased, as both SL projects requested the students to communicate with the citizens via face-to-face meetings and, during pandemic period and schools closure, via email or Google Meet. "During the pandemic, requests for tax support have increased (babysitting bonuses and tax incentives). Students have learned to relate to different types of people and to manage stressful situations" (Teachers 2). Thanks to the public dissemination final event AVC Expo (High valley of Cosa Expo) the students also tested their public speaking skills. As to Learning to Learn area, the SL projects have developed the students' critical thinking skills. The use of digital platforms have not only increased students acquisition of digital skills, but also the ability to use the network in a conscious and safe way. "That is the reason why the soft skills evaluation section has been revised, including new indicators regarding the method of study, the ability to direct the learning in a meaningful way, the ability to select the sources" (Teacher3).

The Technical and Vocational High School "Europa" realized a Distance Public Relation Office in Casalnuovo of Napoli, the "Europa Community Service" (ECS). The interviews highlighted "the students enable to face and solve unexpected problems" (Head Teacher3). The unexpected schools closure during the pandemic has caused the remote opening of the Public Relation Office. "The students have been able to replace the function of supporting citizens in presence with the implementation of a chatbot, an instant messaging service able to offer assistance to users by providing answers and solutions with no waiting times" (Teacher5). The ability to manage the unexpected with creative solutions generating original outcomes are indicators of the increasing of the learning to learn area. At the same time, their active participation in meeting with teachers also after the class time, has shown their flexibility (personal area). As for the learning to learn area "students actively participated in all phases of the project: the identification of the problem, the study of the causes, the identification of solutions and, last but not least, the co-planning of actions, verifying their feasibility in terms of human, material and financial resources needed and evaluating the possibility of activating collaborations with experts, families, associations, local authorities" (Teacher5). As for social skills, "students have demonstrated to be able to face stressful situations thanks to their ability to manage requests from people of all kinds, even those who have suffered greatly from the effects of the pandemic" (Teacher6).

5 Discussion

The outcomes of the research come from a triangulation of the data collected through two different survey tools. Texts have been analyzed by using the content analysis technique [25] through a system of categories and tags corresponding to survey size and LifeComp skill indicators respectively.

As for the personal area, the analysis of both the narrative inquiries and interviews brings out clearly the link between the three SL activities (two of which took place in distance learning mode and one with face-to-face lessons) and the development of the ability to understand and manage one's emotions and behavior, as well as the ability to be flexible. Furthermore, the connections between the three SL activities and the achievement of school well-being, which increased the learning outcomes, are relevant.

As for the social area, the three analyzed experiences have fostered the development of prosocial behaviors, empathy and willingness to help others. Moreover, the three SL activities have increased students' ability to cooperate, negotiate and communicate, critically reflecting on their role in society and in the world.

As for the last area of LifeComp framework, the learning to learn area, the reference is to the development of growth mindset, critical thinking and management of one's learning. The study of both the narrative inquiries and interviews of the three analyzed activities has brought out interesting references to the development of critical thinking skills considered as critical knowledge of the world, and of global themes and issues. From the school leaders' accounts, it has come out that students are able to take responsible decisions and act. Increasing in self-confidence, self-esteem and self-efficacy has produced qualitative changes in students' attitudes in relation to the management of their learning process.

In the analysis the evidences spread over all the three areas (personal, social and learning to learn), the cognitive skills and the responsible relationship with the community confirm the possibility to develop "good worker" with quality SL projects. Teacher 4 of General High School "Bertolucci" links the opportunity to understand better together, social and emotional skills, attitudes and talents of students involved with the opportunity to set up more personalized teaching strategies. His affirmation confirms that SL gives also the possibility to innovate and strengthen teaching strategies. Moreover, teacher 3 of Technical High School "Pertini" underlines the link between digital skills and ability to use the network in a conscious and safe way, that give the reason to revised soft skills evaluation, including more wide-ranging indicators.

Finally, teacher 5 of Technical and Vocational High School "Europa" underlines the ability to manage the unexpected with creative solutions generating original outcomes, referring to a real situation of dialogue between school and his territory. Like teacher 2 of the "Bertolucci", which reports about the increase of the students' awareness of the effects of globalization and the motivation to deepen the sustainable development and environmental issues. Two considerations that show also the intent to break down barriers between education and rest of society. Therefore, we can conclude that quality SL experiences can lead the school along the way of orienting their students as citizens well equipped, with skills to manage the complex and non-linear transitions of economy, technology, social and environmental issues.

References

1. Gardner, H.: Introduction. In: A.A., V.V.: Good Work, Theory and Practice. Excellence Ethics Engagement, pp. 1–24 (2010). www.thegoodproject.org/books-1
2. Gardner, H.: Service-Learning and Good Work. In: Growing to Greatness G2G, pp. 23–28. NYLC, Atlanta (2005)
3. Sala, A., Punie, Y., Garkov, V., Cabrera, M.: LifeComp. The European framework for personal, social and learning to learn key competence. In: JRC Science for Policy Report (2020). https://doi.org/10.2760/302967
4. Bandura, A.: Self-efficacy: The Exercise of Control. Freeman, New York (1997)
5. De Pietro, O.: Service learning e Alternanza Scuola Lavoro: un possibile raccordo per maturare le soft skills richieste dal mondo del lavoro. Una indagine esplorativa. In: Giornale Italiano della Ricerca Educativa – Italian Journal of Educational Research, Pensa MultiMedia Editore, pp.157–177 (2019). https://doi.org/10.7346/SIRD-012019-P157
6. Furco, A.: The community as a resource for learning. In: OECD, the Nature of Learning: Using Research to Inspire Practice, pp. 227–243 (2010). https://doi.org/10.1787/9789264086487-en
7. Billig S.H.: Research on K-12 school-based service learning: the evidence builds. In: Kappan, P.-D. (ed.) Analysis of the Cloud Platform with Learner's perspective, vol. 81, no. 9, pp. 658–664. TEM J. **8**(3), 733 (2000)

8. Cinque M.: Dalle virtùalle competenze alle soft skills. In: Ciappei, C., Cinque, M. (eds.), Soft Skills per il governo dell'agire. La saggezza e le competenze prassico-pragmatiche. FrancoAngeli, Milano (2014)
9. Mortari, L. (eds): Service Learning. Per un apprendimento responsabile. FrancoAngeli, Milano (2017)
10. Astin, A.W., Sax, L.J.: How undergraduates are affected by service participation. J. Coll. Stud. Dev. **39**, 251–263 (1998)
11. Parker-Gwin, R.: Connecting service to learning: how students and communities' matter. Teach. Sociol. **24**, 97–101 (1996)
12. Raskoff, S., Sundeen, R.: Community service programs in high schools. Law Contemp. Probl. **62**(4), 73–111 (1999)
13. Ash, S.L., Clayton, P.H.: Learning through critical reflection: a tutorial for students in service-learning (Instructor Version), Raleigh, NC (2009)
14. Haski-Leventhal, D., Herte J.: Corporate responsibility and responsible management education in the eyes of MBA students. The MGSM – PRME MBA Global Student Survey (2012)
15. Malvey, D.M., Hamby, E.F., Fottler, M.D.: E-service learning: a pedagogic innovation for healthcare management education. J. Health Adm. Educ. **23**, 181–198 (2006)
16. Strait, J., Nordyke, K.: eService-Learning: Creating Experiential Learning and Civic Engagement Through Online and Hybrid Courses. Stylus Publishing, Sterling (2015)
17. Yin, R.K.: Lo studio di caso nella ricerca scientifica. Progetto e metodi. Armando Editore, Roma (2003)
18. Tapia, M.N.: Educazione e solidarietà. La pedagogia dell'apprendimento-servizio. Città Nuova Editrice, Roma (2006)
19. Baldacci, M., Frabboni, F.: Manuale di metodologia della ricerca educativa. Utet Università, Torino (2013)
20. Mortari, L.: Cultura della ricerca in pedagogia. Carocci Editore, Roma (2007)
21. Trinchero, R.: Manuale di ricerca educativa. FrancoAngeli, Milano (2002)
22. Clandinin, D.J., Huber, J.: Narrative inquiry. In: Peterson, P., Baker, E., McGaw, B. (eds.) International Encyclopedia of Education, pp. 436–441 (2010)
23. Perla, L.: Didattica dell'implicito. Ciòche l'insegnante non sa. La Scuola, Brescia (2010)
24. Semeraro, R.: L'analisi qualitativa dei dati di ricerca in educazione. Ital. J. Educ. Res. (7), 97–106 (2011)
25. Losito, B.: L'analisi del contenuto nella ricerca sociale. FrancoAngeli, Milano (2007)

Transitions and Perspectives for the Adoption of the Blended Approach in Higher Education

Barbara Bruschi(✉), Manuela Repetto(✉), and Melania Talarico(✉)

Dipartimento di Filosofia e Scienze dell'Educazione, Università degli Studi di Torino, Turin, Italy
{bruschi,repetto,talarico}@unito.it

Abstract. The pandemic emergency has unpredictably disrupted traditional university teaching and learning practices, depriving faculty members of the possibility of accurately planning at whatever level – personal, collegial, institutional - the transition to online learning.

Starting from the analysis of the results of a national survey lead by the University of Turin on higher education initiatives and learning practices performed during the current crisis, this contribution is aimed at identifying a set of drivers that, according to a socio-constructivist perspective, could transform and innovate, through blended approaches, academic teaching and learning.

Each emerging driver is faced and discussed in the light of the survey results which highlight the attitudes of teachers in the transition from one period to another (normality, emergency, new normality), taking into account also the most prominent literature on online education.

Hence each driver can be considered a sort of quality criterion that, integrated with the other ones, can promote more effective and challenging higher education practices, while inspiring new faculty training initiatives.

Keywords: Higher education · Blended approach · Online teaching and learning strategies

1 Introduction

Covid-19 has undoubtedly affected teaching and learning at higher education institutions worldwide: academics courses had suddenly to switch one's own courses in online mode without a chance to plan this transition with advance notice. Starting from lockdown and in the subsequent academic year, online university teaching represents, in all the various forms through which teachers have expressed it, an element of uncertainty and full of contradictions. Indeed, in the historical phase we are going through, online education constitutes an opportunity for experimentation of new educational approaches.

Nevertheless, it could represent for several faculty members an element of break with tradition, which could also provoke resistance to change, dissent or inertia.

In spite of thirty years of international research experience of educational researchers on the topic of online teaching and learning, the adoption of innovative approaches on this topic among faculty is still scarce [1].

G. Casalino et al. (Eds.): HELMeTO 2021, CCIS 1542, pp. 364–376, 2022.
https://doi.org/10.1007/978-3-030-96060-5_26

However, many universities worldwide have activated through their teaching and learning centres [2] systematic approaches to offer technological, methodological and pedagogical support, by organising faculty training initiatives and providing adequate infrastructure. Even if any form of support is essential to reconfigure one's own university courses in an online structure, the attitudes of each teacher to this challenging shift do not depend only on at what extent she/he is digital literate; rather these are closely linked to the level of experience gained in designing and managing online courses. In this sense, teachers' training is essential to affect and, eventually, modify their attitudes.

University teachers without any previous training on online teaching and learning, who have gained experience only on how to design a traditional academic course, were caught unprepared when they had to switch their lectures online. The majority of them tend spontaneously to replicate what they are used to do under normal conditions during their lectures [3], transferring ordinary teaching practices in a dimension that appears immediate and easy to manage. In this sense, some competences developed for face to face lectures could be useful, but should be integrated with further skills needed for technology enhanced learning.

As a matter of fact, the online context turns out to be complex and multifaceted if the teaching process goes beyond the mere lecture. As soon as a university teacher overcomes the phase of familiarisation with technology and uses competently the video conferencing system for synchronous webinars, being able also to deliver recorded lessons, a new need emerges: how to design online learning activities highly engaging for students.

From a pedagogically point of view, this need can be translated into the requirement to design and deliver courses through active and constructivist approaches focused more on students [4] and on their learning processes than on content domain. Indeed, student population of higher education institution appears highly heterogeneous [5] in terms of their conditions of access to technology, digital competencies, cognitive and social skills, experience, interests, status of student worker and place of provenance and of residence. These preconditions have become even more marked during pandemic, affecting with considerable variability the extent to which students could take advantage of and benefit from the academic courses attended during the emergency.

Thus, higher education should consider the needs of each student by adopting technology-enhanced learning approaches and designing online or integrated learning environments with a sound pedagogy.

The aim of this contribution was identifying some key factors that could innovate and transform higher education teaching and learning starting from the educational experiences of faculty members during the pandemic crisis. Thus, a survey led by the University of Turin was analysed to critically discuss the role of each of these factors and of their connection in the light of the survey achieved results.

2 Faculty Members' Attitudes Towards Online Learning Before, During and Post Pandemic Crisis

2.1 Objectives and Methodology

The Center Luigi Bobbio of the University of Turin, in collaboration with the inter-university center of research on higher education systems (UNIRES), has led a survey in the second semester of the academic year 2019–2020 [6], aimed at identifying teaching and learning practices and trends adopted during the universities closure, a period characterised by the conversion of all the courses into online mode.

The survey has involved a sample of 3398 professors belonging to 40 public universities across Italy and consisted in an online questionnaire organised into seven sections administered through the CAWI method. While the purpose of this survey was multifold and outside the aim of this contribution, in the present study those data dealing with online teaching and learning are selected among the outcomes of the survey. These data provide an overview aimed at achieving the following objectives:

- to compare learning practices before emergency with those activated during the first lockdown;
- to investigate at what extent and at which conditions teachers have adapted their pre-existing courses to the new requirements imposed by the pandemic emergency;
- to identify positive reactions of faculty members counterbalanced by the critical issues;
- to detect the main aspirations of teachers for their future university courses, independently from the evolution of the pandemic.

2.2 The Results

Before the emergency, about one quarter of the sample (23%) used to adopt for their traditional courses a transmissive-dialogical approach, characterized by a traditional lesson enriched with discussion between the teacher and their students. One third of teachers used to follow instead a transmissive-interactive approach, involving even more actively students through exercises and labs. Lastly, 45% of faculty members used to propose an innovative-collaborative approach, whereas students used to transform knowledge in personal competencies thanks to the interaction among them through collaborative learning and to perform specific activities for the development of transversal competencies, of creativity and problem solving.

In our collective imagination, lectures in presence are based mainly on a transmissive approach; nevertheless, according to this survey, traditional university courses for almost half of the sample were very innovative, dynamic and based on active methods. Thus, it could be expected that in the online mode these approaches were maintained. Instead, almost half of faculty members (47%) have paradoxically declared that during the first wave of the pandemic have adopted the more traditional approach, the transmissive-dialogical one, while a percentage of teachers similar to the previous one (31%) have used the transmissive-interactive approach, and only 22% of the sample have chosen the most innovative approach. Therefore, the picture that emerges from these data is of a more simplified and impoverished teaching and learning model for online education, not fully harnessing the potentialities of online educational strategies. The same simplification process has included also students' assessment during the final exams: if with traditional higher education more than half of the teachers used to adopt multiple and mixed approaches like oral and written exams including evaluation of projects, reports, tests and other types of outcomes, with the transition to online education many teachers have reduced both the number and the typologies of assessment.

Besides the approaches used for online education, teachers were asked to declare at what extent have changed structure and contents of their own traditional courses to adapt them to online mode. As can be seen in Fig. 1, the large majority of teachers - about two thirds of them (67%) - declared to have made limited changes; about one quarter (24%) have maintained the same structure of their traditional face to face lectures; only 9% declared to have completely altered the original structure of their courses to adapt them for online education, seizing this emergency as an opportunity to rethink and innovate one's educational approach.

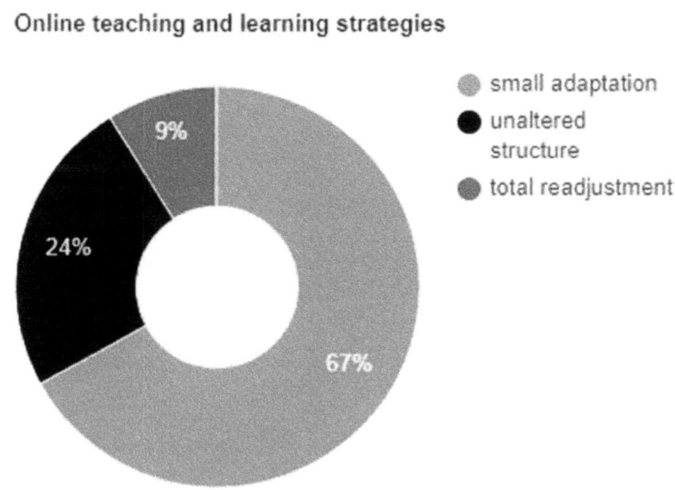

Fig. 1. Level of adaptation of traditional courses to online mode (adapted from [6])

The difficulty in questioning one's methods and habits and the tendency to simplify in order to avoid risks can be inferred also in the typologies of lectures declared by faculty members: two thirds (66%) of them has organised online streaming lectures; 15% of teachers have given both live and recorded lectures; 12% have made available online recorded lectures; finally, only 7% of faculty have organised other types of activities, including the collaborative ones.

Even if the picture emerging from these data appears not to encouraging for the innovation of online higher education, three quarters of teachers were satisfied of their online experience; while more than half of the teachers declared to have enhanced their own professionalism.

As a matter of fact, half of the sample is aware of the need to be trained on online learning approaches. Among the difficulties encountered, 43% of the teachers admitted they have had little time to plan and deliver their online courses; 52% complained of having troubles in achieving practical exercises or laboratory activities, while 75% attributes to online education a lower interaction with students. These types of difficulties attest the low level of experience of faculty members with online education, as well as a probable distorted view of its real potential.

As regards the future, as can be seen in Fig. 2, 54% of faculty members are available to embrace a mixed approach, integrating online and onsite education. They admit that this approach may enhance learning, making possible to make available several kind of digital learning resources and to amplify and differentiate interaction modalities with students. Moreover, groups of teachers are aware that a blended approach could elicit the experimentation of new learning strategies; it could support the achievement of activities more focused on the development of competencies and on interdisciplinary learning; furthermore, it would stimulate students' autonomy and a more intense collaboration. Some teachers declared also that the mixed approach would increase the potential beneficiaries of higher education such as working students, foreign students or lifelong learners, making them also more inclusive.

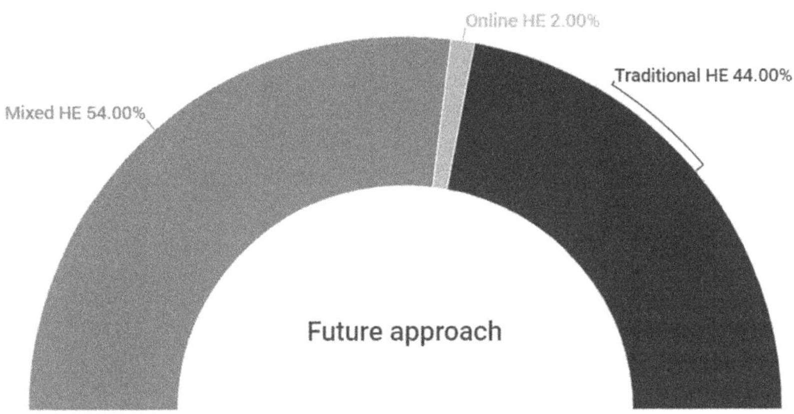

Fig. 2. University teachers' attitudes towards the future approach (adapted from [6])

Nevertheless, this wide and representative number of teachers is counterbalanced by 44% of faculty who want to come back to "normality" and to completely give up online education. Instead, only the remaining 2% would definitely abandon traditional face to face courses for completely delivering them in online mode. This breach of the sample into two opposing attitudes represents a great challenge for the future of universities teaching and learning strategies, especially for the blended approaches.

3 Discussion: Drivers for Transformation of Teaching and Learning Practices

The analysis of the survey led by the University of Turin was undertaken to identify the main elements that, according to the socio-constructivist perspective, could transform and innovate the academic offer. The five selected drivers are blended learning, learning design, personalisation, collaboration and formative and authentic assessment.

In the following paragraphs these drivers are analysed in greater detail in the light of the results of the survey on teachers' perceptions described in the previous section.

3.1 The Blended Approach

The integration between online and onsite higher education through a *blended approach* appears a perspective whose potentialities should be harnessed when the emergency will cease to become the new normality. The results of the survey involving faculty members attest that 54% of them are willing to adopt in the future a mixed approach, that seamlessly integrates online and onsite teaching and learning. And it is very likely that, in the return to the new normality that will characterize the post-pandemic, this approach can continue to represent a reference model for teachers who had experimented online teaching during an emergency and are willing to maintain the advantages of this modality, while not renouncing the teaching activities in presence. Even if the percentage of teachers not willing to abandon traditional teaching is still very high, it's the first time in Italy that such a large number of faculty members are willing to integrate technologies and the online dimension into their teaching.

Also literature in the field of online education confirms that the blended approach could be the most effective solution for higher education: some meta-analysis [7, 8] have found a moderate positive effect size in favour of blended learning, if compared to fully online or traditional courses.

As a matter of fact, blended, hybrid and mixed approaches combine the undeniable advantages of face-to-face training with those of distance learning, seamlessly integrating in person attendance of lectures with participation in online activities delivered through a virtual learning environment. Blended learning give students considerable flexibility in carrying out activities and managing study times at their own pace. In order for blended learning to be effective, the teacher must be able to strategically combine face-to-face and remote activities, becoming aware that the two settings should be integrated making each context functional to the other.

The blended approach is not unique and standardised; rather at least five models of this approach can be applied in the field of higher education [9], arising from different combinations between the variables that characterize the context in presence (led by the teacher, collaborative activity) and the online one (self-managed, guided by the teacher, collaborative activity). One of these five models is the flipped approach, which focuses the online part on digital content, such as videos, handouts, presentations, articles, which students view independently; while the face-to-face part is used for learning activities such as collaborative work, which can also be based on specific strategies such as problem solving, case study, project-based activities. This model could be suitable for teachers who in the survey have declared that in their traditional courses used the innovative-collaborative approach.

Another model of blended learning is the flexible model, in which both the delivery of content and the "collaborative" activities take place online, while in presence the teacher detects the progress of the students' learning and provides them with timely feedback. This model appears instead more suitable for that minority of teachers who are already competent in adopting collaborative online activities.

However, the choice of one model or another one depends not only on the skills and inclinations of the teachers, but also on many contextual elements such as the characteristics and number of students, the available resources, the institutional constraints and, obviously, also from the time available that can be invested, especially for the design of the blended course.

3.2 Learning Design

Faculty members of the sample attributed the lack of time one of the major difficulties in designing suitable courses in the online version. As a matter of fact, time to invest in the design process is essential to ensure the quality of a blended course. The choice of a *learning design* (LD) approach instead of the widespread instructional design approaches (ID) inspired by ADDIE models, reflects the constructivist paradigm shift from a teacher-centric to a student-centric approach.

ID models have a simplified nature so that they can be quickly and easily applied in a linear and cyclical way, under a behavioural approach, helping to make the whole process holistically perceived. However, in the mid-90s of the twentieth century a re-conceptualization of the ID models began, which was caused by a growing interest in constructivism. This cultural movement has led to the development of less rigid design models, which emphasize the complex nature of the design of a course in an authentic learning context.

LD approaches are more flexible, explicit [10] and sharable with other teachers. If in the ID approach the design process is linear and not complex, that of the constructivist ID is recursive, non-linear and sometimes chaotic in its trajectories: there is no predefined order in the development of the project and there is not even a step that must be taken before the others. If problems arise not during the design, but only in the application context and, therefore, during the project implementation phase, the changes can be made on the spot and the project can be reviewed and adapted according to a recursive process.

In addition, LD may engage students making them co-designers in the definition of their own learning objectives or in the iterative redesign of a task.

3.3 Personalisation

In this sense, LD involves *personalisation*, which is based on the principle that students do not achieve all the same goals; rather they reach only the individual goals that enhance their own potential, performing those learning activities responding to their needs. Personalisation of the learning pathways of students is relevant because, as also the faculty members of the survey have admitted, the student population is becoming increasingly heterogeneous for skills, previous experiences and geographical origin, as well as for a set of academic skills such as being able to write an essay, looking for relevant information, or other skills which enable them to profitably attend courses.

If at the technology level personalization translates into the ability of the system to dynamically adapt to the choices made by the student and to track all the progress made [11], the personalization of learning is also a learning strategy, or it can even be considered a pedagogical model, as it can be adopted in blended approaches regardless of the LMS platform or the technological system used. Personalized learning can be considered as that model in which the learning pace, the teaching and learning approach, the learning objectives and the contents are optimized for the needs of each individual student. Furthermore, the activities are relevant and meaningful for that student, guided by his interests and, in some cases, can be initiated independently by the student himself. Therefore, students learn in a different way, planning and taking an active part in their learning process.

If the number of students is too high, design and delivery of personalised and scalable learning pathways can be supported through the use of adaptive learning systems and of microcredentials [3, 12, 13] that can be used in an integrated way. The microcredentials give people the opportunity to build lifelong learning paths also during their working career and to personalize their use according to their needs and aspirations. These are also a device that can help personalize the learning process in adulthood, provided that are not considered individually, but rather included in a broader curricular structure, on the basis of which microcredentials can constellate the training pathway and be accumulated in the personal digital portfolio of each learner. The potential of microcredentials is relevant also in relation to the acquisition of them in international virtual mobility initiatives, thanks to which students can attend online courses in other universities they are not enrolled in, acquiring credit through this system. The experience of the Erasmus + UNITA project, managed by a consortium of universities with the University of Turin as a leader, is moving in this direction as a promoter of this initiative.

Personalisation of learning activities implies that students activate cognitive and meta-cognitive strategies, like self-regulating learning [14, 15], to become progressively more autonomous and able to plan, monitor and regulate his own learning processes, alone or collaborating with others.

3.4 Collaboration

According to a socio-constructivist perspective, *collaboration* in online contexts is essential to make learning processes deeper, relevant, active and engaging. Students, when appropriately scaffolded by the teacher, develop many transversal competencies, like social skills, problem solving, creativity and critical thinking across various collaborative strategies.

Nevertheless, collaboration can be considered the "great absent" in the online courses hold by faculty members during the emergency, as shown by the results of the survey. The majority of them were too cautious, afraid or reticent to the idea of experimenting online what they were already able to do in presence before the pandemic crisis, given the innovative approach they used to take in their traditional courses. The know-how of these teachers concerning collaboration methods for onsite lectures should instead harnessed inviting them to adopt blended approach models that valorise collaboration in presence. Their pre-existence knowledge could be capitalised also within faculty training initiatives, in which teachers could learn the characteristics of online methods and grasp the differences between online and onsite collaboration.

Computers and mobile devices support online collaboration as mediating technologies that shape - and transform - the nature of interactions and their artefacts [13]. Contact between those who collaborate is mediated by network technology, which can have effects that facilitate or inhibit interaction between people. And language is also a medium for transferring meanings from one mind to another through representations of reality.

The recent affordances of ICTs make possible to multiply modalities and settings to deliver and organise collaborative activities, which can take place effectively also synchronously through breakouts rooms [16], that appear more rapid and immediate than those organised in presence.

A recent research on the effectiveness of the collaborative approach for students interacting synchronously in mathematical disciplines [17], emphasizes that synchronous collaboration facilitates reasoning skills and problem solving through the formulation of conjectures, making explicit explanations and criticizing the positions of others. This researcher finds the breakout room a tool functional to this type of collaborative approach, which involves problems solving in small groups.

This plurality of collaborative settings calls into question new strategies for students' assessment.

3.5 Formative and Authentic Assessment

In socio-constructivist oriented approaches, evaluation plays a fundamental role, especially in blended teaching contexts. During the delivery of their online courses, teachers of the sample have resized and simplified approaches of assessment, not being at all aware that evaluation in its formative value takes on greater importance both to evaluate the educational quality of the resources and processes implemented, on which it is possible to intervene in order to improve them, and to make learners more aware of their learning processes, guiding them in their improvement before their learning pathway can be concluded.

The formative evaluation dimensions are formative feedback, self-assessment and peer evaluation [13].

The formative feedback can be given by the teacher or with the support of an intelligent tutoring system (ITS) [18] which provide formative assessment to students giving them a feedback and suggestions on how to move closer to the achievement of a learning goal.

According to a recursive process, the formative assessment of the teacher or of the ITS can be integrated with student's self-assessment, through which he/she becomes progressively autonomous in monitoring his/her own learning. At the same time, the data deriving from the students' self-assessment provide additional information to the teacher regarding the relevance of the proposed activities and their compliance with the student's needs.

Peer assessment conducted within groups carrying out collaborative activities, also supports both the teacher who intends to monitor the progression of students' learning, and the student, who receives an assessment from his peers which makes him more aware of his own learning processes, pushing him to reflect critically on them and to improve himself thanks to the comparison with the judgments of the students who interact with him.

Peer assessment can also be a privileged way to propose collaborative activities, in pairs or in small groups, even in very large classes: the LMS platform or the adaptive systems incorporate tools to implement this type of assessment, which can lighten the teacher's workload by "distributing" it evenly among students, both in the monitoring phase of group dynamics, and in the evaluation of artefacts created by couples or groups.

According to the constructivist approach, some learning objectives cannot be adequately assessed with multiple choice tests, without inevitably diminishing the value of a course and the extent of the knowledge that is promoted and activated. Furthermore, in data collection, there are subjective and qualitative aspects that cannot be captured through tests, scales and batteries; rather, these pregnant aspects present in any educational process, can be detected thanks to the observation processes, the interviews, the questionnaires with open questions and the focus groups [13]. Therefore, there are also other evaluation approaches, such as authentic assessment, which should be taken into more consideration, given that in the context of higher education there is the need to promote, in addition to knowledge, the development of competencies that students can use in their professional future. The development of these skills can be assessed within learning environments in which students perform tasks perceived as meaningful for them.

3.6 A Framework Proposal on Drivers for Transformation of Teaching and Learning Practices

According to a systemic approach and as can be seen in Fig. 3, these drivers are intertwined and not mutually exclusive; along the cycle design – delivery – evaluation, these factors should be interdependently used, so that each of them affect the others as well: *learning design* is the approach to adopt for designing a student-centred course; this course during its delivery should use *collaboration* and *personalisation* as the main learning strategies; finally, *formative and authentic assessment* should be used as evaluation approach to improve teaching and learning processes while enhancing students' assessment. *Blended learning*, positioned at the centre of the chart, is the focal point and could represent the ideal configuration for a seamless integration of online and onsite learning activities.

These drivers represent broad patterns of change that can be promoted from universities at institutional level, but that can emerge also from innovative practices experimented by teachers. Furthermore, these drivers could be considered as reference criteria ensuring a high quality of online and blended courses delivered in the post-pandemic.

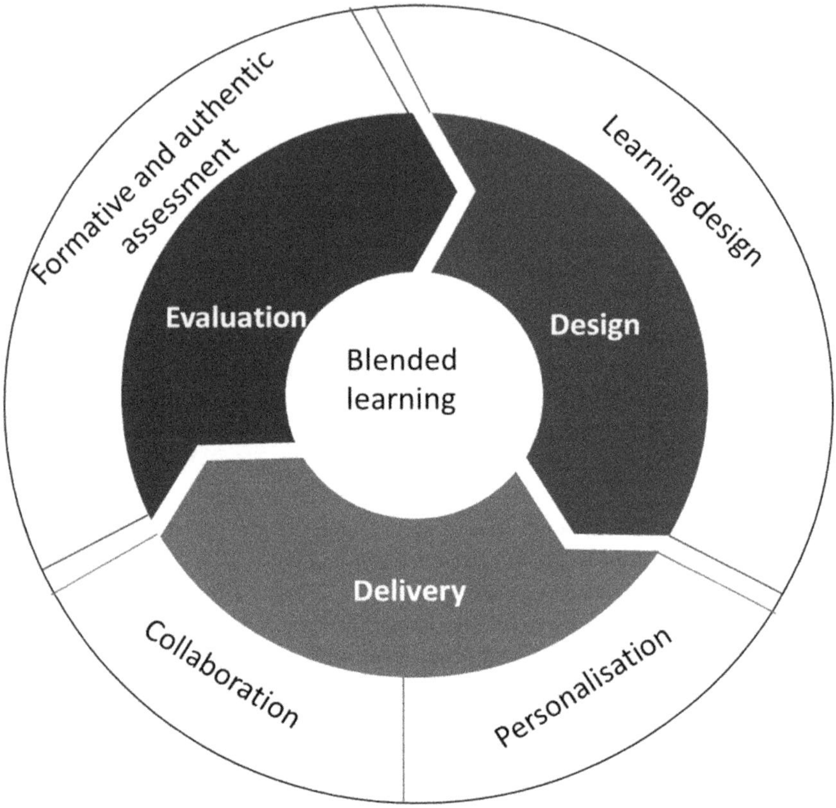

Fig. 3. A framework on the key drivers to reframe HE teaching and learning practices

4 Conclusions

Academics are increasingly aware that they will never go back to normal, even when Covid-19 crisis will be overcome. Lesson learned during this period [1, 2, 4, 5, 14, 19] should be kept in mind to improve higher education teaching and learning: teaching in presence remains undoubtedly a distinctive element of public universities, but the emergency has offered to faculty members new perspectives and insights for improving their teaching and learning strategies.

Now faculty are probably more challenged with the purpose of making their course to evolve from face to face teaching to blended and integrated approaches, mostly if they will be supported through decisions of academic structures at institutional, organisational and political level. Moreover, faculty are challenged use of further BYOD devices available at home, such as smartphone and exergame controllers [20], which amplify the potentialities of blended learning providing an higher level of interactivity and enhancing feedback to the student and allowing ubiquitous assessment.

In this contribution, the analysis of the outcomes of the survey on faculty members' attitudes for online courses hold during pandemic crisis was intersected with results of the recent literature on higher education initiatives and learning practices dealing with current crisis. The limit of this study is that university teachers' attitudes for the second wave of pandemic weren't considered since relevant data for this period were missing; furthers studies are needed to better comprehend trends of teaching and learning practices and to seize any transformation from one period to another, including any change occurring from the post pandemic onwards.

The drivers for transformation emerging in this work were embodied in some online pilot courses delivered during the last academic year at the University of Turin. The joint application of these drivers through different instances combining them, which will be validated in next research, may give a vision to stakeholders of what is changing, while inspiring faculty members in the design and delivery of innovative courses for shaping the future offer of higher education.

References

1. Hofer, S., Nistor, N., Scheibenzuber, C.: Online teaching and learning in higher education: lessons learned in crisis situations. Comput. Hum. Behav. **121** (2021)
2. Bruschi, B.: Università dopo l'emergenza: quali opportunità? Il caso dell'Università di Torino. Scuola democratica **11**(3), 583–590 (2020)
3. Repetto, M., Trentin, G.: Faculty Training for Web Enhanced Learning. Nova Science Publishers, New York (2011)
4. Gaebel, M., Zhang, T., Iucu, R.: Advancing learning and teaching in the EHEA: innovation and links with research. In: Curaj, A., Deca, L., Pricopie, R. (eds.) European Higher Education Area: Challenges for a New Decade, pp. 273–282. Springer, Cham (2020). https://doi.org/10.1007/978-3-030-56316-5_18
5. Curaj, A., Deca, L., Pricopie, R. (eds.) European Higher Education Area: Challenges For a New Decade, p. 596. Springer, Cham (2020)
6. Ramella, F., Rostan, M.: Universi-DaD. Gli accademici italiani e la didattica a distanza durante l'emergenza Covid-19. Working Paper CLB-CPS (2020)
7. Dziuban, C., Graham, C.R., Moskal, P.D., Norberg, A., Sicilia, N.: Blended learning: the new normal and emerging technologies. Int. J. Educ. Technol. High. Educ. **15**(1), 1–16 (2018)
8. Thalheimer, W.: Does eLearning work? What the scientific research says!. Work-Learning Research. Accessed 10 Aug 2021. https://www.worklearning.com/wpcontent/uploads/2017/10/DoeseLearning-Work-Full-Research-Report-FINAL2.pdf
9. Alammary, A.: Blended learning models for introductory programming courses: a systematic review. PloS One **14**, 9 (2019)
10. Laurillard, D.: Teaching as a Design Science. Building Pedagogical Patterns for Learning and Technology. Routledge, London (2012)
11. Grant, P., Basye, D.: Personalized Learning: A Guide for Engaging Students with Technology International Society for Technology in Education Eugene (2014)
12. Alamri, H.A., Watson, S., Watson, W.: Learning technology models that support personalization within blended learning environments in higher education. TechTrends **65**(1), 62–78 (2020)
13. Repetto, M.: La didattica universitaria online nell'era dell'incertezza. Evidenze empiriche e prospettive. Aracne, Roma (2021)
14. Wong, J., Baars, M., Davis, D., Van Der Zee, T., Houben, G.J., Paas, F.: Supporting self-regulated learning in online learning environments and MOOCs: a systematic review. Int. J. Hum.-Comput. Inter. **35**(4–5), 356–373 (2019)

15. Xie, H., Chu, H.C., Hwang, G.J., Wang, C.C.: Trends and development in technology-enhanced adaptive/personalized learning: a systematic review of journal publications from 2007 to 2017. Comput. Educ. **140** (2019)
16. Saltz, J., Heckman, R.: Using structured pair activities in a distributed online breakout room. Online Learn. **24**(1), 227–244 (2020)
17. Morge S.: Collaboration and problem solving in synchronous courses. In: Langran, E. (ed.), Proceedings of Site Interactive 2020 Online Conference, Association for the Advancement of Computing in Education, AACE, pp. 614–617 (2020)
18. Zheng, L.:The effectiveness of self-regulated learning scaffolds on academic performance in computer-based learning environments: a meta-analysis. Asia Pac. Educ. Rev. **17**(2), 187–202 (2016)
19. Cavanagh, T., Chen, B., Lahcen, R.A.M., Paradiso, J.R.: Constructing a design framework and pedagogical approach for adaptive learning in higher education: a practitioner's perspective. Int. Rev. Res. Open Distrib. Learn. **21**(1), 172–196 (2020)
20. Picerno, P., Pecori, R., Raviolo, P., Ducange, P.: Smartphones and exergame controllers as BYOD solutions for the e-tivities of an online sport and exercise sciences university program. In: Burgos, D., et al. (eds.) HELMeTO 2019. CCIS, vol. 1091, pp. 217–227. Springer, Cham (2019). https://doi.org/10.1007/978-3-030-31284-8_17

Author Index

www.ingramcontent.com/pod-product-compliance
Ingram Content Group UK Ltd.
Pitfield, Milton Keynes, MK11 3LW, UK
UKHW021028050925
462611UK00011B/797
* 9 7 8 3 0 3 0 9 6 0 5 9 9 *